How to Design and Improve
MAGAZINE LAYOUTS
2nd Edition

Raymond Dorn

Nelson-Hall Publishers nh Chicago

Library of Congress Cataloging in Publication Data

Dorn, Raymond.
  How to design & improve magazine layouts.

  Includes index.
  1. Magazine design.   2. Printing, Pratical—layout.
I. Title.   II. Title: How to design and improve
magazine layouts.
Z253.5.D67 1986   686   85–21627
ISBN 0–8304–1091–0 (cloth)
ISBN 0–8304–1160–7 (paper)

Manufactured in the United States of America

10 9 8 7 6 5 4 3 2

CONTENTS

CHAPTER ONE

A Brief History of Type

When you stop to think of it, our twenty-six letter alphabet is amazing. With these few letters we can express our every thought and emotion. The dissemination of knowledge—or progress, if you will—would be virtually impossible without the written word. Think of the ancient peoples who had no alternative but to pass on their accumulated knowledge to their successors by word of mouth and by example. How did writing come into being, and why do we stress it in the very beginning of a book about editorial layout?

The letters of the alphabet started with roughly drawn pictures. For example, the letter *S* could have been a very basic picture of a snake. When the sound *s-s-s-s-* went with it, almost anyone who had ever seen a snake would get the same picture. These ''thoughts in pictures'' are called pictographs. Probably the best known pictographs are those on Egyptian scrolls and in tombs. Each picture represents a complete thought or action. This was often awkward, so scribes invented a shorthand method of writing that simplified the complete pictograph. Figure 1.1 shows a typical pictograph. This particular one was used as a seal for a builder and gives a brief description of his achievements. Figure 1.2 is basically the same as figure 1.1, but in the scribe's ''shorthand'' method. This was done quite rapidly with a reed pen. The shorthand method was used in everyday business; many examples found by archeologists consist

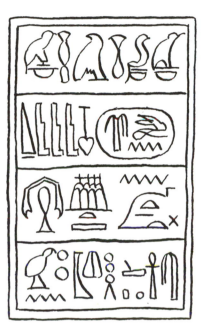

Figure 1.1—A typical Egyptian pictograph. Each stylized picture represented a ''thought.'' When these thoughts were combined they became a statement.

of bills of sale, personal correspondence, and royal decrees. The Sumerians, Assyrians, Babylonians, and Phoenicians in particular developed their own methods of long-distance communication by following this shorthand method. Traders gradually combined most of the accepted pictures into a common jargon that was accepted in their business world.

Perhaps an updated pictograph will illustrate the ''complete thought'' idea. Figure 1.3 shows how a child might draw a stick figure of the father-mother relationship. The father is bigger than the

mother. The father is angular, the mother rounder. If they hold hands, one assumes they are a pair (married). By breaking this pictograph down in steps to the very basics, we get the progression shown in figure 1.3, which might signify that the letter *M* means ''marriage.''

Men and women who have spent their entire careers in the study of alphabets seem to agree that the evolution of our present letters is a matter of conjecture and the result of a great deal of trial and error.

Our present alphabet is Roman and has the same primary shapes that appeared on Trajan's inscription in the second century. In figure 1.4 we have a rough tracing of the letters of this inscription. If you could read Latin, you would find this as easy to understand as your daily newspaper. One must marvel that these letters reached such perfection in A.D. 113.

Even in the rough tracing, notice that the ancient Romans knew a great deal about letter spacing. Note how they handled the grouping of an *A* next to a *V*. They obviously had a great feeling for design for they also created the round letters in such a way as to give ''air'' to the whole. It is a pity that Trajan gets all the credit, while the artist who planned, cut, and developed the lettering receives no recognition.

These Roman letters were cut into stone after they were carefully painted on the stone's surface with a reed pen or a brush. The ''tails'' or the chisel points at the ends are what we now call *serifs*. These serifs are characteristic of all Roman faces.

The traditional Roman face has grace and symmetry, with the serifs adding a finish to its design. Sometimes serifs are lengthened to add a flair to the letters. These are called "swash" letters; see *R* and *Q* in figure 1.4. Serifs also have a historical evolution. Roman faces are subdivided into "traditional," "transitional," and "modern," depending on the serif style.

As seen in figure 1.5, "traditional" can be identified by the wedge-shaped serif that is usually the same size as the stem and tapers into a hairline at the end. The curve into the stem is graceful and gradual. Transitional can be identified by a more pronounced curve into the stem, but with rather blunted and rounded serifs. Modern is quickly identified by the straight-line serifs that have no curve into the stem. The visual impression, however, is still Roman.

Some of the modern Roman typefaces are called "a serif without a serif." These have been specifically designed with just a slight curve at the ends instead of the usual more pronounced serifs. This gives the impression of a wedge, but is not visually true. Optima is a typeface that falls into this class (See the last example in figure 1.5.)

Why this information on Roman typefaces? Your very first reader in school was, in all probability, printed in a Roman face, perhaps Scotch or Bookman, which are used quite often. The letters were large and well formed. You learned to see the shape of each letter and were taught its appropriate sound. Then letters were placed into simple combinations that were called words. You learned to identify words by their shape. This is not as impossible as it sounds. No one reads a letter at a time, unless he or she is just learning to read. Instead, one identifies shapes or groups of shapes. Short words are learned quickly, and recognition is instant. The word *stop* is one we all know. The mental impression is instant—there is no thought involved and no individual letter identification. The shape conveys the meaning.

This is one key to short, easy-to-identify words used in newspaper headlines. The idea is to get the message across as quickly as possible. Good copy, especially if the reader's attention must be caught in a fraction of a second, is composed of word shapes that are recognized instantly and without a great deal of memory digestion.

Figure 1.2—The scribe's "shorthand" method of simplifying statements probably developed around key phrases. Note how the pictographs in figure 1.1 are horizontal, but change to vertical in figure 1.2.

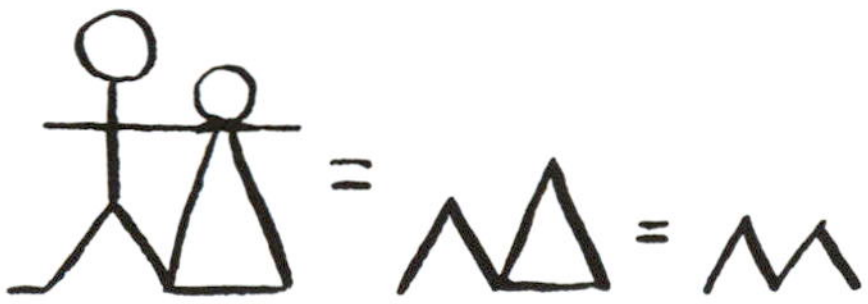

Figure 1.3—This is an oversimplified pictograph of the capital M in a modernized version showing how there could be a natural progression from a pictograph to a letter we all know.

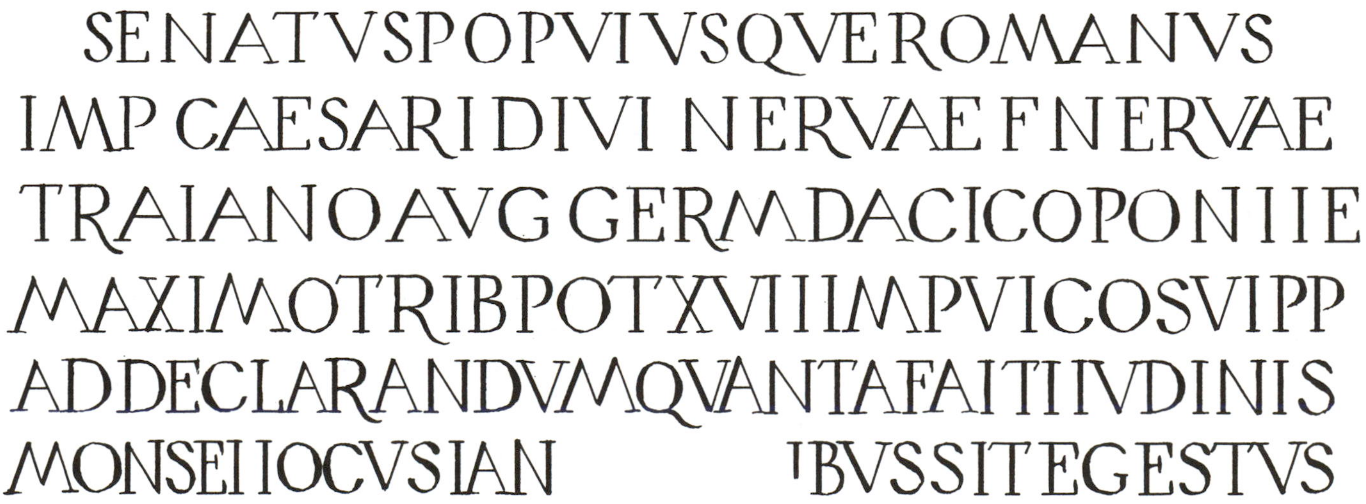

SENATVSPOPVIVSQVEROMANVS
IMP CAESARI DIVI NERVAE F NERVAE
TRAIANOAVG GERMDACICOPONIIE
MAXIMOTRIBPOTXVIIIMPVICOSVIPP
ADDECLARANDVMQVANTAFAITIIVDINIS
MONSEIIOCVSIAN   ᵀBVSSITEGESTVS

Figure 1.4—A rough tracing of Trajan's inscription. Even as a "rough" the letters and words come through loud and clear.

ABCDEFGHIJKLMNF
abcdefghijklmn | 12345

ABCDEFGHIJKLMNOPQRS
abcdefghijklmnopqrst | 12345

ABCDEFGHIJKLMNOPQRS
abcdefghijklmnopqrst | 12345

ABCDEFGHIJKLMNOPQRSTUV
abcdefghijklmnopqrst | 12345

Figure 1.5—The evolution of serif styles is seen in these examples of traditional, transitional, modern, and "serif without a serif."

Compare this to book text, particularly in some scientific publications. Here words must be identified slowly because the memories of certain shapes may not have been used for long periods of time. Longer words, or words with more than three syllables, are identified by groups of shapes. The word *Interactionary*, for example, is put together in short, shape-identified groups.

Words are further identified by their upper half (figure 1.6). You can see this by viewing a line that is set in a conventional Roman face but with a blank sheet of white paper over the lower half. In most cases you can still make much sense of the upper half. This is because the upper half is used, primarily, to complete the major letter characteristics, while the lower half contains fewer of the identifying characteristics.

Our daily consumption of words invariably consists mostly of Roman faces, because this is what people are accustomed to reading. They are the easiest to recognize over years of sight training. A simple proof of this is included in figure 1.7 where two paragraphs of the same copy are placed next to each other. The top one is set in a typical serif face while the bottom

is set in sans-serif (no serif) type. In reading both you will find that the Roman-set copy can be practically skimmed over because word identification is so easy. However, in reading the sans-serif face, you will pause until your eye becomes used to identifying the new word shapes.

Another way of judging type is by its "color." This does not refer to hue, but rather to the overall look of copy set in a certain face. There should be an evenness to the set copy that aids in the flow of reading.

Some Roman faces are "classics," just as some car models are classics. Caslon is one of these classics. The shape of each letter is pure. The shape of each word set in Caslon is a study in symmetry. The "color" of Caslon set in blocks of copy, which creates a relatively "gray" overall tone, is even and appealing. A sample of Caslon 540 is in figure 1.8 for your perusal.

Caslon also has a large "family"; that is, it has been designed for caps, small caps, lower case, bold,

and italic. Other classical Roman faces are Jansen and Garamond. The basic difference between them is in the shape of the letters and in the relationship between the "x-height" and the ascenders and descenders. The x-height is the height of a lower case *x*. An ascender is a letter part that is taller than the *x*, such as in *h, d,* and the upper part of all capital letters. A descender is the part of a letter that extends lower than the *x*, such as in a *p, q,* or *j*. In figure 1.9, compare the relationship between the x-height and ascenders/descenders. Type Script Upright has a very small x-height. News gothic, on the other hand, has a large x-height. These variations create differences in readability. We therefore give typefaces that have short ascenders more leading (i.e., white space between lines) so the word shapes come through clearly. When Romans with short ascenders and descenders are set solid (i.e., with no leading), the "color" is considerably darker and the words are harder to read. It is a good idea to study a Roman face that you might want to use set in body copy to assure yourself that even this small difference will not affect readability.

The transitional Roman typefaces have their classics too. Scotch and Baskerville are two good examples. They are highly readable, though darker in color than most traditionals. The actual shape of the letters is rather blunted, but the word shapes come through clearly. This is why primers and simple word books are printed in these faces. Children can grasp the word forms quicker when they are obvious.

Modern Romans (the Bodoni family is probably the best known of these) are identified by their straight-line serifs. These were created for clarity of individual letter shapes, word shapes, and overall "color." Many newspapers use

The classes of composition for

Figure 1.6—An illustration showing how the upper half of our Roman faces gives the majority of the letter characteristics, making them easy to identify.

Harmonizing is a fixed objective in quality type work. There are many fine types from which to select so that the choice of a face for a particular purpose is not too difficult. But there are several factors that must influence this choice. Types of the same point size vary in the widths of their characters. They may be different *also in their relationships between printing surface and body size. Legibility, which is always desirable, is not an inevitable.*

Harmonizing is a fixed objective in quality type work. There are many fine types from which to select so that the choice of a face for a particular purpose is not too difficult. But there are several factors that must influence this choice. Types of the same point size vary in the widths of their characters. They may be different *also in their relationships between printing surface and body size.*

Figure 1.7—Two identical blocks of copy, the first set in serif type and the other set in sans-serif type. Notice how much easier it is to read the serif letters and, in particular, how your eye pauses for just a moment to fully grasp the new letter shapes in the sans-serif.

Bodoni for just this reason. This is a very "prolific" family, which has light, regular, bold, demibold, ultrabold, and even poster-bold along with small caps and italic. Newspapers often stock the entire family, which gives them many variations in headlines, text, and even advertising, all within the same family, but with all the sizes for variety.

Type design is done by master craftsmen, and too few appear on the scene in one lifetime. A good designer does more than create individual letters in an alphabet. Each letter must not only stand by itself, but blend with every other letter. Capitals must blend with lower case; numbers must blend with letters. The overall feeling must be of the same cloth—finished and cohesive in all respects. We have many display faces, but it is rare that any of them will stand up to a steady reading diet due to their individual character and structure.

Sans-serifs

These are typefaces that have no serifs. They originally appeared about 1820 or so and made such an impression on type design that they have never been discarded. Some sans-serifs look good in mass, but most of them do not. News Gothic, Trade Gothic, Helvetica, and Venus are four that do, and very often they are used in

this way. Because of their readability, they are often used for picture captions or short descriptive blocks of copy. Because of their immediate contrast to Roman faces, they stand away from the rest of the text. Almost all sans-serifs have large families—light, regular, italic, bold, expanded, and condensed. Roman faces usually do not stand condensing or expanding. Sans-serifs, because of their clean lines and straight-forward design, can stand both expanding and condensing. Sans-serifs "marry" well with almost any Roman face. By "marrying" I mean that they are compatible and help complement

each other. By the same token, the use of two similar sans-serifs together causes confusion.

Display Faces

There are, at this writing, some 2,500 different typefaces. A great many of them are used for only one or two lines of copy, such as a title. They do not read well as text or body copy. Display faces are usually created for a specific need or mood. I will go into "mood" faces in greater detail in a later chapter, but will touch on just a few here so you can get the general feeling of why display faces are created.

P.T. Barnum was created and is still generally accepted as a "circus poster" typeface. It creates a mood of circuses, the "Old West," or even "Wanted" posters. Eve was created for and is still used for feminine fashion advertising. Beton Bold was created to simulate the solid-steel structural beams used in skyscrapers. Scripts were created to simulate handwriting. They rarely look good in mass, except for something like wedding invitations. Avoid all-capital words in script—they are almost unreadable. Figure 1.9 shows some one-line specimens of alphabets, some of which have been mentioned. Your local type-house can supply you with its list of available faces.

Caslon 540

HSMANOETRG 23
hsmanoetrguykjwbfp

HSMANOETRGUYK 235
hsmanoetrguykjwbfpcvdqx

HSMANOETRGUYKJWBFPCV 235789
hsmanoetrguykjwbfpcvdqxlizhsmanoetrg

Figure 1.8—The "classic" Caslon. This can always be identified by the slight notch in the capital letter "A," by the high cross bar in the lower case "e," and by the teardrop of the lower case letter "a."

BALLOON BOLD Foundry 10, 12, 14, 18, 24, 30, 36
ABCDEFGHIJKLMNOPQRSTUVWXYZ& *$1234567890*

BARNUM P. T. Foundry 12, 14, 18, 24, 36
ABCDEFGHIJKLMNOPQRSTUVWXYZ&
abcdefghijklmnopqrstuvwxyz $1234567890

BASKERVILLE Lino 6, 8, 10, 12, 14
ABCDEFGHIJKLMNOPQRSTUVWXYZ&
abcdefghijklmnopqrstuvwxyz $1234567890

*BETON BOLD Foundry 48
ABCDEFGHIJKLMNOPQRSTUVWXYZ&
abcdefghijklmnopqrstuvwxyz $1234567890

BODONI REGULAR Lino 6, 8, 10, 12, 14
ABCDEFGHIJKLMNOPQRSTUVWXYZ&
abcdefghijklmnopqrstuvwxyz $1234567890

* NEW CASLON Foundry 18, 36, 48
ABCDEFGHIJKLMNOPQRSTUVWXYZ&
abcdefghijklmnopqrstuvwxyz $1234567890

* EVE Foundry 14, 24, 36, 48
ABCDEFGHIJKLMNOPQRSTUVWXYZ&
abcdefghijklmnopqrstuvwxyz $1234567890

GARAMOND LIGHT Lino 6, 7, 8, 9, 10, 11, 12, 14
ABCDEFGHIJKLMNOPQRSTUVWXYZ&
abcdefghijklmnopqrstuvwxyz $1234567890

* JANSON OLD STYLE—58 Mono 14, 18, 24, 30, 36
ABCDEFGHIJKLMNOPQRSTUVWXYZ&
abcdefghijklmnopqrstuvwxyz $1234567890

NEWS GOTHIC—206 Mono 5, 6, 7, 8, 9, 10, 11, 12
ABCDEFGHIJKLMNOPQRSTUVWXYZ&
abcdefghijklmnopqrstuvwxyz $1234567890

SCOTCH Lino 12
ABCDEFGHIJKLMNOPQRSTUVWXYZ&
abcdefghijklmnopqrstuvwxyz $1234567890

* TYPO SCRIPT UPRIGHT Foundry 18
ABCDEFGHIJKLMNOPQRSTUVWXYZ&
abcdefghijklmnopqrstuvwxyz $1234567890

VENUS LIGHT Foundry 6, 8, 10, 12, 14, 16, 18, 24, 30, 36
ABCDEFGHIJKLMNOPQRSTUVWXYZ&
abcdefghijklmnopqrstuvwxyz $1234567890

Figure 1.9—A typical showing of one-line specimens. Notice that some showings do not have lower case letters. Look for this in specifying type so that you do not assume there is a lower case.

CHAPTER TWO

Handling Copy for Stories

Every story that comes to the editorial layout artist should be typewritten. This is called "copy." Your first job should always be to accurately figure out how much space this copy will occupy *when set in type*. Space for typeset copy occurs in two directions: column width (which will depend on format) and column length (which is the total length, in columns, of the copy in the story). If you visualize the story as being printed on a long piece of adding machine tape, which represents the column width, it becomes apparent that the strip must be cut into segments, each equal to no more than one column in depth.

There may be occasions when the layout artist will want to work with two different column widths. A story may start in a two-column format, but continue later in a three-column format. In this case, one must figure for two different column widths. It is also possible to use a larger typeface on the lead page of a story and to continue the story in a smaller typeface later on. Again, one must figure for two different space items and add them together.

Measuring (Casting) Type

Type fonts are measured by "characters per pica." What this means is that a pica width of type, when set, will contain an average of so many mixed characters and spaces per pica. A "pica" is a uniform unit of measure equal to 12 points. There are 6 picas to 1 inch and 72 points to 1 inch. The character count per pica is usually computed for a "mix" of both capitals and lower case letters. It accounts for some letters that normally take only half a space, such as the lower case *l* and *j*. It also compensates for those letters that normally take more width than the average letter, such as the lower case *m* and *w*.

Occasionally, you might have only a one-line specimen that consists of all the capitals and all the lower case letters, but with no character count per pica given. What can be done to determine the character count per pica? Measure the lower case alphabet in picas. Since this will contain twenty-six letters, divide the pica length by twenty-six, carrying this two decimal points for accuracy. (For example: twenty-six letters are 11 picas long; 26 divided by 11 would give 2.36 characters per pica.) The entire alphabet will include all the individual letter variations. The letter *a*, the letter *m*, and the letter *i* are not the same width. Mixed in sentences, however, they will tend to average out. Other compensations are the spaces between words used to space out sentences to a predetermined measure. This has no reflection on the character count per pica in most cases, but does cause some line variations when actually counting any line for average characters and spaces.

You cannot "cast," or estimate, copy length unless you know how many characters and spaces there are in the copy, as well as the number you can get on a given column width in the typeface being used. The simplest, though most tedious, way is to count *every* character and space in the copy. This is fine for small blocks of copy, such as picture captions or short blurbs, but impractical for the long story. Here are five practical methods for estimating long stretches of copy.

1. Have the copy retyped on typescript paper. This is a sheet that has been prepared and stocked for a specific face and size and on a specific measure. There is an example of typescript paper in figure 2.1.

2. Determine the number of characters and spaces needed to set one typeset line. Count off this number on the copy and draw a faint line down the page, dividing everything to the right of this line into one typeset line plus "leftovers" to the right of this line. Then count the leftovers into units of the number it takes to set another line. This is rather cumbersome, but is used very often.

3. Determine the number of characters and spaces needed for one typeset line and set your typewriter for this count. As you type a line, it should stop at this measure. It will also "set" one typeset line, in most cases, when converted to typeset copy. This will work, but only if you have the time to retype what has been submitted as copy.

4. Prepare a sheet of heavy (.020 gauge) clear acetate as an overlay.

Typescript paper for Genl. Psyche for PICA typewriter, only.

9/11 Century Exp. ———————————————————————— 1 line ———

8/8 and 8/10 Century Exp. (Includes References) ——- 1 line — — ——-

1

2

3

4

5

6

7

8

9

10

11

12

13

14

15

16

17

18

19

20

22

23

24

Figure 2.1—A typical sheet of typescript made specifically for typing on a pica typewriter and for Century Schoolbook, set on a 16-pica measure. Copy typed between the far left line and the first line to the right will set very close to one typeset line in the face used.

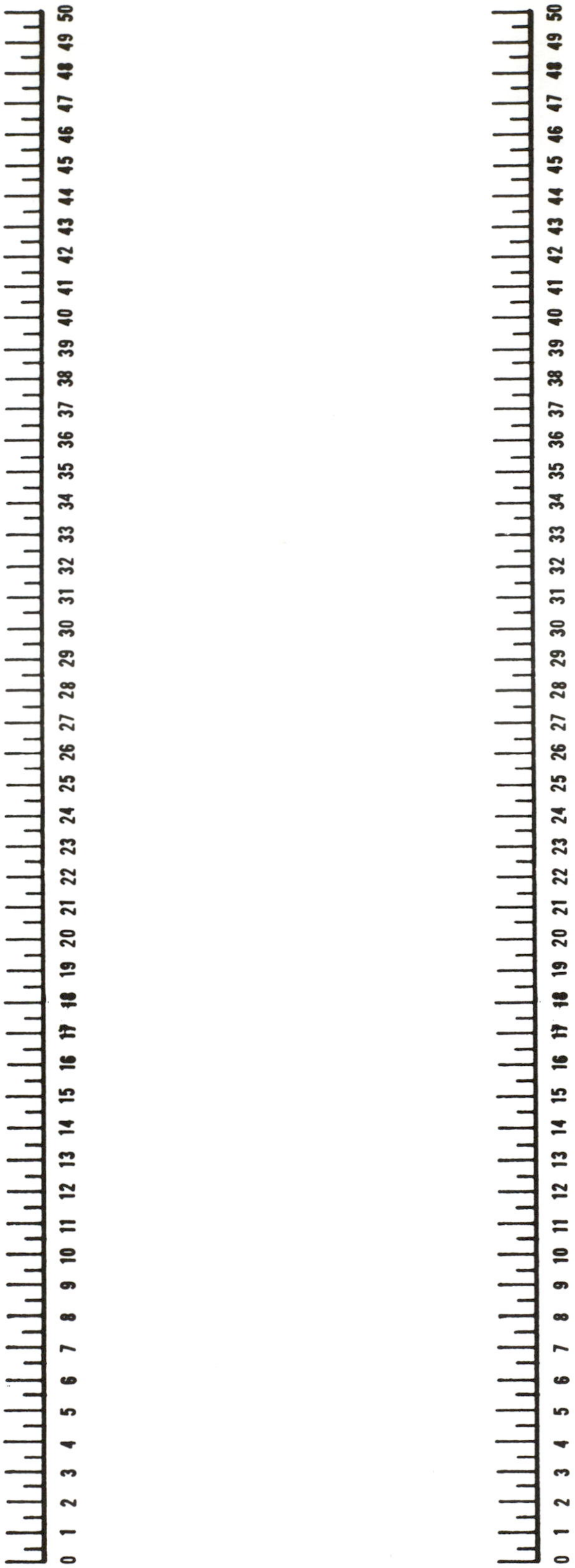

Figure 2.2—These two same-size pica incremented gauges are for your convenience in making up your own "Dorn Estimating Board."

typeset line to the right of the zero line. Use the point of a No. 16 Exacto blade to scratch a fine line into the acetate. Do the same for 1½ typeset lines and for 2 typeset lines, if there is room. Once these lines have been scribed into the acetate, rub India ink into the lines and then rub the surface clean. The ink will remain in the scribed line, leaving a permanent black line that cannot be erased or easily worn away.

When this overlay is placed over the copy and the zero line aligned with the left-hand edge of the copy, it becomes apparent that any number of characters and spaces occurring between zero and the first line will typeset one full line. Two typewritten lines of 1½ units will typeset three lines and so forth. This is excellent when you are using the same typeface and measure for a particular typewriter, but will not work when you change type sizes or typefaces. It is a good idea to prepare sets of acetate sheets to cover most circumstances and to label them properly to prevent confusion.

5. By far the easiest method is to make an "estimating board" (developed by the author and used constantly). Take two pieces of plain white mounting board and cut to 11 by 14 inches. Rubber cement or glue them together for a double-thick board. Then cut eight 1 by 11 inch strips and cement or glue them into two strips, four pieces high. Cement or glue one strip at the top of the board and the other at the bottom of the board. Draw a gauge showing picas and half-picas, 10 inches long. Have this photostated to give two exactly alike. Cement or glue one on the strip at the top of the board and the other at the bottom of the board. Make sure the pica gauge is exactly 1 inch from the left-hand edge. When you slip a rubber band over the board and align it with the zero mark on the pica gauge and then slip another rubber band over the board to a mark exactly one typeset line in the number of characters and spaces needed for one typeset line, you are actually creating a

Scribe a line from top to bottom as a "zero" guide for the left-hand margin. This should be about 1 inch from the left. Scribe another line to exactly the number of characters and spaces needed for one

gauge that will determine how much copy will set for one line. Do the same for 1½ and for 2 lines, if you have room. What this means is that you must count the characters and spaces needed for one typeset line, count off the equivalent number of characters and spaces in the copy, and then "set" the board. By slipping the copy in from the right and moving it under the rubber bands to the left, you can align the rubber bands to calibrate any typeset line for any typewriter, any face, and any size. Those characters and spaces left over, at the right, are then hand-counted for equivalent typeset lines and added to the whole.

In preparing this board for proportional typewritten copy, be sure to average out at least five lines before setting the gauge. The difference between a proportional typewriter and a pica or an elite typewriter is in the number of characters and spaces per inch. In pica there are ten characters per inch. In elite there are twelve characters per inch. However, in proportional typewriters this can vary from eleven per inch to thirteen per inch.

Remember, when casting for small copy, count by hand. When casting for long copy, use one of the methods described above. Figure 2.6 shows an estimating board ready for use.

Computing Copy for Length

Once the number of lines has been determined, it is necessary to examine the typeface chosen for proper leading. Leading is the amount of white space needed between lines to obtain the best readability. For example, if 9 point Century Schoolbook is being used, 2 points of leading sets off the copy to the best advantage. This is specified as 9/11. The 9 means the type size. When 2 points of leading are requested, the 2 is added to the 9, giving 11. Multiply the total number of lines in the copy as predicted to be set by the type size plus the leading. For example, 9/11 would

mean that you multiply the total number of lines by 11, then divide by 12. Since there are 12 points to a pica you will arrive at a total length in picas. If there are 300 lines of 9/11, simply multiply 300 times 11 to get a copy depth of 3,300 points. When you divide by 12, you get 275 picas of typeset copy.

When working with a mixed section, such as 8/10 along with 9/11, each section must be computed as a separate unit, and then all units are added together.

Why is it important to know how long the copy will be? Type does not usually contract or expand but remains as a set unit. You can lengthen or shorten copy by varying the leading, but this may not amount to any great space saving. For instance, in the 300 lines mentioned above, varying the leading by one point will give only 25 picas more or less in length. The copy should be the framework around which the layout evolves. If a copywriter is available, the copy may be cut or expanded to fit an area. However, as a cost-saver, it is better to have the copy set once, as a page layout, and thus eliminate type alterations, which are expensive and time-consuming.

Ordering Type for a Layout

A layout artist can send copy without a layout and ask for "galleys." A galley is no more than the copy, set on column width in arbitrary lengths. These are proofread and corrected. They are then measured, cut apart, and pasted onto a blank layout sheet. This has some advantage in that you can actually see the copy, rather than visualizing what it will look like. When working up a layout that has pictures, knowing exactly how much and where the copy will be can determine the size of the pictures needed to fill out a full page. The disadvantage is that you are asking the printer to set the copy, then pull it apart and rearrange it. It is much simpler to do the job right as a type layout. This also saves double proofreading and money.

The same basic procedures can be followed for both letterpress and offset. The layout artist may be asked to "paste-up" pages from etched proofs. In this case, the copy is set and proofed on white enameled stock, instead of the ordinary proof paper. The layout artist will then actually create a page, ready for camera. This must be done accurately, as any crooked lines will show up like the proverbial sore thumb.

The layout artist can go directly to page proofs if the layout has been handled correctly and the printer follows both the layout and the type instructions. A good layout will act as a blueprint for each page the printer sets.

All layouts have a plan. Usually pages are made up showing the basic format on prepared layout sheets. These sheets show specific locations, such as the column width and height and running foot and folio locations, specifically defining the "live area."

Many of you will paste-up galleys in magazine preparation. The trick to paste-ups is getting all the copy lines and other elements straight and true. Often the errors are not apparent in the original paste-up because there are no guidelines other than the borders and page edges. These don't become apparent until you receive page proofs where any slight misalignment glares at you.

To prevent this from happening, I prepare a sheet of 12½-by-10-inch acetate as an overlay. This sheet has lines scribed into it that accurately define the page edge, borders, margins, alleys, and column widths. Through the copy areas (column widths) I scribe a series of lines 10 points apart. After scribing all the lines and making sure they are "true" I fill in the scribed lines with India ink, rub away all but the ink remaining in the lines, and use it as an overlay. It is quite simple to rubber cement the galleys—place them in position—check the positions with the overlay—and, once placed and aligned with the scribed lines, use the acetate sheet as a burnishing carrier. Since the acetate

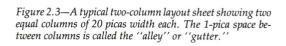

Figure 2.3—A typical two-column layout sheet showing two equal columns of 20 picas width each. The 1-pica space between columns is called the ''alley'' or ''gutter.''

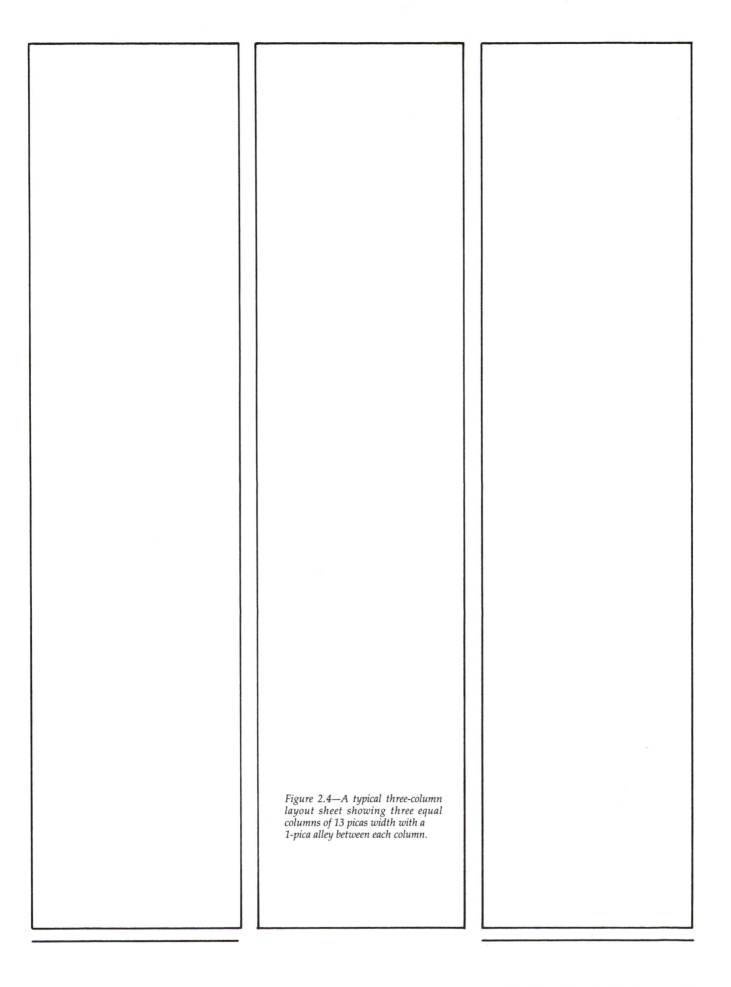

Figure 2.4—A typical three-column layout sheet showing three equal columns of 13 picas width with a 1-pica alley between each column.

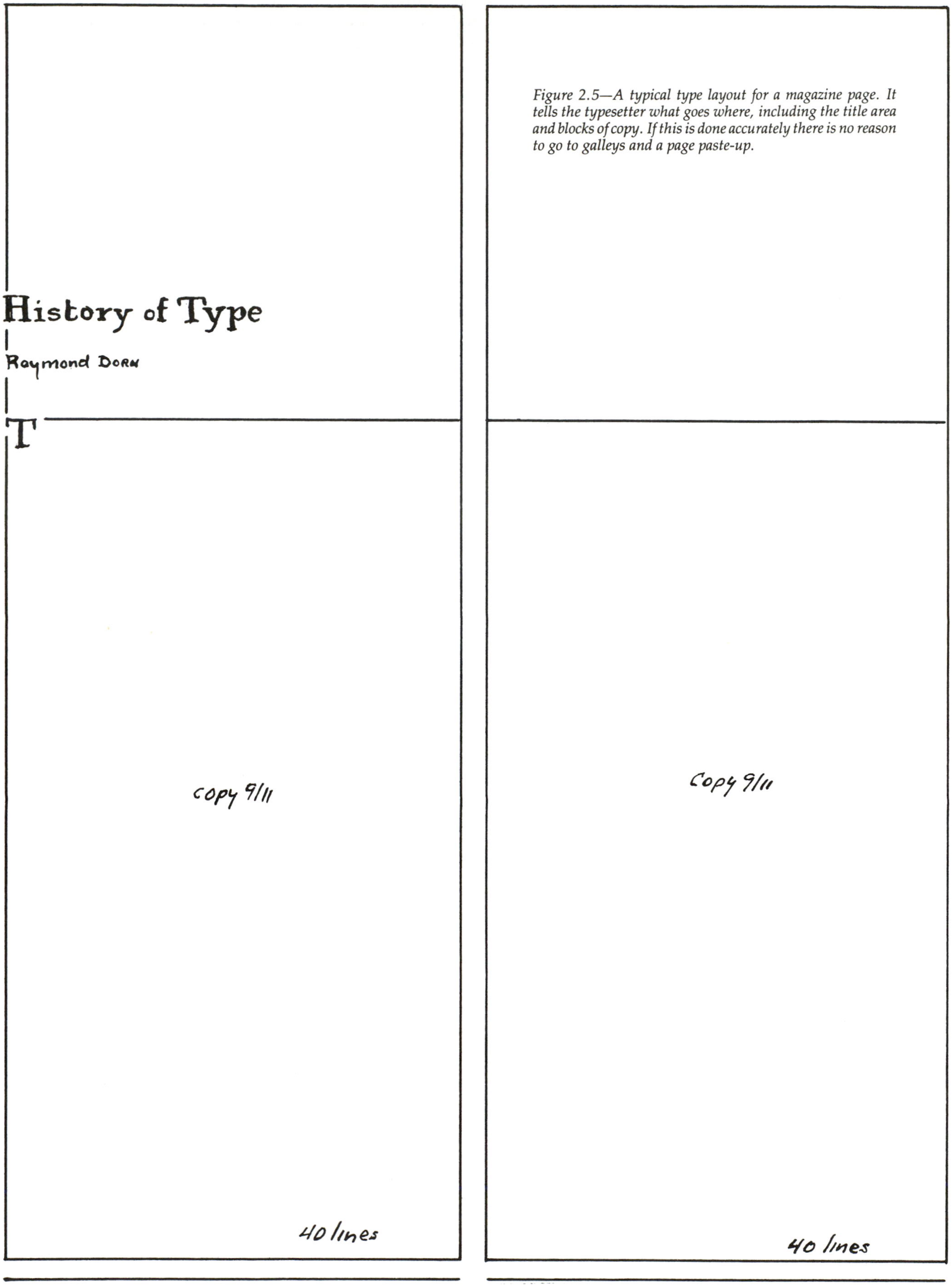

History of Type

Raymond Dorn

T

copy 9/11

copy 9/11

40 lines

40 lines

Figure 2.5—A typical type layout for a magazine page. It tells the typesetter what goes where, including the title area and blocks of copy. If this is done accurately there is no reason to go to galleys and a page paste-up.

sheet is clear it can be placed over the copy and used to check exact alignments. Not only that, but it can take the place of a light table. The sheet can be used again and again with no loss due to shrinkage, warping, or line thickness. It does not affect the galleys in any way. In fact, it preserves them from smearing. You can make one in less than an hour and use it for years.

Another use for the 12½- by-10-inch size is the prepared format overlay. I have prepared an acetate sheet for each of the five formats described in this book. By placing the format (acetate overlay) over the copy or even the original layout, you can quickly see how all elements ''fall'' into the prescribed format or grid. If they do not ''fall into place'' by this quick method,

realign the elements so they will do so.

One word of caution. Do not use anything less than .020 gauge acetate as you might cut completely through it.

Type mark-up is coordinated with the layout. A specific number of lines corresponds to the space shown on the layout sheet. In the example shown, the layout allows

Figure 2.6—The Dorn Estimating Board ready for use. This is adaptable for any typewriter and can be substituted for any of the other four methods of copy estimating. I use rubber bands because they are easily replaceable.

for 48 lines per column. This will accommodate 48 lines of 10/12, or 64 lines of 8/9, and so forth. When moving through the copy, the layout artist specifies the exact number of lines occurring in any area. This tells the typesetter what to set and the printer where to place it.

Proofreader's marks are essential for any layout artist. You should learn them completely. The reason is obvious—you *must* be able to communicate with the printer in the printer's language. If you say, ''Line two should be moved a little to the right under line one,'' you *may* be understood. However, this is not as specific as ''Indent 2 ems,'' which both you and the typesetter understand. Every minute of a typesetter's time is money. The more specific the instructions, the less chance for error and the quicker the job can be done satisfactorily. Accepted proofreader's marks are shown in figure 2.7.

Assuming the layout and copy have gone to the printer in good condition—clear, clean, crisp, and specific—the next thing the layout artist should see are ''page proofs.'' Page proofs are pulled by hand on a proof press in letterpress and by photocopy when set on film. They are ''proof'' that the page has been set as requested. Some errors may occur. The page proofs must be proofread and all corrections noted. Once the pages are correct, the usual custom is to initial them, date them, and return them to the printer.

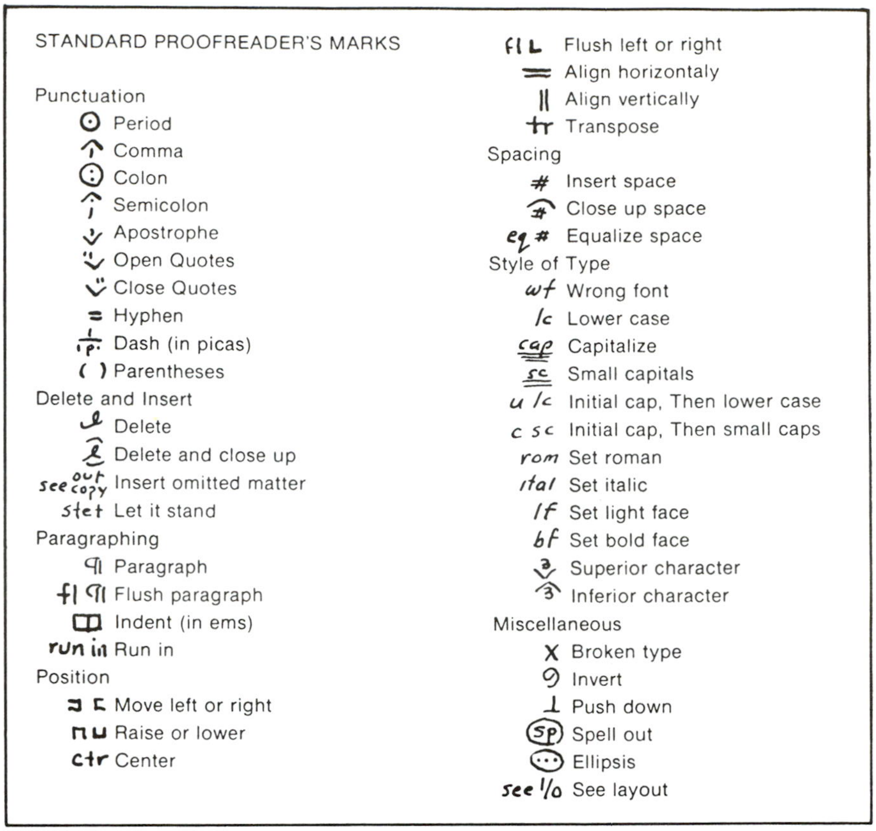

STANDARD PROOFREADER'S MARKS

Punctuation
⊙ Period
⋏ Comma
⊙ Colon
⋏ Semicolon
⋎ Apostrophe
⋎ Open Quotes
⋎ Close Quotes
= Hyphen
⫫ Dash (in picas)
( ) Parentheses

Delete and Insert
⌿ Delete
⌿ Delete and close up
see out copy Insert omitted matter
stet Let it stand

Paragraphing
¶ Paragraph
fl ¶ Flush paragraph
⊓ Indent (in ems)
run in Run in

Position
⊐ ⊏ Move left or right
⊓ ⊔ Raise or lower
ctr Center

fl L Flush left or right
= Align horizontaly
‖ Align vertically
tr Transpose

Spacing
Insert space
⌢ Close up space
eq # Equalize space

Style of Type
wf Wrong font
lc Lower case
cap Capitalize
sc Small capitals
u/lc Initial cap, Then lower case
c sc Initial cap, Then small caps
rom Set roman
ital Set italic
lf Set light face
bf Set bold face
₃ Superior character
₃ Inferior character

Miscellaneous
X Broken type
⊘ Invert
⊥ Push down
(SP) Spell out
⊙ Ellipsis
see l/o See layout

Figure 2.7—Standard proofreader's marks. Copy should always be properly marked up so the typesetter wastes no time in trying to interpret what you meant. Communicating properly will save time and money.

CHAPTER THREE

Display Typefaces and Their Applications

Some typefaces are designed and used to create a certain feeling or mood. These are almost always display faces, which means they are 18 points or larger and usually used in title areas. Since hot metal display faces are hand-set, they can occasionally be letter-spaced with little effort. However, since this is a hand operation, it can get expensive. With cold type (such as Artype, Prestype, and Format, just to mention a few), the layout artist can curve the lines, space them close enough to touch, create overlapping patterns, place them directly over a halftone, interject other faces, and create typographical designs not easily achieved with hot metal. Every would-be layout artist should gather as many ''cold type'' catalogs as possible, purchase at least a few standard sheets, and practice using them. Computer-set display faces also allow the layout artist to use variable letter-spacing, overlapping, and a mixture of faces—plus expanding, compressing, or slanting the type.

Mood typefaces are as hard to define as a personality. While Mr. A may be bright and jolly to his girlfriend, he may be a crashing bore to his male friends. A mood face such as P.T. Barnum (see figure 3.14) may remind one person of the Wild West, but another person of a circus. Correct usage often relates to the story or words used in the title area.

Some typefaces have been identified by continual usage and are synonymous with the subject. Stencil, for instance, is almost always associated with faraway places, because shipping crates have the addresses stenciled on their sides. The use of Stencil (see figure 3.14) on any subject gives the indication that it has been imported. A bowl of cherries, even though domestic, can be made to appear imported just by the use of this particular typeface.

The greatest number of display

ABCDEFGHIJKLMNOPQRSTUVWXYZ
abcdefghijklmnopqrstuvwxyz

Figure 3.1—A specimen of Cooper Black. This is big, bold, and almost brutal.

STRUCTURAL ART ANALYSIS FOUNDATION
A NOT-FOR-PROFIT INSTITUTION

OPEN HOUSE

Sunday, November 18, 1973 — 10 a.m. to 6:00 p.m.
6001 North Drake Avenue
Chicago

We cordially invite you to visit our studio and workshops. You will meet some of our students, observe how our approach to a better understanding of the structure of paintings dramatically expands the imagination, creative ability and self-realization of artists, students and laymen alike.

Please come. Your stay will be most enjoyable and rewarding!

Marshall Salzman
Director

Refreshments

Figure 3.2—An excellent example of a good type ''marriage.'' It is rare to find a sans-serif marrying well with a script. This fine example shows that it can occasionally be done in good taste.

faces are not identified with any single subject. Venus or Futura can be used for any subject, as well as "marrying" with any Roman typeface. Neither Helvetica nor Futura is actually a mood face. What identifies a mood face is the first impression the average person receives when he or she sees it used. The mood created by Cooper Black (figure 3.1) would mean nothing to the indigenous people of Australia, other than the fact that it was darker and heavier than another face. They would be unable to relate the face to an experience or usage.

Certain things relate to other things—ham and eggs; black and white; beer and pretzels. These are called "natural marriages" because the average person has been trained to think of them as related combinations. In type there are also natural marriages—or mixtures—of type. Regular with italic is one. Almost every Roman typeface has this particular combination. Another marriage is a Roman with a sans-serif. For example, Helvetica will marry well with Times Roman. The more subtle marriages constitute the intermingling of two typefaces that go well together. The example shown in figure 3.2 is a reasonably good marriage of a sans-serif with a script.

Chicago vs New York

Chicago vs New York

Chicago vs **New York**

CHICAGO NEW YORK

Chicago New York

Figure 3.3—An example of various "mood" faces comparing New York with Chicago. Notice how your eye cannot settle down to any one face, but keeps moving from face to face.

Figure 3.4—Regardless of the story, can there be any doubt that it must be about the Old South? This is the purpose behind mood faces, when used in title areas.

Figure 3.5—Caslon Antique: worm-eaten and mouse-nibbled wooden faces. Typical of the typesetting of a bygone era.

Figure 3.6—Optima is often called a serif-without-a-serif. This particular face can be used anywhere, anytime, because of its good clean lines.

Figure 3.7—Any doubt that this represents the black-leather-jacketed motorcycle riders? The face is strong, dominant, and almost "pushy."

Figure 3.8—A typical "uncial"—no caps—all lower case and implying that it was hand-lettered with a goose quill. It reminds one of monks handlettering the early Bibles and missals.

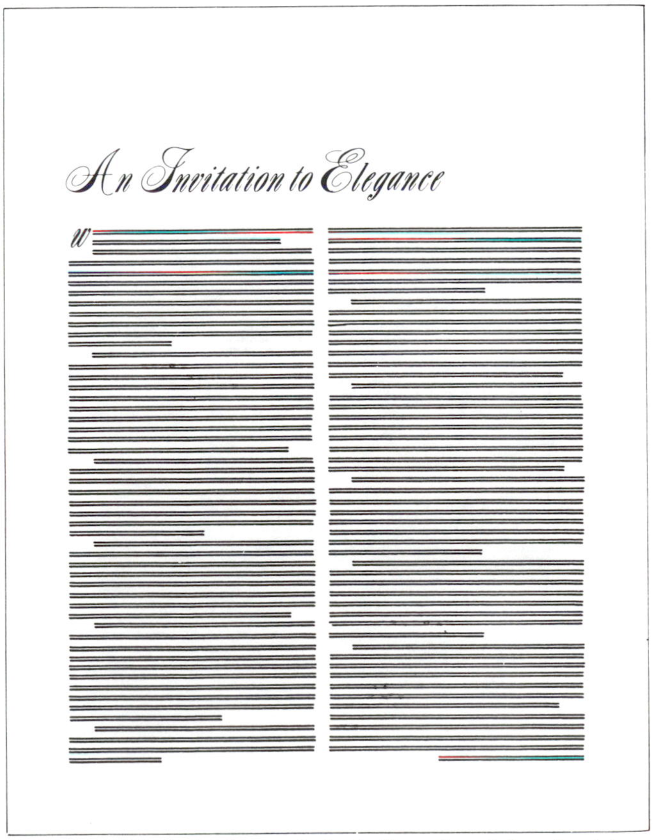

Figure 3.9—This display face speaks for itself; an elegant, formal script.

Figure 3.10—A simple, clean italic, leaning toward the right and implying "flight."

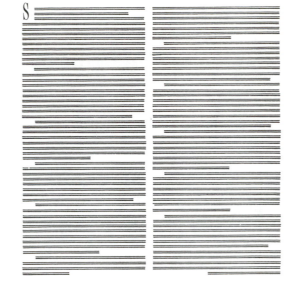
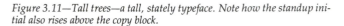

Figure 3.11—Tall trees—a tall, stately typeface. Note how the standup initial also rises above the copy block.

Figure 3.12—Oversimplified but it leaves no doubt that there is a difference between black and white in the story content.

Figure 3.13—The "I-beam" typeface symbolizing the steel girders used in skyscrapers. This is an example of an "Egyptian" face, so called because the style includes faces like Memphis and Cairo.

BALLOON BOLD 12* 18 24 30 36 48 72

ABCDEFGHIJKLMNOPQRSTUVWXYZ .,:;-'""&!? $12345

BANK SCRIPT 14* 18 24

ABCDEFGHIJKLMNOPQRS
abcdefghijklmnopqrstuvwxyz .,:;-'&!? $1234567

BARNUM, P.T. 12* 14 18 24 30 36

ABCDEFGHIJKLMNOPQRSTUVWXYZ
abcdefghijklmnopqrstuvwxyz .,:;-'""&!? $1234

BERNHARD MODERN ROMAN 14* 18

ABCDEFGHIJKLMNOPQRSTUVWXY
abcdefghijklmnopqrstuvwx .,:;-'""&!? $1234

BETON BOLD 18* 24 30 36

ABCDEFGHIJKLMNOPQRST
abcdefghijklm .,:;-"&!? $1234

CASLON OLD STYLE 540 14* 42 48 60 72 84 96

ABCDEFGHIJKLMNOPQRSTUV
abcdefghijklmnopqrst .,:;-'&!? $123+

CHELTENHAM BOLD 86J 6 8 9 10 12* 14 18 24 30 36 42 48 60 72

ABCDEFGHIJKLMNOPQRSTUVWXYZ
abcdefghijklmnopqrstuv .,:;-'&!? $1234

CHISEL 30*

ABCDEFGHIJKLMN
abcdefg .,:;-'&!? $123

CLOISTER TEXT 95J 12* 14 18 24 30 36

ABCDEFGHIJKLMNOPQRSTUVWX
abcdefghijklmnopqrstubw .,:;-'""&!? $123456

EDEN LIGHT 12*

ABCDEFGHIJKLMNOPQRSTUVWXYZ
abcdefghijklmnopqrstuvwxyz .,:;-'&!? $1234567890

FUTURA BOLD 603J 6 8 9 10 11 12* 14 16 18 24 30 36 42 48 60 72

ABCDEFGHIJKLMNOPQRSTUVWXYZ
abcdefghijklmnopqrstuvw .,:;-'&!? $123

GRAYDA NO. 2 18/24* 24 30 36

ABCDEFGHIJKLMNOPQRSTU
abcdefghijklmnopqrstuvwxy .,:;-'""&!? $123

KAUFMANN SCRIPT 14 18* 24 30 36

ABCDEFGHIJKLMNOPQRSTUV
abcdefghijklmnopqrstuv .,:;-'&!? $123

LEADERS
48 leaders

MISTRAL

PALATINO REG. 20* 24 30 42

ABCDEFGHIJKLMNOPQR
abcdefghijklm .,:;-''&!? $123

LEGEND 18* 24 36 48

ABCDEFGHIJKLMNOPQRST
abcdefghijklmnopqrstuvwxyz .,:;-'"" &!? $123

LOMBARDIC 24* 30 36 72

ABCDEFGHIJKL

RIVOLI ITALIC 18* 30 36 48

ABCDEFGHIJKLMNOPQR
abcdefghijklmnopqrstu .,:;= "&!? $123

STENCIL 18* 24 30

ABCDEF .,:;-''&!? $123

UNION PEARL 22*

ABCDEFGHIJKLMNOP
abcdefghijklmnopqrstuvwxyz .,&ff

Figure 3.14—Samples of mood faces.

This is usually not done, but there are occasions when rigid typographical rules can be changed to suit a specific purpose. In this case, for the subject of ''structural art,'' the sans-serif is an ideal choice. The invitation is script, which is also a good choice. This is called a ''marriage.''

Probably the best lesson in this respect is that similar typefaces never marry well. In figure 3.3, Dom Casual will never be comfortable with York Script. Zodiac will never blend with Mistral and Beton and Cheltenham will fight through eternity. Any two similar typefaces will vie for attention. Neuland and Cooper Highlight are two that will do this. However, two very dissimilar typefaces will do the same thing, such as Palatino Italic and Calligraph.

There are several safe rules that apply to type usage:

1. Never mix two similar typefaces. They tend to blend rather than contrast.

2. Sans-serifs and Romans will usually marry well.

3. A script and a Roman will rarely ''marry'' well.

4. Use the complete font of any Roman with impunity.

5. Use the complete font of any one family of sans-serifs with impunity.

6. Never mix two display typefaces.

As the layout artist becomes accustomed to using type, he or she may happen to find a good marriage (in type, that is) either from usage or from another printed piece. Study the blending and compatibility. Once you find a good one, file it away for future reference.

In handling display type for headlines, one might capitalize a whole word within a title area for emphasis with good design results. When a headline consists of more than one line, be sure each line reads as a complete thought or phrase. Watch for peculiar ascenders and descenders that might destroy readability, or divorce one line from another by adding to or lessening the proper spacing. Usually, do not allow the ascenders or descenders to touch. This sometimes creates visual monsters. If you set a headline all caps, set it with tight letter-spacing. If you set all lower case, use ordinary spacing. Don't try to be tricky. Too many tricky headlines look good on the drawing board but fail when the average reader cannot quickly grasp the meaning. Watch for two letters that are the same, one on top of the other (such as two *l*'s). These can create distracting designs. Remember, the layout artist is there to serve the reader. Subtle designs are far more effective than clubs. A neat, clean headline with generous white space is far more attractive than a contrived design that must be identified before it can be read.

CHAPTER FOUR

How to Choose and Handle Type

Every student of magazine design recognizes the fact that all copy should be readable. First, let us define "readable." Webster defines this as "legible, as handwriting; easy to read." We can further define this as "complete word clarity." It stands to reason that clarity is a must if headlines, stories, and captions are meant to be read.

Headlines

A headline is a story title. This is the layout artist's first sales tool in capturing the reader's attention. It makes a great deal of sense to prepare this message loud and clear. "Loud" does not mean "large," but rather well-defined. Roman typefaces are the most comfortable. We are used to seeing them in books and newspapers. However, story titles can get rather dull and, more important, lose their impact, by consistent repetition of the same face. This means other possible choices would include sans-serifs and the wide array of mood typefaces. Before leaving Roman faces, let us study how they should be handled, remembering that many of these concepts will also apply to other typefaces.

The first rule of thumb in handling Roman typefaces in title areas is to use proper leading. Clarity is the deciding factor. Serif letters look best when leading is about one-third the height of the typeface. For example, 18-point type would take about 6 points of leading for maximum clarity and cohesiveness. Even this may not always

be the best leading choice, because some typefaces, such as Century Expanded, have short ascenders and descenders; Garamond is just the opposite. Always study the typeface. Examine the ascenders and descenders. Is the overall effect of a line of type smooth and uninterrupted with excessive ascenders and descenders? Will a multi-line title cause variations in leading? Will a line with no descenders divorce itself from the following line? Will a line with no ascenders divorce itself from the preceding lines? Each of these factors must receive consideration. The reason some Romans are in constant and acceptable use is based on just this sort of examination and judgment. This is not always apparent to the novice when studying one-line specimens of a new typeface. You can see visible proof of the weakness in using consistent leading for all titles in figure 4.1.

Leading is measured from the base of the x-height of one line to the base of the x-height on the following line. The same leading on all lines allows for ascenders and descenders (if one or both of these elements are missing, the white space between lines may appear excessive).

Should letters of one line touch a second line? I do not feel this design trick has application in headlines. It can be used in developing logos or trademarks, where overall and immediate identification is desired, but I feel any title should possess immediate readability, as opposed to requiring a pause to

study and redefine all the letters before it can be read. In the example in figure 4.2, notice how the L and H are joined. This creates a new letter shape that needs to be studied before it makes sense.

Story titles should be brief and limited to not more than five words, if possible. Long and bulky titles are hard to read and lose impact with length. Be careful to break multi-line heads so phrases are not separated.

Computing title lengths is not difficult. One first multiplies the characters per pica by the desired width. This will give an average number of lower case letters needed to fit an area. By counting the capitals as $1\frac{1}{2}$ letters as well as the lower case *m* and *w* and the lower case *f, i, j, l,* and *t* as one-half character, the layout artist can pretty well determine whether a title will fit in an area.

Knowing how many characters and spaces will fit into a given area also determines a workable type size. For example, the title "Mr. Doe visits London" has 21 characters and spaces, counting punctuation marks as one each. Add another $\frac{1}{2}$ character for each capital and we now have $22\frac{1}{2}$. Subtract $\frac{1}{2}$ character for each punctuation mark, two lower case *i*'s, and a lower case *t*, and we find that 20 characters are what we actually have to work with. By measuring 20 characters, lower case, in a one-line specimen, the layout artist can determine a typeface that will fit the area involved.

Sans-serif titles also have ascenders and descenders, but their gen-

Adult Polycystic Disease
of the Kidneys (Potter Type 3)

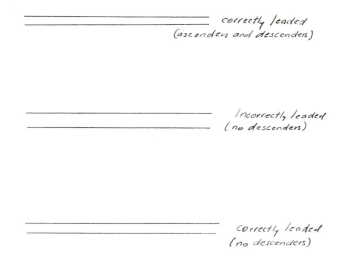

*correctly leaded
(ascenders and descenders)*

Time-Oriented Patient Records
and a Computer Databank

*Incorrectly leaded
(no descenders)*

Tumor Variation
in Families With Breast Cancer

*correctly leaded
(no descenders)*

Britons develop non-invasive diagnostic system

Sentence-style headline

Figure 4.1—Several title areas showing how many layout artists miss the proper leading when the title has no descenders. It is attention to details such as this that separates the average layout artist from the "pro."

eral character and feeling are such that the "one-third leading" rule can be safely applied. Letters are almost always of the same thickness. Romans have many variations in thickness and thinness, particularly in the serifs. The even tone stroke in sans-serifs makes it imperative that letters in one line do not touch letters in the next line. As an example, the letter *T* touching the letter *I* will do several things. It will elongate the *T* and minimize the *I*. This is sometimes used as an eye-catching trick, but such gimmicks have a bad habit of not working.

Sans-serifs can be used in upper and lower case, as well as "all caps," in a title area. Romans rarely look well set all caps. The criterion in working with sans-serifs is the stroke thickness. A thin sans-serif, even though light and airy, is still so structurally sound that it can occupy an area with little trouble. The thick sans-serif, however, will dominate any title area. Sans-serifs, with the possible exception

of some condensed faces, all have one weakness: the circular letters (*C, D, G, O,* and *Q*) are nearly perfect circles and create visual gaps with horizontals next to them. This is apparent in figure 4.3. The sentence structure of titles applies to sans-serifs. They can be measured in the same manner as Romans.

Mood or display faces must always be studied prior to use. Some of them have upper and lower case; some do not. Some have high ascenders but short descenders, and vice versa. Some offer variations of the same letters, such as the letter *S,* depending on where it will be used in a word. Some offer only caps. Some script letters have perfect joining, others do not. I prefer using "cold type" (such as Artype, Format, and the like) for making up some mood typeface titles. The letters can be letter-spaced, moved around, curved, or otherwise manipulated to suit a given area. Both Roman and sans-serifs look best when set mechanically straight (on a printing slug).

Figure 4.2—A typical handling of sans-serif letters into a geometric shape or mass. Notice how hard it is to read, particularly how the L touches the H to create a letter shape that does not exist in our alphabet.

Cold type lettering can also be placed on an acetate flap for perfect alignment over a picture. This is often very difficult when working with typeset etched proofs, even when trimming them close. The paper background between the letters will obliterate the background area. Mood faces can be difficult to lead properly when using etched proofs, which is why cold type sometimes offers the best visual answer for the artist.

Story Copy

Story copy is, basically, a choice of the best Roman face available. It should be a highly readable face, leaded for maximum clarity, and with proper leading to give an exact number of lines in two different sizes to a column depth. For example, fifty lines of 9/11 and fifty-five lines of 8/10 are the same pica and point depth. The face used should also have a bold face and italic face along with the regular. Column width is another factor. A condensed Roman may look good on 13 picas, but become difficult to read on 20 picas. An expanded Roman may look good on 20 picas, but fly apart on 13 picas. Most typesetters stock the most popular fonts and faces.

Casting story copy can be as complex or as simple as the layout artist wishes it to be. The only accurate way to cast story copy is to hand count everything. This is often impractical. The easiest way is to prepare typescript paper, divided into units of ten characters and spaces, and have the staff write their stories on this paper. If this is not feasible, use the ''estimating board'' described in chapter 2. If you use the units-of-ten typescript paper, it is easy to count the total characters and spaces in each paragraph: add the total paragraphs together and total the entire story. The one advantage of the units-of-ten typescript is that one can anticipate ''widows.'' Widow is a word or part of a hyphenated word on the last line of a paragraph. Widows may be eliminated by editing the copy to bring the word up a line or by adding copy so that the last word does not stand alone. Widows are the one sure sign of a non-professional.

Captions

Captions, or legends, are the short descriptive sentences that describe or clarify the illustrations. There are several methods of placing captions—above, below, or to either side. Sometimes they are ''wrapped-around'' a corner. Captions are usually placed *under* a picture when the picture is at the top of a page and *above* the picture when the picture is at the bottom of the page. They can be placed on either side at any time. The wrapped-around caption should be used only in a group or cluster of pictures and should always be a part of the design.

Captions can be set flush left and right, flush left, ragged right, flush right, ragged left and wrap-around. I show examples of each in the diagrams in figure 4.4. When casting, copy for captions should always be hand counted for accuracy. The layout artist should predetermine how many characters and spaces occur within any given measure within the layout format. For example, in the three-column format, captions can occur on one column, two columns, three columns, or one and one-half columns. Each possibility should be accurately charted and a list made. For instance, this might give 32 characters and spaces on 13 picas, 66 characters and spaces on 27 picas, and 100 characters and spaces on 41½ picas. Therefore, a count of the characters and spaces in a caption that totals 78 would be two full lines, plus 14 characters and spaces on the third line. It could also be one full line, plus 12 characters if used over two columns (or 27 picas). A count of 66 characters and spaces for one column would anticipate a widow.

Captions flush on one side and ragged on the other should always be broken at complete words—never hyphenate.

The wrap-around caption has its own method. The caption copy should first be ''scanned'' to be sure there is enough copy for the proper effect. There should be at least three lines above the corner of a picture and three or more lines under the picture. This means two separate measurements: the first three lines on a short measure, and the remainder on a longer measure. The first three lines should not be set on less than a 10-pica measure to prevent ''rivers'' of white space caused by additional word spacing and hyphenations. The count for the first three lines is then deducted from the total. The remainder is divided into three or more relatively equal lines, forming an ''L'' around the corner of the picture. This may take a little more time, but the finished product will show finesse and polish. This type of caption should always be part of a group or cluster page design; it looks much better than captions set flush left and right, which only repeat the shape of the picture.

HIGH POTENCY ANTACID FOR RELIEF OF ULCER PAIN

Figure 4.3—Visually, a horizontal bar with several perfect ''holes'' in it. Notice how the O and C, which are perfect circles, make the line look as if it were punched.

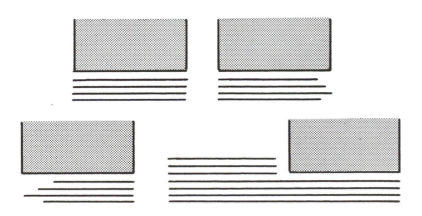

Figure 4.4—The four standard caption setting styles: justified, flush left, flush right, and wrap-around. Be very careful of using flush right-ragged left as it is slightly awkward to read. People are more accustomed to finding the left-hand edge flush.

CHAPTER FIVE

Picture Editing and Cropping

An illustration should invite interest or clarify some specific point within the story. People invariably look at the pictures even before they read the story. Editing pictures requires that one have some general knowledge of the subject. Most editorial layout artists read everything because of their interest in any printed piece. Some knowledge has been acquired from constant exposure to the news media—newspapers, magazines, television, and the like. However, the safest approach to any story is to read it quickly. Exactly what is the picture (or pictures) supposed to do? This must be settled before picture editing. From then on it becomes a matter of judgment. Ask some, if not all, of these questions:

1. How much of the picture should be used?
2. What is the highlight within the picture?
3. Is one picture better than another, when there is a choice of many?
4. If so, why should it be used?
5. What size would you *like* to use?
6. What size might you be restricted to using?
7. Should the picture have a border or special effect?
8. Should the picture bleed off the page?
9. Should it be black and white, two-color, three-color, or four-color?
10. Where will it best illustrate the story?

Let us consider these points individually to determine what the picture editor actually does.

How much of the picture should be used? Suppose you have a picture of a seagull flying over ocean waves. There are several "sight elements" involved—the seagull, the waves, and the sky. Depending on what the story is meant to convey, "edit" or crop the picture to concentrate on one specific sight element. If you concentrate on the seagull, minimize the waves and sky. They might detract from the subject matter by overpowering it.

What is the highlight within the picture? This varies from the first question in that some point *within* the picture will draw interest or attention. Let's use the same example of the "seagull, waves, and sky." It might be that the photographer caught one wing slightly blurred in motion. This slight variation becomes a point of interest because the eye has clearly defined the other parts, but returns and even lingers on the blurred area, trying to redefine it. In some cases design may tie directly into the picture, such as titles that curve with the subject matter.

Is one picture better than another, when there is a choice of many? The expert photo editor has a sense of the unusual. In a dozen pictures of an old man sitting in a rocking chair, all taken at five-second intervals, one picture will reflect a special feeling. Perhaps it is just an added wrinkle around the eyes that indicates a reflection of lost youth. Perhaps it is just a slight extra shadow around the mouth that spells frustration at his age. Often these "little somethings" can be just the special effect needed. In some cases they can be emphasized by enlarging.

What size would you like to use? When there is a given amount of copy and you are restricted to keeping stories to a prescribed number of pages, you must make a choice. If the picture is half a page (most desirable), what will it do to the story? In cases where there is no limit to space requirements, a study of the picture and its relationship to the story is essential. The key word is "relationship." Here is an example of relationship. Suppose there was a story on how to prune roses. The submitted picture consists of a rose bush, a woman kneeling next to it, and some background. The woman has pruning shears in her hand. Now, it is obvious that the woman represents the one being instructed. The highlight would be the pruning shears, and a direct relationship between the shears and the story is essential. Editing the picture down to its barest essentials would show the woman's hands in the act of pruning.

What size might you be restricted to using? These are often called "sacred" pictures, because the usable size is predetermined. Stamps, money, and securities, for example, if shown at all, must be twice-size or half-size, but never same-size. Another instance might be a microscopic slide, where the

Figure 5.1—The original glossy print.

magnification shown in the caption bears a direct relationship to the size being shown.

Relationship also helps to predetermine the size used. This might be illustrated by a picture of a man with his dog standing in front of a house. There is a relationship between the sight elements. The dog is smaller than the man. The man is smaller than the house and so forth. Now, if you had three separate pictures of each sight element, it would not make much sense to make the dog three times the size of the house. The reading public is very much aware of proportions. The only way you might get away with exaggerating is to make the exaggeration obvious.

Should the picture have a border or special effect? Most pictures need nothing more than the subject matter to fully explain the meaning. However, there are cases where borders will do an extra job for a picture. Let us take a "sacred" or predetermined-size picture. It turns out that this does not match the column width. If it is smaller than column width, adding a hairline ruled box around it will help to frame it within the column limits. If a picture is to visually recede from the reader, this can be done by adding a series of lines, starting with a heavy line and progressing to thinner ones. This forces the reader's eye into the center of the picture and helps create an illusion of depth. The reverse would be true to make the picture "flower" out.

A special effect can be created by using tints of color in the form of blocks. A picture centered in a slightly larger tint block will give the picture depth as well as a border. By offsetting the tint block, the picture can be made to "slide" in one direction or the other. Use your imagination. Search, and apply what you see, only be sure it applies to your magazine.

In some instances, photo tricks can give added impact to the picture. One example would be to have the picture reproduced with a coarse screen value by your platemaker. When the proof is returned, take only a part of the picture and "blow it up" (enlarge it photographically). This will explode the dot structure, creating quite a different impression than the original. Another photo trick is reversing out type matter in the picture area. However, be sure the type is large enough to stand a reverse in a dot-structured halftone area.

Should the picture bleed off the page? "Bleeding" means that the picture is no longer within the "live area" (that is the normal page within the margins) but extends off the page. This can be on one side, two sides, three sides, or all four sides. For example, a long, narrow bleed, moving to the top of the page, will help pull the reader's eye in that direction. A bleed off the page at the lower right-hand corner will invite the reader to turn the page. Bleeding comes in handy to emphasize the picture as opposed to the type matter. It also creates special effects impossible to get by keeping everything within the normal page area. Bleeding should be done when you want to create a special effect or movement.

Should it be black-and-white, two-color, three-color, or four-color? Magazines are usually made up in standard printing forms and in multiples of four. A four-page form results in eight printed pages. This is because it is printed on both sides. An eight-page form will become a sixteen-page signature. And a sixteen-page form will become a thirty-two-page signature. What this means to the layout artist is that he may be allowed the use of a second or third color just because of the way advertisements run in any given signature. This color is free, because the color is going to be used anyhow. These "free" colors should be utilized in layout whenever possible.

Let us examine some of the applications of a second color. Most magazines print their advertising in four-color process colors. These are not "true" colors as we imagine them to be. The blue is cyan, which is sort of a robin's egg blue. The red is called magenta and is not a real red, but sort of a rusty pink. The yellow is yellow and the black is black. The combination of these four colors can give almost exact full-color reproductions when handled correctly for plate work.

Presses made to run "four-color" usually use two ink channels for two of these colors. They will usually run the blue and yellow in two channels and on the same run. This prints blue on one side and yellow on the other. The sheet is turned, and the blue then prints on the opposite side, as does the yellow. Next, the press channels the black and red. As each color is laid on top of the other, we get color variations. The yellow and blue make green. The yellow and red make orange, and so forth. The black is usually added last to give final depth and definition.

What can an artist do with a second color (the first one being black) when it is available? One use is for "duotones." A duotone means that for a halftone picture, two plates are made, both of the same image and in the same focus. However, one of these is perhaps 90 percent of a color and 50 percent of black. The result is a picture that combines the two colors and gives another that is neither 100 percent black nor 100 percent of the original color.

Another alternative for using a second color is to have the halftone or line art made 100 percent black and overprint it on a tint block of a color. These tint blocks can be slightly off-center, making the picture move in a determined direction. Or, they can be slightly larger, giving the picture a colored frame.

Line drawings can often use a second color or three different percentages of the same color. These percentages are usually 25 percent, 50 percent, 75 percent, and 100 percent. Tinted areas often help a line drawing with small design spots and help to brighten up a page. One should use color to advantage and never just to decorate. Bar graphs are naturals for the use of a second color, as are most charts and schematic drawings.

Where will it best illustrate the story? The only correct answer here is to put yourself in the reader's place. If the reader is referred to a chart within the story, it makes good sense to place that chart somewhere on the page or facing page in which it is mentioned. If it is a "how to do it" type of story, in which the pictures carry the story rather than the text, the pictures should be in a normal reading pattern, that is, from left to right and top to bottom. Commissioned art for a story (where you hire an outside artist to render a picture based on the story) might be used as part of the title page. This is the most logical place for one good picture to draw the reader into the story. Actually, there are three "positions": there is the ideal position; there are positions that serve a purpose; and there are positions that are not ideal but may have to be used under given circumstances.

The following pages will show you a picture received for a story. Note that there are several "sight elements"—the old man, the old woman, the lamp, and a checkerboard. Using the ten basic questions outlined in the text, "edit" this picture for various story titles.

Figures 5.2 through 5.8 show several variations on the picture as used with different story titles. Each one is different, but all use the same basic picture. Identify each rule, as you see it, in the story layouts and picture handling.

Usually no picture is so well organized or explicit that it should be used from edge to edge. Exceptions might be professional portraits, reproductions of original art, or specific items that must be shown in their complete form. Even then, the platemaker should have enough room, on all four sides, to square off the picture.

Picture cropping usually means the removal of superfluous subject matter from any or all four sides, so that the final result will contain just the meat of the picture. The difference between "editing" and "cropping" is that cropping shows size, and editing shows how much. Cropping is usually done with a Stabilo pencil. This has a very soft lead that will not mar the picture. Two lines are drawn on the white border of the photograph at the top and two more along the right hand side. The top shows width desired; the side shows depth desired. These give the camera person exact boundaries and permit exact 90-degree corners. Why are these

Ma and Pa Retire to Arizona

Figure 5.2—Cropping the original into two specific parts changes the original into two very individual character studies. Notice how both faces look into the text.

Old "Doc" Jonas

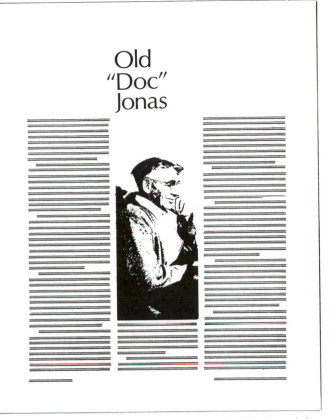

Figure 5.3—A character study tied into the heading. Could be done only by cropping.

Checker Champs of Sun City

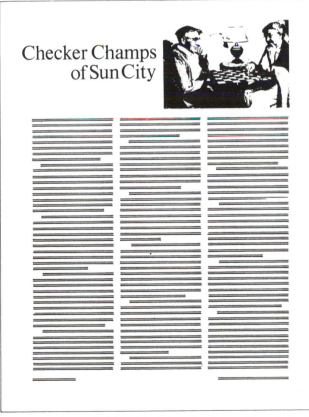

Figure 5.4—Almost all of the original picture has been used to make the title area and the picture into a cohesive unit.

Retirement: The golden years

Figure 5.5—A "split" into two character studies.

Sweet Sixty and still enjoying life!

Figure 5.6—Cropping has now made the original rectangle into a stronger horizontal shape.

Peace and Contentment

Figure 5.7—Cropping and sizing (with a bleed) pulls the reader's eye off the page and "leads" into the following page.

right-angle corners necessary? The type matter for the stories is set as straight, horizontal lines, which square up with the edges of each page. If the picture is crooked, or tilted, this becomes very obvious when placed in a field of true horizontals.

Cropping can also be indicated by placing a tissue flap directly over the photograph and drawing a box, at right angles, on the tissue. This box indicates exactly what is to be taken from the picture. This is used when a photograph has been borrowed and cannot be marred in any way, such as a portrait photo. The tissue overlay method also can be used to tell the platemaker what areas you may want "dropped out." These drop outs are areas within the picture that serve no purpose and can be eliminated. This is called "outlining," and the result would be a picture that has free form instead of the usual box shape. *Do not* use a ball-point pen or hard-lead pencil to crop or show drop outs. This will dent the surface of the emulsion and create

So you think there's no skill to the game of Checkers?

Figure 5.8—Sizing and cropping to give some white space or airy feeling to the picture. Notice how the title area setting creates an invisible line that leads directly down into the picture.

"valleys" or shadows that are hard to eliminate.

Line drawings, as a rule, are not cropped. The reason is that the edges of the drawing are already clearly defined. There may be line drawings that have superfluous material that bears no direct reference to the caption. These can be trimmed by cropping, by cutting a mask, or simply by covering with white paper or correction tape. If one visualizes any cropped picture as being contained within a frame, the whole concept becomes clearer.

Picture Sizing

The space allowed in a layout for a picture will seldom be the same as the size received. Very often magazines will specify that they accept only 5×7 inch glossy prints, or some other standard size. Suppose a story called for three pictures and all were 5×7 inch prints. How would the layout artist get these three pictures "sized" proportionally down to areas desired? The rule that applies here is: "things equal to a third thing are equal to each other." More simply, this would be "direct relationship." The John Hancock Building in Chicago is 100 stories high. Twenty different-sized photographs of this building will do nothing to change its height in relationship to its surroundings.

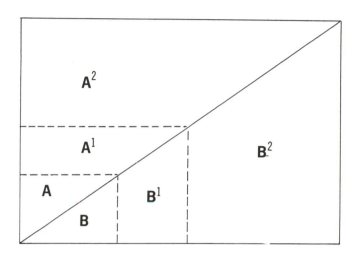

Figure 5.9—The "diagonal principle" illustrated.

Using the Proportional Wheel

The layout artist might have a picture 30 picas long by 18 picas high. The artist wants this to be 16 picas long but does not know the new height. Align the proportional wheel with 30 on the inside circle and 16 on the outside circle. By reading the scale back for 30 to 16, we find the new height is 9⁹/₁₆ picas. By reading the figure in the "percentage of original size" window, we find we will instruct the printer to shoot this photograph at 53 percent. No matter what the original size, this method can be used to determine the new size.

How to "Size" without the Proportional Wheel

The theory of the proportional wheel can be defined as the "diagonal principle." Any rectangle that has a line (diagonal) drawn from the lower left-hand corner to the upper right-hand corner is divided into two equal parts.

As one can see in figure 5.9, A equals B because the area is divided into two equal parts. Any line drawn parallel to the base, and intersecting the diagonal, and any line drawn parallel to the right-hand side and intersecting the diagonal will create a new rectangle in direct proportion to the original rectangle. No matter how many

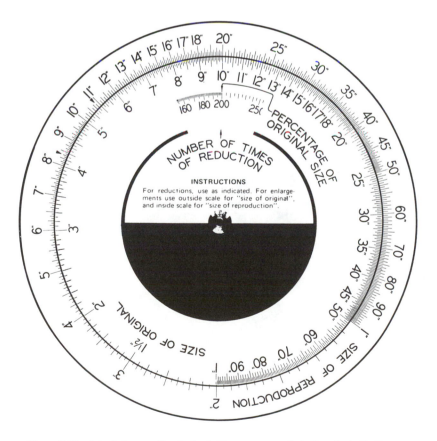

Figure 5.10—A typical proportional wheel. There are many, but all are basically the same.

Figure 5.11—The picture to be used in the assignment on cropping and sizing.

lines are drawn, as long as they are parallel and intersect the diagonal they will bear the same relationship to the original.

Lay a sheet of translucent paper over the photograph. Using the crop marks as a starting point, draw the rectangle of the picture. (Use your drawing board, T-square, and triangles to make this accurate.) When the tissue is removed from the photo, you have an accurate rectangle of the box (or area) being sized. To get the size you want, draw a diagonal from the lower left corner to the upper right corner. Strike off the desired width at the bottom and draw a line parallel with the side, up to the diagonal. This will intersect the diagonal line at exactly the new height. A line drawn parallel with the base to the intersection will give the width. For instance, in figure 5.9, the photo A^2B^2 is 20×14 picas. Using the diagonal method, we learn that if we want the photo to be $10\frac{1}{2}$ picas wide, its new height will be $7\frac{1}{4}$ picas (A^1B^1).

This method can be used to enlarge photos and to get a new width when you know what height you want the photo or picture to be. Again, using figure 5.9, suppose AB is your original photo. Draw the diagonal from the lower left to the upper right corner and extend it beyond the original box. If you want the illustration to be 14 picas high, extend the left-hand vertical to 14 picas. Draw a horizontal line parallel to the bottom of the photo to the diagonal line; the new width is 20 picas. This comes in handy for quick sizing or when no wheel is available.

Use figure 5.11 to practice sizing with these two methods.

CHAPTER SIX

Magazine Elements: Purpose and Design

Cover

The cover is the first thing anyone sees. As such it is a powerful selling tool. A person may never purchase a very interesting magazine if the cover has no visual appeal. Several elements occur on the cover. Each has its own position for a purpose. The title, or "logo," for instance, is rarely anywhere else but at the top. This is because magazines compete with other magazines on the newstands. For display ease, racks are provided that stack magazines so that not much more than the title shows. If a magazine had the title at the bottom, which might very well be an ideal position from a design standpoint, it would sell few copies. No one would be able to locate the title on a display rack. It would be covered by other magazines.

This does not obviate the possibility that some "in-house" magazines or "by subscription only" magazines may have the title elsewhere than at the top. Many have them running down the side. However, from a sales standpoint, the title should appear where it can be quickly seen and identified. Once the title becomes easily recognizable, it starts being called a logo.

The price should also be shown. There are two schools of thought on the price type size. One school states that, if the magazine appeals to you, you will buy it regardless of the price. The other school feels that the price should be easy to read so that the buyer does not have to ask about it.

Every magazine has an issue date. This is usually interwoven into the magazine title area as part of the logo design.

Cover design is very important. This is the first customer contact. It must do the sales job. Along with this active sales approach, one usually finds story titles on the cover: these help persuade the observer to purchase the magazine. Short titles are a sales pitch, after the reader has learned to recognize the magazine by its logo or title. The editor usually chooses the titles that have the most sales appeal. The cover is "built" around these titles. As an example, a magazine may carry a story on mountain climbing. The cover features mountains or something related to the story. Supplementary titles are then added to catch those readers not directly interested in mountain climbing. Story titles are usually placed at the left so that they are not hidden, or covered, by other magazines on the same flat surface.

From the preceding, you should have some basic concept of the cover elements and their general placement. *How* you handle them is called "design." A casual look through a magazine rack or display reveals some interesting things. The title is short and rather positive. An example is *Time*. The title contains four letters and is in bold type. In other cases the logo identification predominates. *House Beautiful* and *Natural History* are rather long and designed for recognition. A title should never become tricky or forced. The buying impulse lasts for only a fraction of a second. If the reader's eye is lost amid flourishes and tricky letter positioning, it

might very well move on to something easier to identify. This is the last thing the publisher wants.

There are eight commonly accepted cover design formats, with enough visual variations from the general format to multiply into many more. However, you will find that they are all mostly variations of the basic eight. These are covered in the next few pages.

It is possible that you may discover others. These will usually be in-house or subscription-only publications. Even then, many will follow the original eight, because most designers will operate where they feel comfortable.

Mastheads

Every magazine publishes a list, usually by departments, of the staff involved. This not only tells who is responsible for what but also where to write and whom to address in specific areas. Once you start reading mastheads and get familiar with who does what, you will start identifying layout styles with names. It won't be long after that when you may identify art directors with styles and spot them as they move from magazine to magazine. The art director for *Fortune* magazine, for example, has a style, as does the art director for *Glamour*. Neither will ever accept a job on the opposite's magazine because oil and water don't mix. What works for the business press

Figure 6.1 (A through H)—These are the eight basic cover designs. Almost every other cover design is simply an adaptation of one of these basics.

January **topic** 50¢

"Speedy Gonzales" Strikes Again

Full Color Whaling Pictures

From Office Desk to Sea

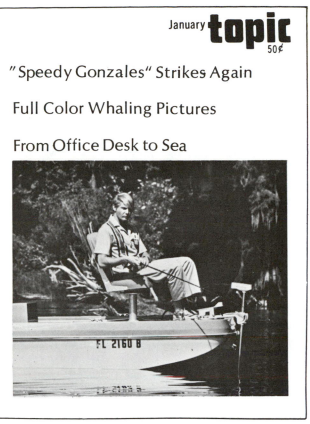

A. This is a variation on the two-fifths by three-fifths design with the picture framed in white. This leaves room for at least three interesting story titles.

January **topic** 50¢

Monsters of the Swamps
Fly Rod versus Plug

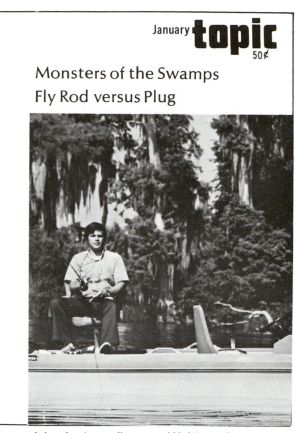

B. This example has the picture off-center and bled in two directions. The white space panel at the left helps to counterbalance the whole design. The picture leads the reader directly into the magazine.

January **topic** 50¢

Fishing the Big Sur

Trailing The Grey Fox

Build Your Own Cabin

C. This page has a panel that is two-fifths of the width, leaving three-fifths for story titles. The panel and the area shown as white space can be in color. Variations include using mood faces for titles and having small blocks of copy. The panel may also have rounded corners or be centered in a ruled box.

January **topic** 50¢

Casting for the "biggies"

D. This example uses the five-to-one ratio. The logo will appear in a color panel with one title for the most appeal. The bottom four-fifths contains a picture, bled on three sides. With this format, there are usually no variations. It is rather straightforward.

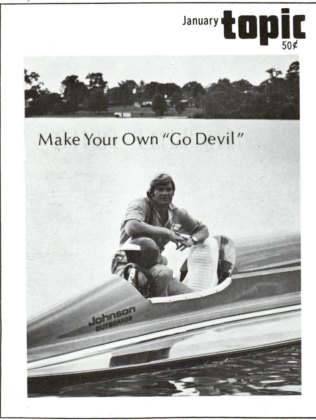

Roaring, Raging Torrent of Fear

E. This example uses a full bleed. The logo can be reversed out if the picture is dark enough or overprinted if not. Story titles can appear in one, two, or even several lines. Full bleeds tend to expand the area. Mood faces can be added for interest.

A Taxpayer's Revolt

An Answer From Outer Space

"What Do I Do Now?" - McGovern

Why Embargo is the Answer

Olympic Review

Pollution - A National Shame

Sexual Supremacy

F. This example is rather simple in format, but has a lot of room to "sell" a wide variety of story titles, sure to please someone. This can be in color with titles reversed out, or in mood faces to add some additional interest.

Make Your Own "Go Devil"

G. This example has the picture framed with white space. The logo is usually outside the picture area, and one title, matching the picture, is used to "sell" the cover. A picture in full color is very attractive in this format. The white space around it tends to make the colors brighter.

H. This is an example of an outline picture. The cover contains nothing but one very striking picture and the logo. This makes for good design and salesmanship. The fact that no story title appears invites one to open it and see what's inside. It is simple and direct.

has no place in the fashion design field.

The masthead might lead you to some other interesting observations. If you see a succession of art directors through a year's time, you can almost take bets there is something disagreeable to contend with. If the same art director is there for as long as you continue to read the masthead and the style is good, it not only reflects stability but also job satisfaction. You can learn from both. In the first case, how each art director tries to overcome the disagreeable element, and in the second, what makes for good design.

No publication should be without a masthead of some kind, even though you may be the only one on it, wearing seven hats.

The design of a masthead should always be handled as a listing of information and, most often, is set in boldface type for departments and lighter face type for the people involved. Mastheads should have ''air'' (or generous white space) because of the mass of material involved.

Table of Contents

The listing of stories is essential to every magazine. The design of the table of contents must be carefully considered for style. This is usually the first design element in any magazine after the cover. Once the design has been chosen, it rarely changes. People want what they are accustomed to finding in the same position, in the same format, and with little or no change from what they have been trained to see.

In terms of design, the table of contents should present the information in the best possible way. This narrows down to a few functional rules.

1. Story title: first in importance. Usually boldface and in the same wording as the story title within the magazine.

2. Authors: second in importance. Usually in the same face, but not boldface.

3. Page number: third in importance. Usually boldface because there is a direct relationship between the story title and the page

where it is located.

4. Synopsis (or selling paragraph for a story): fourth in importance. This is occasionally used to further sell the story or identify its contents if the story title might be vague. It is not used in all magazines, but does add a nice touch if the magazine is technical and copies of the magazine are filed for reference.

With these simple rules in mind, and knowing that people read from top left to right, horizontally, you can see that the best arrangement would be a horizontal one. In terms of design, a repetition of horizontal lines tends to compress a page. This can be counteracted by using generous white space, to help expand it. This type of reading material *needs* white space.

Editor's Column

A great many magazines carry an editor's page or at least a special space. This may be used to point out sidelights to stories, echo the magazine's editorial concepts, or for casual chatter that might inter-

est the reader. This column usually receives special treatment in design format because it is very dear to the editor. A good art director knows how to combine both a desired format and style with good graphics to minimize whatever errors in judgment might occur.

Fillers

Fillers are exactly that—space elements used to fill out pages that might otherwise have empty spaces. The *Reader's Digest* does this exceptionally well. In terms of design, fillers are usually set in short measure in the two-column format so there is sufficient white space to set them off. In the three-column format, they are more often the column width but set off with ruled boxes. Both the narrow and wide fillers can utilize decorative rules. All printers stock rules in a wide variety of designs and widths. Fillers draw attention when framed. The attention factor can be strengthened by decorative rules and minimized by plain line rules.

ARTHUR M. HETTICH / Editor
JOHN C. BRADFORD / Art Director
BEATRICE BUCKLER / Executive Editor
AARON SCHINDLER / Managing Editor
LAWRENCE L. KANE / Associate Editor
LESLIE R. FORESTER / Copy Director

EDITORS

Articles: BABETTE ASHBY / *Beauty:* MARY MILO / *Health:* MAXINE LEWIS
Child Care and Education: BARBARA SEAMAN / *Senior Editor:* PATRICIA CURTIS
Creative Crafts and Needlework: DEBORAH HARDING
Editorial Services: ANNA MARIE DOHERTY / *Photography:* GEORGE NORDHAUSEN
Fashion and Home Sewing: JANE BENFORD / *Food:* JANE M. O'KEEFE
Home Furnishings and Equipment: CAROLYN BISHOP
Interior Design: DELPHENE RICHARDS / *Special Projects:* ROBERT L. ANDERSON
Shopping Circle: FLORENCE SIMON / *Assistant Managing Editor:* JOSEPH G. HOLD
Editor-Reporters: NANCY HECHT, LA VERNE POWLIS *and* LINDA DANNENBERG
Contributing Editors: LOUISE BATES AMES, Child Care Consultant;
JASON BERGER, *Travel and Leisure;* MARY BASS GIBSON; NIKA HAZLETON;
EVELYN E. SMITH; A. M. WATKINS, Money Management
Associate Fashion Editor: JEANIE C. ALBERT / *Poetry Editor:* ELEANORE LEWIS
Copy Editors: AGNES M. BOS *and* HEATHER FRAYNE
Associate Equipment Editor: SUSANNE McGUIRE CURRY

ASSOCIATES

EDITORIAL: Helen T. Boasi, Anita Counsman, Al Drayton,
Edythe Greissman, Lilian Kyrkos, Alberta Russell, Celeste Villegas,
Juta Virkmaa, Ann Wesbecker, Lois G. Williams
FOOD: Ruth K. Mumbauer, *Nutrition;* Marie T. Walsh, *Director, Test Kitchen;*
Carole Burde Semel, Alyce W. Lienhard, Julia Lee Wright
ART: Carl Herrforth, *Manager* / Teresa Montalvo, *Associate Art Director;*
Karen Brown, Angelo T. Sperrazza, Elizabeth M. Steidel, Erika Douglas
PHOTOGRAPHY STUDIO: William McGinn, René Velez, John James
Editorial office: Family Circle, 488 Madison Ave., New York, N.Y. 10022
Unsolicited material must be accompanied by self-addressed, stamped return envelope

Figure 6.2—A clean, functional masthead. This is an excellent example of good typography. Not many designers give this type area that much attention.

CHAPTER SEVEN

Page Design

Proportion

Proportion is the principle of design that involves a pleasing relationship among all parts of the page design and the page's relationship to what precedes or follows it. Remember that no one story is an entity. It relates to the preceding page as well as the following pages.

Basic Shapes

Editorial pages almost always consist of a basic vertical design in their general format. This is because pages that consist of copy are in either a two-column or three-column format. Straight copy, therefore, creates two or three gray-tone vertical shapes, separated by a thin strip of white space

called an "alley." Pictures placed within this vertical design should complement it. Here are several points to remember.

1. A vertical *plus* a vertical is usually monotonous.

2. A "change of direction" will make a page more interesting. A strong horizontal picture, for instance, will cause a visual change of direction. See figure 7.1 for an example of this effect.

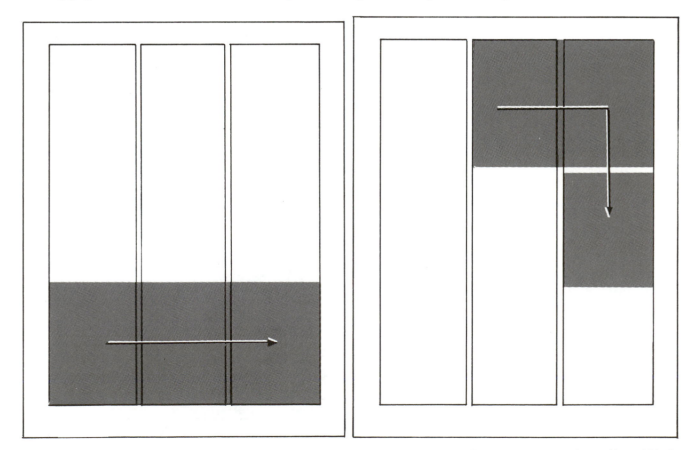

Figure 7.1—*A strong horizontal will create a change in direction and help relieve the vertical feeling of three same-width columns.*

Figure 7.2.—*The L-shaped arrangement creates a change of form within the basically vertical design.*

3. A change of form will also make the page more interesting. An outline halftone picture will add interest. An L-shaped grouping will provide a change of direction as well as a change in form. See figure 7.2.

4. White space used as a design element complements the verticals. White space used as a deep sink (starting the type columns lower on the page) is actually a horizontal movement, which will complement the verticals. See figure 7.3.

5. A change of form *within* the picture will create its own center of interest. An example would be a picture, or even a chart, with a strong sawtooth design. This gives movement within a controlled area. See figure 7.4.

6. Color used as ''spot designs'' can draw interest away from the vertical pattern. An example of this would be a chart already vertical in design (as the columns might be). When the chart carries the same design as the columns, it creates a feeling of repetition. Adding color, or even a change of tone values of gray, can effect a diversion from the verticals. These added ''spots'' are just enough to provide a seasoning of interest from the design. See figure 7.5.

7. Optical illusions that create interrelationships within the page are easy to achieve by placing the pictures so they pull the reader's eye away from the verticals. This is particularly effective when using bleeds. Do not ''nail down the corners.'' This means placing a picture in each of the four corners. While this may distract from the vertical pattern, it creates another pattern equally monotonous. See figure 7.6.

8. Space division, or how one utilizes white space *within* pictures, can also create sufficient interest to detract from strong verticals. An example of this would be a halftone placed within a ruled border or box. A frame such as this, if equal on all four sides, will keep the picture placid. If the top and right are equal and the left and bottom are unequal, the picture will optically move in one direction. See figure 7.7.

9. Variety can be defined by John Dewey's remark, ''There is no excellent beauty that hath not some strangeness in the proportion.'' Variety, as far as the layout artist is concerned, is the interjection of just enough strangeness to create interest. An example would be three pictures—two of them square, and the third round, oval, or outlined. See figure 7.8.

Texture or Pattern

An example using fabric patterns will illustrate this point. Utilizing texture or the ''feel'' of pictures within a page can highlight them. Silk and tweed are good examples; one can emphasize the ''feeling'' of each by placing one next to the

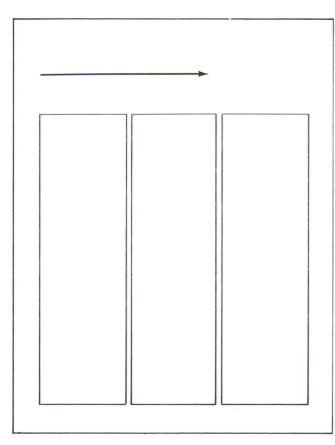

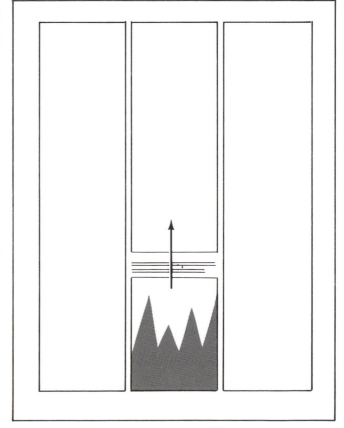

Figure 7.3—Even a pure white ''sink'' will create a horizontal form that will relieve the vertical design.

Figure 7.4—The sawtooth form within a rectangular form is an example of what we call ''a form within a form.'' The sawtooth is minimized by placing it within another form, particularly when the second form blends with the verticals.

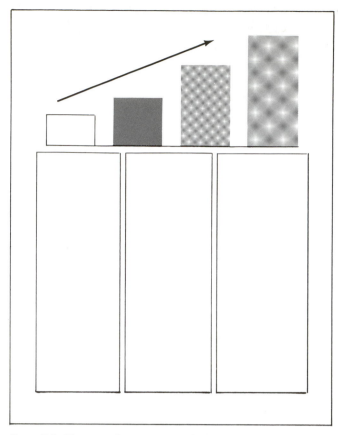

Figure 7.5—The screened patterns not only draw interest but also create their own movement by the variations in size.

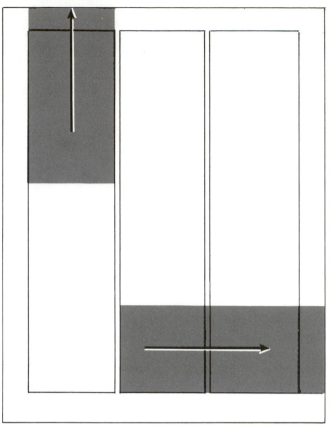

Figure 7.6—Bleeding creates an optical illusion by making the pictures seem to move off the page.

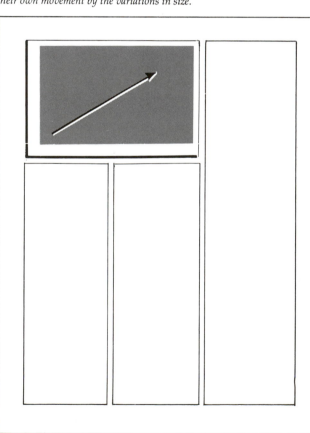

Figure 7.7—Borders and picture positions on the page can also create movement.

Figure 7.8—Variety in shapes within a panel can break the vertical arrangement.

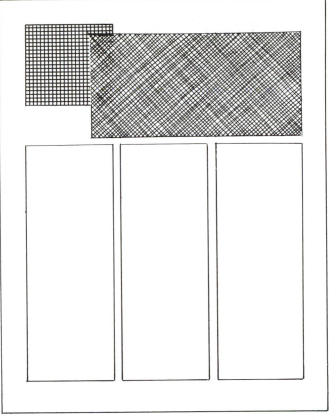

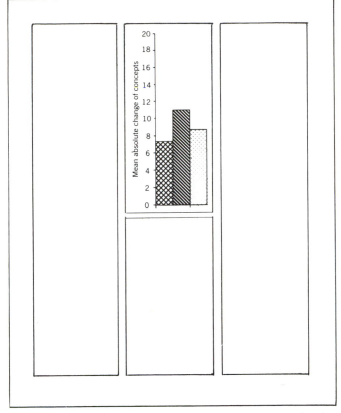

Figure 7.9—Different screen values, with interplay in textures, can also be a good diverting device.

Figure 7.10—One way to solve the light and airy vertical is to enclose it within two columns of text. This creates an invisible box, which is open at the top for interest and variety.

other. In pictures the layout artist looks for patterns and designs that can be utilized to play against each other. This helps divert the reader from the page-column verticals. See figure 7.9.

Charts or Graphs

Many trade magazines have few halftone pictures but are replete with line drawings. This includes charts, graphs, and schematics. These should first be examined for classification. Most fall within groups defined as "strong horizontally," "strong vertically," "light and airy," and "dark, with massed detail." There are problems and answers with each.

1. Strong vertically
Problem: How to utilize, when the page is predominantly vertical.
Possible answers: Spots of color in the chart content; a two-point color border, changing optical direction; the addition of a textured area other than simple tint values;

placement next to a horizontal or "light and airy" shape. See figure 7.10.

2. Strong horizontally.
Problem: How to keep this from dominating the page.
Possible answers: Reduce to a proportion that will balance the rest of the page; place next to an equally strong vertical; have the plate-maker use a percentage of black, rather than 100 percent; change the straight lines into tints of a light color; put it at the top of a page so the "sink" will help subdue it. See figure 7.11.

3. Light and airy.
Problem: How to keep the art from flying apart.
Possible answers: Enclose with a border; enclose the art with text on both sides; place rules in color, or tint values of gray, at both top and bottom. See figure 7.12.

4. Dark, with massed detail.
Problem: How to keep this from dominating the page.
Possible answers: Allow extra white space around it; put it at the top of a

page so the "sink" will help minimize it; change the dark black areas to tints of gray (if possible); relieve some of the dark areas by using patterns instead of solids; relate with a light picture or table. See figure 7.13.

The same techniques apply to pictures that have these characteristics.

Interest

Every design needs some note of interest that catches the eye and arrests the attention. These can be divided into the following groups.

1. Emphasis. When emphasizing an area, do so by drawing the reader's eye to it. An example of this would be the use of a contrast in colors (or hues), values, or intensities. This can be done on a chart or graph by the use of a color and variations of the same color. It can also be done by the use of unusual detail or grouping. See figure 7.14.

2. Center of Interest. This can be

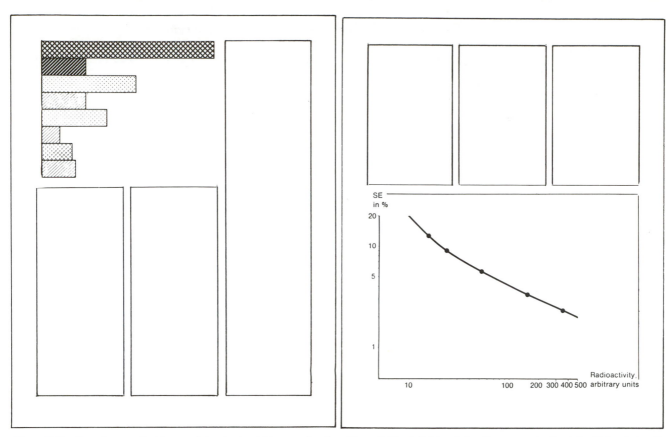

Figure 7.11—Changing a vertical bar graph to a horizontal bar graph will help to create diversion. A vertical plus a vertical is poor design.

Figure 7.12—A light and airy diagram can be "contained" by placing the text above it. The hairline-ruled box helps keep it from "floating." If the diagram were placed at the top of a page, it would "float" off into space.

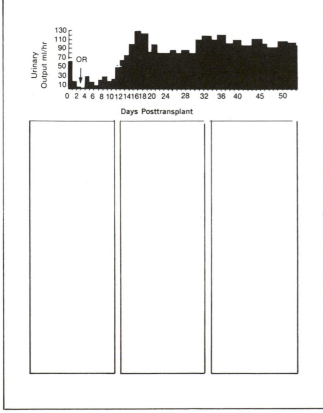
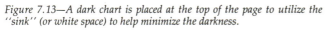
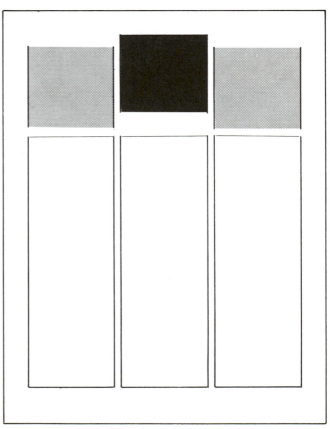

Figure 7.13—A dark chart is placed at the top of the page to utilize the "sink" (or white space) to help minimize the darkness.

Figure 7.14—Emphasis, or a diversion from the vertical design, can be created by placing one dark or dominant picture slightly above column level.

defined by the question, What draws the eye to any particular spot or area on the page? Center of interest can be planned and can, in effect, direct the reader's eye almost anywhere the layout artist chooses to move it. Probably "optical center" is the easiest. This is in the middle and two-fifths down from the top of a page. Remember that every page has a point of interest, even if it's only the upper left-hand corner, where the reader's normal eye movement takes him. Creating a center of interest may be a little more difficult when all the layout artist has to work with is straight copy. Title areas *can* be utilized to advantage. Standup, indented, or decorative initials are other ways to create a center of interest. See figure 7.15.

3. Rhythm. This is a change from one line to another, from one dimension to another, from one value to another, or from one color (or tone) to another. In application, this would mean establishing a pattern to the layout and then utilizing that pattern to create interest.

A design is not necessarily good just because it sets out to *deliberately* achieve balance or pleasing proportion, or to locate a center of interest. Often such a positive approach results in a flat monotone or stereotyped format. The design just lies there in its functional form. Leaving something to the imagina-

tion is always more interesting.
Some things to remember:
1. Horizontal lines suggest repose or calmness, as well as width.
2. Vertical lines suggest activity as well as height.
3. Zigzag lines suggest activity or motion.
4. Squares, rectangles, and triangles suggest stability.
5. Circles, ovals, spheres, and ellipses suggest movement.
6. Round corners, diagonal corners, and mortises change the "feel" of a square, rectangle, or triangle.

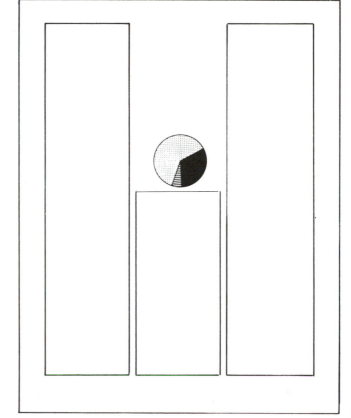

Figure 7.15—Optical center for drawing power also emphasizes the white space and diverts the eye from the vertical patterns.

CHAPTER EIGHT

The Title Area as a Space Unit

Display typefaces, particularly in the commercially prepared alphabets, such as Format, can be shaped to almost any form. They

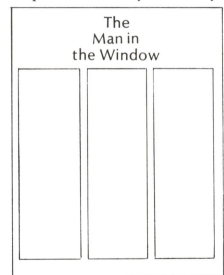

Figure 8.1—The pyramid shaped title.

can curve, touch, overlap, or combine with any other size or font. This is because they are made up of individual letters that can be cut out and placed any way you wish. The backs are coated with a pressure-sensitive backing, which means they will adhere to almost any clean surface. Many magazines, however, use only one specific typeface for all headlines, with variations in size, regular, bold, and italic, but in the same font. Under these circumstances, the title area may often be the only space element available to create interest in the story. Being limited to size and face means the layout artist has only one alternative—to use "shapes" and provocative words in the title areas. Some of the basic shapes follow.

1. Pyramid. Centered head where the first line is short, fol-

lowed by another line that is longer and, perhaps, a third line, longer yet. This creates a "pyramid" shape. Since the peak of this shape points *away* from the story, it is not always the ideal choice. See figure 8.1.

2. Inverted pyramid. The opposite of the pyramid, but with the peak pointing *into* the story area. This shape is probably the simplest way to invite the reader into the story. See figure 8.2.

3. Oval. Where three lines form a visual oval, with the top line short, the middle line longer, and the bottom line short. This is usually centered on a page and gives a rather formal look to the page. See figure 8.3.

4. Square. Where the title lines are lined up at both ends, or flush left-ragged right, but with lines nearly equal. This particular shape

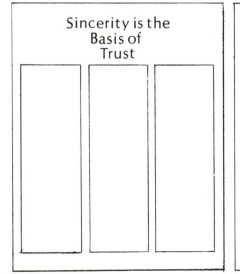

Figure 8.2—The inverted pyramid shaped title.

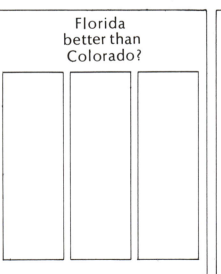

Figure 8.3—The oval shaped title.

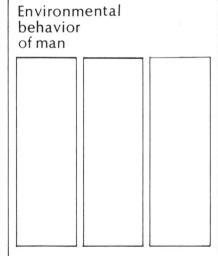

Figure 8.4—The square shaped title, often half a triangle or ragged on one side.

Figure 8.5—A title in a well.

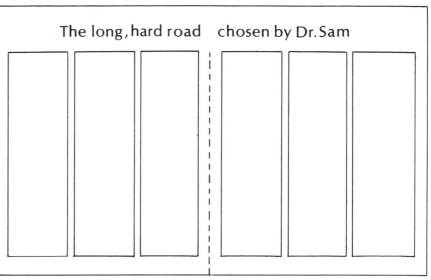

Figure 8.6—A long one-line title across two pages. Notice that the title extends slightly into the gutter to "bridge the gutter" without disturbing the word spacing.

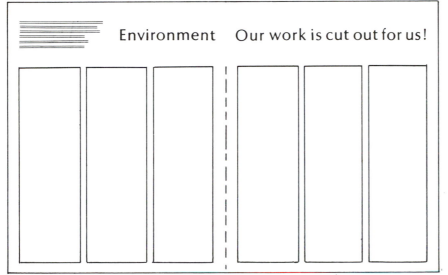

Figure 8.7—A long one-line title across two pages with a blurb. The blurb also leads directly into the story.

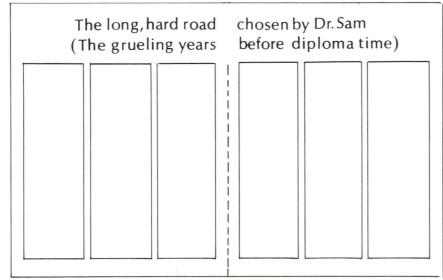

Figure 8.8—An example of too much title and how awkward it is to handle, let alone read.

can line up with the beginning column of a story and provide a "lead" into the story. This is also the easiest and cheapest to set. See figure 8.4.

5. "In a well." Where the title area can be set in any of the above, but appears no wider than one column in the two-column format, and no more than two columns in the three-column format. The story copy forms a wall around at least one side of the title area. See figure 8.5.

6. Double-page spreads. Where title areas are long and cumbersome and are, therefore, spread over a longer area. The "double-page spread" must always start left and face a right-hand page. There are several ways to handle the long title, depending on how many characters and spaces are involved.

a. A long title, across both pages, with the byline usually over or directly above the first column. The sink must be considered as a part of this design problem, and proper spacing must be allowed between the title area and the story so it does not crowd the copy or stand out as a "floating entity." Since a double-page spread occupies twice as much space as a single page, the type face and size must be compatible with the body face and size. See figure 8.6

b. A long title line across both pages, with a "blurb" or quick story synopsis woven into the title area, is interesting because the blurb becomes another design element. It should be an integral design part of the title area. See figure 8.7.

c. Two long lines are rarely good from a design standpoint. This will always be cumbersome and difficult for the reader to assimilate in one visual bite. If possible, shorten the title or make it into a title and subtitle. If this is not possible, try to create a title design that will occupy the area, but use a great deal of white space to help clarify it. See figure 8.8.

d. A practical solution to a long title area is to use a picture as a connector between the long title and the story. If the picture bleeds in a direction opposite to the long title diagonal, there may be sufficient movement between the two to create a diversion. See figure 8.9.

Remember to ''bridge the gutter'' in handling any title across two pages. This means that the words must be arranged so that no word is broken in the middle of the page. When pages are bound together, it is hardly ever possible to get a perfect alignment (unless, of course, this is the center spread). When words appear slightly off alignment, the error is magnified.

Title areas should draw attention to and be at, or near, optical center. Visualize the title lines as strong horizontals and use them to complement the verticals created by the columns of the story. Use any ''sink'' to advantage. Most magazines can take up to an 8-pica sink without losing any design factor on the page. Be sure to watch for correct spellings. A word misspelled in a title area will draw more attention than one occurring within a story because it is more obvious. Title areas should be neatly lettered on the layout and closely simulate the typeface being used.

Blurbs as a part of any title area

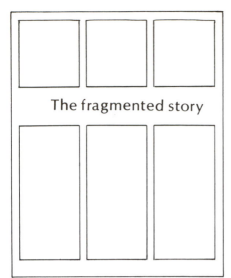

Figure 8.10—The fragmented story. How would you read the copy, across or up and down?

should have sufficient air (or white space) around them to draw attention, but not so much as to detract from the title itself or to isolate the blurb. The blurb is a secondary selling tool and should not dominate the title area.

Continuity is a must for editorial layout. For good reading, nothing should be fragmented. Copy, in particular, should always flow from one page to another in the same general pattern we are all accustomed to reading. This is also the most comfortable. In no case should the reader be forced to break an established reading pattern to satisfy some design point. Figure 8.10 shows how a title *may look good* from a design standpoint but fragment the reading pattern. There will always be indecision. Does column one read up and down, or across? This can turn any reader off.

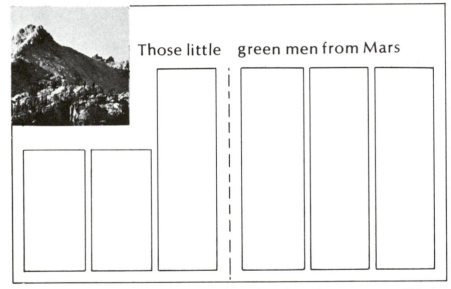

Figure 8.9—A picture used as a layout device to distract from a long title across two pages. This also uses two geometric shapes to distract from the six verticals.

CHAPTER NINE

Tools Needed for Layouts

All layouts depend on the format being used. The first ''tool'' needed would be layout sheets. These are preprinted and show all measurements accurately. They show the format (either two- or three-column or the grid pattern being used), as well as border, alleys, gutters, and column widths. Each column represents a column width as well as depth. The depth is figured in equivalent number of lines to the actual pica depth. For instance, a 54-pica column (in depth) will accommodate 59 *lines* of copy with leading that totals 11. For instance, this 54-pica depth will accommodate 59 lines of 9/11 or 8/11. The same pica depth will also accommodate 65 *lines* of copy with leading that totals 10. For instance, 8/10 or 9/10. The same depth will accommodate 72 lines of any typeface with leading that equals 9, 8/9 or 7/9, for example. Figures 2.4 and 2.5 show two standard layout sheets, in both the two-column and three-column formats.

Along with the layout sheets, a ''line counter'' is essential. This is shown in figure 9.1. The line counter is a gauge that indicates how many lines, with leading, occur within a given depth. The line counter is used on the layout sheets to determine the actual line

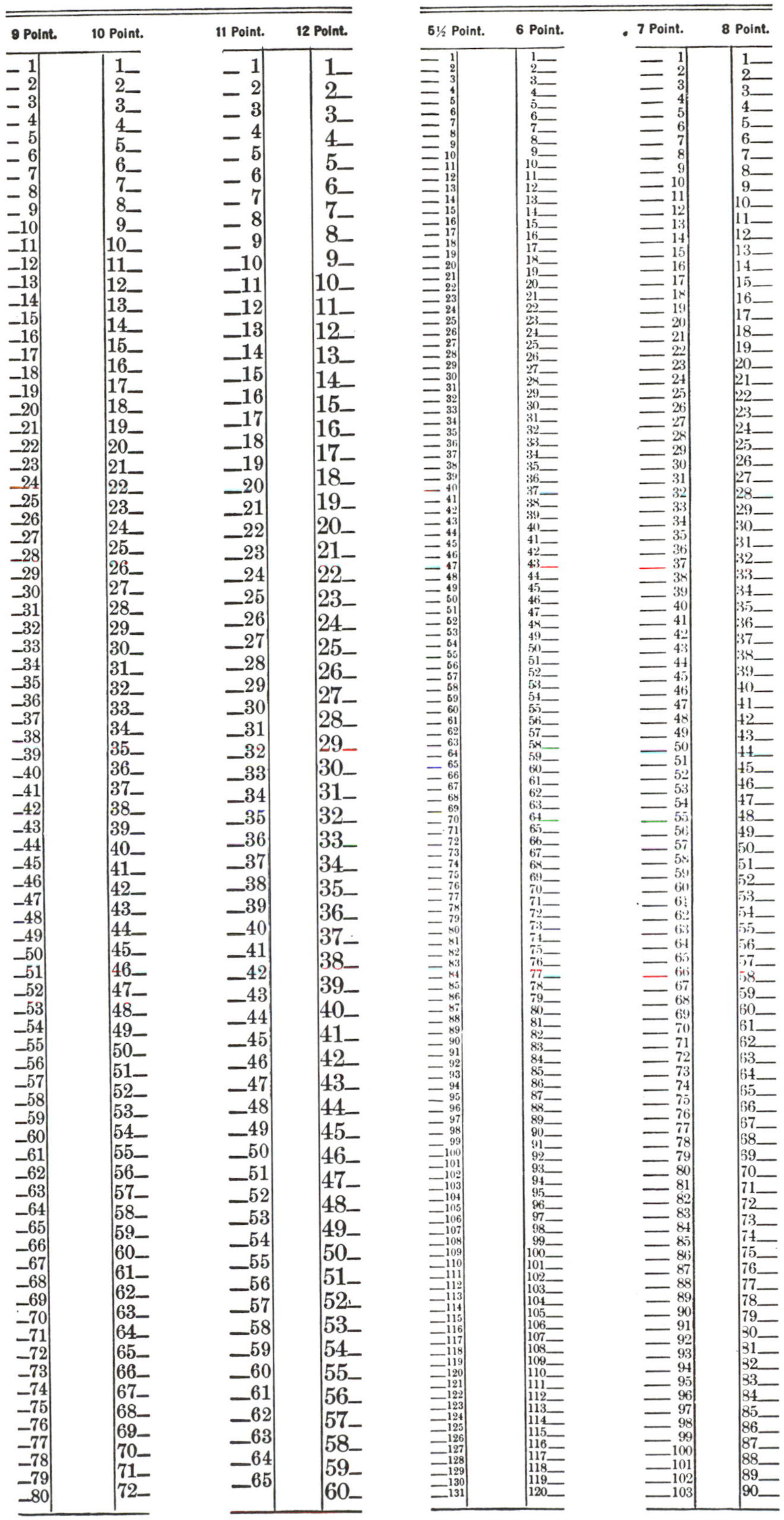

9 Point.	10 Point.	11 Point.	12 Point.	5½ Point.	6 Point.	7 Point.	8 Point.

Figure 9.1—A line counter, showing both sides. This is used to determine how many lines (based on leading) there are in a given depth.

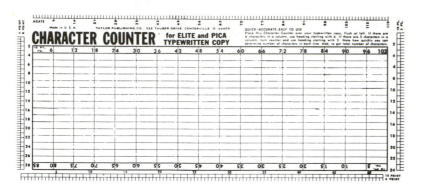

Figure 9.2—A character counter, divided into characters and spaces for both pica and elite typewriters.

count for various sections and tells the typesetter and make-up person exactly what occurs where.

When laying in the copy, the line counter is placed at the required number of lines and a "tic mark" is made. Two right triangles, or a T-square and a triangle, are then used to line up the column edge with the tic mark and a horizontal line is drawn across the column. This indicates exactly where the copy begins and ends. It becomes a master plan for the make-up person.

The character counter, another excellent tool, is shown in figure 9.2. This is divided into both pica and elite gradations. There are 10 units for pica typewritten copy (characters and spaces), and 12 units for elite typewritten copy (character and spaces). This is used to quickly compute captions or other small blocks of copy. It gives an exact count of characters and spaces in a given line. It will *not* give an accurate count for a proportional typewriter.

A good layout artist will prepare a sheet of specific characters and spaces for most possibilities in a particular magazine. For instance, captions being set as 8/10 News Gothic would have the following counts: 34 characters and spaces on 13 picas; 70 characters and spaces on 27 picas; 110 characters and spaces on 42 picas. This predicts the number of lines any given caption will "set." For example, 412 characters and spaces will set 12 lines, plus part of another line, on 13 picas. It will also set 6 full lines, or nearly so, on 27 picas. It will set 4 nearly full lines on 42 picas. In the case of a 13-pica measure, it alerts the layout artist to anticipate a "widow" of 4 characters, depending on how tight or loose the copy is set.

A "pica stick" and the proportional wheel are essentials, particularly when sizing figures. The pica stick is used to measure between crop marks and determine what is set on the wheel. Proper picture sizing and cropping are essential and must be accurate. Once the final picture size has been determined, it must be transferred to the layout sheet as an open space. This open space will be filled with the picture in its final size. The pica stick is used to measure this space accurately in both width and depth.

A pad of tracing paper comes in handy. This is used to trace mood typefaces for accurate size and position on the layout. It is also used as an easy way to determine other possible picture sizes in the various column widths prior to doing the actual layout. For instance, a picture is placed under a piece of tracing paper, and a rectangle of the picture size is drawn. A diagonal line is then drawn from the lower left-hand corner to the upper right-hand corner. Three rectangles are then drawn over (and within) the original size. Each rectangle is equal to the three possible sizes one might use. This saves using the proportional wheel three times and helps you to visualize what the wheel may not show. See figure 5.9.

Pencils are tools, and at least two should be used on the layout. A No. 3 hard, which holds a good point, should be used on the lines and copy. A No. 2 soft should be used in title areas. Since the softer pencil lead tends to smear, it is ad-visable to spray the final result with a good fixative after lettering.

Scratch pads are also considered "tools." They will be used for the necessary arithmetic and to sketch quick "roughs" or "thumbnails."

Layout sheets should be printed front and back and double-page width. This lets the layout artist know which pages face each other. The sheets are then made up into a "book" consisting of as many pages as there will be in the story. For instance, three layout sheets will make a twelve-page "book."

Sometimes layouts are handled as single units so the art director, or layout artist, can get full command of the ad positions. In this case, proofs of the ads are cemented into the position they will occupy and the stories built around them.

Some additional "tools" are needed—scissors, rubber cement, rubber cement pick-ups, and an Exacto knife or editorial scissors. If you use an Exacto knife, use a No. 16 blade. This has not only a point but also a flat surface handy to slip under proofs or photostats while carrying them to the layout. Use a steel triangle for cutting proofs or photostats. A plastic triangle should not be used for cutting as the edges soon become nicked and useless for drawing and aligning.

A list, or diagram, of all proofreader's marks is a must. Copy should be marked up correctly, preferably with red or blue pencil, to match the layout. Pages should be numbered and special instructions given to the make-up person in the margins. The layout artist must remember that no one person will handle all of the layout once it goes for work. Typesetting goes one place, pictures to another, plates a third, and the final pages to still another person. Good cooperation and specific instructions are essential to make sure the layout comes out exactly as you want it.

Since the layout is a "master plan," it *must* be clean, accurate, and well done, and every precaution should be taken to make sure the people involved will rarely make any costly error. Page proofs are "proof" that all instructions have been followed and the job completed as instructed.

CHAPTER TEN

Layout Methods

Almost all editorial layouts can be broken into some basic formulas. We will identify them by code letters: C equals copy (or the story); P equals pictures; S equals space, including sink and desired white space as a design element; T equals the title area, if handled as a unit and not overprinting a picture. Ordinarily, $C + P + S + T = L/O$, all the elements involved in the layout. However, it is not always quite that simple because of the many intangibles involved. If layout were strictly a mechanical procedure, machines could be scheduled to turn out layouts in stereotyped fashion. While it is true that there are some layout devices presently entering the field, machines have no personality, and the final results tend to look machine manufactured.

There is no element in an editorial layout that cannot vary. *Copy*, as an example, can be varied by setting in a variety of sizes and faces, even though the word content does not change. Copy can be set to fit almost any existing area. A given amount of copy can be set 12/15, in two columns, at the very

beginning of a story, but change to 9/11 later on in the magazine. Copy originally intended for 9/11 can be varied by changing the leading to 9/12, thereby adding an additional pica of space for every 12 lines. *Pictures* can be varied by sizing or cropping to almost any desired space or area. *Space*, such as sink, can be varied by as much as the upper fifth of a page without any great loss in design. Other space elements, such as a "natural column ending," can cause variations on every page, depending on how it is used. *Titles* can be varied in many ways. It is therefore apparent that the formula of $C + P + S + T = L/O$ does not always tell the whole story.

Usually, the type size throughout magazine stories tends to remain constant. This is because of a cost factor. It is easier to set all the copy at one time, in one size and one face, and even on one measure. Time is money. You are paying for any variations. Under the assumption that the copy will be in one face and size, let us propose that the layout artist is trying to fill a five-page layout. Three of these

pages (in area) will amount to story copy, leaving two pages in which to put the pictures and story title.

The sizing of the pictures is usually the first step in filling the space left over from the story copy. Titles and other space areas are ignored at this stage, because they are not really prime space fillers. The arrangement of the pictures within the allotted space is often dependent on the number of pictures available. The solution is not simple because of the many variables in picture size, content, and placement, and whether they will be grouped, overlapped, bled, or clustered.

Pictures should accomplish a purpose other than merely filling space. For example, bleeding off the lower right-hand corner will lead the reader into the next page. Grouping all the pictures into full pages has its advantages, but it is often much better to intersperse them throughout the story for added interest. Use a "thumbnail" or "rough" and indicate the *preferred* positions for the pictures. This will give some idea of their size and location in the layout. Imagine that the story copy will be set on one strip of tape, one column wide. This imaginary tape will be "x" number of picas long. When the total length is divided by the number of picas in each column and the number of columns on each page, it is easy to see that cutting the tape into segments and building the layout from the segments is the easiest way to handle the total layout.

Figure 10.1 shows a thumbnail of

Figure 10.1—A "thumbnail" or "rough" (sometimes called a "miniature") of a proposed five page story layout. This is only to give one an idea of how the elements will be arranged.

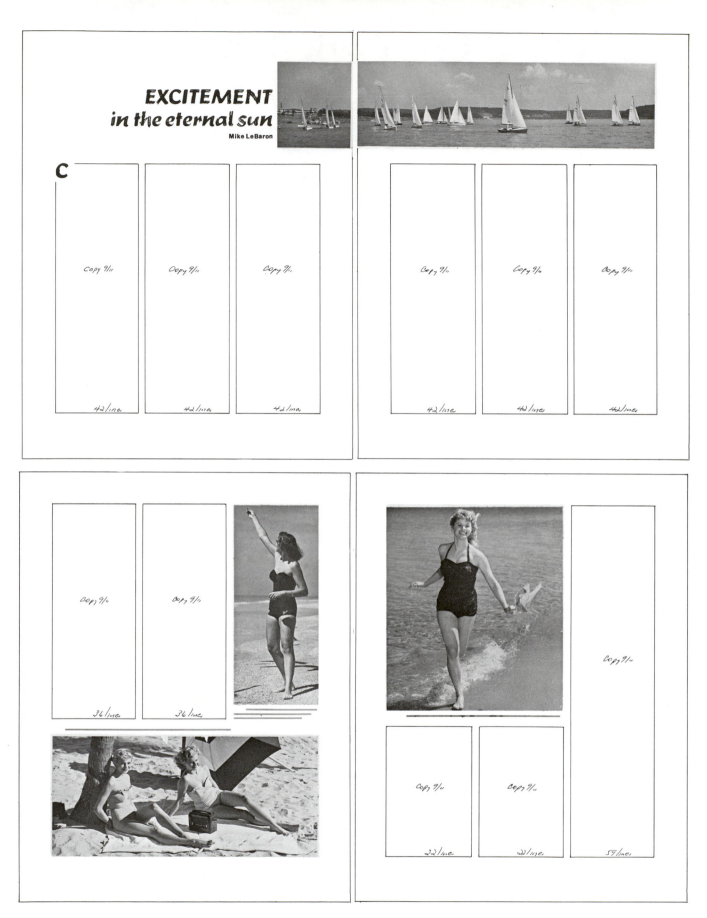

Figure 10.2—A layout, with photostats of the pictures in place, ready to go to page proofs.

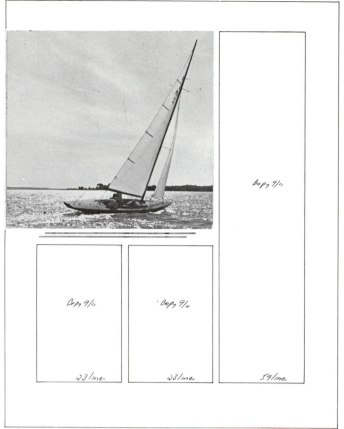
Copy 9/11

Copy 9/11   Copy 9/11   Copy 9/11

23/line   23/line   59/line

Figure 10.2—Continued.

the example cited above for a five-page layout. This is the rough plan. The first step in deciding a layout is one of arithmetic. What does the layout artist have to fill, in picas? How much of this space will the story take up, in picas? How much will the title area and/or sink take up, in picas? Whatever space is left over will then be used for pictures. What does this amount to, in picas? In the example given, the format is three-column. Each of the three columns measures 54-picas deep. This means that there are 162 picas per page, or 810 picas in the five pages.

Our story title is "Excitement in the Eternal Sun" by Mike LeBaron. Copy has been computed as 532 lines of 9/11 Times Roman. When this is converted into picas, we have 488 picas. The title area and byline have a depth of 8 picas. This must be multiplied by 3 because it goes over three columns. This takes up an additional 24 picas. By adding the picas for the story to the picas for the title area, we find that there are still 298 picas left to fill.

Once this simple arithmetic is out of the way, the next step is the thumbnail in which the ideal positions for the pictures are picked and sketched in. Remember that this thumbnail is just a preliminary guide and may have to change somewhat to suit the actual circumstances.

This now resolves into sort of a "which came first, the chicken or the egg?" proposition. Which comes first, the copy or the pictures? Sometimes it is difficult for the novice. We suggest that the copy be worked with *first* because it is a tangible. The other elements are intangibles. In our example, the first double-page spread is handled as six equal columns of 42 lines, or 252 lines of the 532 involved. We then consider a full column on page four, as well as a full column on page five. This gives 59 lines in each, or an additional 118 lines subtracted from the total. This now leaves 162 lines to be used in six partial columns. Since the pictures are contemplated as rectangles, each of the three sets of two should

be of equal depth. This can vary, slightly, as the layout progresses and the pictures are sized to fit spaces.

The lead picture is tentatively planned for the same space as the title area, as sort of a counterbalance in the design. This plays a light horizontal (the title area) against a dark horizontal, the halftone picture. These two horizontals are further counterbalanced against the six equal gray verticals (columns of copy) in the story. Pictures 2, 3, and 4 are planned as a double-page spread, and the arrangement is such that it balances across twice the normal page area. A possible arrangement would be the "Z" form, creating a center of balance that is at optical center, as well as the center of the double-page spread. Picture 5 is tentatively planned as an outline halftone, giving some relief from the previous four picture rectangles.

After the thumbnail is completed, the next step will be to see if it can be made to fit the "mechanical," which is an accurate arrangement of all the elements. Quite often, the difference between thumbnail and mechanical will not be so great that the original plan is upset, but this can happen.

The layout for this particular problem is shown in figure 10.2. On reexamining the first picture, it was found that cropping could not make it fit into the originally planned area. To compensate for this, and to keep the same original planned space over the six equal columns, the picture was changed to a long, across-the-gutter bleed and tied directly into the title, creating a slightly off-balance panel. Pages 3 and 4 are still workable. It was just a matter of sizing the pictures to fit the areas chosen. There is a slight difference in the actual depths of the columns of copy because cropping the pictures to get the essential areas in made them slightly longer than originally planned. However, this variation is minor in the overall plan.

Page 5 presented a problem. Reexamination of the next story (which would be on page 6) shows considerable space facing page 5.

Following the original intention of using an outline halftone would create a bad layout problem in relationships. There would be only one column of copy separating the two stories. While story separations have their place, this would look awkward and segmented. Rather than submit to awkwardness, the picture is reexamined, and a bleed (to the left) is used. The slanted movement of the sail is then emphasized. This tends to minimize the verticals of the story columns and solves the white-space problem. Remember that no story is an entity. It relates to its components, to other stories, and to the issue as a whole.

When the printer gets the mechanical, there will be no doubt as to where all the elements go. The pictures are shown, in position, and sized. The copy is shown, for line count and position. The title area is exactly as it will appear in print. The original pictures should have been marked (on the back) with a Stabilo pencil, showing the size wanted, with the crop marks to follow on the front.

"Squaring off a page" is sometimes difficult for the novice. In our preceding example, suppose an ad occurred on two of the outside columns within the story area. This forces the story to jump to another page in the rear of the magazine, but will give only two-thirds of a page. (A "jump" is the same as "continued on page . . .") If there were another column ad on this jump page, the solution would be simple. The ad, plus two columns of story copy would equal one full page. If no ad is available, how does the layout artist get three equal columns from what is left over? The answer is to divide what's left over by three (the number of columns involved). If this cannot be divided equally (for instance, 32 lines in each of the three columns), either pull one line back into this page from the preceding page, giving a little more space under the picture and caption, use a hairline rule as a substitute for an imaginary last line, *or* use a symbol such as a "ballot box" indicating that this is the end of the story.

"Natural endings" come in two ways. One has the copy ending in the last column, as it naturally occurs. This would give two full columns and part of a third. Since this leaves a white "hole" in the layout, these are most often filled with cartoons or small fillers of some kind. If this area is left open, the white hole will not only draw attention, but will serve no design function. This can be minimized by decreasing the sink of the first page or using a variable sink on all pages of this particular story. It can also be eliminated by increasing the size of the pictures or even by increasing the size of the type used in the story. This is a good reason why a "thumbnail" is a good approach. It tells you pretty much where you are going before you start.

The other natural ending, used so successfully in *Psychology Today,* is the natural ending at the bottom of each column. Copy should break at full paragraphs and should vary just enough to adjust each page. The procedure is to cut the imaginary tape into relatively equal lengths, to the nearest paragraph, and let the white space fall as it may. If one is working with "galleys" and doing a paste-up, this is considerably easier. The columns in natural endings always look neater and cleaner when there is a hairline rule between the columns and another at the bottom. This helps contain the white space and prevents a ragged-looking page bottom.

One advantage in using natural endings is apparent in our five-page layout example. Here we handle the *pictures first,* rather than the copy. The thumbnail locates the pictures ideally, and the copy is then woven into the remaining space. For example, page 1 could have 42 lines/38 lines/ and 42 lines. Page 2 could have 40 lines/36 lines/ and 42 lines. Page 3 could have 34 lines and 36 lines. Page 4 could have 20 lines/18 lines/ and 57 lines. Page 5 would then have 20 lines/23 lines/ and 44 lines. This represents a loss of 36 lines of the total needed for the story. However, it means that the picture on page 5 could then be used as an outline halftone, as originally intended. The first two columns would have been 18 lines higher, minimizing the white space problem and ignoring the problem area on page 6, which would have followed the same natural ending procedure.

"Stories in sequence" means that stories follow each other, but are all short and none takes up more than part of a page. In this instance, each story must be handled as a part of the whole. Each story can follow "naturally" or be squared off and followed immediately by another story.

CHAPTER ELEVEN

Laying Out Spreads

A "spread" can have several definitions. The one most commonly used in editorial layout is the "double-page spread," which means "spread across two pages, left to right." However, I define a spread as a *total* story, whether one page, two pages as a double-page spread, or even the whole story.

A Left-Hand Spread

This is a complete story contained on one left-hand page. This means it faces a right-hand page. It must, therefore, be planned to complement the facing page, whether this is a full-page ad or the end of another story. The layout artist should be reminded that *no* story is an entity, but is always part of the whole magazine.

Left-hand pages contain some interesting sight element locations. In reviewing reading habits we know that the upper left-hand corner is the beginning of our American reading pattern. This becomes a preferred position for sight elements, such as a title area, a picture, or a blurb of some sort. This area has, or can have, sufficient white space at the upper right to help break up the facing page.

The bottom right-hand corner, on left-hand pages, is deadly if used for a bleed. Since the bleed pulls the eye to the right, it actually pulls the reader away from the story. This is particularly true if the bleed is a strong horizontal one. If pictures are used in the right-hand column (on left-hand pages) the same weakness is apparent—they seem to relate to the right-hand page. This limits the layout artist to a few preferred positions for story elements—upper left, the middle (in a three-column format), or optical center, with run-around copy (in a two-column format). See figure 11.1.

A Right-Hand Spread

This is a complete story contained on a right-hand page. "Lead" (or major) stories almost always start on a right-hand page. This means that the first story will almost always face an ad or ads plus small copy. The layout artist usually has no control over this, accepting ads as a fact of editorial life. The page facing the first right-hand page of stories should be examined for content to prevent any conflict between the advertiser and the story title or content. Disregarding this principle can lead to the loss of an advertiser should some inadvertent *faux pas* occur.

Titles on the *first* right-hand page should take advantage of white space and be as far right as feasible. At first, this would seem to conflict with the accepted reading patterns. One must view the full-page ad as a visual point of interest and handle the ad and the right-hand page story as a double-page spread.

Titles on *any other* right-hand page can occur according to normal reading patterns. It is better to keep story titles out of the gutter area, however, because they tend to push into the left-hand page.

The lower right-hand area is a natural location for bleeds because they will lead the reader into the following page. Preferred positions for any sight elements can be in the right-hand column in a two-column format and the two right-hand columns in a three-column format.

The Double-Page Spread

This is always a left-hand page and the facing right-hand page. The first consideration is always one of space, if for no other reason than the layout artist has twice as much of it. The area to fill is no longer a vertical rectangle, but rather a horizontal rectangle. See figure 11.2.

Picture locations no longer have any preferred positions, nor do titles or blurbs. We are now considering a rather unrestricted unit, with the exception of the gutter area. The following questions will help somewhat in determining picture location.

1. Which picture will create a center of interest?
2. Which picture, or pictures, should dominate the spread?
3. Which picture or pictures are secondary in importance?
4. What sizes should they be? Can they become one sight unit by mortising or overlapping?

Figure 11.1—Left- and right-hand variables for both two- and three-column formats. Notice how the same basic arrangements are applicable regardless of format.

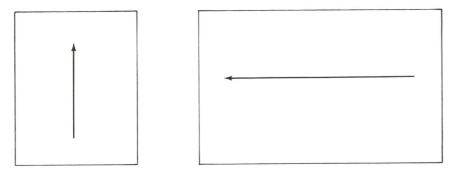

Figure 11.2—A single page spread (or layout) is basically a vertical rectangle. The double-page spread is basically a horizontal rectangle. This "change in direction" also controls how you handle the elements.

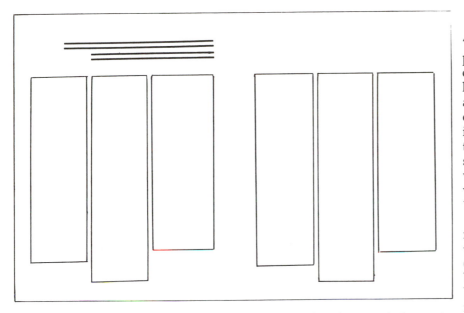

Figure 11.3—A double-page spread with straight copy illustrating how the "natural column endings" give some relief to the monotony of six verticals.

Figure 11.4—A double-page spread with one picture dominating. This is a sure attention-getter if the picture is worth the size.

5. How do the pictures relate to the whole spread? Every double-page spread should have a cohesive composition and relationship.
6. Will a shape other than a rectangle create impact?
7. What relationship do captions have to the design and to the pictures?
8. If using a picture across the gutter: how can it be placed so that nothing essential occurs in the gutter area?

Let us discuss these one at a time.

1. Which picture will create a "center of interest"? If a double-page spread has nothing but story copy, it will have a dull, monotone look, with the possible exception of a display title, a decorative initial, or perhaps natural column endings. The straight-copy spread then becomes a design built on a series of vertical gray columns, with the title area and sink the only variables in the design. See figure 11.3.

Double-page spreads, in most magazines, are of sufficient importance to call for either pictures (halftones) or created art. This brings us to "center of interest." We know our title can be a center of interest, but a good picture will draw more interest than just words. People like pictures. They are simple and easy to relate to and are quickly understood, even without words.

There are unlimited positions in the double-page spread even for only *one* picture. The layout artist, realizing this, will try placing the picture to the *best* advantage within the design. Consider the elements—a horizontal (the title area), several verticals (the story columns), and the arbitrary picture size. The picture can take as many as three of the four columns available in a two-column format or as many as five of the six available in the three-column format. Figure 11.4 shows an example of one picture dominating a double-page spread. This can be quite effective, provided the subject matter will carry it. It is certainly a "center of interest."

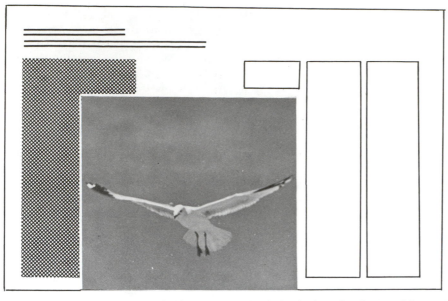

Figure 11.5—A double-page spread with two pictures. One is the "leader," the other is a "follower," but both combine into one unit. The large photo is mortised into the horizontal one.

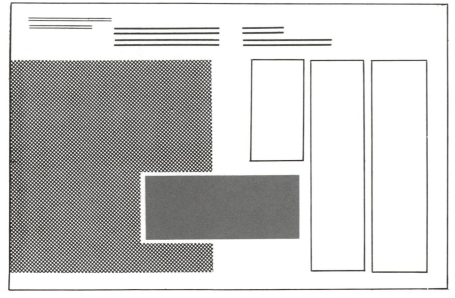

Figure 11.6—An example of a "mortise" arrangement.

2. Which picture, or pictures, should dominate the spread? This question is based on two or more pictures being used and is rather basic. If there is more than one picture, a choice must be made as to which one will "lead" and which one will "follow." Making them both the same size is poor design. "Leading" and "following" is usually a matter of size, subject matter, tonal variations, or even color. Location is another factor. In figure 11.5, we have two pictures, one dominating just by size. There are three horizontals, a rectangle, and three verticals in the design.

The relationship of all elements, as well as the white space used, is one of design, although the larger picture dominates the spread.

3. Which picture, or pictures, are secondary in importance? Here we consider three or more pictures. One will be the "leader," all others, "followers." Arrangement becomes the primary job—should the sizes follow large/medium/small? Should they be rectangle/rectangle/square? Should they be rectangle/rectangle/outline? Should they be dark/light/dark (in tone values)? Each deserves consideration. They should be so arranged that they

form a design within the page form. They should start with a center of interest, grab the reader, hold him with consecutive points, and then pull him into the story.

4. Relative sizes and combining into units has been fairly well covered in the discussions on questions 1, 2, and 3. Combining into design units is a little more difficult. "Mortising" is combining two or more pictures into a unit by having the platemaker saw straight lines into each, creating corners. This can result in an "L" shape, a square shape, an inverted "U" shape, almost any shape that will interlock (see figure 11.6). Overlapping is a little different, because one picture intrudes in another picture's area, with no white line separating the two pictures. Be careful when mortising or overlapping that the pictures have enough contrast so the viewer is not confused about where one picture ends and another begins. The contrast can be in tone (as in black-and-white photos) or in color.

The combined unit must relate to the whole, and design is often created by the use of counterpoint. This means "light versus dark," "shape versus shape," "horizontal versus vertical," "size versus size." Counterpoint causes an eye movement between opposites.

5. How do the pictures relate to the whole spread? In terms of design, all pictures should have a relationship to the page spread as well as to each other. There can be either a symmetrical or an asymmetrical balance of all units. There are several basic design considerations in black-and-white layouts, which are multiplied by all the colors in the spectrum if color is available. Basically, the layout artist is working within a white rectangle. It may be close to the "golden rectangle" with proportions of three to five so much favored by the ancient Greeks. If the double-page spread were 11x18½ inches, it would be ideal. However, since paper sizes are based on multiples of 8½ by 11 inches, the double page is actually 11 by 17 inches.

The layout artist must balance all the elements within this white rec-

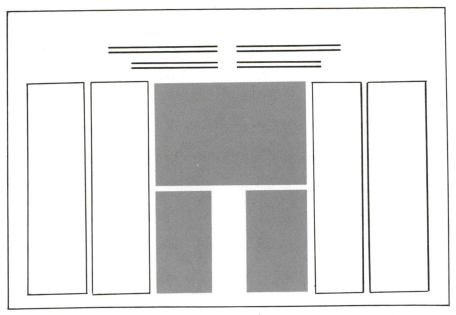

Figure 11.7—A ''symmetrical'' layout. Notice that all elements balance down the middle.

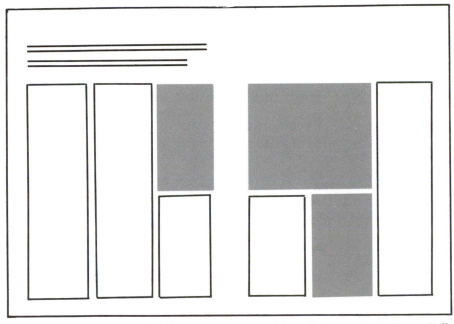

Figure 11.8—An ''asymmetrical'' layout. The elements are balanced by shape and weight but are ''off-center.''

strong whites versus strong blacks, and color versus color are all examples of complete changes. Three identical shapes will look or feel different when there is high contrast. See figure 11.9.

Figure 11.9—Changes in ''weight'' also reflect changes in ''value.''

7. What relationship do captions have to the design and to the pictures? Captions fall into a field by themselves. We almost always see captions (which are picture word descriptions) flush left and right in most newspapers. This forms a neat block of copy that fits well with the rectangles of the pictures. They are clean and simple and accomplish their job in a straightforward manner. There are four basic styles of picture captions in magazines: (1) flush left and right, (2) flush left, ragged right, (3) flush right, ragged left, and (4) the wrap-around or staggered. See figure 11.10.

Within these four, we also have equal copy blocks, as opposed to one block. A one-column picture would have one copy block, no matter how long it was. A two-column picture can have either one copy block or two equal copy blocks. A three-column picture can have two equal copy blocks or, on occasion, even three blocks. It will rarely have just one copy block because it would become too difficult to read on long measure.

Flush left, ragged right captions are usually placed to the right of a picture, so the caption lines up with the side of the picture. The opposite is true of flush right, ragged left. The wrap-around caption is a little difficult because it must be accurately handled. The copy must be hand-counted for exact word breaks to be effective.

Location of captions must always relate to the picture being described. I prefer no captions under pictures at the bottom of a page because they give a ragged alignment to the page. A good rule of thumb

tangle. One's first tendency is usually to accept the gutter as center and try for equal balance in proportions (sizes, values, and shapes) on both sides of the gutter. This, more often than not, results in a rather stylized, mechanical sort of layout. There may be nothing wrong with this in developing a special feeling. However, an asymmetrical layout using the same elements can often be more interesting. See figures 11.7 and 11.8.

Rhythm is also important in cre-

ating interest. Three same-size pictures in a row are often dull and monotonous. Rhythm means a change in pattern, be it a change in size, a change in value, or a change in shape.

6. Will a shape other than a rectangle create interest? Remember, when working within a rectangle, repetition is poor design. Therefore, almost any other shape will create some interest. I prefer a *complete* change in shape. Outline halftones, contrasts in tone value,

Figure 11.10—These are the four basic caption formations described in the text.

would be *under* the picture if the picture is at the top of the page, *over* the picture when the picture is at the bottom of the page, and *to either side* when the picture is anywhere else on the page, as long as the caption forms a unit with the pictures involved.

8. Pictures crossing the gutter *must* be examined and sized so that no important area will be lost during binding or stitching. Visually, no magazine lies as flat as a single sheet of paper. There is always a slight loss due to the depth created by the two stacks of pages on either side, as well as a slight curve in the middle. This may seem of little importance to the beginner, but this ''shingling'' tends to push one page closer to the opposite page, making all sight elements move closer to each other. Pictures of people should never be chopped into left- and right-hand parts. Pictures with continuity (such as buildings or anything having a perfect alignment) should be planned so the gutter crossing does not warp the reader's impression of the whole picture. If the magazine is stitched, the stitch pattern should also be studied so that a stitch or staple does not fall into a vital area.

The Full Story

Every story should be considered as a ''spread'' if for no other reason than it will be read as a unit. Normally, the first page of a story spread will have a title and an illustration. The picture acts as sort of a ''teaser,'' which will pull the reader into the story. The title (words) and picture are there to tempt the reader. If the story starts on a right-hand page, it will be followed by a double-page spread, and will utilize a ''leader'' into the following pages. A horizontal bleed at lower right will do this. Once the reader is into the story on two or three pages, the layout artist will usually have no problem in jumping the story back into the magazine. Try not to use more than one jump. It causes reader discomfort and can be irritating.

Stories heavily illustrated can ''carry'' a story with just the pictures and captions. Stories with minimal pictures need all the help they can get on the first page. Stories in the ''how to do it'' class should follow normal reading patterns—that is, from left to right and from top to bottom. Pictures should be as close to written descriptions of them as possible.

No one can set down specific rules on how to lay out spreads because of the variations in sizes, shapes, relationships, and elements. Each should be considered as a fresh unit and decided on its own merits and design. Good spreads can be defined as the most pleasing arrangements under the circumstances.

I feel that the best double-page spreads are never planned from the *outside in* but start from the inside and blossom out. Starting from the outer margins and working in tends immediately to define boundaries. This almost always produces a mechanical effect.

CHAPTER TWELVE

Grouping and Clustering; Panels and Bleeds

Picture arranging within the framework of a magazine page or spread falls into four areas. These are grouping, clustering, panels, and bleeds. Let us take each one and discuss it.

Grouping

Grouping means making an arrangement around a central point of interest with two or more pictures. Groups can be arranged in a circle, in a spiral, in steps, or in a radial formation. In each case, one picture will draw the reader's interest, while the remaining pictures form a pattern around it. Every picture has some movement within the picture itself. Simply arranging an ideal group will not be enough if the movements within each picture do not enhance the group. The layout artist should study each picture within a grouping and plan to harness the interior movements with the overall movement of the grouping. These movements should be free-flowing and cohesive. Groupings can be particularly effective when a second color holds them together. It can also be particularly jarring when a second color detracts from the free-flowing movements. See figure 12.1 for some simple grouping arrangements.

Clustering

Clustering differs from grouping in that white space is used as a design element. All the pictures "cluster" around the white design. These white space designs are a "cross," a "T," an "H," an "L," a double "T," a "Z," a double "I," and a square "U." The pictures hang from the white space design and form their own structure. In figure 12.2 are illustrations of clustering. In no case do the pictures have to be equal in size, nor does the picture content play an important role. The white space design holds them invisibly together. This is particularly effective with plenty of white space outside the clustered area and is excellent as a "picture page." The layout artist should study the pictures for relationship but, as a rule, clustering allows much more freedom than grouping. It is often harder to achieve without planning, but is quite effective.

Panels

Panels are pictures arranged in a straight line, usually across a full page or up and down one column of a page. Panels always create a strong directional pull or movement in the direction of the horizontal or vertical placement. This movement should be realized and utilized.

Pictures in a panel will usually be the same size in one dimension (such as the vertical size or the horizontal size), but not the same size in the other dimension. Three same-size squares will not be as interesting as two squares and a circle, or a diagonal with two odd sizes, or a square with two outline halftones. Three different widths but a common height will also create interest. See figure 12.3 for some examples of panels. Panels can take on individuality by variations in tone, size, or color and can be made to create motions other than simple horizontals and verticals merely by "invisible movements" within them.

Bleeds

Bleeds mean the picture continues up to the edge of the page and visually seems to continue beyond the page edge. Bleeds will expand either a column or a page because they seem to go beyond the "live area" formed by the borders of the page format. See figure 12.4 for examples of bleeds, and notice the directional pull in each case.

In the picture arranging techniques outlined here, each contains a "motion" or "directional pull." How does the layout artist utilize them? In grouping, the movements will help make the page more interesting and cohesive. They will detract from the strong verticals of the column format as well as the strong horizontals formed by title areas or sinks. They will also make any page more interesting from a design viewpoint. The layout artist will harness a movement, balance it, create counterpoints, and generally mold

Figure 12.1—Some examples of grouping. Notice how there is almost always a "leader" and "followers." This is determined by picture size, as size will draw attention first, before what's actually within the picture area.

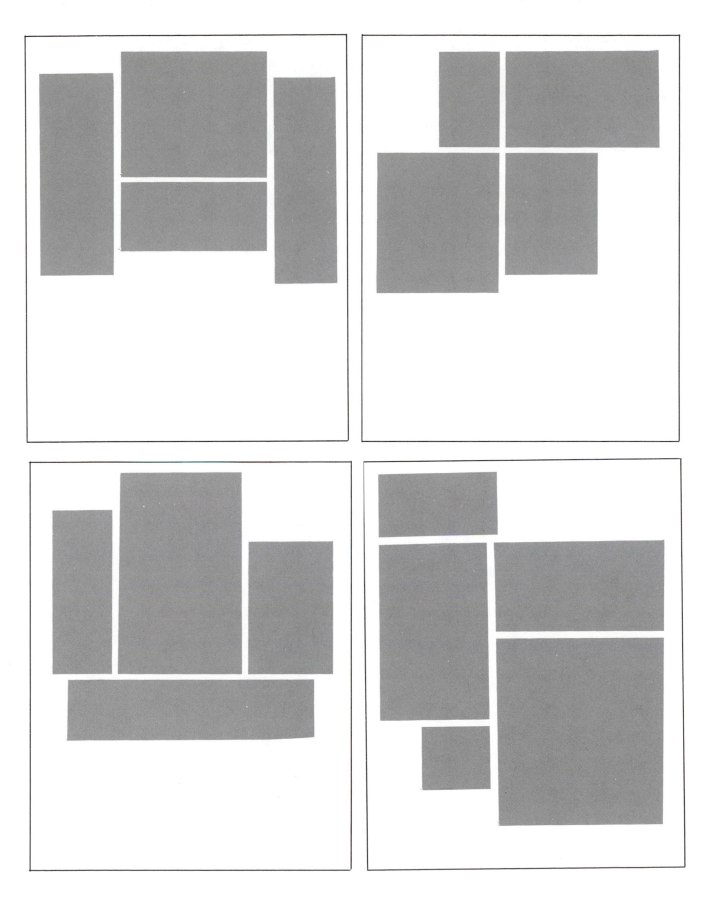

Figure 12.2—Some examples of clustering. These illustrate the H-shape, the cross-shape, the squared-U shape, and the arbitrary-shape. In each case, the white space design draws attention and holds the formation together. Pictures can be any size and are "hung" from the geometric shape.

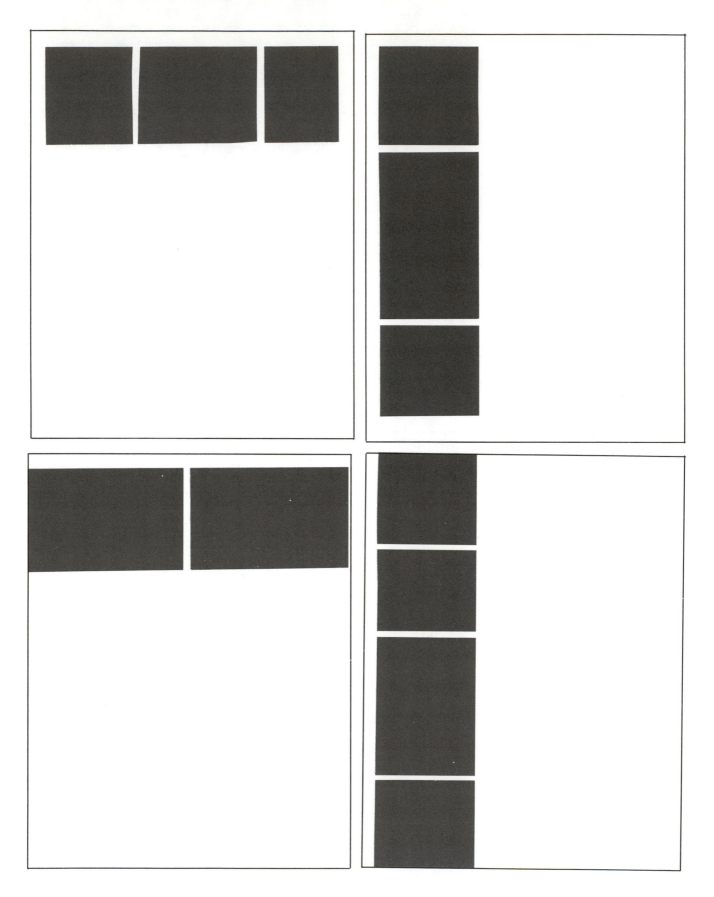

Figure 12.3—Panels are created by using several pictures and either a full horizontal or full vertical on the page area. They can be within the live area or bleed off the page.

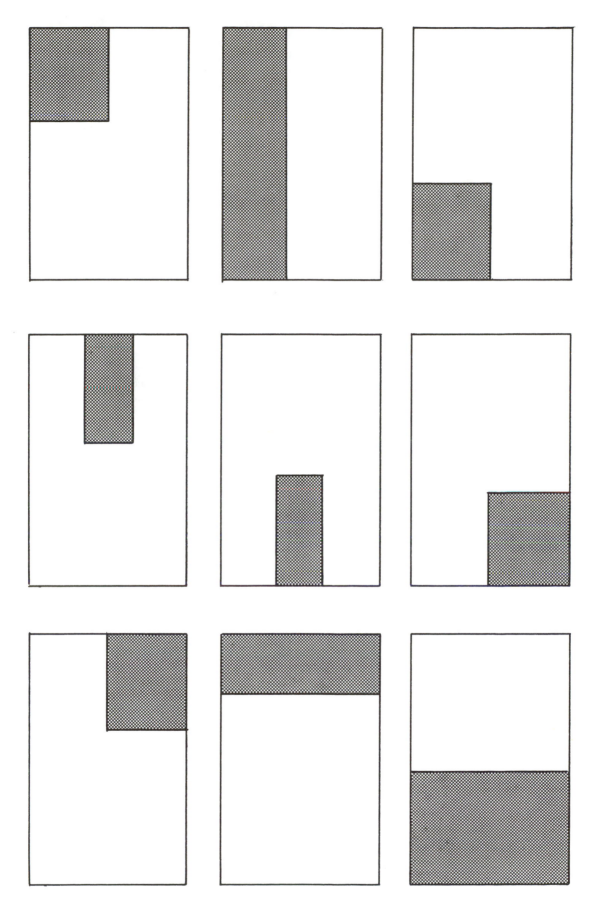

Figure 12.4—The basic bleed positions for one picture.

all movements to suit the design purpose.

In clustering, the layout artist already has a captivating design and should use it to face a page of relatively straight copy. This makes the "picture page" form a counterpoint to the columns of copy. In panels, the motion, or inner motion within the pictures, can offer either counterpoint or balance to a page of copy, provided a ratio of light and dark is maintained. For instance, a panel more than one-fourth of a page in depth will start to dominate the page. Often a more subtle balance may be desired. Panels at the top of a page should not be as high as panels at the bottom of a page. When panels are at the bottom, they tend to lift or carry the copy. When they are at the top of a page, they tend to "cap" or press down on the copy. Panels down the middle of a page will segment the story. Bleeds, other than full-page bleeds, take advantage of white space, be it sink or margins. This white space should be considered as a part of the bleed design to be balanced against the other page elements. Often, the white space tends to tie all elements together.

White space can also be "trapped," or surrounded by other elements of various densities (text, pictures, and so forth). When this occurs, the white space no longer serves a design purpose. Rather, it becomes an obvious *faux pas* and will draw attention. Since there is nothing in this area, it becomes obvious that drawing attention to it is an error and it can "divorce" elements which should be united. Page design must serve a purpose. When no purpose is served, the page design falls apart.

CHAPTER THIRTEEN

Magazine Formats

There are three basic magazine formats generally accepted in America. They are two-column, three-column, and tabloid.

Two-Column Format

A typical two-column format, on a standard 8½ by 11 inch page, may have a sink, left-hand border, and right-hand border of 5 picas. Each column is 20 picas wide, with a 1-pica alley and 6 picas at the bottom of the page to allow for the running foot and folio number. This will give the equivalent of 55 lines of any type size (with leading) that totals 12; it will give 60 lines of any type size (with leading) that totals 11; and 66 lines of any type size

(with leading) that totals 10. Each column is 55 picas deep.

The two-column format, with typeset lines 20 picas wide, is generally considered as "editorial" reading lines, and settles about halfway between "book" measure, which is 30 picas, and "news" measure, which varies from 11 to 13 picas wide. It is often used in scientific publications and is conducive to slow, methodical reading patterns, where the reader does not necessarily want quick impressions.

The two-column format limits the layout artist to pictures on either one or two columns. Expansion of these limits, such as half-column pictures or pictures at optical center, invariably results in

run-around copy. This must be carefully and accurately done. Time costs money, and an error of even one line can throw off an entire layout, resulting in resetting and added cost.

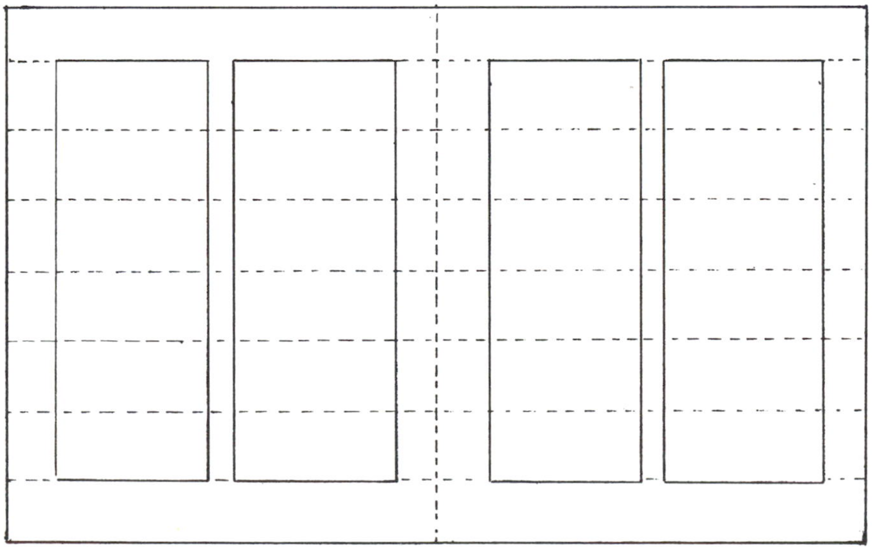

The two-column format has other weaknesses. Ads are sold as half page or full page, as a general rule. This means that an ad will take one-half of any available page, often detracting from the reading material. Titles can rarely be placed in a well because this would leave white space that is difficult to rationalize in good page design. Even though the columns are basically verticals, their width tends to give the impression that they are as much horizontal as vertical. It also gives the pages a "block" appearance. This can be minimized somewhat by setting two columns on 18 picas, using the added page margins (white space) for counterbalance and slightly expanding the alley to 1½ picas.

Three-Column Format

A three-column format, on a standard 8½ by 11 inch page, will give the same number of lines per column, but *not* the same number of lines per page. The two-column format will give 120 lines of 9/11. The three-column page will give 180 lines, although on a shorter measure. This does *not* mean the layout artist will get one-third more copy per page. As a matter of fact, you will lose the additional alley, 1

Figure 13.1—"Modules" in a two-column format. There are twelve modules to each page and twenty-four modules in a double-page spread.

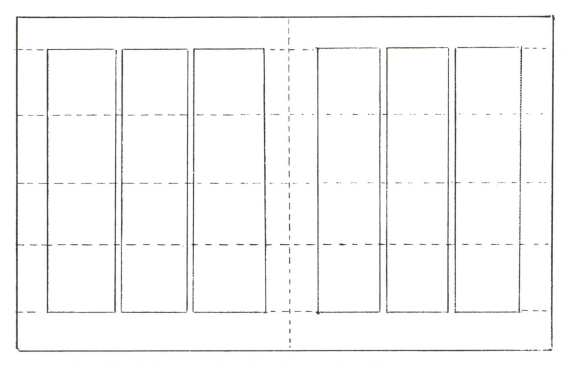

Figure 13.2—Modules in a three-column format. There are twelve modules to each page and twenty-four modules in a double-page spread.

pica wide and 55 picas long, which would accommodate, roughly, three more lines of 20-pica copy. This means that the three-column format will set three lines less per page than the two-column format (of 9/11 copy). However, when estimating copy, or handling copy in the form of galleys, the actual number of lines per page is more important than the area covered.

The three-column format is usually set on 13 picas. This is used in magazines where stories are read quickly in "paragraph-absorbing gulps." The format allows for a great many picture placement variations. One column, two columns, three columns, squares, horizontals, and verticals are all usable in three columns.

There is rarely any run-around copy in three-column formats. Setting copy on any measure shorter than 13 picas creates "rivers" in the copy, word breaks, and hyphenated words that just do not look good. The extra alley gives a little break to the solid block impression apparent in the two-column format. The three-column format permits titles in a well with no trouble. Ads are often sold as outside one-column ads, which

create less reading distraction. The three verticals are natural design elements for pictures and complement nearly all possible horizontal picture arrangements.

Tabloids

Tabloid formats are most often half a newspaper in size. The most commonly used size is 11 inches by 17 inches, though this can drop down to 11 inches by 14 inches, depending on the press requirements. They use three-, four-, five-, six-, and even seven-column designs. See chapter 35 for more on tabloids.

Modular Systems

All three formats can also be handled in a "modular" type layout format. This is deceptively simple. The pages are divided into equal units, all the same size, called "modules." A three-column format may be subdivided into four equal units within each column, giving twelve modules per page, three across and four deep. All story elements are then sized to fit a full, or nearly full, module. A pic-

ture that does not fit a complete module is then moved left or right, up or down, within the module, utilizing the white space as a design element. There are almost unlimited variations to a twelve-module page. Perhaps figures 13.1 and 13.2 will help illustrate. All of the variations cannot possibly be shown. The added white space factor is one of delicate balance to prevent the page from looking like a checkerboard. Accurate sizing of pictures is the key to modular formats. Even then, a "grid" look develops that is hard to cope with.

Grid Systems

Grids are pages preplanned to accommodate many variations, with variables in pictures, copy, titles, and blurbs. Margins are also considered as part of the grid. Elements are placed within the grid to form repeated design patterns. The variables are picture content, size, or gray tone in text.

Both modules and grids form a highly regimented format and are often difficult to live with. They are handy guides for the novice but restrict layout freedom.

CHAPTER FOURTEEN

Using a Second
and a Third Color

Color has several layout advantages. It adds impact to the page. It adds a design element to the page. It adds interest to items *within* the page. It should rarely be used to decorate, but, rather, be used to advantage, to prove or clarify a point, to create a mood, perhaps, but always for a definite reason.

Using a Second Color

A second color usually means black with another color. Black is almost always used for story copy because of its readability, as well as its availability at all printers. This does not exclude the possibility of using another color for copy if the conditions are right.

Color has impact. By definition, impact means "a striking together; a collision communicating force." Color is the first thing to "hit" the reader. A page containing copy (gray tones) and white (space) and a black bar graph contains monotones. In design construction, this may be perfect, but it has no life or impact. Add red to the bars in the graph and the page immediately comes "alive." The red creates a "communicating force" by attracting the reader's eye to the bars at once.

Colors have "weight" as do the grays of the copy, the white in the page design, and all other page elements. Reds, for example, have about the same visual weight as blacks, but more impact. Dark blues, dark greens, browns, and purples have a medium visual weight. Orange falls into a middle weight, while yellow has no weight at all.

Tints of most colors less than 50 percent are in the same visual weight as grays. The layout artist uses these visual weights to create design, balance, and counterpoint within those pages where color is available.

Design is "to fashion according to a plan; to execute as a whole." Page design is the layout artist's prime job. The purpose of every page is good balance and design, according to a plan. The layout artist achieves this by balancing weights and sizes and color against the total page design.

Color emphasizes movement. A simple comparison shows that the red bars in a bar graph dominate the directional movement even more than black bars, because color draws attention to the movement.

Interest is immediately created by the use of a second color on any page. The fact that the color is something different makes it stand apart from the monotones. Attention is another word used to describe interest. Color should never be used just to decorate. When color is available it should be used for a specific purpose or for special effects, which include clarification of the art, story, graphs, or statements within the story.

Many magazines cater to a specific audience. Business publications make great use of facts and figures, which are presented as graphs, charts, or schematic drawings. These are all naturals for the use of a second color. Graphics will draw more attention than simple tabular material. Adding color helps in every case. In magazines for general reading consumption, a second color can be used successfully in duotones, panels, posterization, or in line art of any description. This color usage seems to be a vast untapped field. Perhaps many layout artists do not feel they have the necessary "know-how" to cope with it.

Second-color usage is easy to prepare, even for the beginner. There are two basic methods. In the first method, the layout artist prepares an acetate flap, with the second color "keylined" over the black plate. The art is then made in two parts, each registered to the other, so that the final result is two "plates" that can be shot and plated in register. They are printed in two colors, each covering its own area. A second method is to place a tissue overlay over the art. On this tissue, give specific instructions to the platemaker to separate them mechanically, that is, by making two negatives but deleting parts from each to make a two-color composite. The second method is preferred.

Perhaps a refresher paragraph is in order so that the layout artist may review some color terms. *Chromatics* are all the true colors. *Achromatics* are not colors, but monotones. *Hue* is pure color. *Tone* is a gradation of a color. *Shades* are the addition of black, to create a deeper color. *Tints* are the addition of white to create a lighter color. *Chroma* is the density of color.

There are three primary colors—red, blue, and yellow. There are also three secondary colors, which are made by combining any two primary colors. Red and yellow, for example, make orange. Blue and yellow make green. Red and blue make purple. The tertiary colors are made by combining any two secondary colors. Intermediate is any primary mixed with a secondary. Red mixed with orange, for instance, will give a red-orange color.

There are warm colors such as red, orange, and yellow. There are also cold colors such as blue, green, and purple. Warm colors will project outward while cool colors will recede, or move inward. Children like bright primary and secondary colors. Older people tend to prefer tints or shades.

Colors have a few generally accepted connotations. Red is considered bold and powerful. Blue gives a feeling of hope and patience. Yellow is happy and frivolous. Orange is also happy, with indications of power. Greens are universally popular because they give a feeling of freshness and renewed life. Purple indicates a feeling of pomp and dignity.

The ''color wheel'' as we know it has colors arranged in a circle. We can begin with red, then move to orange, yellow, green, blue, purple and back to red. *Monochromatic* means two or more tones of the same color. *Analogous* means two adjacent colors. *Complementary* means opposite colors (like red and green, orange and blue, yellow and purple). *Triads* are either the three primary colors or any three delicate colors. When red and green are used together, the green should dominate. When yellow and purple are used together they can remain equals. When blue and orange are used together, the blue should dominate.

Why the lecture on color? Layouts are created for reading audiences. The use of color should be appropriate to the audience and subject matter. Red and green are rarely used on the Fourth of July. One can almost always relegate some color usage to the seasons of the year without being in error: strong blacks and whites for late winter, greens for spring, browns and golds for autumn. These colors are accepted by implication. Other stereotyped color usages exist, such as pink for baby girls and light blue for baby boys. Deep purple suggests royalty. Red, white, and blue indicate patriotism. Reds, golds, and browns will rarely look good in a story about spring planting.

Using a Third Color

''Third color'' means that black and two other colors will be used. The procedure in preparing art is similar to that for two colors, that is, you can use the keyline or tissue method. The main difference between two-color and three-color is that the third color can be used to give a *fourth* color. For example, red and black can only give shades and tints of pink and gray. When yellow is added as a third color, we not only have red and black, but also tints of pink, gray, yellow, and orange. When yellow is added to blue and black, we can get yellow, green, blue, and gray. When red is added to blue, we can get red, blue, violet, purple, and gray. This is particularly effective in posterization, when specific shades or tints are not required, but the color combinations are allowed to fall as they mix.

Both two-color and three-color have some qualifications when reversing or overprinting copy. This simple guide will help illustrate this point.

Red: Reverse type from solid to 50 percent. Overprint from 10 percent to 30 percent. Notice that 40 percent is a middle zone, and neither reversed type nor overprinted type will look good.

Orange: Reverse type from solid to 80 percent. Overprint from solid to 10 percent. Note that a reverse, though acceptable in the higher percentages, is not really good. Overprinting on all percentages of orange is best.

Yellow: Reverse type is never good on yellow. instead, overprint on all percentages.

Green (depending on the shade): Reverse from solid to 60 percent. Overprint from 10 percent to 30 percent. Again, notice that 40 percent is a middle zone in which neither looks good.

Blue: Reverse type from solid to 50 percent. Overprint from 10 percent to 50 percent. This depends on the shade of blue, of course. Navy blue, for example, will accept a reverse from 20 percent to solid, while cyan, or process blue (a light blue), will not.

Violet: Overprint all values. Rarely will a reverse look good on any pale color.

Purple: Reverse all but 10 percent and 20 percent. This color is generally too dark for overprints.

Blacks and grays: Reverse all blacks, except those very light tints of gray. Do *not* overprint blacks or grays, as the type will blend into the color.

When you use a third color, take color ''vibration'' into consideration. Some colors will stand by themselves with no trouble. However, as soon as you add another color, particularly right next to it, they will both strive for attention, creating a visual vibration. This is particularly true of the ''primitives,'' or true colors. Red and green will vibrate when placed next to each other. Blue and orange, orange and green, and blue and red will also vibrate when placed next to each other. The delicate colors will not vibrate, but have another vice. They blend into each other. Violet and yellow, light blues and light greens, and tints of orange and red will blend. Vibration can be minimized by separating the true color with white space or even gray values.

Colors on tinted stock will assume still another shade or tint, depending on the color of the ink and of the stock. White paper will give more or less true colors. Tinted stocks will never give true colors. A color on a tinted stock, if the same basic color as the stock, will blend into the background. There are some cases where this muted effect may be desirable, but generally speaking, one should not use the same color on tinted stock.

In terms of cost, it is better to use a standard ink color, such as the PMS color system or the 4-A colors. If you want a specific shade or tint, the ink most often will have to be "matched." This gets expensive. Some colors, like the true golds, silvers, or bronzes, may need an extra pass through the press—once to place a sizing (or undercoat) and a second time to place the metallic inks. This is necessary to get a true color. If you are printing on colored stock, the ink color should be adjusted so the shade is the same color you originally chose. You must tell the printer to make this adjustment.

CHAPTER FIFTEEN

Four-Color Printing

Four-color printing here means *all* the colors. It gives a graphic representation, more or less, of things the way the eye sees them. Fresh fruit can be presented in all its delicate tints, tones, and hues, very much as in nature. Color adds impact and reality that no black-and-white halftone can ever show.

In ''four-color process,'' four specific colors are used. When combined, these inks give the entire spectrum. The four colors are magenta (a slightly purple-colored red), process blue or cyan (a light blue), yellow, and black. Any other blue would not give the correct combination with the other three colors to give tints and shades necessary for light blue skies, green foliage, and the whole scale of reds, purples, and violets. A darker blue would tend to make the greens dull, the reds off-color, and the violets and purples much darker.

These particular four colors are laid down in specific sequences and degrees, giving a dot pattern that resembles a rosette. Each dot in the screen and rosette pattern is a pure color, but the overlapping and exact percentages give a visual impression of all the colors in the rainbow. The four colors are not mixed, *per se,* to give other colors, but combined in dot patterns and dot sizes to give the viewer the full color range.

The technicalities of four-color process do not really belong in this chapter on usage. We are primarily concerned with *use,* not mechanics. The layout artist should trust the platemaker with the actual mechanics, striving for good final color results.

Four-color has some ramifications. While it is basically true to the subject matter, it lacks several things we usually add in actually ''seeing'' a subject. One of these is depth. Color pictures are a slice of reality simply reproduced on a flat surface. Because the surface is flat, they will all lack this third dimension. They also lack peripheral vision, which is the area surrounding the subject on all sides. When our eye concentrates on a subject, we see not only the subject, but also an area considerably larger—in some cases even as much as 200 degrees to the left and right of the subject. Peripheral vision can be illustrated by extending your arm, full length, with one finger held upright. Move your arm as far away from your center of vision as you can. You will see when moving your arm to the right that the upright finger is still visible even when it passes your shoulder. While it is true that your eye is not focusing on what happens outside the direct line of vision, it still picks up much of what happens outside this line of vision.

A photograph, whether black-and-white or four-color, also has ''sides.'' When a picture ends, so does the effect. This is particularly true of a television or movie screen. The picture is *contained*; it forces your eye to focus on a specific area. When we ''see'' things in actual life, we have a complete view. All dimensions are included. One of these dimensions is ''time.'' When we look at a flat picture, we lack both depth and time. For example, when we watch a football game, we can see the play unfold from beginning to end. This action contains time, motion, depth, and peripheral vision.

There are several important things four-color *can* give us that a black-and-white halftone cannot. One of these is impact; others are reality, special effects, and designs based on the colors. Let us take these one at a time. Impact follows the same concept in four-color as it does in two- and three-color. Something with impact draws the eye and attracts attention. Reality means things appear exactly as they should be. This is essential in some stories, particularly stories about nature or fashions. In both, reality is a selling point and helps clarify the editorial statements. Special effects are, more or less, a comparison factor. An example may help clarify this. A picture of a Christmas tree, fully decorated and lit, would provide little impact when shown in black-and-white. Again, four-color can be used to arouse attention, even though it's not the truth as we know it. Picture a fire—alive with yellow, golds, reds, and oranges. Now, replace these colors with greens, blues, and yellows. We still have ''flames,'' but they are not ''fire'' by our usual perception.

Designs based on color revert to composition and design *within* the pictures, as well as composition and design within the page. Picture size and location are factors. Hardly any four-color picture contains an equal amount of all the colors. Study each picture to find out which color dominates the picture. Then balance or design the page with other elements around it. An exa...

ate a more controlled interest.

Full-color pictures often can be controlled by their background. A full-color picture of autumn foliage can gain increased color brilliance with a broad white border. Conversely, it can be dulled with a black border. Tinted stock will always dull, or at least mute, the col-

ally soften flesh tones. The cool colors will harden them. Patterns will accentuate the softness of skin tones. Solid colors and smooth fabrics will overemphasize them.

How does the layout artist prepare four-color art for the platemaker? Full-color art comes to the artist either as a transparency or as

. Reflective art is a pic-
done in full color on a
Study the picture for
at enlargement or re-
ll give the best final
t do you want out of
? If you are working
pictures, is it to your
o have them all sized
opposed to a variety of
ou restricted to only
four-color, one form,
ature, or can you use
roughout the maga-

decision has been
photostats made of the
es to be used. Again,
nal size, comparing it
original. What impact
n the new size that it
in the original size?
u see now that wasn't
the smaller transpar-
e effect what you
o, place the photostat
nd build your layout.
d that good color lay-
m the inside and work
A common mistake is
the outside and work
iddle. This is an obvi-
hen we remember the
an only *help* color. En-
, by starting from the
nd working inward,
ken the color impact.
ve that one effective
has more impact than
less a meaningful
achieved. Again, one
n weaknesses in color
much color! This not
it difficult for the
est, but minimizes the
f presenting some-
mashing instead of a
. An example of ''too
be a four-color illus-
plus a bright colored

CHAPTER SIXTEEN

Design and Function

To design, according to Webster, is "to plan mentally, to outline, to scheme; to fashion according to plan." Design, then, has two active stages—planning and execution, or conception and results.

A design must be conceived and planned for a purpose. Good design is pure, simple, and functional. Conversely, poor design is almost always cluttered, crowded, full of gimmicks, or without purpose. A shower faucet may serve to illustrate. Its function is to turn water on or off. Whether it is plain chrome or highly ornate gold plate, its function does not change. When people say something is "overdesigned," they mean the function has been obliterated with gingerbread.

How does this principle operate in magazine design? Let us look at covers, stories, pictures, and endings.

Covers

Covers have a function—to sell the magazine and to provide a showplace for stories that appear inside. What would help, in terms of design, to accomplish this function?

The logo (magazine title) should be at the top. It should be readable. It should be quickly identified. The price and issue should be part of the logo area. These are factual building pieces that must occur within a few inches of the top so that the area involved will not be

buried when the magazine is displayed with others in a stand.

What can be done, within this restricted area, that will fulfill the function and yet achieve good design results? Since the magazine logo is the most important element, a great deal of consideration must be given to its construction and readability. Many magazines depend on large type running across the very top and often using a slight bleed. This is an effective but blunt approach. The larger letters, of course, can be reversed out to minimize the bluntness or even filled with a tint of a color used on the page. The theory behind this blunt approach is quite obvious. The observer is captivated by sheer size.

A large logo is restricted to three basic positions—left-hand corner, right-hand corner, and top center. A well-developed logo that does not depend on size but on recognition is preferable. In this case the logo has a secondary effect. It acts like a combination title and trademark.

Since the 2-inch area at the top is the logo domain, this usually leaves about 9 inches of the 11 inches to fill unless the cover is a four-sided bleed.

Once the magazine is picked up, there is still another way to persuade the reader to purchase it— story titles. Since all prospective readers are not interested in the same things, one title is rarely sufficient unless it is for a special issue. The editor provides several choices, and their arrangement be-

Figure 16.1—The "standard' newsstand elements; logo, issue date, and price in the upper 2-inch area.

Figure 16.2—In "controlled circulation" the logo and issue (no price) can appear anywhere on the cover. The logo can also be any size and moved at will to suit the cover picture or pictures.

The Headline

The "Blurb" areas

The Byline

divisions of the supraorbital and supratrochlear arteries (Fig 1).[26] Angiography in cases of internal carotid occlusion due to thrombosis[3] or ligation of an aneurysm[11] has demonstrated retrograde flow from the temporal artery to the ophthalmic artery and internal carotid siphon. (Injection of the scalp in such cases warrants particular caution.)

Anomalous arterial supply to the ophthalmic artery (and thence to its ocular-orbital branches) was found by Singh-Hayreh and Dass[21,24] in about 4% of cadaveric orbits. The luminal caliber of the ophthalmic artery between its origin from the internal carotid and the point of origin of the lacrimal artery was either constricted or entirely obliterated. The respective major or sole blood supply to the patent remainder of the ophthalmic artery was then from the middle meningeal artery through a substantial enlargement of the normal anastomosis between the orbital branch of the middle meningeal artery and the recurrent meningeal branch of the lacrimal artery (Fig 2 and Table).

The Subhead

collateral pathway has been suspected in the rare cases of amaurosis in conjunction with intraoral injections of anesthetic solutions for mandibular nerve block (Fig 2).[11] Precautions to be taken with local injections (described in this article) are not only warranted with intraoral infiltration of anesthetic solutions, as in the situation just mentioned, but also with submucosal injections of corticosteroid suspensions, as in the treatment of oral lesions of lichen planus, lupus erythematosus, and pemphigus. Rarer collateral pathways from submucosal or subcutaneous arteries to the orbital vessels are discussed by Singh-Hayreh and Dass.[21]

The usual course of the central retinal artery is tortuous and coiled in the orbit and multiangulated where the optic nerve membranes are penetrated.[24] The diameter of the artery has been estimated to be a mere 0.28 mm.[27] After many subdivisions derived from the central retinal artery, the minimal luminal accommodation is reached in the superficial and deep capillary plexuses of the retina.

Though clinical findings and recent opinions favor the arterial route of the embolism for most cases in point, suggestions involving the venous circulation may be rarely tenable. In isolated cases involving subcutaneous nasal injections of paraffins, funduscopy showed substantial venous engorgement and hemorrhages as seen with retinal vein occlusion.[3] Timm, as quoted by Hager and Heise,[6] sug-

---

The "Blurb" areas

---

gested that some cases of amaurosis concurrent with intranasal injection were initiated by intravenous injection into an ethmoidal vein, followed by passage of the injected material into the ophthalmic vein.

Generally, there are rough parallels in the courses of the superior ophthalmic vein and the ophthalmic artery and the veins of the scalp with their corresponding arteries. A preparation injected into the supraorbital or supratrochlear vein would flow into the superior ophthalmic vein. However in the cases of amaurosis associated with scalp injection, funduscopic and other clinical findings were compatible with arterial embolism.[3]

Early explanations for uniocular amaurosis concurrent with subcutaneous injections of paraffins suggested more circuitous routes, whereby accidental injection of material into a peripheral vein was thought to be followed by systemic arterial dissemination, perhaps with a bypass of the pulmonary circulation through a patent foramen ovale.[14] Other atrial septal defects deserve similar consideration.

It has been repeatedly noted that ocular accidents that followed paraf-

jected material via group 1 branches. Evidence for the intra-arterial route have included funduscopic visualization of emboli in the retinal arterial branches[1-3,9] and roentgenographic visualization of the central retinal artery in a patient who received intranasal thorium dioxide injections as a treatment for ozena.[6]

Blood pressure is reduced in the ophthalmic artery system to protect the eye from the systolic pressure elsewhere. Sometimes the ophthalmic artery is snuggly fitted between the internal carotid trunk and the optic nerve when the latter cannot deviate upwards because of a superimposed fold of dura mater.[21] The pulse wave on the carotid artery may further reduce space for the opthalmic artery to the degree that during cerebral angiography the ophthalmic artery may not fill if the radiopaque material was injected during a compression phase. The counterpressure of a forceful injection into a group 2 artery may then exceeed the local blood pressure and thereby effect retrograde flow to the ocular-orbital supply junctions,

The Picture Caption

23

TOPIC April 1976

Figure 16.3—*The basic page functional elements: title (or headline), "blurb," author (or by-line), picture captions, folio number, and running foot. Headlines can vary in size and face, but there should be good "type marriages" in all other type elements—for instance, a "mix" with regular, bold, italic, caps, and caps and lower case, but all in the same face.*

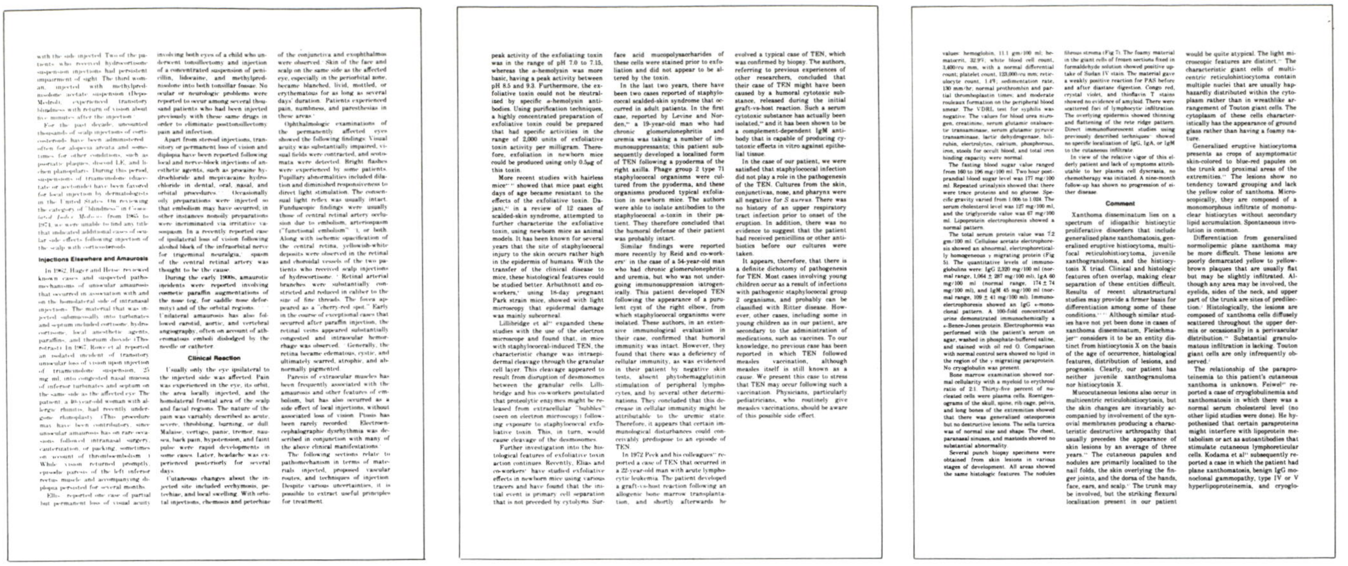

Figure 16.4—*The three basic story endings are: squared off at the bottom (left); natural (center); and natural column (right).*

comes a design that is sales oriented. This may present some difficulty when all the artist has is typography and color to work with.

Typography in story titles should never conflict with the logo. Rather, the story titles should become a married unit. Title arrangements are balanced against the logo area. In an average story title area, one story is usually featured and several more are subordinated to it. Some publishers may feel all story titles are equal and want them to be handled in that way. Title areas consisting of three or four titles (or as many as six) are often run down one side of the cover as separate units. This creates a panel of black and counterbalances the logo area. The titles can also appear in a strong color other than black.

Cover design often depends on subject matter, with the logo occupying its established position but everything else built around the subject. For instance, a picture of a person, with full four-sided bleed, would lose impact if obliterated by story titles. Instead, the story titles are molded around the person's face to create a form within a form.

In the eight standard cover designs, each unit (except the full bleed and free form) is basically composed of rectangles. The common practice is to handle each as a separate entity and as a part of a cohesive unit, and all are contained within the 8½-by-11-inch rectangle. There is nothing wrong with this. There is nothing wrong with using interlocking devices, either, although they are not used often. By interlocking devices, I mean that all, or part of, the units are arranged tighter and seem to overlap into other units. This creates motion in some cases and placidity in others.

Stories

Stories should be read with ease and continuity. The heads create interest, as do the illustrations, but the main thrust is "to be read." Continuity in design means a natural flow of all the elements. No one likes to read in segments. This is particularly true with jump pages and stories interspersed with small ads. Yes—ads pay our salaries—but the good story designer also thinks of the reader.

Reading patterns are interesting. A high percentage of *Reader's Digest* readers will concentrate on the fillers, putting the feature stories to one side for later reading. For *Time* or *Newsweek*, reading patterns depend on interest and some areas are skipped completely. *Look* and *Life* pictures and captions were read as a unit. In scientific or specialty fields, the reader will often clip and file those stories of special interest. The reader will turn first to what interests him or her most. This brings us right back to continuity, the crux of every story layout and design. What constitutes continuity besides uninterrupted flow? The titles (or heads) should be part of the story and lead directly into the story. A headline at the bottom of a page means a visual jump from the bottom back to where the story starts. This is interrupted continuity. The movement from headline to story should be smooth, uninterrupted, and yet viable. The visual line can be straight, spiral, curved, or any uninterrupted movement.

Pictures

Pictures should never segment the copy. They create visual roadblocks to continuity if they do. Pictures belong at the top, bottom, or sides of copy, but never in between blocks of copy. Pictures can create "leaders" in reading patterns by bleeding into the next page. Design patterns may be a challenge to the layout artist and give a feeling of design accomplishment. The same design patterns may be quite distracting to the reader. Copy tricks such as wrapping copy around an object, for instance, are often unwarranted and an annoyance to the reader.

vocal alarm. Do your best to avoid problem situations. Don't go out alone after dark. Stay away from lonely areas and make sure you're not stuck in a confined area, such as an elevator, alone with a stranger. Enroll in a good self-defense course. This will give you practical skills and will help you feel more secure. You can't always prevent someone from trying to take advantage of you, but you can be prepared.

Twinkle, Little Star

[Continued from page 28]

go on! And so I left the theater with a courageous smile and continued to bore both friends and delivery boys with an advance review of Eve-Lynn's four minutes and 53 potentially show-stopping seconds.

"She marches so well," I told them, "that I'm either going to send her to the New York City Ballet or the New York National Guard."

Two days later, the golden moment was upon us at last: opening night, which was opening afternoon, for the first performance of The Nutcracker was a Saturday matinee. On the way to McCarter, I said to Eve-Lynn anxiously, "Now don't be nervous, honey. Just go out there and break a leg."

"Daddy," she said, "if I break a leg, then I won't be able to dance."

"It's just an expression we theatrical fathers use."

"Well, it sounds very stupid to me."

"Atta girl, let all your emotions out. Then you won't be tight up there. Hey,

Picture Credits

Cover	Chuck Hamrick
Page 2	Bill Rogers
	Geoffrey Gove-R.G.
8	Alfred Gescheidt
17	Ralph Cowan
20-23	Roger Harvey
26	Jack Haesly
29	Lucky Curtis
32-33	Swanson, Pearson, Haugaard
34-35	Lonnie Warren
38	Joe Fletcher
42-47	Bill Rogers
48	Richard Tomlinson
51	Allan Price-R.G.
53	Bruce Roberts-R.G.
55	Arnold Zann
56	Burton McNeely-Van Cleve

R.G.—Rapho Guillumette

Fear and Wallendas

[Continued from page 47]

his palms sweaty now, shouting soft encouragement as Delilah eased up on the chair. "Careful, Delilah," said Karl, and his voice could be heard all through the armory. "Don't lean too far." Delilah smiling, looking only at her grandfather, inching up on her feet. "Careful,

guess what I've got in my pocket."

"What?"

"This." I held up her favorite green hairband. "For good luck."

"Mommy and I were looking all over for that this morning."

And then, after a lingering hug, I left her backstage and walked toward the seats to sweat out the show. A few minutes later, I greeted a grand procession of relatives whose tickets had been underwritten by paternal pride. I couldn't afford a seat for myself, but luckily I didn't need one because I planned to make a little movie from the rear of the orchestra with an equipment and indoor film, a movie Johnny Carson would need for his interview with Eve-Lynn and me.

Suddenly the theater went dark, the music came on, and the curtain rose to reveal a bunch of forgettable kids. I watched the meaningless first 40 minutes through the viewfinder of my Bell and Howell, trying to steady my hand against the pounding of my heart. At last the soldiers' music sounded. I zoomed in on the entering troops, and felt a sharp tap on my back.

"No picture-taking in the theater, sir," said an usherette.

"Oh, you don't understand," I told her. "My daughter's in the show."

So I turned with just my adoring naked eyes to watch the theatrical debut of Eve-Lynn Schoenstein, who had to be up there someplace; I just couldn't be sure of where because I couldn't pick her out from the rear of the orchestra. After a frantic scanning of the troops, I finally discovered her: She wasn't in the front row. Some treacherous mother had deliberately shrunken her kid! So that's how the game was played! Well, next year Eve-Lynn and I would be back and not for a clogged up chorus line. There was a sugar plum in act two who had 46 seconds more than any first act child. And she was far enough from the next sugar plum so you could nudge an uncle to see her 50 yards away.

Delilah, careful." Finally, the lithe sequined body straightens completely upward and the hands slowly go out and up in a graceful arc. And now the applause, the deafening applause, and the crashing upbeat music, and the Wallenda family standing together on the platform throwing kisses and bowing to the crowd far below. Quick, dramatic slides down a rope to the grimy stage and more kisses and bows, and for these several minutes Detroit and Mario's wheelchair and all of the ones who are under the ground now are forgotten. Only the cheers and the music and the glistening wire—conquered, once more—and the sheer exhilaration of it all. You need to walk the wire. A little tension is good. Even if they do know fear, they are trying to prove they aren't afraid. Karl is afraid of dying in bed. What else could he do for a living? When I have walked the wire, I have two strong martinis and I forget it. Karl is crazy. The one that killed all them people. We don't do the pyramid anymore, there are only four of us now.

Anti-smoking

[Continued from page 13]

than half as harmful as the one of 15 years ago. But since we know that some people will continue to smoke, against their own best interests, we must encourage further development in this area. We should be able to reduce the harmfulness of the average cigarette by an additional 50 percent within the next few years.

Combined with continued efforts to discourage young people from starting to smoke and helping smokers give up the habit, it will be possible to reduce cigarette smoking in America by another 50 percent in the very near future. Then, the next strategic objective—to reduce cigarette smoking to an absolute minimum—will be within striking distance. It can and must be done.

Dr. Terry is on leave from the University of Pennsylvania, in order to serve as part-time special consultant to the American Cancer Society, and as a staff member of University Associates, Inc., a non-profit academic consulting firm in Washington, D.C.

Diabetes

[Continued from page 37]

son is not the kind of kid who stands still very long. In fact, he's usually the one the other kids follow." It seems that Rich had even given the coach some candy to keep on hand in case there was any problem with his diabetes.

He was even doing better in his classroom subjects. His concentration had improved, said his homeroom teacher, and he didn't seem so worried.

Two days later, Rich came home with a story about Louise, the only other diabetic in the school. "All the kids in her class came down at lunch and started yelling that Louise went crazy in class . . ." I held my breath. "Of course, she was having an insulin reaction and Mr. Lash didn't figure it out." I waited, still uneasy despite his cool tone, wondering how much it had upset him. "There's really no excuse for having an insulin reaction," he said. "She must be pretty stupid."

Perhaps Rich is sure now that he could handle his own insulin. Perhaps he realizes now that diabetes is a problem, but just one part of his life.

It's the loneliness of it that bothers him sometimes. Knowing that his other friends are somehow separate from this thing is a heavy burden, even for a young child.

But there can be a camaraderie, too, and a little pride in a job being well done. Like the time last spring Rich figured out that one of his baseball teammates, from another school, also was diabetic. "You have diabetes?" he asked. The boy nodded. "Me, too," said Rich.

"How much insulin do you take," the boy asked.

"Thirty-two units."

"I take twenty-eight. Give it yourself?"

Richard said he did. Small talk, shop talk. Once over, they got back to the game. And I doubt if they ever spoke about it again.

I asked Rich later how he knew the boy had diabetes. "I could tell by the way he got a Lifesaver out of the pack with one hand while he was catching with the other. Only diabetics can get so good at sneaking candy without other kids noticing."

And only parents can get so good at knowing their son is growing up.

[Please turn page]

Figure 16.5—An example of "slush pages" containing two "jumps" and four "continued from's."

Endings

Endings consist of squared-off columns, natural endings in a column, and natural endings with fillers.

Where the end falls is always cause for concern. Good story layouts are continuous, with no more than one jump. The jump page should complete the story if at all possible. Continual jumps are distracting and should be avoided. A "slush" page, consisting of short left-overs, is a sure sign of unprofessionalism.

What is the design factor in endings? The answer is in what the layout artist does with the white space. Simply leaving it white would create a feeling that the story is incomplete. Breaking up the white space into uneven blocks (as in natural column endings) at least indicates an attempt at solving the problem. The squared-off columns are the most professional: the real pro starts layouts from the end and works forward.

Ideally, stories are preplanned for no more than one jump. This means ending the jump page full and deducting the remainder of the stories and pictures to fill the front page allotment for the story. (For example, for a five-page story with one jump, you would deduct one or two or three columns of straight copy on the jump page and fill the front five pages with story, pictures, and title.) Far too many layout artists complete the first five pages and then find openings in the rear of the magazine to fill with leftover story. This is not only the lazy way, but full of traps. It often means cutting copy from the end of a story, as well as adding poor or partial jumps, and very often conflicts with ads.

You may plan to leave white space at the story ending for fillers, cartoons, and the like, if they are available or if you have an artist on the staff to create spot drawings to fill certain areas.

CHAPTER SEVENTEEN

Designing and Redesigning Magazines

Until the late 1960s, established magazines like *Time, Look, Life,* and *Ladies Home Journal*—all household words—had the industry firmly in hand. The formats were set. They worked. They accomplished their purpose, as they had for many years. There was no reason to change.

Suddenly, *Look* folded. *Psychology Today* burst on the scene with an exciting new format. *Sports Illustrated* proved the feasibility of the specialist publication. The industry stopped to examine itself.

The facts are these: postal rates had gone up (and are still rising), television had made tremendous inroads into the news media field, the special-fields markets had been mostly neglected, and sex had become a prime selling force. *Playboy* had been there for years and was practically printing its own money. *Cosmopolitan* had been hovering in the background and also making money with sex as its prime subject. What resulted? A veritable rash of sex-oriented magazines— all copying *Playboy's* style and format. However, the more realistic publishers pulled more out of this than the "girlie" concept. They realized that the magazine market was fast becoming a specialty-oriented one.

Why this brief history? Simply because this is the time for the magazine designer. Even a casual examination of a dozen magazines indicates two things. First, very few vary from the old, reliable standard formats (two- or three-column), and second they all tend to "over-reach" in each issue. By this I mean

that each successive issue tries to contain some gimmick or embellishment that the previous issue did not have. This "shotgun" designing is distracting, to say the least. Out of this mess of new magazines, the true designer must create a workable format, a design based on purity, simplicity, and grace, with the capability of standing the test of continued repetition without creating monotony.

What is a definition of good magazine design? Rob Cuscaden, in a tribute to Leo Burnett published in the *Chicago Sun-Times*, said it quite well: "The work accomplished [by Leo Burnett] was and is distinguished by a certain straightforward expression of directness, honesty, and humaneness: an absence of tricks and gimmicks: the presence of substance instead of shallowness." He was talking about advertising, but the same principles apply to good magazine design.

Designing with these concepts in mind is indeed difficult. One must assemble, at least mentally, the wide variety of formats and layout ideas available. If the designer has mastered the discipline, he will have developed a sense of "rights" and "wrongs." Years of viewing and analyzing sharpen this sense.

Are you designing or redesigning? The difference is that designing generally means starting out with something new and fresh. Redesigning generally means working with an established format or editorial style.

The real challenge would seem to be starting with something new.

This has many traps. Some designers are inclined to develop a style and push it beyond its capabilities. For example, a format that is good in every way for a building-services magazine would not work well for a high-fashion magazine. The designer who does this is trying to push a square peg into a round hole—to force a design to meet a purpose. *Psychology Today* developed its own style and format. In copying it, other magazines brutalized it.

Designs are created to serve a specific purpose—not to solve all problems. Some designers are merely copycats. In copying, they fail to realize the basic design concept—designs *must* serve a specific purpose. Copying can be as dangerous as quicksand.

Redesigning has its weaknesses, too. One's first inclination is to start with the cover and carry that design throughout the magazine. The good designer looks at the whole. A display-type logo may look great on the cover. The same display type may also look good on individual pages. But what happens when these pages contain fractional ads that also are replete with display faces? The whole impact is lost. No design or format should be attempted without a complete study of the entire magazine, ads included.

Since redesigning is harder than creating a new design, the first step must be one of analysis. What do you have to work with? Why should it be changed? Does the present format serve its maximum purpose? What factors will an ad-

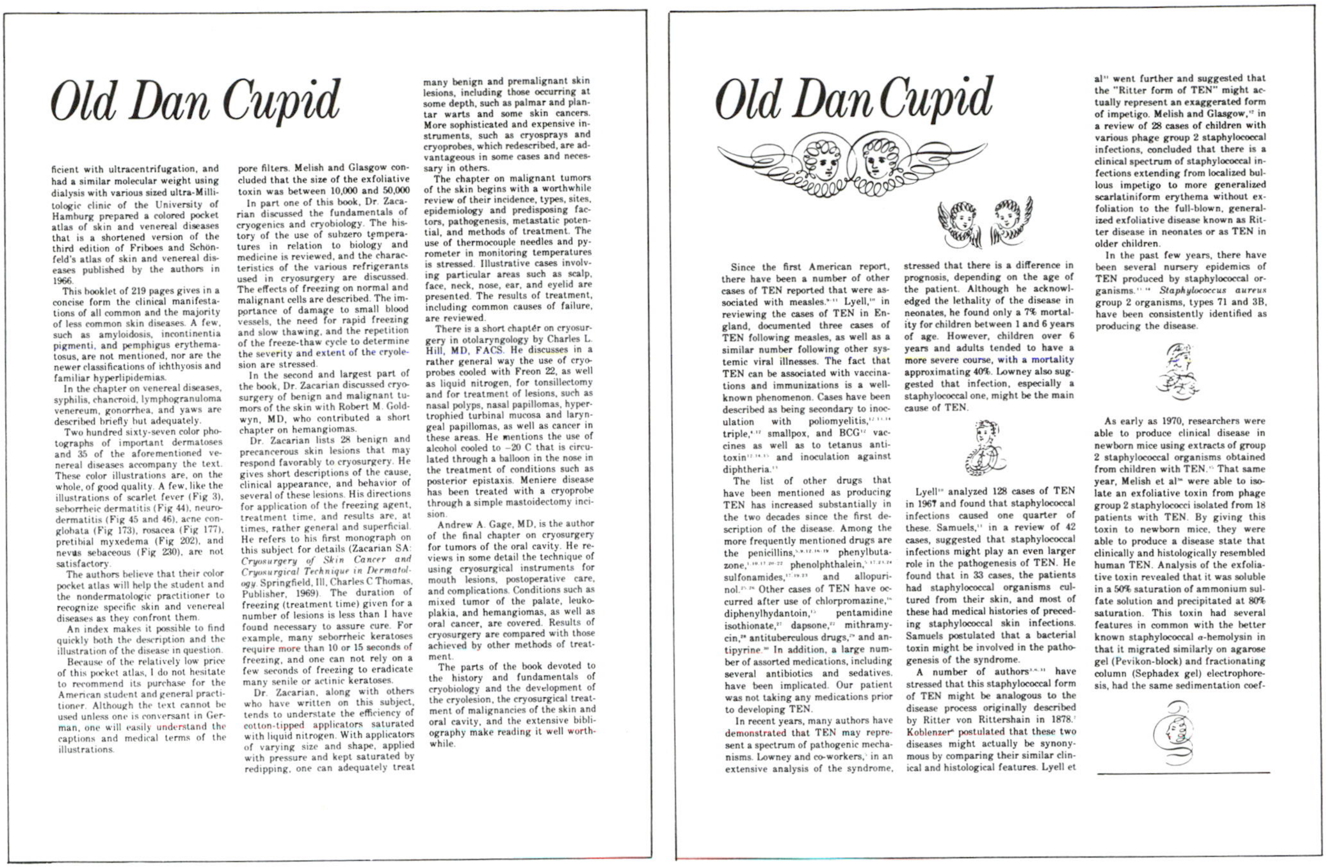

Old Dan Cupid

ficient with ultracentrifugation, and had a similar molecular weight using dialysis with various sized ultra-Millitologic clinic of the University of Hamburg prepared a colored pocket atlas of skin and venereal diseases that is a shortened version of the third edition of Friboes and Schönfeld's atlas of skin and venereal diseases published by the authors in 1966.

This booklet of 219 pages gives in a concise form the clinical manifestations of all common and the majority of less common skin diseases. A few, such as amyloidosis, incontinentia pigmenti, and pemphigus erythematosus, are not mentioned, nor are the newer classifications of ichthyosis and familiar hyperlipidemias.

In the chapter on venereal diseases, syphilis, chancroid, lymphogranuloma venereum, gonorrhea, and yaws are described briefly but adequately.

Two hundred sixty-seven color photographs of important dermatoses and 35 of the aforementioned venereal diseases accompany the text. These color illustrations are, on the whole, of good quality. A few, like the illustrations of scarlet fever (Fig 3), seborrheic dermatitis (Fig 44), neurodermatitis (Fig 45 and 46), acne conglobata (Fig 173), rosacea (Fig 177), pretibial myxedema (Fig 202), and nevus sebaceous (Fig 230), are not satisfactory.

The authors believe that their color pocket atlas will help the student and the nondermatologic practitioner to recognize specific skin and venereal diseases as they confront them.

An index makes it possible to find quickly both the description and the illustration of the disease in question.

Because of the relatively low price of this pocket atlas, I do not hesitate to recommend its purchase for the American student and general practitioner. Although the text cannot be used unless one is conversant in German, one will easily understand the captions and medical terms of the illustrations.

pore filters. Melish and Glasgow concluded that the size of the exfoliative toxin was between 10,000 and 50,000

In part one of this book, Dr. Zacarian discussed the fundamentals of cryogenics and cryobiology. The history of the use of subzero temperatures in relation to biology and medicine is reviewed, and the characteristics of the various refrigerants used in cryosurgery are discussed. The effects of freezing on normal and malignant cells are described. The importance of damage to small blood vessels, the need for rapid freezing and slow thawing, and the repetition of the freeze-thaw cycle to determine the severity and extent of the cryolesion are stressed.

In the second and largest part of the book, Dr. Zacarian discussed cryosurgery of benign and malignant tumors of the skin with Robert M. Goldwyn, MD, who contributed a short chapter on hemangiomas.

Dr. Zacarian lists 28 benign and precancerous skin lesions that may respond favorably to cryosurgery. He gives short descriptions of the cause, clinical appearance, and behavior of several of these lesions. His directions for application of the freezing agent, treatment time, and results are, at times, rather general and superficial. He refers to his first monograph on this subject for details (Zacarian SA: *Cryosurgery of Skin Cancer and Cryosurgical Technique in Dermatology.* Springfield, Ill, Charles C Thomas, Publisher, 1969). The duration of freezing (treatment time) given for a number of lesions is less than I have found necessary to assure cure. For example, many seborrheic keratoses require more than 10 or 15 seconds of freezing, and one can not rely on a few seconds of freezing to eradicate many senile or actinic keratoses.

Dr. Zacarian, along with others who have written on this subject, tends to understate the efficiency of cotton-tipped applicators saturated with liquid nitrogen. With applicators of varying size and shape, applied with pressure and kept saturated by redipping, one can adequately treat many benign and premalignant skin lesions, including those occurring at some depth, such as palmar and plantar warts and some skin cancers. More sophisticated and expensive instruments, such as cryosprays and cryoprobes, which redescribed, are advantageous in some cases and necessary in others.

The chapter on malignant tumors of the skin begins with a worthwhile review of their incidence, types, sites, epidemiology and predisposing factors, pathogenesis, metastatic potential, and methods of treatment. The use of thermocouple needles and pyrometer in monitoring temperatures is stressed. Illustrative cases involving particular areas such as scalp, face, neck, nose, ear, and eyelid are presented. The results of treatment, including common causes of failure, are reviewed.

There is a short chaptér on cryosurgery in otolaryngology by Charles L. Hill, MD, FACS. He discusses in a rather general way the use of cryoprobes cooled with Freon 22, as well as liquid nitrogen, for tonsillectomy and for treatment of lesions, such as nasal polyps, nasal papillomas, hypertrophied turbinal mucosa and laryngeal papillomas, as well as cancer in these areas. He mentions the use of alcohol cooled to −20 C that is circulated through a balloon in the nose in the treatment of conditions such as posterior epistaxis. Meniere disease has been treated with a cryoprobe through a simple mastoidectomy incision.

Andrew A. Gage, MD, is the author of the final chapter on cryosurgery for tumors of the oral cavity. He reviews in some detail the technique of using cryosurgical instruments for mouth lesions, postoperative care, and complications. Conditions such as mixed tumor of the palate, leukoplakia, and hemangiomas, as well as oral cancer, are covered. Results of cryosurgery are compared with those achieved by other methods of treatment.

The parts of the book devoted to the history and fundamentals of cryobiology and the development of the cryolesion, the cryosurgical treatment of malignancies of the skin and oral cavity, and the extensive bibliography make reading it well worthwhile.

Old Dan Cupid

Since the first American report, there have been a number of other cases of TEN reported that were associated with measles.[9-11] Lyell,[10] in reviewing the cases of TEN in England, documented three cases of TEN following measles, as well as a similar number following other systemic viral illnesses. The fact that TEN can be associated with vaccinations and immunizations is a well-known phenomenon. Cases have been described as being secondary to inoculation with poliomyelitis,[12,13,14] triple,[4,12] smallpox, and BCG[12] vaccines as well as to tetanus antitoxin[12,14,15] and inoculation against diphtheria.[11]

The list of other drugs that have been mentioned as producing TEN has increased substantially in the two decades since the first description of the disease. Among the more frequently mentioned drugs are the penicillins,[5,9,12,16-19] phenylbutazone,[1,10,17,20-22] phenolphthalein,[5,17,23,24] sulfonamides,[17,19,23] and allopurinol.[25,26] Other cases of TEN have occurred after use of chlorpromazine,[16] diphenylhydantoin,[15] pentamidine isothionate,[27] dapsone,[22] mithramycin,[28] antituberculous drugs,[29] and antipyrine.[30] In addition, a large number of assorted medications, including several antibiotics and sedatives, have been implicated. Our patient was not taking any medications prior to developing TEN.

In recent years, many authors have demonstrated that TEN may represent a spectrum of pathogenic mechanisms. Lowney and co-workers,[5] in an extensive analysis of the syndrome, stressed that there is a difference in prognosis, depending on the age of the patient. Although he acknowledged the lethality of the disease in neonates, he found only a 7% mortality for children between 1 and 6 years of age. However, children over 6 years and adults tended to have a more severe course, with a mortality approximating 40%. Lowney also suggested that infection, especially a staphylococcal one, might be the main cause of TEN.

Lyell[10] analyzed 128 cases of TEN in 1967 and found that staphylococcal infections caused one quarter of these. Samuels,[11] in a review of 42 cases, suggested that staphylococcal infections might play an even larger role in the pathogenesis of TEN. He found that in 33 cases, the patients had staphylococcal organisms cultured from their skin, and most of these had medical histories of preceding staphylococcal skin infections. Samuels postulated that a bacterial toxin might be involved in the pathogenesis of the syndrome.

A number of authors[3,6,11] have stressed that this staphylococcal form of TEN might be analogous to the disease process originally described by Ritter von Rittershain in 1878.[7] Koblenzer[6] postulated that these two diseases might actually be synonymous by comparing their similar clinical and histological features. Lyell et al[11] went further and suggested that the "Ritter form of TEN" might actually represent an exaggerated form of impetigo. Melish and Glasgow,[12] in a review of 28 cases of children with various phage group 2 staphylococcal infections, concluded that there is a clinical spectrum of staphylococcal infections extending from localized bullous impetigo to more generalized scarlatiniform erythema without exfoliation to the full-blown, generalized exfoliative disease known as Ritter disease in neonates or as TEN in older children.

In the past few years, there have been several nursery epidemics of TEN produced by staphylococcal organisms.[11,14] *Staphylococcus aureus* group 2 organisms, types 71 and 3B, have been consistently identified as producing the disease.

As early as 1970, researchers were able to produce clinical disease in newborn mice using extracts of group 2 staphylococcal organisms obtained from children with TEN.[15] That same year, Melish et al[16] were able to isolate an exfoliative toxin from phage group 2 staphylococci isolated from 18 patients with TEN. By giving this toxin to newborn mice, they were able to produce a disease state that clinically and histologically resembled human TEN. Analysis of the exfoliative toxin revealed that it was soluble in a 50% saturation of ammonium sulfate solution and precipitated at 80% saturation. This toxin had several features in common with the better known staphylococcal α-hemolysin in that it migrated similarly on agarose gel (Pevikon-block) and fractionating column (Sephadex gel) electrophoresis, had the same sedimentation coef-

Figure 17.1—''Functional'' versus ''embellishments.'' As you can see, the gingerbread really adds nothing to the story but decoration. It also chops up the story into segments, which is never good layout.

vertising analysis show? What printing process is now being used? What about typesetting and prep-work? Can or should it be changed, and why? Let's take these one at a time.

What do you have to work with? A designer begins with an audience, a format, and an editorial style. The audience consists of the people who read the magazine (and, in some cases, the advertisers in the magazine). In the current concept, this would tend to be a specialty group, both of readers and advertisers. Mass audience magazines are fighting for their share of a market and losing to television. What kind of people are in your audience? This very often will help determine the format and editorial style. Engineers tend to prefer a highly regimented and precise format because their nature is to be factual. Sports-minded audiences prefer lots of full-color action pictures carried throughout the entire magazine. Fashion magazines will have lots of full-page, full-color spreads, with copy becoming secondary. Scientific publications are highly regimented with much ''sacred'' copy and pictures of a predetermined size. ''Sacred'' means that neither copy nor pictures can be cut or expanded, but must be used as they are.

Also included is the present format, either two- or three-column in 95 percent of the cases. Will changing from one to the other affect advertising? Remember that a 13-pica outside ad has no place in a two-column format where the column width is 20 picas. One of the commandments of magazine publishing is that the advertiser pays your salary. This may be the first restriction—that is, format limits imposed by advertising sizes. Your first impulse may be to feel you are at a dead end. Changing a format sounds impossible without also changing the advertising rates, sizes, and positions. It is possible to ''mix and match,'' but only in the Midwest style (see chapter 22).

Suppose management will not approve of a format innovation? This leaves the designer with a problem that is, however, not insurmountable. It means only that your basic design must start with the present format.

Besides the basic two- and three-column formats, there are other factors that need analysis. What about ads? Are they black and white, two color, or four color? A knowledge of impositions is essential. If black and white, where are they most likely to occur? Is there a section composed of fractional ads? If a second color is used in the ads, can this be utilized in the editorial pages? Can it be used to advantage? This is often neglected. Four-color pages also give the opportunity to use three colors on many pages.

What about typography? (This means the typeface used in the head, copy, and captions.) You may be committed to a typesetter that has few available faces and sizes (though this is now rare). By changing typefaces, sizes, and leading, it is entirely possible to create a new look.

What does the art reflect? Does

the present issue contain many halftones or is it a mixture of halftones and line art? Are the line drawings bar graphs, charts, or tables? Is the designer expected to delineate an art style? Remember, what might look good in an original concept may become deadly with constant repetition. So, we have several "design factors"—ads, format, typography, and art. Each must be considered separately but also in combination as an entity.

Does the present format serve its maximum purpose? By format, I mean all the design factors. Perhaps redesigning will dictate changes in only one or two areas. Change just for the sake of change is an exercise in futility. The change must serve a purpose.

What process is being used for prep-work, plates, and printing? The present trend is to divide services into prep-house (typography and platemaking) and printer (printing, binding, and distributing). However, the printing process may determine the direction and cost. Offset lithography seems to offer the greatest variety and cost saving. The use of computerized typesetting offers an even greater variety of typefaces and sizes, while type on film (as well as plates) cuts shipping costs and handling. Advances in pre-prep are made almost daily. Cost, service, and quality are all involved.

You can save money if you train yourself or the people using your design to handle layouts without the use of galleys or paste-ups. Going directly to page proofs cuts out this middle cost. It saves the prep-house from handling the copy twice and minimizes alteration costs. It gives you an immediate proof of what the page will look like. Film also allows one to enlarge or reduce type to fit certain areas without resetting.

So far, we have brought up a lot of unanswered questions which need resolving. Let's start by saying that all the "design factors" have been analyzed and all need changing. In this way, one can discard what need not be used. In each case we will compare the design factors with design and redesigning.

Ads

Advertisers contract for space in magazines. These spaces generally are the back cover, inside front cover, inside back cover, the center spread, full-page ads, fractional ads (less than a full page), and "mail order" ads. The covers and spread rarely affect any design format. Full-page ads can affect the magazine design by their placement. Care must be taken that a full-page ad does not face the first page of a story that might cause conflict. Ads must also be placed so there is no conflict for the reader's attention. This is resolved in make-up.

The two types of ads that cause the most trouble in magazine design are the fractional ads and the mail order ads. Fractional ads can be one column or a part of one column in the two-column format. They can be one column, two columns, or parts thereof in the three-column format. At least one column in the format should contain copy. Ads can also be half page in either format (that is, from the top down or from the bottom up). Mail order ads are small ads, usually several to a column, in any format.

The ad spaces are determined by the format, and advertising space is prepared to meet format requirements. However, design decisions must also tie in directly with typography. In this case I do not mean the choice of type, but the way in which it will be used. If columns are set flush left and right, there is no problem. If copy is set flush left ragged right, the visual impression given will be an uneven or ragged edge to one side of the column. An ad placed next to this will carry the ragged edge unless a hairline rule is used to separate them.

If copy (or format) is being set with a natural column ending and ads are full column in depth, the bottom of the page will present a ragged appearance. The solution is to square off each column with hairline rules. Half-page ads seldom give design problems, although they should always be separated from the text with generous white space.

In redesigning a format or design, the layout artist usually begins with either a two- or three-column format. The ads will stay the same. However, they must be studied for general context and typography. Study one year's back issues, and you will get a sense of

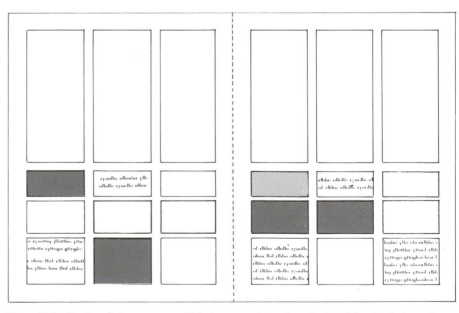

Figure 17.2—Fractional ads versus copy. This shows a variation from placing all fractional ads on the outside columns. This divides the reader's attention into two separate units—story and ads are separated by the page design.

the kind and amount of display faces used.

Mail order ads create problems in both designing and redesigning. Every effort should be made to segregate them. The reasons are simple. Mail order ads bring in the least amount of revenue and cause the most make-up problems. There is no good reason to tear up a page make-up for a small ad. The revenue will never equal the cost. Even when you use fillers the odds are never good that the space needed will equal the space the ad might occupy. This can mean re-editing or even resetting copy. This is expensive.

In terms of design, segregation has some weaknesses. Rather than a full page of mail order ads, the designer will stack building-block formations into partial pages, perhaps even one-half or one-third of a page, with text above them.

Format

In designing, "format" covers more than just a decision to use two or three columns. It also covers the construction and placement of the table of contents, masthead, the editorial section, stories, fillers, next month's previews, and special sections of any kind. The entire sequence *must* be handled as a cohesive unit. Good magazine design means the whole thing, not just the stories.

The table of contents is rarely placed anywhere but in the front of any magazine. This position is firmly established. Very often, a table of contents seems to be handled as a separate entity. This is because there is usually an abundance of type faces used in it. The same feeling used in the rest of the magazine should prevail in the table of contents. It can be smaller or tighter, but it should always be a variation of the same format.

Mastheads are often combined with the table of contents, unless the staff is so large that additional space is needed. Mastheads should follow the general feeling and format. Editorial pages (and by this I mean the pages assigned to the editor to air the magazine's editorial

concepts) can vary in some way from the regular format, usually by setting copy on a different measure, just to draw attention. Fillers, too, can vary, but only by setting them on a different measure. The preview of next month's issue can be almost identical to the table of contents except for information.

Typography

The first place new or exciting typography can be used is on the magazine cover. Everyone wants to design covers—publishers, editors, art directors, layout people, designers, even the lowliest person in the office. The problem is that they have widely divergent ideas about what a cover logo should be. It's a sad fact that anything created by committee is doomed to failure. A cover logo is the first thing the buyer or reader sees. It conveys a meaning and establishes a feeling along with the corporate identity. This should be left to the designer or at least to the art director. Either one should have a firm grasp of the editorial content and general feeling of the magazine. Only the designer has a grasp of how big and what color the logo should be and even where to place it.

More often than not, the simplest way is the best way. Cleverly designed logos for covers must compete with the type faces used for story titles and other subject matter used on the cover. All should blend into a cohesive unit. The cover logo is repeated over the table of contents and, often, over the masthead when the masthead is on a different page. Here, again, it conflicts with a variety of type faces and sizes. The cover logo will also appear on letterheads, envelopes, invoices, mailing labels, statements, checks, literally everything the publisher has that bears the magazine's identity. Is it any wonder, then, that it should be handled by a professional?

Heads

Heads, or title areas, are another rich field for the designer. Heads

need to create a mood or story feeling and require variety. This is achieved through different faces, sizes, colors, locations—every trick imaginable. This is one place where the designer's imagination can run free without actually using creative art.

Body Copy

Type for body copy should *always* be chosen for readability, including correct leading. There are many highly readable body faces—almost all are Roman. The only recent addition to body faces that is not Roman is called Optima. Sansserifs in large masses usually create reading problems. The reader must identify word shapes that are out of the ordinary. We are accustomed to reading Roman faces. It is a good practice to stick to the ideal reading faces.

Look at the ascenders and descenders when planning for correct leading. This was mentioned previously, but bears repeating. The longer the ascenders and descenders, the less leading will be necessary for easy reading. When planning a page layout, remember that there is no leading above the first line or below the last line. While this seems to be a small thing, it can vary page depths by several points. Look for "color" in body faces. This means the weight of the characters and how they will look in mass. Some faces, like Garamond, are fragile and present a light gray mass. Others, Cheltenham for instance, are quite heavy and the feeling, in mass, is very dark. This is also a factor in page design, particularly when there may be nothing but copy on the page.

Body copy sometimes seems to lack something without a "stand-up" or "indented" initial to begin the story. This is usually three lines deep. Anything larger will tend to make the first word lose its capital. The portion standing above the line will be dependent on the size and leading used. For example, a 9/11 face will allow 4 points to extend above the first line. If one were to use 10/12 and a 24-point capital, there would be only 2 points above the first line. Occasionally, larger letters are used, but they should "hang" outside the first column.

Once the typefaces and sizes have been chosen, it is essential that an accurate character count per pica be firmly established. Why is this essential? Good page layouts are planned. A good plan means knowing *all* the variables and standards that may occur within any area. When handling stories, the page designer must know, within a small margin, exactly how much space the stories will occupy. This applies not only to the column widths in a chosen format, but also to the possible variations. For example, a special section may call for variations in column widths. The occasion may arise when variables in line widths may be a factor. It is good practice to set up guide tables for frequently used column or line variables.

Captions

Captions are the descriptive sentences used to tell the reader what the pictures are about. Captions should *never* be in the same face or size as the text. This will cause reading confusion. The present design trend is to emulate conversation—that is, flush left, ragged right, with appropriate line breaks to match the pauses and conversational nuances. The typeface used most often is a sans-serif, provided the captions are short. This helps differentiate them from the text copy. Guide tables should also be set up for all caption possibilities, and widows should be scrupulously avoided. This is a mark of the professional.

Filler Copy

Filler copy is copy used to pad areas that would otherwise be white spaces. They can be line drawings, cartoons, or trivia set as copy blocks. Fillers are gradually fading away in favor of the natural column endings. However, a look at *Reader's Digest* shows the value of interesting trivia, which is often read first and quoted the most often.

Fillers should be pre-set on any desirable width, measured for depth, and then filed by both subject matter and depth. This gives a quick index of appropriate fillers as they are needed. Occasionally, they can also be written to fit spaces. This, again, is where an accurate character count per pica is needed. Line drawings or cartoons can usually be enlarged or reduced to fit any given area, with no great loss in detail.

Column endings are in between typography and format. Ending a story evenly is sometimes troublesome, as no story is written to fill an exact space. The usual procedure is to build pictures, heads, and sinks into such variables that they can all be used to make stories end full and complete on the last page. The natural column ending format makes this a little easier because the white space at the bottom of each column can be used as a variable. Care and judgment should be used on natural column endings to make them look professional. For example, the best way to end each column is at a full paragraph break or, at least, a full sentence. Anything else looks haphazard and unprofessional.

Along with natural column endings, there is still another "natural" way to deal with type. This is setting copy flush left ragged right, with no hyphens and with every line an almost self-contained phrase. Copy is marked up for specific breaks, rather than setting it flush left and right. Like anything else, this can be overdone. The repetition of the ragged edges, particularly in the three-column format, creates a pattern of looseness. The page might look better if more firmly controlled.

Art

Art is classified as anything that cannot be set in type. This would cover all halftones, combinations, line drawings, reflective art, transparencies, tables, charts, and graphs. Art can be divided into submitted, bought, free, and in-house.

Submitted Art

Submitted art comes from the author. Often, there is a writer/photographer team. They cover a story, and you may receive many contact prints or transparencies in the same size as the camera film. First, read the story. Then examine the art. The first shuffle will likely include many photos that are eye-catching and descriptive of the story. These are reexamined for specifics. Continual culling will probably result in a few very good shots. These are then printed in a 5-by-7-inch size for closer examination. This size is good for cropping and viewing for details. The story and these few pictures are used for the story layout.

Bought Art

Bought art is art purchased outside the staff. An artist is called in and, quite often, told exactly what the subject matter and rendering style should be. It is always a good practice to clarify what the final size will be. The artist should present a rough for your examination and approval before going into final art. Fees should be openly discussed. Neither you nor the artist wants to buy a "pig in a poke."

Free Art

Free art consists of glossy halftone prints obtained from travel agencies, tourist bureaus, historical societies, convention bureaus, and so on. They can be used with only a credit line and at no cost to you. There are also some excellent "clip art" services available for a small fee. This is usually line art and can be used without a credit line.

In-House Art

In-house art is art that either you, your staff, or the company photographer creates on demand.

Art of any kind can be glorified, diffused, and changed somewhat with the help of your platemaker. Ideas often reach fruition by a short conference. Mezzotints and camera tricks often make an art director look somewhat better than he or she may be. Do not look down on mechanical art renderings. They have their place.

CHAPTER EIGHTEEN

Analyzing and Redesigning Magazines

The possibility of redesigning a magazine is often overlooked. The editor or publisher already has a salable product. It it weren't, it wouldn't be in business.

Some magazines, such as *Time, Sports Illustrated, House and Garden,* and *Scientific American* fulfill a complete function within each issue. They have an editorial style that withstands time and is based on function *plus* a lot of hard work to get there. I am not talking about these, but rather the ones that have had their formats so patched and repaired over the years that the original concept is no longer clear. I am talking about the magazines that may be using a two-column format and have been for the past fifty years simply because "the old man liked it." When he left the business, his successors chose to forget that there might be anything else.

Not all of us are lucky enough to be art directors on a "slick." Many more of us are on the "trades," those good, reliable, no-nonsense publications that serve their function in the least obtrusive manner. It is the bulk of publishing I shall talk about: limited size, limited formats, limited distribution, limited money, and, more often that we might care to admit, limited abilities.

Magazines are redesigned from the *back*. This may come as a surprise to many, but it's logical. A new logo or cover design indicates there is something new on the inside. When the inside is the same as the last issue, the impact and real thrust of redesigning are lost.

In planning an entirely new design, solving all the problems beforehand is often impractical. You still must "put issues to bed." The subtle approach is much better.

Redesigning generally starts from the back because that's where most of the trouble areas lie. The first sign that any magazine needs help can be found in the last six pages or so. I have seen some publications that have as many as three tag-ends to stories on one page, *plus* fractional ads taking up the remaining space. Mail order ads, fractional ads, and jumps often congregate here. Weed out these problems *first*. Your impulse will be to start with formats and feature stories. Control that impulse. They will fall into place as you progress. The professional starts all designs, formats, and layouts from the back. He or she *plans* the stories, including jumps, to establish, as nearly as possible, an uninterrupted reading pattern.

What all this means is facing up to certain facts. We *have* fractional ads. We *have* jumps. We may even have want ads or obituaries. How do we solve the problem of organizing many pieces?

The first step should be one of sorting and analyzing the pieces. How many fractional ads are there? What general typographical "feeling" do they have? Are they loud and blatant, with large type and distinctive faces? Are they small, with lots of copy? Are they a combination of pictures and type? Separate them into groups. Arrange the groups by sizes. This will often indicate an organizational format.

The main problem with fractional ads is that there are often so many "pieces" that the average reader tends to see them in clumps. This is all the more reason to organize them. The publisher rarely sees fractionals as anything other than segments that equal revenue. At $15 a column inch and ten ads deep, he has $450. Here we have a viable design item that already has two strikes against it. How can you satisfy both the publisher and the advertiser? Put them all on one page? Don't kid yourself! Even the $15 advertiser realizes that an ad that is lost in the crowd will get little response. The most hackneyed layout device is to put a batch of fractionals on an outside column. Many vertical ads are half a column long. It would make more sense to place the ads at the bottom of a page, and place story copy across the top of the pages. The reader can move easily from page to page *either* reading the story *or* perusing the ads.

Mail order ads *can* be grouped and placed on one page. They appeal to a group of readers who would like nothing better than to be able to read them all at one time. In this case it would be well to establish this area as a "constant" and to develop a special location and department heading for it. This would further tend to free-up space for the reader to move uninterrupted through stories.

Special departments call for special analysis. These seem to fall into two generally weak areas. There are either too many or too few. By "too many" I mean things like

"Sports Shorts," "Hobbies," "Household Hints," "Driving Tips," and so on. The problem here is getting enough copy to fill each department in each issue. This is closely followed by another problem area—the constant repetition of department heads. In the "too few" class, we have one generic heading used to cover too many small items. Many of these may be lost in the shuffle. What is the ideal? That depends on the reading audience. It should depend on subject matter *directly* related to readership. It should not be a side issue (for example, a stamp collector's column in an engineering magazine). Many short items could be expanded into a short story instead of being buried in a special "generic" column.

Readers develop reading patterns. Many of these are inviolate, such as starting at the upper left-hand corner of any page. Others are equally pertinent. A reader is *accustomed* to finding certain sections in certain places. Try to establish what these patterns are before reorganizing or redesigning.

What makes a good department head? We must return to the basic requirement of any good design. It must be clean, simple, direct, and functional. This means a department head, such as "New Products," should be: (1) a good type marriage with the copy; (2) compatible with ads that may occur on the same page; (3) not cluttered with a picture or line drawing that may become dated; (4) a type design, with perhaps rules or a simple box to set it off; (5) workable in various column widths to permit changes from three columns to two; and (6) succinct!

Some magazines carry many special departments successfully. *Time* magazine does it quite well. Most of the "trades," however, seem to carry too many. The theory that "more is better" should be revised to say "less is more." It is better to have a few well-written, well laid out departments than many weak ones. The ideal magazine would probably have from three to five "features," from five to seven "short stories," and three to five "special departments."

How do you solve the problem of too many special departments? The simplest way is to reevaluate. How many *must* be in every month? How many could just as well be in every other month? How many quarterly? How many semi-annually? This approach can satisfy almost everybody except the editor who feels his or her favorite department must *stay*!

Short stories should never contain jumps. It is apparent that a short story, by definition, won't be very long. Why aggravate the reader by cutting the short story into pieces? Short stories should be planned with just as much care as a feature. They should never be treated as "leftovers." It's true that many short stories give the layout artist more problems than the feature. This is all the more reason to give them special attention.

In analyzing feature stories one must consider several things. Where the ads occur is certainly important. Generally speaking the first, or lead, story faces a full-page ad. The lead story is almost always on a right-hand page and contains the logo and issue date. The center-page spread almost always falls within the features section. Full-page ads or pages that consist entirely of ads are often interspersed in the features section as story dividers. Occasionally this can lead to problems. Suppose you lay out a picture-oriented six-page story. In

CONT FROM PAGE 22

the exercise quotient (Eq), (peak heart rate in beats per minute times the peak systolic blood pressure in millimeters of mercury divided by STET time in minutes) decreased in all but one of the patients. The mean Eq for all patients decreased from 2,500.8 initially to 1,370.9 at three-month testing and to 1,221.6 at six-month testing. This was statistically significant, both as to initial compared to three-month testing ($P<.01$) and as to initial compared to six-month testing ($P<.01$) (Fig 5).

Only three patients had positive ECG evidence for ischemic heart disease on initial STET. Two of these had a normal test after three months. Several patients who were receiving antianginal medication required less short-acting medication as they progressed in the exercise program.

Of the 42 patients who completed three or more months of the program, all but four are gainfully employed. Of the seven subjects who dropped out of the program before the end of three months of training, one had worsening of his Eq as well as a decreased follow-up STET time; of the other six, three improved their Eq (one of them did not change his STET time, however). Three had no follow-up testing.

Several patients who remained in the program have had minor injuries such as soft tissue ecchymoses, pulled hamstrings, sprained ankles, and generalized muscular soreness that caused temporary cessation of their activity. However, all of these patients have returned to the program without consequence.

Regarding body weight and fasting blood chemistry and blood lipid studies, no specific patterns or correlations have evolved. Of the 42 patients, 20 (47%) had a decrease in weight of at least 1.8 kg (4 lb) or more. Twenty-five (60%) had a decrease in serum cholesterol level of 20 mg/100 ml or more, 22 (52%) had a decrease in serum triglyceride value of 15 mg/100 ml or more, and 20 (47%) had a decrease of 0.3 mg/100 ml or more in serum uric acid level. In 12 of the total 42, both cholesterol and

triglyceride levels were decreased. For 22 patients reviewed at the six-month follow-up period, a statistically significant mean weight decrease ($P<.01$) of 79.4 kg (175.1 lb) to 73.8 kg (162.7 lb) was recorded. For the 16 patients who had another triglyceride determination at the six-month follow-up period, there was a mean decrease from 190.4 mg/100 ml to 143.8 mg/100 ml that was also statistically significant ($P<.01$).

All patients who remained in the program for at least three months (42 at this point), enjoy the program and feel it is beneficial. They find that tensions are relieved, that they feel better, and that they are acquiring confidence in their ability to perform physical tasks during the exercise classes and in their daily activity at work and at home.

CONT FROM PAGE 34

In the 1960s, Frank et al[5] reported local observations derived from the first clinically manifested myocardial infarction occurring in a population of 55,000 male adults enrolled in the Health Insurance Plan of Greater New York during an observation period of 18 months (301 cases). More than one fourth of these men who were experiencing their first myocardial infarction were in the least-active group with regard to their customary physical activities on and off the job. This study confirmed other previous observations, such as that of Morris et al[16] in London in 1953, that physical inactivity is associated with a higher incidence of myocardial infarction. Fox and Oglesby,[11] in a review in 1969, submitted that it is prudent to include increased habitual physical activity in a program to prevent or manage nonacute coronary disease. With these reports as a basis, several investigations over the last few years have reported favorable results with various types of organized physical activity for patients with recent myocardial infarction.

CONT FROM PAGE 41

In 1966, Naughton et al[1] reported the results in a small group of 16 patients who engaged in a one-hour

session of competitive games, calisthenics and noncompetitive jogging after having had a myocardial infarction. Twelve patients who underwent training for eight months, after serving as their own controls, had a significant training effect as manifest by the decrease in the systolic and diastolic blood pressure and pulse rate during rest, standing, and comparable energy expenditure.

CONT FROM PAGE 53

Gottheiner[2] reported on a larger number of patients (1,103), 548 of whom had had a previous myocardial infarction. No information is available on exercise testing. The program began with several months of mild strength building activities (including weight lifting), the specifics of which are not provided. After nine months, the men engaged in rhythmic endurance exercises such as running, hiking, swimming, cycling, rowing, and volleyball. Later, the better trained subjects participated in competitive games. The participants in the program practiced on their own without medical supervision. The most impressive results of the study are in the mortality, which was 3.6% for the entire group over the five-year period, in contrast to 12.0% of an apparently comparable nonexercise group of Israelis with previous myocardial infarction. Also, these authors described other objective effects of the training such as reduction of resting heart rate and of resting and exercise blood pressure.

Frick and Katila[3] in 1968 reported a small group of seven patients with recent (one to two months) myocardial infarction who were studied by cardiac catheterization before and after a seven-week period of twice-weekly bicycle ergometer work. The training was followed by a reduction in exercise heart rate and tension time index. Increased stroke volume and improved left ventricular function were also observed. Concomitant with the hemodynamic changes, general exercise et al.[18] Of those affected, 31 manifested diabetes mellitus and optic atrophy; 11 had diabetes mellitus, optic

Figure 18.1—An example of a slush page or "garbage area." This is a sure sign that the layout person didn't plan the layouts. It indicates the line of least resistance.

Figure 18.2—While overemphasized and roughly done, these are examples of too many special departments. It would be much better to limit these to no more than six and give those six emphasis instead of trying to please everyone.

the layout stage, each page "relates" to the others and the whole is a cohesive unit. But imagine this sequence occurring three pages prior to the center page spread and three pages after it. The advertiser neatly chops the story into two unrelated halves. Feature stories should be planned to appear *between* ads.

Are the feature stories really features or just long stories? Are they picture-oriented or copy-oriented? Are the pictures black-and-white, four-color, or a mix of both? All of these questions are part of the original analysis because they give direction toward redesigning. One should always ask, "Do my features accomplish their maximum function?" If they do not, their thrust and importance will be lost.

We have gone through an average magazine and broken the analysis down into individual parts. Now let's start putting these parts together into a logical sequence and try to develop a format and style that will solve as many problems as possible. Let's first list them into general "areas": late news; mail order page(s); fractionals and jumps; special departments; short stories; feature stories; table of contents, masthead; postal information; and cover.

What format will be optimal for all groups? At first we think two-column and three-column. That's

not bad. It's what you are used to handling. Let's operate within this framework. Probably the easiest way to indicate change without too much trouble is to "mix and match." Divide the "areas" into the two- and three-column formats, with possibilities of "mixing and matching" any of them. The most logical arrangement would then be: (1) late news: one, two, or three columns (either in the front or back of the magazine); (2) mail order page(s): two or three columns, depending on present ad space sizes; (3) fractionals and jumps: two or three columns, depending on present ad space and size; (4) special departments: two or three *or* two *and* three mixed; (5) short stories: two or three *or* two *and* three mixed; (6) features: two or three *or* two *and* three mixed. This gives us certain areas in which we can also vary from the vertical feeling to the horizontal feeling, causing natural breaks in separate stories appearing on the same pages (see figure 19.3).

There are also variables that work *within* certain areas such as short stories and features. One of these might be the "Double-18" which could be used instead of the standard format. This gives a white space area of 4 picas on the outside of every page within the section. In this white space you can place titles, blurbs, or pictures for design

interest. It also gives you the possibility of using the "Midwest style" or the arrangement of 7-13-20 picas. *Do not* try to use either of these on ad pages where the space has already been predetermined by ad spaces.

Another issue reverts back to the question posed: "Are the areas 'picture oriented' or 'copy oriented'?" If picture oriented, try for better groupings or clusterings, or fewer *good* pictures instead of a mass of mediocre pictures. If copy oriented, try to learn some simple rendering techniques that will add some life to these otherwise dull pages. It will help.

Feel you're ready to tackle the problem? Wait! No good magazine works without a plan. Don't just jump in and think the general plan will solve all the problems. Instead, take a section at a time, again working from the back. Spread the redesigning over several issues. Save the cover for last. You will find that each area you cover will have individual problems. Solve these as you design. Polish each before releasing it. Don't place them within the issue until you are completely satisfied that they will stand the test of time. Always look to the complete job, but assimilate it in parts. When all the parts are in and functional, then add the new logo and cover design.

Good magazines have their ads

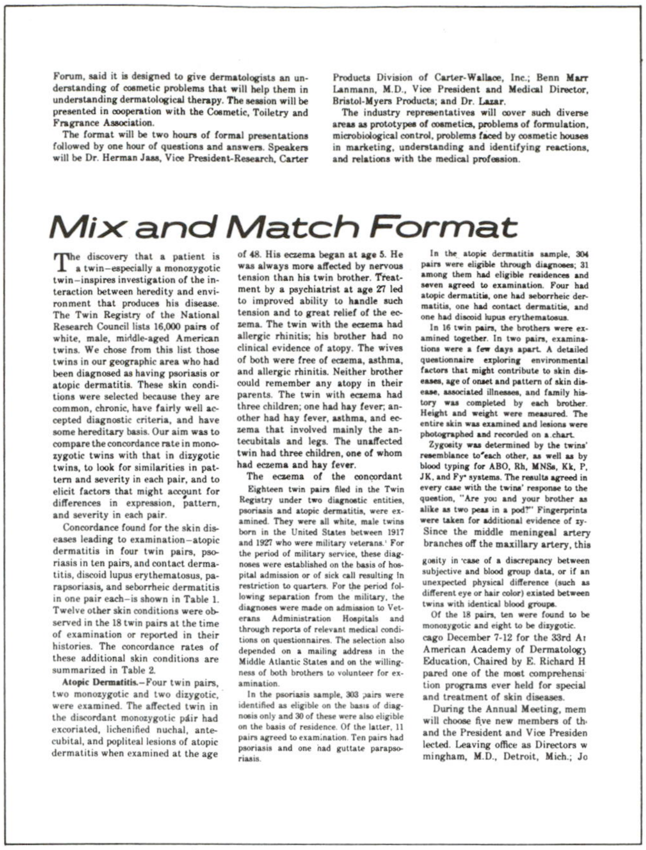

Figure 18.3—"Mix and match."

Figure 18.4—The "Double-18" design.

placed and "paced" well. You may not even realize it, but they, too, are part of the whole cloth. Ad rates are determined by size and position. Four-color ads cost more to produce than black-and-white ads, so are charged at a higher premium. Certain "positions" receive more exposure than others. These are the back cover, inside front cover, inside back cover, and center-page spread. These, too, carry a higher premium. In graduated importance, after these come the full-page ad facing the table of contents, and full-page ads separating stories. These are usually easy to place and handled as prime advertising positions.

Our main concern is placing and pacing ads that are one-column, two-column, half-page, quarter-page, and fractional. These cannot be placed without knowledge of the printer's page impositions. No ad should be placed without some knowledge of the printing processes, as letterpress and offset have differences in bleed areas, gripper edges, and other special problems. The mechanics of plac-

ing ads within the page impositions is rather basic. Keep black-and-white ads on the same sheet side. Color ads depend on channels and ad location. Try to keep all ads in the same color on the same form. Advertisers will rarely use the same shades, even though the industry keeps on specifying "AAAA standard colors." This creates problems, for example, a Salem ad, which uses a particular shade of green, may appear on the same form as a Campbell Soup ad, which can give the tomato soup an ugly green cast. This is a press problem, however, and doesn't really concern us.

Black-and-white ads that do not include an illustration have only two ways to draw attention—distinctive typefaces and type sizes. In either case, black-and-white ads almost always "scream" for attention. They are usually created to appear on either a left- or right-hand page, so there is usually no "directional movement" within them. In placing ads remember that there should be a visual difference between ads and text. Loud,

screaming ads will pull the reader's eye away from the copy. Subdued, quiet ads will tend to blend with the copy and become indistinct.

There are several methods of placing ads: by subject matter; by counterpoint (that is, quiet ads next to loud ads); as short separators; and as space fillers. The good art director will try to place ads to prevent story conflict and will *never* place two ads that might cancel each other out next to each other, such as a diet ad next to a chocolate ad.

Ideally, the stories are laid out on a storyboard ahead of time. This gives you a good idea of the story sequence and open positions for ads and spreads. As an ad is received it can be "placed" in an opening best suited for it.

How do we place ads? Rather than simply putting the ads in open positions as they are received, it is better to wait until the last possible moment. Place the ads on a table and arrange by size (one column, half column, full page, fractional, and so forth). Then group same-size ads by subject

Cancer-The Quiet Killer

artery through a substantial nent of the normal anastomosis between the orbital branch of the middle meningeal artery and the recurrent meningeal branch of the lacrimal artery (Fig 2 and Table). Since the middle meningeal artery branches off the maxillary artery, this collateral pathway has been suspected in the rare cases of amaurosis in conjunction with intraoral injections of anesthetic solutions for mandibular nerve block (Fig 2).[1] Precautions to be taken with local injections (described in this article) are not only warranted with intraoral infiltration of anesthetic solutions, as in the situation just mentioned, but also with submucosal injections of corticosteroid suspensions, as in the treatment of oral lesions of lichen planus, lupus erythematosus, and pemphigus. Rarer collateral pathways from submucosal or subcutaneous arteries to the orbital vessels are discussed by Singh-Hayreh and Dass.[1]

The usual course of the central retinal artery is tortuous and coiled in the orbit and multiangulated where the optic nerve membranes are penetrated.[1] The diameter of the artery has been estimated to be a mere 0.28 mm.[1] After many subdivisions derived from the central retinal artery, the 'minimal luminal accommodation is reached in the superficial and deep capillary plexuses of the retina.

Though clinical findings and recent opinions favor the arterial route of the embolism for most cases in point, suggestions involving the venous circulation may be rarely tenable. In isolated cases involving subcutaneous nasal injections of paraffins, funduscopy showed substantial venous engorgement and hemorrhages as seen with retinal vein occlusion.[1] Timm, as quoted by Hager and Heise,[1] suggested that some cases of amaurosis concurrent with intranasal injection were initiated by intravenous injection into an ethmoidal vein, followed by passage of the injected material

Evidence for the intra-arterial route have included funduscopic visualization of emboli in the retinal arterial branches[1] and roentgenographic visualization of the central retinal artery in a patient who received intranasal thorium dioxide injections as a treatment for osena.[1]

Blood pressure is reduced in the ophthalmic artery system to protect the eye from the systolic pressure elsewhere. Sometimes the ophthalmic artery is snuggly fitted between the internal carotid trunk and the optic nerve when the latter cannot deviate upwards because of a superimposed fold of dura mater.[1] The pulse wave on the carotid artery may further reduce space for the opthalmic artery to the degree that during cerebral angiography the ophthalmic artery may not fill if the radiopaque material was injected during a compression phase. The counterpressure of a forceful injection into a group 2 artery may then exceeed the local blood pressure and thereby effect retrograde flow to the ocular-orbital supply junctions, whereupon group 1 arteries would propel the injected material to the eye and its surroundings.

In the scalp, the occipital, posterior auricular, and superficial temporal arteries—derivatives of the external carotid—form extensive arborizations that anastomose freely with the subdivisions of the supraorbital and supratrochlear arteries (Fig 1).[1] Angiography in cases of internal carotid occlusion due to thrombosis' or ligation of an aneurysm[1] has demonstrated retrograde flow from the temporal artery to the ophthalmic artery and internal carotid siphon. (Injection of the scalp in such cases warrants particular caution.)

Anomalous arterial supply to the ophthalmic artery (and thence to its ocular-orbital branches) was found by Singh-Hayreh and Dass[1] in about 4% of cadaveric orbits. The luminal caliber of the ophthalmic artery between its origin from the internal ca-

Figure 18.5—Bad ad placement—overemphasized but entirely possible without preplanning. The reader will catch this ad, ''Try it! You'll like it!''—''Cancer–The Quiet Killer.'' Do not place ads and stories without examining both for this sort of juxtaposition.

matter and further divide them into general ad feeling (loud, subdued, diagonal, pictures dominating, copy dominating, same second color, and four color). While it is difficult to give specific rules, *generally* place loud ads on pages consisting mainly of copy. Subdued ads on pages that have a strong picture will create counterpoint. Diagonal arrangements should be controlled to perform a service such as pointing to a blurb or picture. Picture-dominated ads should appear on quiet editorial pages. A good second color can be used in a filler or cartoon to help draw interest away from the single-color use.

When placing ads look for things that might affect the copy. For instance, two very dark outside ads will tend to fence-in the copy. Two light or airy ads will expand the copy area. A dark ad and a light ad would be most effective with the dark ad at the bottom. When placing fractional ads one above the other, try to arrange them by ''weight,'' with the darkest at the bottom and the lightest at the top. When arranging two quarter-page ads, place the darkest at the outside. When arranging four quarter-page ads, try to stay away from a checkerboard arrangement. Rather, place the two heaviest at the bottom or outside and the two lightest at the top or inside. Always relate ads to each other as well as to the total picture.

Color will draw attention. In handling a second color try to counterbalance the color by using the same color within the copy (text).

General Rules for Analyzing Magazines

These rules of thumb will often provide guidelines in deciding whether a magazine is well designed and laid out. Some magazines develop recognizable styles in defiance of rules, but these are rare.

1. Are page margins and gutters narrow, giving a feeling of congestion? If so, the design feeling throughout will be the same.

2. Are editorial content and ad content clearly defined? If not, the whole design tends to blend into a mass.

3. Are story titles well chosen and constructed? Are type marriages compatible? The first sign of design weakness is constantly changing title faces. This indicates only ''change for change's sake.'' Good type marriages—titles, blurbs, text, and captions—are the sign of professionalism.

4. Are pictures arranged for geometric shapes or for content? If arranged for geometric shapes and balance only, the layouts are still basic. If for content, does the internal movement play an important part in holding them together, or does your eye move in an uncontrolled way? If so, the style is still that of a beginner.

5. Do special departments have their proper perspective? Are there too many? Too few?

6. Look at the last six pages. Are they slush pages or are they well organized?

7. Look at the table of contents. Is it clean, neat, and functional?

8. Are stories laid out as individual pieces and then simply linked together within an issue or are they coordinated into one flowing cohesive unit? If there is any disjointed feeling, it can be attributed to poor planning and layout.

9. Are there many pages where story material is simply used to pad out ad pages? This is often a sign of greed. A magazine is rarely well designed when greed predominates.

10. Is the editorial content so superior that you could forgive poor design? If so, do so. Even then, is the typeface readable? Is leading proper? Are stories handled in an uninterrupted flow?

11. Is there art for art's sake? Gingerbread? Gimmicks? Useless decoration? Are stories laid out as an art director's dream and a reader's nightmare? Are the layouts functional? Anything that does not fall within the concept of ''clean, neat, and functional'' is a waste.

CHAPTER NINETEEN

Creative Layout Thinking: Covers

Almost all magazines now in print fall into eight general formats. They are shown in figure 6.1 (see chapter 6). An analysis shows that all but one (free form) follow the same general lines of the rectangular shaped cover. Here we have a ''form within a form.'' The subject matter, of course, creates other visual effects, but the form is static. Even color does not change the form.

This seems to be a fertile field for design. Your first thought should be: just because this is the way it has been done for a hundred years does *not* mean there is no other way. The simplest way is always the easiest, and a well-worn path is easy to follow.

Let us follow the principles of creative thinking. First, list all possibilities. Analyze the possibilities into probabilities. Expand the probabilities into any saving values. Expand on the saving values.

Try to distill one or two workable ideas. Finally, design, if possible, from the ideas.

List as many possibilities as you can in fifteen minutes. At this stage, do not analyze for ''practicality'' or ''impracticality.'' Simply let ideas flow. Here are some to get you started.

1. Die-cut into another form—circular?
2. Die-cut the cover over a page to give a new effect?
3. New dimensions? Square?
4. Three panels, each different in size, overlapping each other?
5. Gatefold—expanding area?
6. Molded into a three-dimensional shape?
7. Cover opens in opposite direction?
8. Cover wraps-around, top or bottom?
9. Rounded corners—diagonal corners?
10. A new material—cloth, plastic?

We now have ten ''raw ideas.'' Let us take each and see how practical it is.

Die-cutting into another form, such as an oval or circle, will give ''production fits'' to both the editorial staff and the printer. How does one work on individual page designs when the form of each page is fixed? The costs would be fantastic. Not only that, but a monthly repetition of the odd shape would lose its novelty in short order. Before we discard this, ask the pertinent question, Is anything in this idea worth saving? Probably a scrap—the die-cutting needn't be as obvious as a circle. Die-cutting a form into the cover (like a circle or oval) to show part of a picture underneath it means you must have a ''double cover.'' In the normal course of events, the first page (after the cover) is usually an ad. This means covering the ad. This has some other weaknesses. Die-

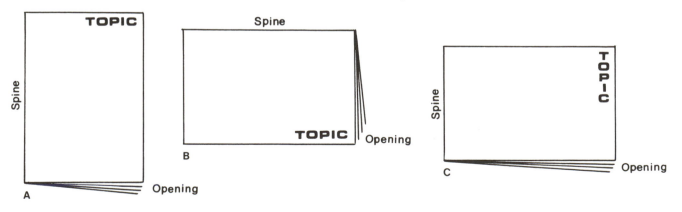

Figure 19.1—Three possible openings. Left is the standard form with the opening at the right. Center is a variation with the opening at the bottom. Right is a change from a vertical rectangle to a horizontal rectangle, but still opening at the right.

TOPIC

Figure 19.2—A rough result of creative cover thinking as outlined in the text.

cutting eventually means easy tearing, not a desirable end result. What's worth saving? On the surface, nothing.

The idea of new dimensions certainly has some merit, provided paper and press specifications will meet your requirements. Remember that page sizes are in multiples of 8½ by 11 inches in most circumstances. In "sheet fed," this means a sheet size 17 by 22 inches (after trim). Any new dimension would have to be an economical cut from this size, with little or no waste. An inch of paper doesn't sound like much, but on a sheet 17 by 22 inches, every inch less than 22 inches means a loss of a sheet for every 17 sheets. In a press run of 100,000 this would mean about

5,800 sheets thrown away. Since paper is sold by weight, visualize 5,800 sheets on a scale that registers dollars thrown away on a whim.

Your first reaction might be, "I might as well bend to the cost factor," but *think* for a moment! A good designer molds basic requirements to his or her purpose. What else might give "even cuts" from a 17-by-22-inch sheet? You already know 8½ by 11 inches. What about 11 by 8½ inches? What would this mean? First of all, it would mean the magazine would be short and wide. This means something in newsstand display, where all magazines in competition would stand on the short side, with the long side up. Ready to throw up your

hands? Look at figure 19.1. Samples A and C are similar, with the spine at the left, even though the width and height dimensions are reversed. Sample B, however, is different. In this case, the spine is at the top, and the opening is at the bottom. This creates an immediate change in reading pattern because people aren't accustomed to turning pages up. Let's table this idea for a moment and go to paper other than sheet fed.

In web offset the paper is on a roll and moves through the press on a ribbon of paper called a web. This comes in standard widths (22 inches) but *not* lengths. It can be cut to any length! Give you any ideas? How about square (11 by 11 inches)? A square magazine *does* give new dimensions and breaks the traditional mold of the rectangle. Again—let's table this idea. Let it settle in the back of your mind and develop.

Three panels, each a different size and overlapping, has some excitement. Visualize, for a moment, a cover (full bleed) of a woman's head. Perhaps it is a famous personality, like Elizabeth Taylor. The 8½-inch dimension is cut into two panels, over the bottom page. One panel 2½-inches wide and another 5-inches wide are staggered over the final 8½-inch wide panel. Each is printed in a different color—red duotone (for her fiery nature), violet duotone (for her love of the color), and full color. Here we might have a cover keyed to her personality tied in with a specific story. This is good for one issue. What do we do for an issue on football or needlecraft? Think! How about a line drawing—a duotone and a full-color of the same subject? Still sounds exciting. Table it for further investigation.

A gatefold expanding the cover area means you could have a long horizontal rectangle instead of a short vertical rectangle. What does this mean in terms of design? It means one of two things: either giving up the back page (ad revenue) for an area 25½ by 11 inches or the equivalent of a double-page spread (17 by 11 inches). This might have possibilities for a special issue, provided the back-page advertiser will accept another position for the one issue. It has no apparent design merit.

Impressing a shape into a cover calls for immediate rejection. This would mean male and female dies, individual pressing of each, and shipping problems.

A cover opening in the opposite direction would mean that the average reader would turn it over so that it opens normally, thereby starting at the back of the magazine. Not very functional.

A cover wrap-around from top to bottom has the same rejection factor. Design must accomplish a function. Simplicity is a key factor. If you force the reader into an unfamiliar reading pattern, you'd better have a good functional reason.

Round or diagonal corners, while novel, would accomplish nothing.

A new material brings to mind cloth or plastic—something with a "feel" different from paper. It opens the door to a new approach, which is exactly what we are trying for.

Now, let's see what we can use from the pieces.

1. A new size, compatible to press and paper specifications.
2. Three overlapping panels.

Certainly doesn't sound like much, does it? Let's distill the problem into a few simple sentences. We are looking for a new cover design—one that will adapt to standard paper and press specifications and that is *not* one of the standard eight, if for no other reason than we don't want to copy. The first time around, all we could salvage from our thinking process was three overlapping panels and a new size.

Let's further expand on "a new size" or "feeling." Almost all mag-

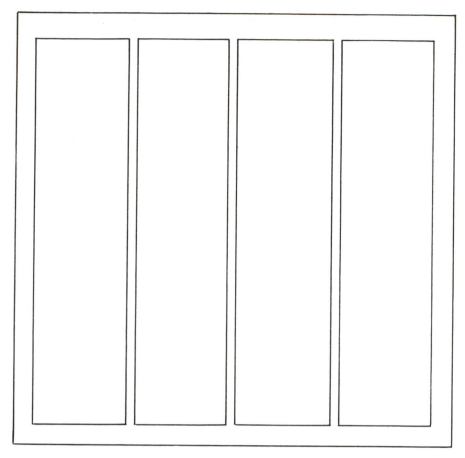

Figure 19.3—The four-column format in the "square size" used by Prism *magazine.*

azines have two general formats, two columns on 20 picas and three columns on 13 picas. Each is properly scaled to the standard 8½-by-11-inch page size. Suppose one were to use two columns on 13 picas. This would mean a new width, 6 by 11 inches, or a long skinny magazine. There is also a 2½-inch paper waste on sheet fed. We could also go in the opposite direction, four columns on 13 picas or 11 by 11 inches (Web-offset). There is a subtle difference between a narrow and a wide new size. The "narrow" would give an impression that you've been cheated and the

wide that you are getting more for your money.

This is exactly what *Prism* did. It was redesigned to 11 by 11 inches, not a newsstand size, but okay for a controlled circulation publication. Column widths vary from three to four columns, depending on story content. The magazine cannot be hidden under a pile of standard sizes. The square format lends itself to all kinds of vertical and horizontal patterns.

The only real objection is the look of the ads, which are standard 8½-by-11-inch sizes and which look out of place.

CHAPTER TWENTY

Creative Layout Thinking: Table of Contents

The first step in creative layout thinking for a contents page is to define the purpose. Ask yourself questions like: What is it? How will it be used? What are the basic elements? What has already been done? Why have these been accepted? What direction does redesigning indicate? What will a new design have in reaction value to the reader?

A table of contents is a sequential list of stories or departments in any magazine. It gives the story or department titles and, sometimes, the authors. It may give an epitome (or brief "teaser" for the story) and will always show the page number for the story location. This fairly well describes what it is.

How will it be used? It will be used as a guide to story locations within the issue. It should be very close to the front of the magazine. This is the "accepted" location. However, the majority of right-handed people will pick up a magazine and start looking at it from the back and move forward. There seems to be no logic to this reading, or scanning, pattern. It makes one wonder why the table of contents is not placed at the rear of magazines. In the September issue of *Woman's Home Companion* of 1934, this is exactly where the table of contents was placed. And it failed. Probably because the logic of location was overpowered by the "acceptable" location in other magazines.

What are the basics? Succinctly, the story title and page number and more often than not the au-thor's name and a "teaser" paragraph make up a contents entry. The typography is also basic. Story titles are usually boldface, along with the page numbers, and anything else is either regular or italic since they are subordinate.

What has already been done? A look at a dozen tables of contents will indicate they all follow the established rules. Some are spaced differently, some simply move the elements around to simulate change, but all are pretty much alike. This is a job that has to be done without a great deal of fanfare or designing effort. I feel the designer must accept this as a challenge.

Why is it accepted? A table of contents is functional. It has a job to perform. As long as that job is done, the "form" it takes will usually be accepted.

What direction does redesigning indicate? Let's look at what we have. We need a directory, preferably near the front of the magazine, that will accomplish its purpose, *but in a different form*. With this in mind, what are some of the steps necessary for redesigning?

In creative layout thinking the purpose should be secondary (that is, in the initial thinking stages). The first step should be to list all possibilities, even though these possibilities may seem unrelated and even foolish at the start. The idea is to stimulate your mind and let ideas simply roll off the top of your head, as fast as possible. Here are some examples to illustrate this creative thinking process.

1. A long, vertical panel on the outside page edge, with arrows pointing into the issue.
2. A horizontal panel, either at the top or bottom, as a page guide index.
3. A cover with a gatefold containing the table of contents.
4. A form other than square or rectangular.
5. Titles and authors on a page index along the edge of each page of the story, with the page indented, or trimmed, for viewing.
6. A central location, with the table of contents split into two locations, pointing both front and back, from a double-page or center-page spread.

The six possibilities were all listed in less than ten minutes. As one can see, they don't make much sense in their present stage. Each will now be used as a springboard for further examination just to see how ideas develop.

1. A long vertical panel on the outside of a page, with arrows pointing into the issue, has some possibilities, provided the stories are departmentalized, as they are in *Time* magazine. However, adding arrows with page numbers inside them creates a rather cumbersome format. The constant repetition of the arrows is a design weakness. Repetition is deadly, no matter where it is used. Before leaving this idea, let's see if there is anything worth saving. The change in format from either a

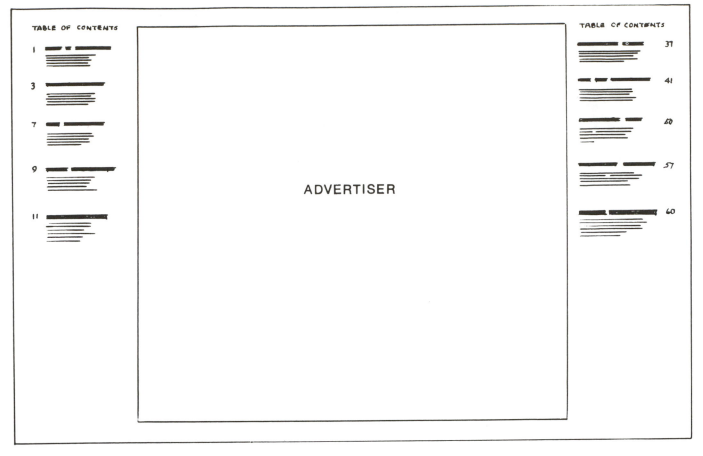

ADVERTISER

Figure 20.1—A "rough" of a possible table of contents area in a center page spread. This would be used with the advertiser's cooperation.

square or rectangle (as most tables of contents are) to a long vertical panel might be put to one side as a future possibility.

2. A horizontal page index might have some merit if used to present the information in some other form. However, a horizontal is limited to the page width, which means information must be concentrated in a smaller space. This creates some type congestion and typesetting problems. It would seem there is nothing to "save" from this rough idea.

3. A cover with a gatefold flap has been used, but this presents a press problem and cost factor that often makes it impractical. Designers must be aware of the cost of their ideas. Let us discard this idea as impractical.

4. A form other than a square or rectangle duplicates idea number 1. But one must also think of a "change of form" as being oval, circular, free form, triangular, or maybe even L-shaped. All of these

would present typesetting problems. However, a "change of form" has some merit.

5. Titles and authors on a tabbed page edge has several weaknesses. Once the magazine is trimmed, they would be hidden, unless the outside edge has an index type format. Without the index tabs, all story titles would lie one under the other and the whole separation purpose would be lost. This seems highly impractical, but before discarding it, let us decide if anything is worth saving. Expanding on the idea of an index format with the outside vertical panel we have previously "saved" might result in a panel in various colors, with a color index for each section. This might be attractive and even interesting, but the possibility of color changes and matching bars on page sections presents a highly impractical production problem. The designer must also think of the others involved.

6. A central location would

mean the center-page spread. This is prime advertising space and is usually a "no-no." However, a little salesmanship *might* persuade an advertiser that a table of contents on his page would give him double or even triple exposure. The spread could be arranged to utilize an outside panel on each page edge, with listings pointing forward and backward. This has some interesting possibilities, but would need an advertiser who is quite understanding.

Whichever ideas appealed to you bear detailed study. If none of them gave even a faint *glimmer* of success, then go back and redefine the problem. Break it down into just the bare essentials. Once the problem has been distilled, put it into the back of your mind and let it simmer for a few days. The subconscious mind has a marvelous capacity for remembering everything you observe. This "inner mind" will chew on the idea, match the problem with other, seemingly ca-

inside BROOKS

DYNAMICS of VIOLENCE

This is a remarkably comple scholarly synopsis of what we and can conjecture about the changes in medicine and public in China since the proclamation People's Republic in 1949. Arti 14 experts now working in the States, Canada, and England major topics, ranging from the impressive history of Chinese macology to the latest advance ral health care, limb replaceme gery, and acupuncture anes

see pg 12

Talwin

Authors display no politic though all are cautious ab generalizations for a coun that population estimate more than 100 million per

see pg 33

break out a new flag

The book has technical flaws. offset printing is small, smeary sometimes difficult to read, and are a distracting number of graphical errors. An index, would be very useful in such a field, is lacking. These are points, however. What remains the reader are some fascinating

see pg 54

QUESTIONS

The authors present an en tic and chatty case for an e: care facility as part of a gene pital. In describing their exp with "continuing care" befor

see pg 67

After describing the facilit the circumstances of their st authors describe their team and detail the method of case

see pg 83

Other features and special departments

Figure 20.2—A table of contents using miniatures of the lead pages of each story.

sual observations, and begin feeding you ideas. *No idea* should be discarded without analysis.

Using this process (this chapter, so far, is based on an actual problem) I received nothing on the first attempt. However, after a few days of letting my subconscious wrestle with the problem, the key phrase "a change of form" seemed to be an answer. What evolved from this phrase was a takeoff on what was already being done in *Playboy, Gallery,* and *Psychology Today.* In each case, these magazines took the art from a story and repeated it as part of the table of contents. My concept of this idea is *the entire first page of the story* should be reproduced, in miniature, on the table of contents page. This can be done by photographing the page or pages involved just before going to press. Each story page fits into a format that allows for two double-page spreads and three single-page stories and is placed just inside the cover page. This allows the reader to get a quick peek at the stories involved, establishes a *complete* visual picture, and gives the page number for location. This is a synopsis of the prime stories in graphic form. It is simple and easy to use. It gives the reader an immediate identification of each story.

No idea loses merit by analysis. Learn to develop ideas. Learn to keep your mind open to the possibilities of ideas already used. *Search and apply.* Remember, someone may have had the same idea but just didn't expand on it enough.

CHAPTER TWENTY-ONE

Midwest Style

In magazine publishing, there are two generally accepted formats, two column and three column. These are quite old, as is the one column used in very old textbooks.

Designers have accepted the two basic formats as practical and easy to work with and have built most magazine designs around them, with some innovations, of course. The last relatively new innovation was the natural column ending used so well in *Psychology Today.* Some magazines mix the two- and three-column formats in different sections. They are just variations of the same theme.

Several years of research and experimentation have resulted in a new format. This is neither three narrow columns nor two wide columns. It is a delicate balance of a white panel, a narrow column, and a wide column. The proportions of each are critical and *must* be 7 picas, 13 picas, and 20 picas. This gives exactly the correct symmetry and balance of a white, a narrow gray, and a wide gray area, even when pictures or ads are used.

Pictures fall within the "golden rectangle" (3 by 5 inches) when laid out in a modified modular format, which is not as restrictive as the two- and three-column formats are.

Proper balance and symmetry are realized by limiting pictures to the following: 13 by 10½ picas, 13 by 21 picas, 13 by 30½ picas, 20 by

10½ picas, 20 by 21 picas, 20 by 30½ picas, 34½ by 10½ picas, 34½ by 21 picas, 34½ by 30½ picas, 41½ by 10½ picas, 41½ by 21 picas, 41½ by 30½ picas, from *either* the top down *or* the bottom up, but none in between; and 20 by 52½ picas (wide column), 13 by 52½ picas (narrow column), 34½ by 52½ picas (both columns in width), 41½ by 52½ picas (both columns in width, plus the white panel). There are seventeen possible variations, covering almost every picture size, with little or no cropping.

Ad locations maintain the page balance and symmetry by becoming a part of the editorial content in both size and location. A one-column narrow ad is always on the outside page edge, but has a 7-pica white panel between it and the page edge. A one-column wide ad is always on the inside and is separated from either another ad or text by wide gutters. Fractional ads, either on 13 or 20 picas, are placed within the columns but separated from the text with a 6-point space plus a 1-point rule and 2 picas more of white space. In this position, they will blend into the format and yet maintain their individuality. It also limits confusion with the text.

What are the advantages of the Midwest style?

1. The format is new and exciting.
2. Specific rules can be followed that bring exciting results.
3. When one uses proper type-

script paper, copy can be estimated accurately enough to predict widows.
4. The layout artist can skip galleys and go immediately to page proofs. This is a money saver as well as a time saver.
5. The format, even on facing pages of straight copy, is as easy to read as it is to look at.
6. Titles can "hang" into the white panel area, visually drawing attention. This can minimize the use of display faces to draw attention.
7. Natural column endings minimize the need for exact squaring off of pages.

What are the disadvantages of the Midwest style? Almost all the disadvantages have been weeded out through extensive experimentation. The biggest disadvantage was (past tense) predicting copy length. By using typescript paper, created specifically for the typewriter used, and tabulating it into units of ten characters and spaces, the layout artist knows exactly how many characters and spaces there are to a given story. This is done by counting a paragraph at a time for accuracy.

A tabulated sheet, in the faces and sizes being used, must be made. This tells the layout artist that an average of so many characters and spaces will occur within any given measure. This is made for 13 picas and for 20 picas, and

Whatever in the world do they Want!

Figure 21.1—An example of Midwest style.

carried through for fifty-seven lines deep.

When characters and spaces in any given paragraph have been tabulated, the total is checked against the totals on the tabulated sheet for either 13 or 20 picas. For instance, a paragraph containing 473 characters and spaces and being set Times Roman, 9/11, may give 35 characters and spaces on 13 picas, and 50 characters and spaces on 20 picas. This would mean the paragraph will set twelve full lines on 13 picas, plus 10 characters and spaces on the thirteenth line. It would also set eleven lines on 20 picas, with 23 characters and spaces on the twelfth line.

Total character and space count for all copy is first computed. This is divided into the equivalent of a full page, consisting of a narrow 13-pica column and a wide 20-pica column on each full page. For example, the 9/11 copy will set fifty-seven lines deep on the page. The characters and spaces used above, that is, 35 characters and spaces on 13 picas and 50 characters and spaces on 20 picas, will give 1,995 characters and spaces for the 13-pica column and 2,850 characters and spaces for the wide column *or a* total of 4,845 per page of just straight copy.

What is left over is filled with pictures, title, or sinks. As an example, we have 12,000 characters and spaces to fill three full pages of a story. Of this 9,690 consists of copy (two columns each of 13 picas and 20 picas), leaving a total of 2,310 characters and spaces to fill with other elements. This is converted to picas. The pica conversion is then put into picture space, or title space, or sinks, or all of these.

Copy must be accurately determined. A total of characters and space is used for the base of this format. As you use up characters and spaces per desired area, they are then deducted from the total.

This means making a "rough" prior to actually doing the layout. The rough will help you predetermine how much copy is involved and how you want it placed. The space left over will then be used for title areas, blurbs or pictures with their captions.

Figure 21.2 (next page)—The basic grid formation in Midwest style. Title areas can occur in 2 plus 3 plus 4 plus 5, or in 2 plus 3 plus 4 plus 5 and 8 plus 9 plus 10 plus 11. This creates a variable "sink" that can be as much as 14 picas deep. Copy occurs in areas 3, 9, 15, and 21 (when set on 13 picas) and 4, 5, 10, 11, 16, and 17 (when set on 20 picas) for left-hand pages. The opposite is true for right-hand pages. In either case, the 7 picas of white space should always be on the outside edge. Titles should "hang" into the 7 picas white space. Pictues can be any single or multiple of any grid or grids, except 2, 8, 5, or 11, which are too small. The numbers 1, 6, 7, 11, 13, 18, 19, and 24 are bleed areas. Try not to bleed at top or bottom. Plan your layouts from the gutter area out. This means bleeding to the outside, where bleeding is used.

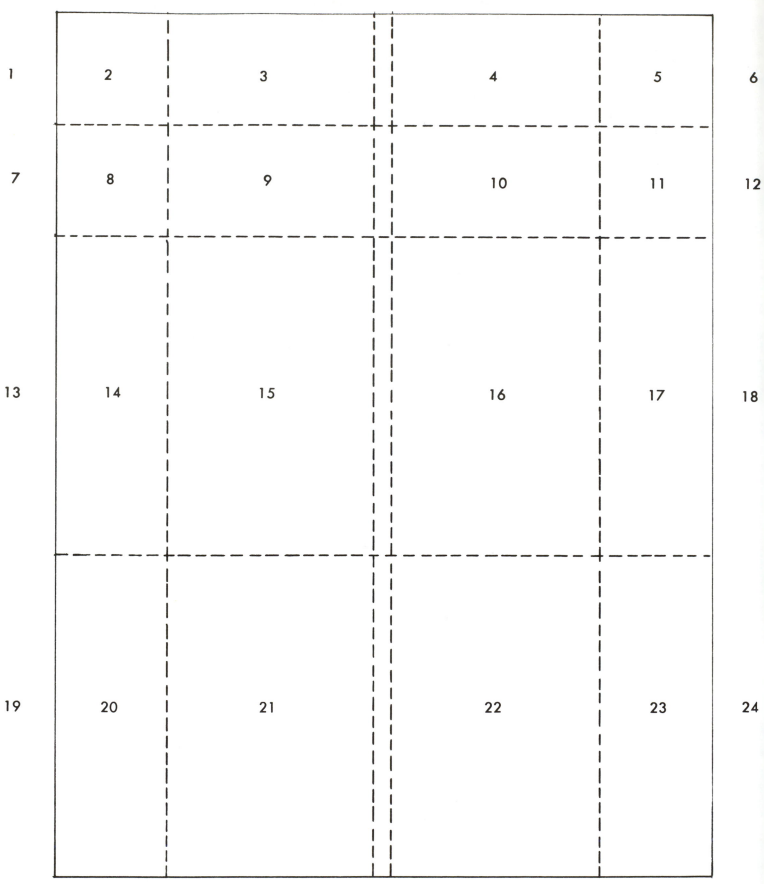

Figure 21.2—The basic grid formation in Midwest style.

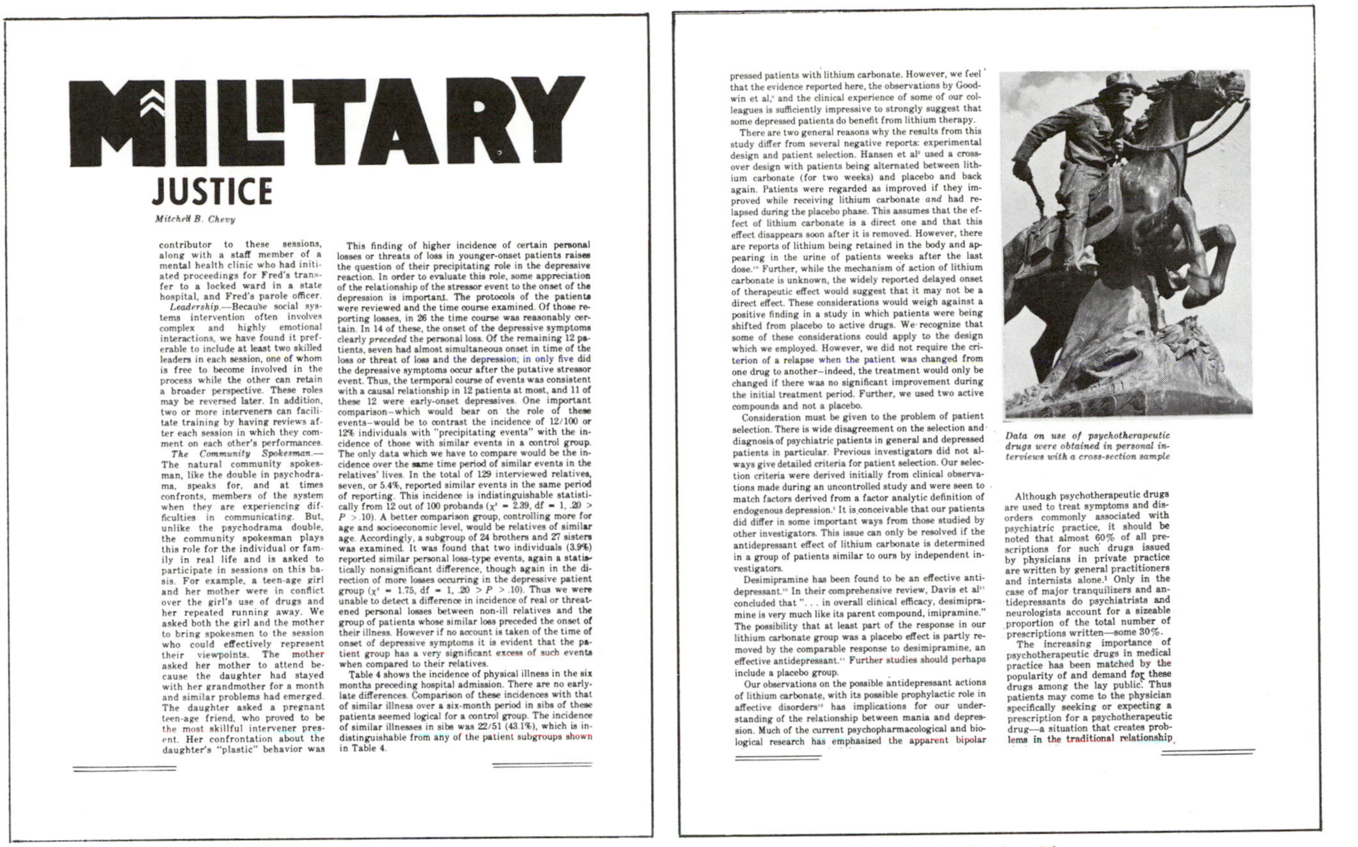

MILITARY

JUSTICE

Mitchell B. Chevy

contributor to these sessions, along with a staff member of a mental health clinic who had initiated proceedings for Fred's transfer to a locked ward in a state hospital, and Fred's parole officer.

Leadership.—Because social systems intervention often involves complex and highly emotional interactions, we have found it preferable to include at least two skilled leaders in each session, one of whom is free to become involved in the process while the other can retain a broader perspective. These roles may be reversed later. In addition, two or more interveners can facilitate training by having reviews after each session in which they comment on each other's performances.

The Community Spokesman.—The natural community spokesman, like the double in psychodrama, speaks for, and at times confronts, members of the system when they are experiencing difficulties in communicating. But, unlike the psychodrama double, the community spokesman plays this role for the individual or family in real life and is asked to participate in sessions on this basis. For example, a teen-age girl and her mother were in conflict over the girl's use of drugs and her repeated running away. We asked both the girl and the mother to bring spokesmen to the session who could effectively represent their viewpoints. The mother asked her mother to attend because the daughter had stayed with her grandmother for a month and similar problems had emerged. The daughter asked a pregnant teen-age friend, who proved to be the most skillful intervener present. Her confrontation about the daughter's "plastic" behavior was

This finding of higher incidence of certain personal losses or threats of loss in younger-onset patients raises the question of their precipitating role in the depressive reaction. In order to evaluate this role, some appreciation of the relationship of the stressor event to the onset of the depression is important. The protocols of the patients were reviewed and the time course examined. Of those reporting losses, in 26 the time course was reasonably certain. In 14 of these, the onset of the depressive symptoms clearly *preceded* the personal loss. Of the remaining 12 patients, seven had almost simultaneous onset in time of the loss or threat of loss and the depression; in only five did the depressive symptoms occur after the putative stressor event. Thus, the termporal course of events was consistent with a causal relationship in 12 patients at most, and 11 of these 12 were early-onset depressives. One important comparison—which would bear on the role of these events—would be to contrast the incidence of 12/100 or 12% individuals with "precipitating events" with the incidence of those with similar events in a control group. The only data which we have to compare would be the incidence over the same time period of similar events in the relatives' lives. In the total of 129 interviewed relatives, seven, or 5.4%, reported similar events in the same period of reporting. This incidence is indistinguishable statistically from 12 out of 100 probands ($\chi^2 = 2.39$, df $= 1$, $.20 > P > .10$). A better comparison group, controlling more for age and socioeconomic level, would be relatives of similar age. Accordingly, a subgroup of 24 brothers and 27 sisters was examined. It was found that two individuals (3.9%) reported similar personal loss-type events, again a statistically nonsignificant difference, though again in the direction of more losses occurring in the depressive patient group ($\chi^2 = 1.75$, df $= 1$, $.20 > P > .10$). Thus we were unable to detect a difference in incidence of real or threatened personal losses between non-ill relatives and the group of patients whose similar loss preceded the onset of their illness. However if no account is taken of the time of onset of depressive symptoms it is evident that the patient group has a very significant excess of such events when compared to their relatives.

Table 4 shows the incidence of physical illness in the six months preceding hospital admission. There are no early-late differences. Comparison of these incidences with that of similar illness over a six-month period in sibs of these patients seemed logical for a control group. The incidence of similar illnesses in sibs was 22/51 (43.1%), which is indistinguishable from any of the patient subgroups shown in Table 4.

pressed patients with lithium carbonate. However, we feel that the evidence reported here, the observations by Goodwin et al,[9] and the clinical experience of some of our colleagues is sufficiently impressive to strongly suggest that some depressed patients do benefit from lithium therapy.

There are two general reasons why the results from this study differ from several negative reports: experimental design and patient selection. Hansen et al[2] used a crossover design with patients being alternated between lithium carbonate (for two weeks) and placebo and back again. Patients were regarded as improved if they improved while receiving lithium carbonate *and* had relapsed during the placebo phase. This assumes that the effect of lithium carbonate is a direct one and that this effect disappears soon after it is removed. However, there are reports of lithium being retained in the body and appearing in the urine of patients weeks after the last dose.[10] Further, while the mechanism of action of lithium carbonate is unknown, the widely reported delayed onset of therapeutic effect would suggest that it may not be a direct effect. These considerations would weigh against a positive finding in a study in which patients were being shifted from placebo to active drugs. We recognize that some of these considerations could apply to the design which we employed. However, we did not require the criterion of a relapse when the patient was changed from one drug to another—indeed, the treatment would only be changed if there was no significant improvement during the initial treatment period. Further, we used two active compounds and not a placebo.

Consideration must be given to the problem of patient selection. There is wide disagreement on the selection and diagnosis of psychiatric patients in general and depressed patients in particular. Previous investigators did not always give detailed criteria for patient selection. Our selection criteria were derived initially from clinical observations made during an uncontrolled study and were seen to match factors derived from a factor analytic definition of endogenous depression.[5] It is conceivable that our patients did differ in some important ways from those studied by other investigators. This issue can only be resolved if the antidepressant effect of lithium carbonate is determined in a group of patients similar to ours by independent investigators.

Desimipramine has been found to be an effective antidepressant.[10] In their comprehensive review, Davis et al[11] concluded that ". . . in overall clinical efficacy, desimipramine is very much like its parent compound, imipramine." The possibility that at least part of the response in our lithium carbonate group was a placebo effect is partly removed by the comparable response to desimipramine, an effective antidepressant.[11] Further studies should perhaps include a placebo group.

Our observations on the possible antidepressant actions of lithium carbonate, with its possible prophylactic role in affective disorders[12] has implications for our understanding of the relationship between mania and depression. Much of the current psychopharmacological and biological research has emphasized the apparent bipolar

Data on use of psychotherapeutic drugs were obtained in personal interviews with a cross-section sample

Although psychotherapeutic drugs are used to treat symptoms and disorders commonly associated with psychiatric practice, it should be noted that almost 60% of all prescriptions for such drugs issued by physicians in private practice are written by general practitioners and internists alone.[1] Only in the case of major tranquilizers and antidepressants do psychiatrists and neurologists account for a sizeable proportion of the total number of prescriptions written—some 30%.

The increasing importance of psychotherapeutic drugs in medical practice has been matched by the popularity of and demand for these drugs among the lay public. Thus patients may come to the physician specifically seeking or expecting a prescription for a psychotherapeutic drug—a situation that creates problems in the traditional relationship

Figure 21.3—An example of Midwest style. Notice the interesting variation in the display title.

Nine informed volunteers having previous ministered drugs were given small, doses of dextroamphetamine sulfate. Within pervised administration, eight subjects chosis which rapidly abated with drug

as sleep deprivation, predrug personality, or have been thought crucial in the origin proved to be insufficient as explanations prisingly, it was found that large long-term mine caused the subjects to feel depressed

The Wonders of Ireland

SUITS against psychiatrists or psychiatric hospitals occasionally arise from the use of electroconvulsive therapy (ECT). At one time, some professional liability insurers apparently thought that the risk of injury from ECT was so great that they were reluctant to insure physicians or others who administered ECT.[1] The current incidence of these suits is difficult to ascertain. It seems reasonably certain that the incidence has declined as the use of effective muscle relaxants has become more widespread.[2] While few such cases reached the state appeals courts in 1968 and 1969,[3-6] it is unclear whether they accurately reflect the extent of litigation in this area. Most professional liability cases are settled before trial and only a small fraction ever go as far as a state appeals court. Professional liability insurers are reluctant to release information about the number and type of cases they settle out of court. My conversations with counsel for companies which write malpractice insurance policies indicate that suits against psychiatrists for injuries arising from ECT are uncommon. Even though suits relating to ECT are probably waning, it is still predictable that occasional patients who incur injury during or after ECT will bring suits against allegedly culpable physicians or hospitals.

This study surveys the recent experience with ECT in a loosely selected group of psychiatric units, and, against this background, raises and briefly discusses some of the legal issues relating to ECT.

units, decreased in 30 units, and had not changed substantially in 14 units. During 1968 alone, over

tivities. They quickly became irritable and fault-finding, were anorexic, and related to clinical personnel in a highly dependent manner. This dysphoric affect was modulated by the environment, however, and the content of thought was otherwise entirely realistic. This reversal of response was most evident in subjects who received dextroamphetamine for four and five days.

A prepsychotic phase lasting several hours was observed in all subjects who later developed extreme paranoia. Subjects who were previously quite verbal and relatively trusting became quite taciturn, reserved, and negativistic. Most confined themselves to their rooms, made periodic inspection of their surroundings, and asked questions that indicated suspicion of events. If directly questioned, however, they gave oblique answers and specifically denied any paranoid feelings. Later, after the subjects ceased taking dextroamphetamine, they explained that they were aware of being abnormally suspicious during this period and had tried to conceal their paranoia.

The onset of obvious paranoia was usually abrupt. Subjects spoke freely about their paranoid ideas and often thought they had gained sudden insight into the "real" reason for the project. For example, one volunteer thought that the study was an elaborate subterfuge to have him hospitalized for "heart trouble." He felt that he knew his condition was terminal and thanked the physicians for "doing all they could." Despite his belief in his near death, his affect was essentially blunt and matter-of-fact. Not all delusions were this minor. Another subject turned off the room lights and sat lotus-fashion in his bed. When questioned about this behavior, he stated that he was aware of a "giant oscillator" placed in the ceiling to control his thoughts and the behavior of others in the hall. When told there was no oscillator, he gave the oblique answer that he did not mind being subjected to the oscillator but felt he should have been informed about its presence. Still another volunteer felt that his ex-wife had hired an assassin to dispatch him, and grew most disturbed when the physician would not guard the window while he guarded the door. Although paranoid delusions were common in all the psychotic patients, there was no evidence of disorientation, clouding of consciousness, or memory disturbance.

Ideas of reference were also common. Two patients felt

Seven schizophrenics and three patients with severe character disorders

single study in which clinical experience on a crisis-oriented inpatient service is examined to determine the extent to which the crisis theory model fits that experience.

It is the purpose of this communication, first, to briefly review certain aspects of crisis theory; and second, to examine the applicability of crisis theory to clinical practice on a general hospital psychiatric inpatient service which is part of a community mental health center.

The term "crisis" has been applied both to a reality situation,[5] and to the person's response to that situation.[6] Caplan writes

> We have seen that crisis involves a relatively short period of psychological disequilibrium in a person who confronts a hazardous circumstance that for him constitutes an important problem which he can for the time being neither escape nor solve with his customary problem solving resources.[6(p 53)]

We shall follow Caplan by referring to an antecedent hazardous situation or circumstance, and reserve the term *crisis* to refer to the consequent state of psychological disequilibrium.

The quality of hazardousness is one which is present in varying amounts in any life situation. Caplan notes that any particular life situation may be seen as more or less hazardous by members of a particular cultural or social group.[6(p 42)] According to crisis theory, situations which are especially hazardous will be followed by major crises in a significant portion of the population.

Certain hazardous life situations or events are thought to be especially likely to precipitate the state of crisis. These include death or addition of a family member, loss of a job, threat to body or family integrity, and role transitions such as graduating from college, beginning a new job, or marrying. Starting from Lindemann's study of grief reactions following a catastrophic fire, there has been a steady increase in the number and kinds of situations which are thought to precede crisis, as well as in the amount and kinds of pathology which are thought to follow hazardous situations. Porter, for example, defines crises as "precipitating stresses leading to emotional disorder or mental illness."[7(p 11)]

Sensory Profile.—Aside from recording quantitative data pertaining to the number of button presses for each kind of sensory input in each of the three sensory conditions, this paradigm also generates a qualitative overview of sensory preferences and the intensity of these preferences for each individual subject. This overview, which may be regarded as a "sensory profile" or "sensory print," may serve as a basis for clinical interpretation in the same manner that the Minnesota Multiphasic Personality Inventory, California Psychological Inventory or other psychological test profiles do. Naturally, before these interpretations can be regarded as clinically valid, norms will have to be established by testing large groups of subjects. Statistical analyses to discover the types and incidence of certain patterns to other clinical parameters will also be performed. In any event, to illustrate what is meant by a sensory profile, I should like to present some representative samples selected from the 36 normal subjects already tested. So far, profiles also have been obtained on over 50 psychiatric patients.

Figure 2 depicts four different types of sensory profiles *(A, B, C, D)* found in the normal sample. The length of the vertical lines for each condition indicates the number of button presses and the nature of the lines indicates the particular sensory modality (see Key). Although all this information could be presented by raw data, this visual display represents a more convenient way

Figure 21.4—An example of Midwest style.

Figure 21.5—An example of Midwest style. Notice how the headline gives the feeling of "pushing"—visual impact reinforcing the words.

Until you can visualize and make accurate roughs, I suggest that you use pieces of paper cut to 13 picas wide and 20 picas wide and column depth. On each piece mark off how many typeset characters and spaces this will accommodate. This should help you in visualizing what these "blocks" of copy will do when placed on a layout sheet. Then, cut these pieces to required depths, using a line counter to determine how many lines of typeset copy are involved. By placing these on your layout sheet you can quickly determine what areas are left over for other sight elements. Once you get the hang of it, you can soon forget the "cut-out" system.

Several "keys" are necessary to make the format work. One is that the layout *must* be created from the *end* forward. Another is to set the rather rigid rule, "Simplicity must govern." No embellishments or gimmicks. No filling of the white space panel just because it's there. The entire format is capable of standing by itself. It utilizes the white space and all elements perfectly. It doesn't need anything else.

CHAPTER TWENTY-TWO

The Dynamics of Ratios within Geometric Shapes

Probably one of the most important things you will discover about interesting magazine layouts is the design conception that "equals are static, unevens are exciting." I shall start by making another statement: "People want to be comfortable." On the surface this sounds rather trite and most people will raise an eyebrow and mutter, "So what?" It is exactly this desire for creature comfort that carries the key to flat or exciting magazine layouts. Want a reader to be "comfortable"? Give him squares or rectangles, perfectly balanced. You won't disturb him. You won't excite him either. Equals cancel each other. Perfect balance, in reality, is no more than a form of "comfort."

Where are we most likely to see the principle of "evens"? You will find it in any publication that insists on a majority of equal geometric shapes. The editorial content had better carry the publication, because the graphics won't do it. It is also true that editors and art directors like to be comfortable. You can spot this in numerous publications.

Publications in the standard size (8½ by 11 inches) are most easily adapted to the 1 to 3, 1 to 5, and 3 to 5 ratios. Any publication size evenly divisible by two will be an even. The 1 to 3, 1 to 5, and 3 to 5 ratios will become exciting. The reason, again, goes back to the comfort theory. People look at pages and mentally try to achieve balance. If there is an even balance, they feel comfortable. If there is an uneven or asymmetrical balance, they feel uncomfortable. This serves two very important functions. It incites interest and it gently nudges the reader to examine the page. Once the reader realizes there is no comfortable balance, he or she will move on. It is the slight pause that means you have the reader hooked. This is not enough! Reward him! Give him something of value, a good arrangement, a good group or cluster of interesting pictures, a blurb with a key phrase, even an intriguing title area.

How do we achieve unevens? Multiples, of course, but there are other ways: rhythm, pace, values, sizes, color, *anything* uneven. Rhythm means a flow, or cadence. This can be done with column variables, such as the Midwest style, or a "mix and match" as far as copy is concerned. It can also be done with counterpoint, or variations in sight elements, such as large versus small, light versus dark, black-and-white versus four-color, color versus color. Pace is an intangible as far as specifics are concerned. Every magazine has to develop its own pace, the sequence of presentation between stories. Values, provided they are uneven, are closely related to both rhythm and pace. An example would be a large gray area complemented by two smaller areas, giving a 3 multiple. Sizes are also closely related to the uneven theme. Any publisher that continues to make all pictures column-width size has no grasp of the even/uneven principle. Along with sizes we must also consider placement. Again, the even approach is stagnant.

Color always has impact. If your publication is limited to two-color, use the uneven principle in tone or tint values. Remember that "1" is also an uneven. By this I mean that "one use" may have more impact than any multiple will, and will often draw more attention.

Let me repeat, for just a moment. Ratios of 1 to 3, 1 to 5, and 3 to 5 are exciting because one's mental effort to balance cannot succeed. The thought process quickens (*ergo*, excitement). An even arrangement offers no such challenge. There are still other ways to achieve imbalance: values versus tints (in color), color opposites, color vibrations, arrangement of unequals, left versus right, and changing points of interest.

The word *dynamics* means a branch of mechanics pertaining to the motion of bodies. I apply this principle in magazine layout on the theory that pages can "move" depending on size, weight, placement, color, and the interrelationships of all elements to the whole.

In magazine layout and design there are several accepted formats: one-column (digest size), two-column (digest size and standard size), three-column (standard size), four-column (standard size and tabloid size), and mix-and-match in all but the digest size and the Midwest style, which is the narrow-wide column format and usually applicable to the standard size.

In every case we are faced with gray, vertical, rectangular shapes as the beginning of any page design. These verticals are formed by the "color" of the columns of type. Americans start at upper left and read down the columns. They also read from left to right across the page. Changing reading patterns in an effort to develop new geometric shapes would mean a complete retraining program for readers. The effort would hardly be worth the result. We will have to face the premise that all magazine designs start with gray verticals. Any multiple that can be divided evenly by two will remain static. There can be no motion if things are equal in size, color, or placement. Three of the magazine formats are shown in outline form. As you can see, the "evens" remain placid and uninteresting (see figures 22.1 to 22.9).

The reasoning behind uneven multiples is apparent when you look at the structure of these three formats. Two-column is a "divide-by-two" design. Three-column and the Midwest style are unevens. You cannot get an even design from them. It is also apparent simply by viewing the three formats that three-column is more interesting than two-column and the Midwest style is more interesting than either. Why?

The answer may become apparent with explanation. People do not wish to remain uncomfortable. They will try to achieve balance when it does not exist. A two-column format is easy to balance. A three-column format is also relatively easy when one considers that three columns will face an opposite page of three columns. Six is divisible by two. In the Midwest style, facing pages will have "matching shapes," creating equals.

In a two-column format, we can use uneven variables, but the effect is not as striking as it is in the other two formats. One reason is that white space, so necessary in good design, becomes painfully apparent. The column widths give too much white space within the live area. Pictures at column widths are also larger than three-column pictures.

What will complement a set of vertical rectangles? Several things. A horizontal will do it, as will a break in the geometric pattern, a change in form *within* the rectangle, color or counterpoint, spatial variations, rhythm, or optical variations. These can be called "known variables."

A horizontal causes a change of direction. Horizontals include the sink (actually a white horizontal, even though there is nothing in it but space); title areas (with still further variations in typefaces, spacing, and the normally accepted "shapes"—triangular, inverted triangles, square, and flush left or flush right); pictures with many variations; and, on occasion, tint blocks within title areas used as design motifs and as a way to bridge the gutter.

A break in the geometric pattern

Figure 22.1—"Evens" cancel each other and have very little page interest.

Figure 22.2—"Unevens" catch attention and create interest in two-column formats.

simply means that the vertical rectangle has some variable within the rectangle that breaks it up into segments. This can change the basic form. Bleeds, blurbs, titles in a well, running commentaries, an outside column stand-up initial, and natural column endings segment the vertical into uneven pieces.

A change of form within the vertical might be a vignette halftone, an outline halftone, an oval or circular picture, or a line drawing that also causes spatial variations within its own shape. Color and counterpoint will give vertical differences in values. Color will almost always pull the reader's eye away from a monotonous repetition. The judicious use of white space creates rhythm, relief of monotony, space around titles, and space around pictures, and balances specific areas. White space is used as a design element to balance the whole. White space has "weight" and should be used as a counterbalance.

Optical variations, much like any other layout device, are used to pull the reader's eye toward a specific area. All of these tend to reduce the "tombstone" effect of pictures on the tops of vertical gray columns.

Now that I have roughly defined some of the known variables—and they have their place in magazine layout—let's see how these "shapes" can affect the page as a design unit.

Title areas have many variations within the horizontal theme. They may be classified into "controlled" and "uncontrolled." For example, an all-caps title gives the impression of being controlled simply because there is perfect alignment of the characters and words. The shape is a dark horizontal. When this is placed with a sink, with white space above and between it and the body copy, we usually have a "bar formation" composed of a white horizontal, a dark horizontal, and a white horizontal. This can cause enough design variation to draw attention away from the verticals.

Caps and lower case titles, although uneven in form, still fall into the controlled class. Ascenders and descenders do not cause that much variation since the type is still in perfect alignment.

When I talk of uncontrolled title areas I mean titles that curve, warp, interlock, or create shapes that must be viewed as a design element before they can be read and title areas that include elements other than words (such as a picture or tint block).

In an uncontrolled title area, such as a title that curves up and then down, the white space will still cover the same area, but the space shifts to occupy different positions. A curved title will use the sink, creating two corners, at the page corners. What this amounts to is that the "curve" actually occurs only at the lower edge of the title.

When title areas (title, subtitle, blurbs, or any combination of them) are created as shapes, white space should always be used to emphasize that shape. If not, the shape gets lost or confused by crowding. Any title set other than in a straight line falls into the un-

Figure 22.3—"Unevens" with tint values in two column.   *Figure 22.4—"Evens" in three-column formats—dull and uninteresting.*

Figure 22.5—"Unevens" in three-column formats.

Figure 22.6—"Unevens" in three-column formats.

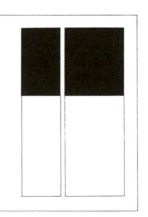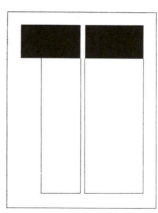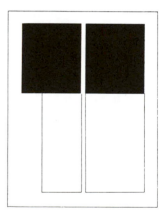

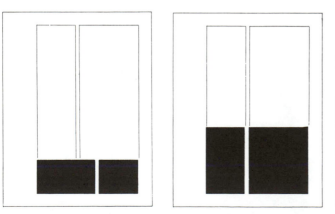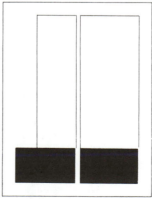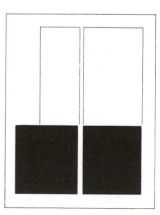

Figure 22.7—There is no way to get "evens" in Midwest style if used at column widths.

Figure 22.8—"Evens" in Midwest style. The pictures move into the white space creating a diversion from the "evens."

controlled pattern.

Remember that black is the "strongest" color you can use against white. Any other color will give tonal variations. Even "bright" colors do not have the impact that black has against white.

Size is an important rhythm factor. Change creates rhythm. When combining size with color, remember that color values decrease from solids to tints and shades.

Titles should be attention getters. Great care should be used to get optimal use from them. Handle them as "designing units." This means use the white space. Crowding will decrease impact.

Traditionally, when handling pictures within a horizontal, designers have been limited to several basic formations. I say traditionally because the basic formations were devised for letterpress printing, and one was charged extra for *anything* that varied from the basic square cornered "cuts" or copy that was cast on a single measure. I cannot overemphasize this letterpress background. We are still trying to rid ourselves of it.

In the letterpress "ideal," page layouts consisted of shapes that brought no additional charges. They were the horizontal panel, the vertical panel, the T-shaped group, the L-shaped group, the U-shaped group, and the inverted U-shaped group. These were all square cornered shapes and column widths. The traditionalists firmly believed in "a place for everything and everything in its place." They loved perfect alignment. They hated any layout that did not fill every corner. They originated the term "tombstoning" by placing all the "cuts" directly over a column of copy. It is part of our purpose to place a tombstone over this kind of thinking.

Let's look at some of the "groups" and examine the variables that will prevent tombstoning. The easiest example would be variations in widths. "Cuts" immediately look better if they are anything *but* column widths. The break in design pattern is more interesting than the tombstone at the top of each column and creates a strong horizontal that cannot easily be divested from the verticals.

Even such a basic change as tone values can help detract from the gray verticals. Color will always do so. Bleeds will strengthen the horizontals. Outline halftones within the horizontal will also do it. Changes from halftones to line drawings, if this is possible, will do it. The idea, of course, is to create so much attention that the verticals are optically lost.

In grouping by geometric shapes, the largest will draw the most attention. The larger the subject, the closer it seems. Conversely, the smaller the subject, the farther away it seems. This rule of opposites can be used to draw attention to special areas. The premise that the largest would draw the most attention was used with deadly effect by traditionalists. Most groupings started out with a

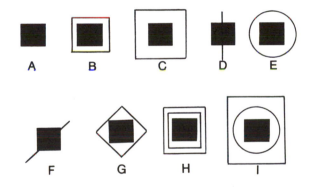

Figure 22.10—"Enclosures" or strong line divisions affect the basic shape.

A. Floats free.
B. Form emphasized by repeating the shape.
C. Form "floats" but is relatively controlled.
D. Line draws attention first.
E. Visually a "bull's-eye," optical change to round corners.
F. Line draws attention.
G. Form within a form decreases the inner form.
H. Receding and restricted.
I. Too many forms. The eye picks up the outer form only.

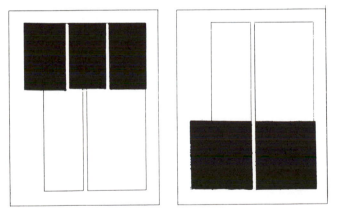

Figure 22.9—"Evens" and "unevens" in Midwest style still create interest.

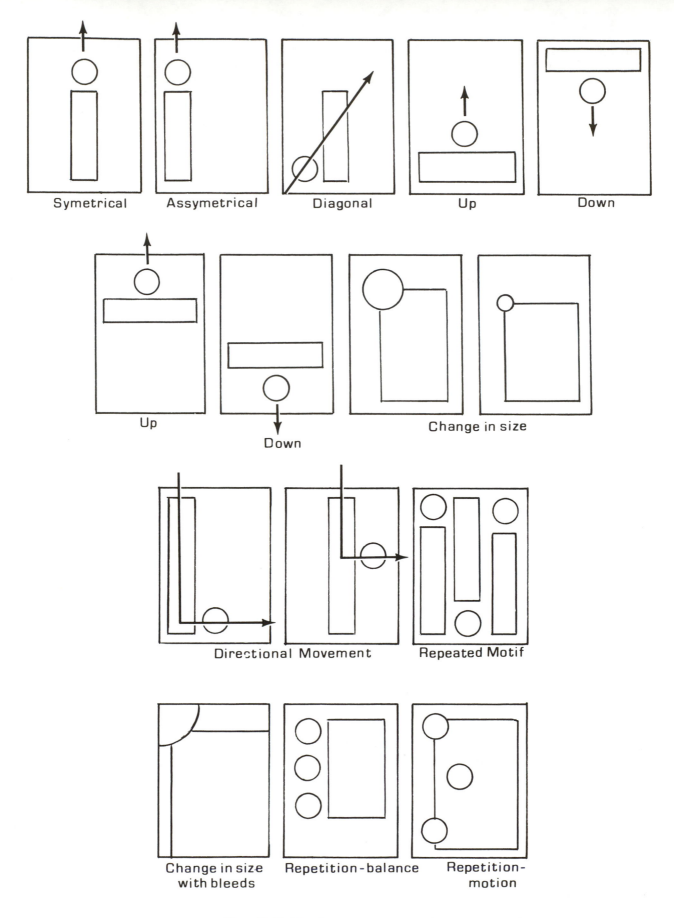

Figure 22.11—How shapes create eye movement.

large shape; then this was surrounded by shapes that were any size smaller than the original. Grouping presumes that one picture is the leader and all others are followers. The leader was almost always identified by size, shape, or color, but the basic shape still remained a square-cornered rectangle.

We all know that color will draw attention before size. Color will "draw" depending on brightness in any size; even a half-inch colored circle will receive attention before a gray halftone. If you don't believe this, try cutting out a half-inch circle of orange and placing it anywhere on a page of halftone pictures.

Sometimes the daring traditionalist used mortising and was willing to pay the extra charges for the massing effect. The sad fact was that anything other than perfect alignment was billed as additional costs and the designer had to be willing to defend these costs. We no longer have this problem. With offset printing and film stripping one can do almost anything. In particular, you can now set type on *any measure* simply by giving a command to the typesetter.

Good grouping *always* uses white space as a frame, counterbalance, or attention getter. The traditionalist was afraid of white space because it represented an area that was not used. Good grouping ideally should be less than column width for the best effect. Get away from filling every corner. Your layouts will show immediate improvement.

A few years ago a new geometric shape called clustering was devised. This was never used by the traditionalists. In clustering, one arranges the pictures around a white geometric pattern. This differs from "mortising" in that the pictures are not joined together but rather held together by patterns.

Let's return for just a moment to known variables as applied to ads and ad placements. Here, again, we had the letterpress ideal. Ads were placed according to prescribed "shapes" that were made to fit open editorial areas. The rea-

soning was simple. Squares and rectangles could be placed in the chase (a metal frame that holds type for printing) and locked up with little or no trouble or additional cost. This ad placement dictum is still with us. I believe that once a magazine breaks away from traditionalism there will be advertisers who will create ads to complement the new designs.

Line drawings differ from halftones. They can be created to almost any irregular shape. In letterpress, the "cut" was shot "image edge to image edge." The cut was then square cornered. If you wanted a caption within the image area, you had to pay extra to have it mortised in. On film this is just a matter of stripping. More often than not the caption belongs within the line area instead of below or above it.

Second-color and four-color designs should *always* use white space to help emphasize the color. Colors used on tinted stock will invariably lose impact. Probably the best example of four-color in high-gloss whites for emphasis are seen in the *National Geographic* and *Arizona Highways* magazines. They *know* the value of color against white.

As you can see, none of the items discussed above have utilized the theory of evens/unevens. They were all ploys to get your attention away from the gray verticals. Let's examine the other illustrative pages that show the principles of the theory. We have used the same three formats—two-column, three-column, and Midwest style. Note that the multiples 1 to 3, 1 to 5, and 3 to 5 are uneven. Compare these against the first set of example pages. Note the differences in design appeal.

Let's discuss what happens when you purposely create those stabilizing lines that help the reader achieve balance, even though true balance does not exist. In grouping, start with the leader-follower concept. Arrange the pictures by sizes and harness the internal movement within the pictures. You invariably will end up with one "point" (usually of interest) that will attract the reader. It is this point you should study to find what you can balance it with on the opposite page. For instance, if the point (center of interest or balance) is below optical center on one page, the same point should be used as a starting point on the opposite page. The structure of the elements need not be the same. In fact, it is better if they are not. But the "invisible line" should be utilized. In the example at the left in figure 22.12 the invisible line carries the reader's eye from upper left to lower right and *away* from the copy. In the example at the right, the invisible line is used to control the eye movement.

Instead of doing two facing pages and sensing the invisible line *afterwards*, it is better to create one good page, find the center of interest, and balance the pages by drawing a line across the gutter to the facing page. This will give you a point on which to start creating a group, cluster, or design that will utilize the point. The invisible line will also help you in deciding where spatial balance may occur and how to use the white space. Remember that white space *has* weight, space, size, and a place in the total page design.

Let us summarize by repeating several pertinent points.

1. Evens are dull, comfortable, and unmoving.

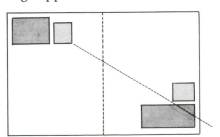

Figure 22.12—Invisible construction lines.

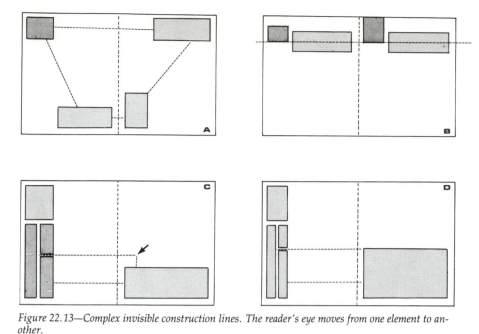

Figure 22.13—Complex invisible construction lines. The reader's eye moves from one element to another.

2. Unevens are uncomfortable and, therefore, exciting.
3. The uneven approach is realized by the use of any multiple that cannot be evenly divided by two.
4. The simplest approach in standard sizes is in multiples of 1 to 3, 1 to 5, and 3 to 5.
5. Breaks in patterns within the verticals should be unevens.
6. Bleeds will help to emphasize unevens.
7. White space will help to emphasize unevens.
8. Unevens can be achieved by changes in rhythm, size, color, tint, value, or shape.
9. In pacing your layouts, give the reader a "resting place" where evens predominate and where everything comes out all right.
10. Once you capture the reader with a challenge, reward him or her.
11. Utilize points and invisible lines to control the reader's eye movements.
12. Forget the letterpress ideal of perfect alignment. Think "white space" and forget about filling every corner.

CHAPTER TWENTY-THREE

The Clock-Grid System

Many layout artists do not feel competent or comfortable when faced with most grid systems. The purpose of this discussion is to show that a mechanically simple grid *can* give professional results.

Each grid in the clock-grid system is based on starting at optical center, two-fifths down from the top and at page center from each side. The reasoning is simple. Optical center gives an ideal balancing point for every page. It means facing pages will complement each other regardless of the grid composition.

Starting at optical center, a protractor is used to extend a set of lines equal to the hour positions on a clock, that is, 30 degrees, 60 degrees, 90 degrees, 120 degrees, 150 degrees, and 180 degrees for the hours 10, 11, 12, 1, 2, and 3. The opposite is then used for the hours 4, 5, 6, 7, 8, and 9. We now have a series of lines that can be extended to the edges of the live area (42 picas by 54 picas on the normal $8^1/_2$ by 11 inch page). Figure 23.1 illustrates the resulting "grids."

This breaks each page into 24 grid units. In the top panel, the grid units are equal on both sides of center but unequal in sizes. The next two panels are equal on both sides of center as well as above and below optical center. The bottom panel is similar to the top panel, except that the depth is almost twice as deep. The grid multiples are so varied that it is difficult to create any even balance. Balance on each page will invariably occur at optical center. Copy can be set on any grid width except the two outer grids, which are too small to accommodate copy without chopping it up. The best copy blocks are $17^1/_2$ picas or 18 picas. The two outer grids are used to "hang" title areas or pictures. Pictures can be any grid size except the outer two on both sides, although bleeding can utilize these two grids quite well and should be used in that way. All pictures will include their captions when falling within any grid or combination of grids. Proper spacing between ele-ments should be 1 pica. This means that the picture *and* caption will actually "fall" one-half pica inside the grid pattern, giving 1 full pica between elements.

All pictures are examined mechanically for location and size within the grid structure. A picture can be any complete grid *or* combination of grids. Titles should always occur at the top and in the top panel of grids. This means the white space within the sink area will always be a variable.

It becomes apparent from figures 23.15 A, B, C, and D that pictures arrange themselves into either clusters or panels with irregularly shaped widths. The movement *within* the pictures can be controlled, but this is not essential. The page presentation does not depend on controlled movement but rather on optically balanced units.

Following the grids will rarely give an even or placid page unless the page is all copy. Page interest is invariably uneven and, therefore, captivating.

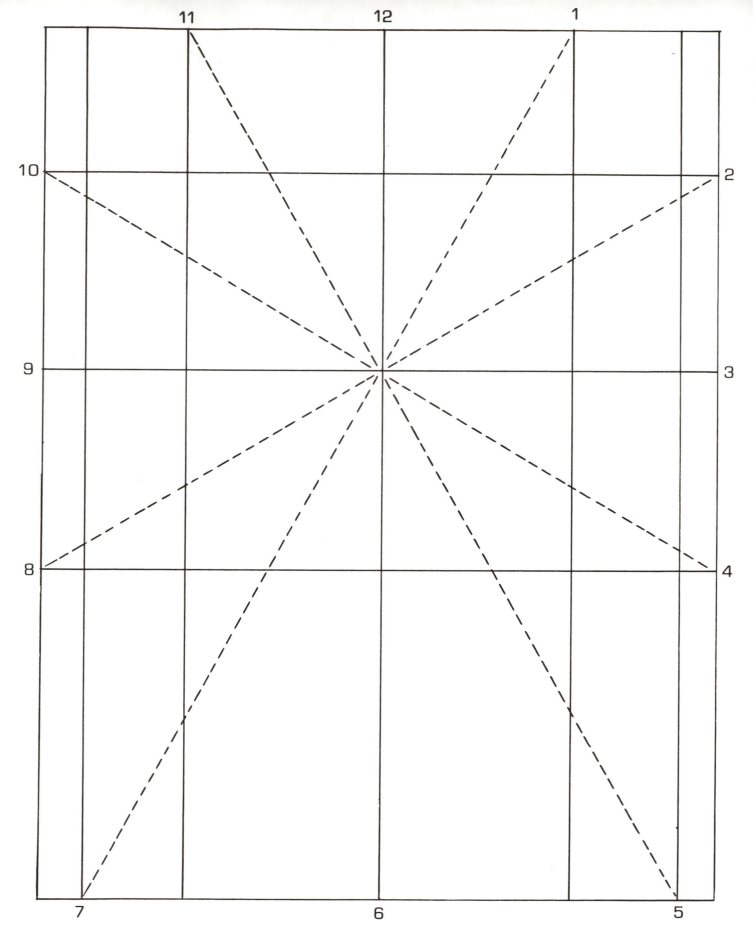

Figure 23.1—The clock-grid system basic plan or format.

How to Design and Improve Magazine Layouts

The "Clock Grid System"

The cause of this patient's death appears to have self-induced water intoxication secondary to comp water drinking during an acute psychotic episode symptoms of increased agitation, confusion, fearfu head discomfort, weakness, nausea, polyuria, and ab nal fullness are compatible with classic description o idly progressive water intoxication.[11] Her subse unresponsiveness, apparent central neurogenic h ventilation, decerebrate posturing, and apnea su transtentorial herniation.[11] At postmortem examin transtentorial herniation was indeed present and th demonstrable cause was generalized cerebral edema certain etiology. That cerebral edema is the abnorm of acute water intoxication was demonstrated in the nal case of Helwig et al of fatal water intoxicatio ondary to proctolysis.[1] Helwig et al produced ide brain abnormality by producing water intoxication i bits, and Wasterlain and Posner[15] recently conf these pathologic findings in a sophisticated study of water intoxication in rats.

Why this patient developed a rapidly fatal cour mains problematic. Several factors must be consider cluding the effect of a thiazide diuretic on free clearance, and the possibility that the psychotic p itself may have been accompanied by neuroend changes affecting the organism's ability to meta

type or pattern of movements but rather to a sub need or desire to move."[4] This urge to move is alwa companied by affective distress and, objectively, is fested by restless pacing, inability to sit still, and c uous alterations in posture. With the more subc akathisias, the patient may not use the word, "re and complain instead of "jitteriness," inability t "comfortable," "impatience," "irritability," "feeling ' up," or being a "bundle of nerves." The well-estab interaction between anxiety and extrapyramidal toms makes it even more difficult to distinguish a su cal akathisia from anxiety.

Mental manifestations do occur in documented ganglia disease. Schwabb et al[1] have reported parox attacks of altered mental functioning in Parkinso ease. These attacks are often associated with ocul crisis and frequently disappear when antiparkin drugs are administered. Davison and Bagley[15] also an increased incidence of schizophrenia-like psycho such basal ganglia disorders as Huntington chore son disease, torsion spasm, essential hereditary t and midbrain reticulosis. They conclude that "basa glia dysfunction often has a prominent mental comp which may take a psychotic form."

Since biperiden—an anticholinergic drug—re these decompensations, the question arises whet

MD, et al, 1973, unpublished data). Type I suppressi sociated with pronounced REM compensation, appe timately related to pontine-geniculo-occipital (PGO ing in cats, events considered the most obligatory of REM sleep.[14] Recent studies on PGO spiking in a and phasic-integrated potentials in man sugges REM-sleep rebounds are more dependent on effe PGO-spike activity than effects on REM-sleep time. contrast, the type of REM-sleep suppression with li type II suppression, is due to the decreased length o REM period, rather than a lengthening of the R REM cycle, and is unassociated with REM rebound. dition, the number of abnormal REM minutes ten increase during the drug periods.

With respect to delta sleep the increases in delta on lithium averaged 30 minutes per night. Durin drug period there was a significant inverse correlati tween REM percent and delta-sleep percent. While sleep latency did not change significantly on lithium latency did change significantly and also correlate serum lithium levels, findings that suggest REM changes are more responsive to varying dosages o

ium than delta sleep. The differential changes of o REM-sleep parameters in patient No. 3 on differen ium dosages support this argument.

Since both the major reduction in REM sleep and creases in delta sleep occur mainly during the fir second thirds of the night, it may be that the effe sleep are related to the dosage schedule of lithiur cause postabsorptive serum level peaks of lithium o occur two to four hours after the dose, the postabso peak in this study was probably reached between 11 and 1:00 AM (or during the first third of the night). T whether lithium's effect on sleep is related to bloo levels, one would need to administer lithium durir the medication periods. In fact the longitudinal da patient No. 3 show almost no variance of the sleep ti gardless of time period. Lithium's lack of sedative at the usual clinical dosages may partially explai

As previously noted, lithium by itself should not b sidered a sedative drug and in this investigation was no significant change in the time spent asleep d the medication periods.

improved by the piperazine drugs, one should consi possible bias that may have resulted from some pa receiving a drug other than the one their physician have preferred. In a "physician's choice" research c each patient is treated with the drug that the phy believes to be best for him. It has been argued that should result in a uniform positive bias, if any, and not prejudice the comparison of treatment outcom "random assignment" design, such as the presen causes most patients to receive drugs other than the cian's choice. A comparison of the "physician's choi sults with results from the "random assignment" de of methodological interest.

To eliminate the possibility that a selective bia have been introduced by the fact that some patient: not treated with the drug that the psychiatrist woul chosen, the total sample was divided into "preferre "nonpreferred" medication groups. A three-way di physician's preference × Global Improvement ar was undertaken using methods described by Shaffer results provided no evidence that the physician's p ence influenced the Global Improvement ratings, that is comforting with regard to this and other no research designs.

The patients who actually received the type of dru treating physician would have selected anyway cons a "physician's choice" research design within the "random assignment" design. The frequencies in v categories of improvement for patients who receive sician's choice medication are shown in Table 6. Th tingency test yielded χ^2 = 10.66 with 4 df, a value tha most identical to that derived from the complete ra assignment design. Thus, had this study been done context of a "physician's choice" design, the same c sions would have followed. This comparison is of me logical interest in considering the value of observat type research conducted in natural treatment se, without random assignment of patients.[8]

Age was the primary variable that distinguish tients who responded best to the piperazines in the ses of BPRS scores. For comparison, the frequenc various categories of Global Response ratings ar sented in the lower portion of Table 5 for patients 40 years of age and for patients over 40 years of ag difference between drug treatments and statistical nificant (χ^2 = 13.45 with 4 df) in older patients, while younger patients the Global Improvement ratings d differ significantly among the three treatment g Thus, the Global Improvement ratings confirm the symptom ratings as indicating the superiority of p zines for older schizophrenics patients.

Next, a series of analyses attempted to identify ty patients for whom the piperazine drugs were best tients were grouped according to the various clinical ria, such as paranoid vs nonparanoid. They were grouped according to BPRS profile pattern into ' thinking disorder," "withdrawn disorganized thi disturbance," and "hostile and affective types."[7] I other analysis they were grouped on the basis of

Vacations Unlimited

That no differences were found among the three of phenothiazines in terms of total degree of re comes as no surprise. Numerous large-scale coope studies have failed to show differences in overall e among "peer" antipsychotic drugs.[10,11] Despite thes sistent failures, a common clinical experience ha that some patients respond preferentially to one t drug as compared with another. This study attemp throw some light on these more subtle differences.

Such differences as were found were internally tent and largely consonant with prevailing clinical b Piperazine phenothiazines were more effective tha other two classes for treating patients over 40 ye age. This age group, however, was more heavily we toward patients classified as nonparanoid, core, s phrenics with primary disturbances of thinking, for the piperazines also were the preferred drug class. patients generally exhibited better responses to thiazine treatment than did the younger, paranoid In short, the idea that piperazine derivatives have specific antipsychotic activity was given some supp the present study.

One should caution that past experiences in try delineate specific indications for antipsychotic drug been highly discouraging. We ourselves were una replicate an initial finding that paranoid schizophre

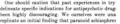

Figure 23.2—The clock-grid system in application.

CHAPTER TWENTY-FOUR

Innovation

The following is a lecture I gave to the Business Publication Production Club of Chicago. Some items have been mentioned before. On the whole, the art of innovating belongs to those who want to improve their style, rather than to the followers. The result of this lecture was a rather interesting hour of discussion.

Innovation is defined as the "act of introducing something new or novel." Most magazine designers who have made a serious study of magazine layout seem to accept the fact that there are *accepted* ways of doing things. Because they are accepted, they have become almost sacred. The "hack" patiently learns the rules and then complacently sits back and religiously applies them. The industry has too many of these people who are *afraid* to dare, to innovate.

Let's start with the basic magazine formats. You have two-column and three-column, almost without exception. In the two-column format you invariably place the cuts in any, or all, of the four corners, or at optical center, or within the golden rectangle, or bleed them off the page. Sometimes, if you feel daring, you might use an outline halftone or mortise a couple of cuts. You say to yourself, "After all, there are only a limited number of positions for pictures in the two-column format." The three-column designer says the same thing. You casually look around and, since everyone else is doing the same thing, you feel it must be right. Did you know that

the three-column format goes back to the Rosetta stone three thousand years ago, and the two-column format goes back to Gutenberg, some five hundred years ago? I'm sure the introduction of a three-column format, in magazines, seemed like the "ultimate" to the person using the two-column format. It *did* prevent wrap-around copy. It *did* offer half again as many possible picture locations. It *did* seem easier to read. However, you might want to use a picture or art that doesn't really look good in either format.

Another disadvantage of *both* formats is that you are stuck with a monotonous pace—straight copy marching along in two or three gray columns, much like rows of tombstones.

What would the innovator do? First of all, he or she would study the problem and actually tear it apart and rebuild it, if necessary. In rebuilding this particular problem, I came up with what I call the Midwest style. In this format we can still use the standard 8½ by 11 inch page size, but we use a format consisting of one column on 13 picas and another on 20 picas. What does this give? First of all it establishes a rhythmic beat. It's no longer in lockstep, because it has a well-paced rhythm.

This format accommodates all the standard two- and three-column picture sizes as well as many more. Even facing pages of all copy have some feeling of rhythm. This leads me to some interesting sidelights on picture sizes, particularly the wrap-around

bleed. We all know the theory behind bleeds—how the bleed visually increases the picture size as well as creating a visual directional pull. The wrap-around bleed is something else! First of all, you don't have to worry about exact registration, as you might in a double-page spread. There is no "crossing the gutter" to worry about or page alignment when the magazine is bound. You actually *lose* minor registration problems as soon as you turn the page. You also create a wide variety of curiosity devices that can be satisfied by turning the page. You have a "continuing" device to pull the reader along. We all know what happens when we have a long diagonal figure that causes problems that cannot be readily solved by cropping to page size. The wrap-around bleed can solve many of these problems.

The wrap-around bleed will not solve all your problems but is a device that is seldom used and that *can* solve many a problem.

Another rich field for the innovator is page impositions. Many of us overlook this because we are so engrossed with what each page or spread will look like, *as we lay it out*.

Let's take an example. You have a story of five pages, already laid out, in line and black-and-white halftones. In the imposition pattern, page three of your story falls in line with a two-color ad. If you disregard the imposition and send the story on its way, you entirely miss an opportunity to use one of the following—duotones, a tint block overprint, a mezzotint pattern on color, posterization, the use of white as a ''third color,'' or the special handling of tabular material.

I sometimes wonder if the *mechanics* of handling two or three colors causes the designer to have a mental block. I see immediate jumps from straight black-and-white to four-color, with little or no attention paid to the great possibilities in between. If it's the mechanics that bother you, call your platemaker, who will not only explain how to do it, but, if time factors are involved, will often do it for you with minimal instructions.

Let us return briefly to innovation in the use of second or third colors. Sometimes I think we should all take a short course in ''creative thinking.'' This can be broken down into four basic steps:
1. Totally disregard the final result and list all the *possibilities*. Here is where many of us fail, because we think in reverse; that is, we think of the *final* result before we actually tackle the problem.
2. After this list is prepared, eliminate all but the *probabilities*.
3. Analyze the probabilities.
4. Eliminate, with cost factors in mind; then choose the best.

Now, let's apply this. Your imposition shows that an advertiser is using a ''match brown.'' Your picture is a half-page, halftone of a group of executives. In listing the possibilities you should think of *not only* the *applications*, but also the *implications*, of brown. Brown, for instance, is an earth color, a warm color, a basic color. Brown is also dark enough to utilize white as an opposite. The picture could go as a Van Dyke brown print, as a duotone, a mezzotint, or to spotlight a main point of interest with either a circle or a design on white.

Let me show you the possibilities of handling tabular material in a different way. Tables are a concentration of factual material usually arranged in columns, reading up and down and from left to right. The easiest arrangement is tabular typesetting. Nice even rows of information. The next easiest is to enclose the table in a ruled box, which helps set it off from the gray

text background material. The innovator recognizes that there is more than one way to skin a cat. You might convert the data into bar graphs, using either a color or gray screen values. You might convert the data into pie-graphs, and implement their structure by using color or tints of colors. You might convert the data into another form, such as pyramids, symbols, stacks of money, buildings, people, almost any graphic form other than just straight material. You might even utilize motion, such as changes in direction. Since the text is primarily vertical, change the table to primarily horizontal. Use color to strengthen the horizontals.

Here is still another innovative idea for your perusal. I call it the theory of the ''double cover.''

The double cover carries the normal, acceptable second, third, and fourth covers. The cover for a November issue, for example, appears in its normal place. However, immediately inside the cover, and in place of a normal ad position or table of contents, show the cover for December. This carries a ''banner'' saying, ''This is next month's cover. Look for it on November 20th'' along with the entire cover page for the next month's issue. The double cover is carried through, *complete*, creating *two* second, third, and fourth covers.

What does this mean to you? First of all, it is a sales tool: next month's cover creates expectation and a visual identity. It subconsciously plants an image in the reader's mind. When the December issue hits the stands, the image has already been established.

Second, ad revenue for three covers is doubled. You now have six to sell! You save money printing two covers at the same time. The only additional cost is press time and paper for the first issue. This can easily be absorbed in the additional ad revenue. Third, no fractional ads need appear in the issue. A center spread, or double-page full-color ads, or only full-page ads need appear inside the issue. Fourth, ads can be sold on a yearly contract basis. New, full-color one-page or double-page full-color ads can be added at will. Fifth, editorial

content will not be disturbed by fractional ads, jumps, or clutter. The labor-saving costs and retaining a good esthetic quality inside are money in the bank.

Sixth, with advertising locations fixed, you can ''bank'' stories. This means making up an issue will only be a one- or two-day job. You merely compile the issue with sufficient pages to make a quota. With the issue made up of full-page ads there will be no story disturbance. Seventh, there is little or no need for a space salesperson, except to tie the advertisers to yearly contracts.

Eighth, editorial staffs can be minimized. The office space and salary saving can also be considered money in the bank. Ninth, you can give the reader pure reading enjoyment. Nothing will disturb his or her reading. All stories are complete. No junk pages. No clutter. No small ads to contend with.

Think about it, and ask yourself, Why not?

Innovation is ''the act of introducing something new or novel,'' as well as ''a change effected by innovating.'' We might also define it as a creative act effectively used. Since no lecture is complete unless one can define all their terms, let us also define ''leaders'' and ''followers.''

Leaders are people who take command, followers are people who fulfill those commands. It is apparent that leader and follower can never be the same person. A leader sets the pace, makes the decisions, assumes responsibility, accepts challenges. He or she is never static, for leadership implies movement. The follower is the opposite: he or she rarely sets the pace, avoids a decision, may, on occasion, assume some responsibility, but would rather make no move that might be subject to criticism. Accepting a challenge seems beyond the follower's capabilities.

These definitions certainly apply to many magazine layout and design people. You can recognize leaders and followers by their work. However, before becoming too harsh, let's examine the reasons why some publications never seem to change.

Tradition is the natural enemy of innovation. You all know the time-worn excuses for not innovating. They include: our editor *likes* two-column, we have been using three-column for thirty years and wouldn't feel comfortable with anything else, we have people on the staff who cannot cope with change, and, the old stand-by, we have always done it this way. It seems that everyone falls back on the comfort of tradition. You always know exactly where you are.

There are some reasons for remaining constant. Newsstand sales depend on logo (title) identification. Tables of contents have a logical and acceptable position that rarely calls for changing. Advertising still pays most of the cost. Ad sizes as well as many of the accepted ad positions (back cover, inside front cover, and inside back cover) are so functional and revenue producing that there would be no valid reason to change.

Magazines with controlled circulation and no newsstand sales have good reasons for remaining relatively constant. What distresses me are controlled circulation publications that have been "tradition-oriented" and that still follow newsstand sales formats and ideas. Here are magazines that are wide open and yet show little or no innovative layouts or approaches. They merely copy the others and remain stagnant. The logo invariably appears at the top, in one size and in the same position. Strong, immovable, and dull. There is no reason why it could not be either larger or smaller, or in another position, or moved from the top to the bottom or to one side, should the need arise. Many of you have faced the problem of the "inviolate logo" when trying for a good cover design. You may feel it should be reversed out, only to find that, in its fixed position, you have both light and dark areas involved, which makes the reverse unworkable. Or the logo occurs on the edge of an important area. Or the logo causes conflict with the cover design as a unit.

The leader grabs the challenge and moves the logo for a better pur-

pose. The follower says, "I'll be happy if the editor or publisher doesn't notice that the logo destroys the cover design."

And what about tinted stock for a cover in controlled circulation? The follower says, "But the back page contains a black-and-white ad and black-and-white *means* that and nothing else." The leader might say, "This cover and ad would both look better printed on a beige-tinted stock." He or she then prepares arguments, calls the advertiser or agency, and lays it on the line with the art director. The designer tries to "sell" the art director on an idea that will do *both* of them some good. It is rare that any black-and-white ad *must* appear only on white stock. Many advertisers would be only too happy to take advantage of a tinted background, as long as it didn't cost them anything. After all, art directors know a little bit about the use of color, too. You say it won't work? Have you tried it? After all, you'll never know unless you try. Part of innovation is trying what others have not attempted.

How can you innovate within the traditionalist structure? This may be easier than you think. Let's just talk about four new ideas. The first is the wrap-around bleed. This is a picture that bleeds off a right-hand page to the right and continues on the left of the following page. It accomplishes several things. It increases the width of the original picture area. It satisfies curiosity. It does not need perfect registration. It gives you a three-page spread instead of a double-page spread. We also have the stand-up initial that occurs outside the column in the border, instead of in the traditional position of being flush with the first paragraph. Another is the "miniature page" table of contents. Still another is the "mix and match" layout format. Each of these was created to serve a specific purpose at a specific time. To simply let these ideas die after using them once is a waste. Good ideas should be simple, direct, and never need explanation. They should be so well designed and thought out that they could stand repeated use without bordering on monotony.

In the four ideas presented, perhaps the wrap-around bleed would be the only one that could not bear constant use. The others can.

How does one develop the ability to innovate? Perhaps the following hints may help you in developing your potentials.

Develop idea files. Prepare yourself. Have "starters," like yeast, for your own thinking process. These come in four categories: (1) ideas others have used; (2) ideas others have used *plus* your adaptations; (3) ideas in the raw stage that you have not used; and (4) experimental ideas from 3 that you develop in your spare time.

Adapt ideas others have used to suit a specific problem when you have so little time that you need immediate help. These would include such things as posterization, converting halftones to line by the tracing method, mirror-images, "flopping," and many of the solutions we see in everyday use. This means establishing a "how to do it" file. When you see a good layout idea, clip it, accurately describe how it was done, and file it for future reference. This is relatively easy and can be the beginning of the other files. This will be the largest file, for a while a least, because you will be adding to it almost immediately. *Never* pass up a good layout idea because you couldn't figure out how it was done. If you can't figure it out for yourself, call your platemaker or printing salesperson. They will both be happy to advise you. Talk it over with other people. Nail it down. You can only profit from the experience.

Next, we have ideas others have used (from your starter file) and which you then supplement with your own individual application. For instance, you used a line drawing in the tracing technique. Enlarge on this idea. Make another and offset one over the other to create double lines instead of single lines. Or, have a photostat made to a slightly smaller reduction and use the tracing as an overlay to get the double line effect. Try using the two drawings in two different colors to give a new effect. Or make one solid and the other gray for a depth effect. As you can see, this now becomes a beginning of your second file. In the long run, this file will probably be the largest one you will have because every idea has many applications.

The difficult file is the one you develop from raw ideas entirely on your own. These are ideas that have no specific application at the present, but are built up toward the future. You keep them, nurture them, return to them as your subconscious builds on the original concept, and, eventually, you have them in a polished form, ready to apply. Many of these ideas may be the ones you put to one side in the press of business because they didn't apply at the time. This file should also contain "related ideas" that you pick up from observation, things like billboards, matchbook folders, place mats, television commercials, ads that strike you as well done, typographical tricks—anything that might have an idea future. At this stage you don't have to develop any of them. They are put there as reminders to help you when you run out of ideas. Instead of a file, this could be a simple sketch book of ideas.

The hardest of all is the experimental file because this indicates you will have to do some work on your own time. This is the synthesis of the other three files. Here is where you run an experimental lab. Say you have an idea on a layout that just won't gel by thinking or roughing it out. In this case you actually use dummy copy and dummy pictures, and paste up a layout with all elements in position. This helps you visualize a final result. It also helps uncover errors in thinking.

Ideas are nebulous things at best. Truly creative people are rare. But we can all develop a good, workable "idea file" system. There is another facet to the "idea file" system. Publishing is a fluid field. New publications are always opening up. People move, become unhappy with their present jobs, relocate, or sometimes just give up publishing for greener pastures. This creates openings. Publishers look for people with ideas. The best resumé you can present is a portfolio of ideas you have mastered. If you are now using two-column formats, experiment with three-column. If you are well acquainted with both, try the Midwest style. If that doesn't appeal to you, try the grid or modular formats.

Does innovation have a saturation point? I think this may well depend on how far you go and can find applications within your publication. Examine other magazines. Follow the good ones. You will notice that the good ones have an acceptable style and use innovation only for impact. There are others that feel innovation means topping each issue with something they haven't used before. Beware of them. Each issue becomes a continual exercise in futility.

Where does one find ideas? Another pertinent question. Besides searching other publications, write for free brochures that might interest you. Paper companies offer good ones. Keep your eyes open and all your senses alert. You never know when an idea will occur. Even such simple, mundane things as floor tile arrangement means someone has already solved a problem in arranging geometric shapes in a different or provocative way. Look for two-color combinations. Here again, you must realize that people may face different problems in different ways, but the final result could solve a problem for you once you apply the premise. An example of the mundane would be shoe ads and wedding ring ads. Here are two products that have almost the same shape to work with every time. Yet creative people manage to solve the problem on a weekly basis. Observe, search, and apply.

By all means, study your competition. You can rarely defeat an opponent without doing this. Often the competition can give you an edge in persuading management to try an innovative idea. This is a competitive business. Learn all the tricks you can, short of direct copying.

The hardest place to apply innovative ideas is in trade journals. Assume you have a position on a magazine that has a building-products market. Doing layouts that illustrate sheets of plywood, cement blocks, or machinery seems pretty dull. Your first thought might be, "How many possible ways can I illustrate a building block?" The innovative approach here is a little more subtle. There are two approaches. Call a building-block manufacturer. Explain that you have a problem and would like information on building blocks. If possible, take notes. You will find, as in copywriting, that there are some "key words" or "key phrases." List these. Handle each one as an idea starter and list all possibilities. These key words could give you a new approach, and your readership will feel you know something about the product.

The other is to list *all* possible ways you might use a building block or blocks, even though they have no *direct* application at the time. For instance, paint the blocks bright colors and use them as flower pots; paint them white and use fluorescent paint on them for house numbers at your curbstone; use them as umbrella stands; visualize the cement texture as a background shape for a blurb. Remember, each of these ideas should be only a starter.

Innovative layouts almost always depend on how you use the pictures. You can be innovative once with a table of contents, with a masthead, with an editorial page, and perhaps with a format, but you simply can't change every month. You should have some knowledge of photography. It would do you good to go to your local library and review past issues of photography and camera magazines. This is where much of the experimental work is being done that could affect you in the future. By all means talk things over with your platemaker or printing salesperson. Once they know you are interested, many of them will simply flood you with related information.

The hardest part about innovation is that it indicates you might have to do something extra. That's also the hardest part of being a leader in anything. If you don't take the time, you may be a follower all your life.

CHAPTER TWENTY-FIVE

Counterpoint

Magazine pages should have good balance and design. Balance and design should be subtle but positive. The best page designs are functional without gimmicks or design tricks.

Good page designs can be achieved by the use of functional positioning of all the page elements. It is a good idea to keep a "morgue" of interesting ideas to supplement the basics. The difference between a "hack" and a

"pro" is how the basic positions are made to serve a purpose. There is a great similarity between good page layouts and good music. The melody (or theme) is there, but it is the "counterpoint" that emphasizes it, shapes it, accentuates it, and increases the value of the melody. Another simile might be a master chef who turns a beef roast into a culinary delight by adding one's own "counterpoints" in seasonings.

In each of the following counterpoint discussions, I will use one elemental and basic layout design. One design and the subtle variations on it can apply to any design function.

White versus Black

Since the majority of magazines are printed in monotones, that is, blacks, whites, and grays, one

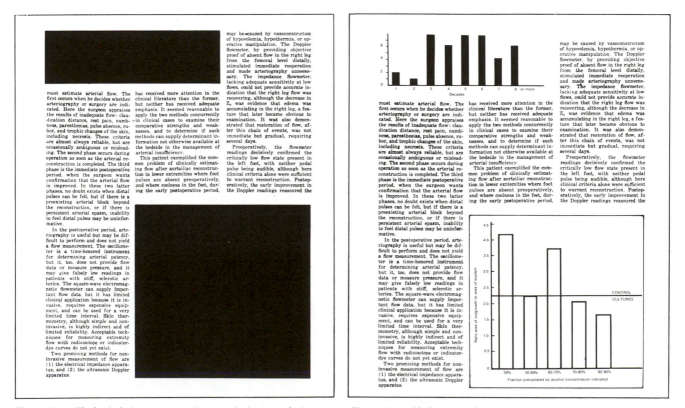

Figure 25.1—The basic design, a square picture and a horizontal picture.

Figure 25.2—Black versus white. Notice how your eye moves back and forth on a diagonal, comparing both size and weight.

must start with these three tone values as basics. Figure 25.1 shows a page with a square picture area and a horizontal picture area. This idea is often used, with the square and horizontal "played" against each other. Where does counterpoint come in? One must look *within* the pictures. For example, if the square picture were a forest of pine trees, it would have a feeling of many verticals. This "pattern" can be increased by placing it within a horizontal area. Strong vertical patterns within pictures also have a tendency to accentuate the vertical patterns of the copy columns. Changing the tone values of the pictures will also change their layout values. For instance, a square that is very dark will dominate a larger horizontal that is light. Black (or dark) horizontals will also increase the value if bled off the page.

What if both pictures were line drawings? One might be inclined to say that the relative "values" are the same. A simple counterpoint is to reverse the smaller area, making the copy white against a dark background. This gives a white versus black counterpoint.

Halftones versus Four-Color

One error many layout artists make is to use four-color just because it is available. It is true that color talks and carries messages with power. But this can be lost when overdone. Actually, color receives more attention when countered with an opposite, such as a halftone (black, gray, and white) or a line drawing in black or a strong color.

There are two basic variations in a "one-page functional design." One picture can be in four-color, with the other as a halftone or one-color rendering. This can become a trap for the unwary because both four-color pictures and halftones have variations in tonal values. The color may be sharp and brilliant and the halftone washed out and gray. Or, the color might be subdued and the halftone sharp and clear. If the color and halftone are similar in tone values, there is no

counterpoint but rather a balance. The brighter the smaller of the two areas, the more page interaction there is.

Color versus Color

Color creates movement and attention. This is particularly true of color opposites. It is *not* true of pastels or similar shades of the same color. Light blue versus light blue, for example, has no movement at all. Light blue with pink is the same, even though they are two different colors. Counterpoint means using color interaction for a purpose.

Motion versus Stability

Every picture has some movement within it. In many cases, this movement can be accentuated, emphasized, minimized, expanded, or contained. Basically, horizontal forms cause your eyes to move left and right. Verticals cause your eyes to move up and down. Squares are

Figure 25.3—Visualize the larger picture in four-color. Notice how your eye will move back and forth on a diagonal trying to decide if both pictures are identical. This illustrates how a halftone can detract from four-color, even though smaller in size.

Figure 25.4—Two identical tone values. Even though one is larger, there is very little counterpoint because they are similar.

must estimate arterial flow. The first occurs when he decides whether arteriography or surgery are indicated. Here the surgeon appraises the results of inadequate flow: claudication distance, rest pain, numbness, paresthesias, pulse absence, rubor, and trophic changes of the skin, including necrosis. These criteria are almost always reliable, but are occasionally ambiguous or misleading. The second phase occurs during operation as soon as the arterial reconstruction is completed. The third phase is the immediate postoperative period, when the surgeon wants confirmation that the arterial flow is improved. In these two latter phases, no doubt exists when distal pulses can be felt, but if there is a preexisting arterial block beyond the reconstruction, or if there is persistent arterial spasm, inability to feel distal pulses may be uninformative.

In the postoperative period, arteriography is useful but may be difficult to perform and does not yield a flow measurement. The oscillometer is a time-honored instrument for determining arterial patency, but it, too, does not provide flow data or measure pressure, and it may give falsely low readings in patients with stiff, sclerotic arteries. The square-wave electromagnetic flowmeter can supply important flow data, but it has limited clinical application because it is invasive, requires expensive equipment, and can be used for a very limited time interval. Skin thermometry, although simple and noninvasive, is highly indirect and of limited reliability. Acceptable techniques for measuring extremity flow with radioisotope or indicator-dye curves do not yet exist.

Two promising methods for noninvasive measurement of flow are (1) the electrical impedance apparatus, and (2) the ultrasonic Doppler apparatus.

has received more attention in the clinical literature than the former, but neither has received adequate emphasis. It seemed reasonable to apply the two methods concurrently in clinical cases to examine their comparative strengths and weaknesses, and to determine if such methods can supply determinant information not otherwise available at the bedside in the management of arterial insufficiency.

This patient exemplified the common problem of clinically estimating flow after aortoiliac reconstruction in lower extremities where foot pulses are absent preoperatively, and where coolness in the feet, during the early postoperative period,

may be caused by vasoconstriction of hypovolemia, hypothermia, or operative manipulation. The Doppler flowmeter, by providing objective proof of absent flow in the right leg from the femoral level distally, stimulated immediate reoperation and made arteriography unnecessary. The impedance flowmeter, lacking adequate sensitivity at low flows, could not provide accurate indication that the right leg flow was recovering, although the decrease in Z_0 was evidence that edema was accumulating in the right leg, a feature that later became obvious to examination. It was also demonstrated that restoration of flow, after this chain of events, was not immediate but gradual, requiring several days.

Preoperatively, the flowmeter readings decisively confirmed the critically low flow state present in the left foot, with neither pedal pulse being audible, although here clinical criteria alone were sufficient to warrant reconstruction. Postoperatively, the early improvement in the Doppler readings reassured the

Figure 25.5—Two different tone values. Now we have weight (or color) versus weight (or color), and there is counterpoint.

must estimate arterial flow. The first occurs when he decides whether arteriography or surgery are indicated. Here the surgeon appraises the results of inadequate flow: claudication distance, rest pain, numbness, paresthesias, pulse absence, rubor, and trophic changes of the skin, including necrosis. These criteria are almost always reliable, but are occasionally ambiguous or misleading. The second phase occurs during operation as soon as the arterial reconstruction is completed. The third phase is the immediate postoperative period, when the surgeon wants confirmation that the arterial flow is improved. In these two latter phases, no doubt exists when distal pulses can be felt, but if there is a preexisting arterial block beyond the reconstruction, or if there is persistent arterial spasm, inability to feel distal pulses may be uninformative.

In the postoperative period, arteriography is useful but may be difficult to perform and does not yield a flow measurement. The oscillometer is a time-honored instrument for determining arterial patency, but it, too, does not provide flow data or measure pressure, and it may give falsely low readings in patients with stiff, sclerotic arteries. The square-wave electromagnetic flowmeter can supply important flow data, but it has limited clinical application because it is invasive, requires expensive equipment, and can be used for a very limited time interval. Skin thermometry, although simple and noninvasive, is highly indirect and of limited reliability. Acceptable techniques for measuring extremity flow with radioisotope or indicator-dye curves do not yet exist.

Two promising methods for noninvasive measurement of flow are (1) the electrical impedance apparatus, and (2) the ultrasonic Doppler apparatus.

has received more attention in the clinical literature than the former, but neither has received adequate emphasis. It seemed reasonable to apply the two methods concurrently in clinical cases to examine their comparative strengths and weaknesses, and to determine if such methods can supply determinant information not otherwise available at the bedside in the management of arterial insufficiency.

This patient exemplified the common problem of clinically estimating flow after aortoiliac reconstruction in lower extremities where foot pulses are absent preoperatively, and where coolness in the feet, during the early postoperative period,

may be caused by vasoconstriction of hypovolemia, hypothermia, or operative manipulation. The Doppler flowmeter, by providing objective proof of absent flow in the right leg from the femoral level distally, stimulated immediate reoperation and made arteriography unnecessary. The impedance flowmeter, lacking adequate sensitivity at low flows, could not provide accurate indication that the right leg flow was recovering, although the decrease in Z_0 was evidence that edema was accumulating in the right leg, a feature that later became obvious to examination. It was also demonstrated that restoration of flow, after this chain of events, was not immediate but gradual, requiring several days.

Preoperatively, the flowmeter readings decisively confirmed the critically low flow state present in the left foot, with neither pedal pulse being audible, although here clinical criteria alone were sufficient to warrant reconstruction. Postoperatively, the early improvement in the Doppler readings reassured the

Figure 25.6—Motion versus stability. Notice how the motion at lower right continually points you back to the picture at upper left.

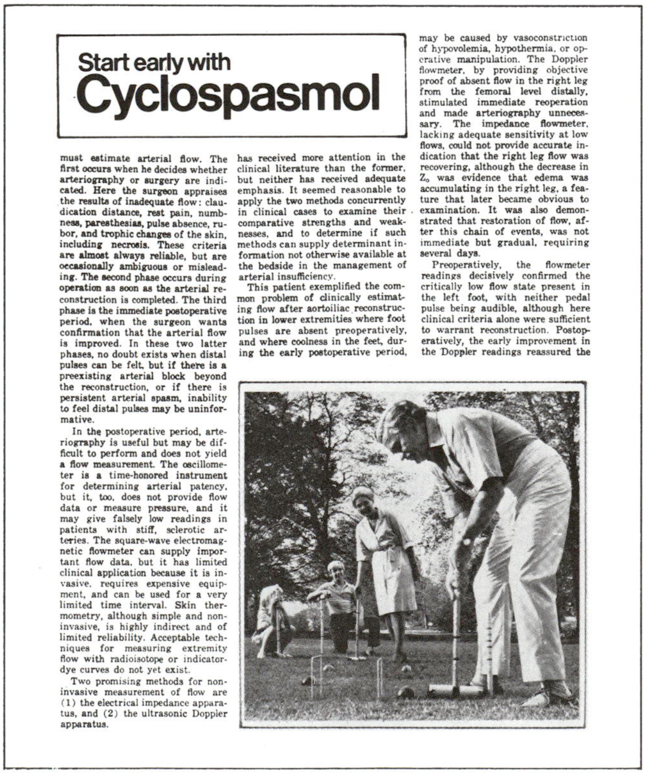

Start early with
Cyclospasmol

must estimate arterial flow. The first occurs when he decides whether arteriography or surgery are indicated. Here the surgeon appraises the results of inadequate flow: claudication distance, rest pain, numbness, paresthesias, pulse absence, rubor, and trophic changes of the skin, including necrosis. These criteria are almost always reliable, but are occasionally ambiguous or misleading. The second phase occurs during operation as soon as the arterial reconstruction is completed. The third phase is the immediate postoperative period, when the surgeon wants confirmation that the arterial flow is improved. In these two latter phases, no doubt exists when distal pulses can be felt, but if there is a preexisting arterial block beyond the reconstruction, or if there is persistent arterial spasm, inability to feel distal pulses may be uninformative.

In the postoperative period, arteriography is useful but may be difficult to perform and does not yield a flow measurement. The oscillometer is a time-honored instrument for determining arterial patency, but it, too, does not provide flow data or measure pressure, and it may give falsely low readings in patients with stiff, sclerotic arteries. The square-wave electromagnetic flowmeter can supply important flow data, but it has limited clinical application because it is invasive, requires expensive equipment, and can be used for a very limited time interval. Skin thermometry, although simple and noninvasive, is highly indirect and of limited reliability. Acceptable techniques for measuring extremity flow with radioisotope or indicator-dye curves do not yet exist.

Two promising methods for noninvasive measurement of flow are (1) the electrical impedance apparatus, and (2) the ultrasonic Doppler apparatus.

has received more attention in the clinical literature than the former, but neither has received adequate emphasis. It seemed reasonable to apply the two methods concurrently in clinical cases to examine their comparative strengths and weaknesses, and to determine if such methods can supply determinant information not otherwise available at the bedside in the management of arterial insufficiency.

This patient exemplified the common problem of clinically estimating flow after aortoiliac reconstruction in lower extremities where foot pulses are absent preoperatively, and where coolness in the feet, during the early postoperative period,

may be caused by vasoconstriction of hypovolemia, hypothermia, or operative manipulation. The Doppler flowmeter, by providing objective proof of absent flow in the right leg from the femoral level distally, stimulated immediate reoperation and made arteriography unnecessary. The impedance flowmeter, lacking adequate sensitivity at low flows, could not provide accurate indication that the right leg flow was recovering, although the decrease in Z_0 was evidence that edema was accumulating in the right leg, a feature that later became obvious to examination. It was also demonstrated that restoration of flow, after this chain of events, was not immediate but gradual, requiring several days.

Preoperatively, the flowmeter readings decisively confirmed the critically low flow state present in the left foot, with neither pedal pulse being audible, although here clinical criteria alone were sufficient to warrant reconstruction. Postoperatively, the early improvement in the Doppler readings reassured the

Figure 25.7—Line versus halftone. The title is read first, but then the eye moves down to the picture.

must estimate arterial flow. The first occurs when he decides whether arteriography or surgery are indicated. Here the surgeon appraises the results of inadequate flow: claudication distance, rest pain, numbness, paresthesias, pulse absence, rubor, and trophic changes of the skin, including necrosis. These criteria are almost always reliable, but are occasionally ambiguous or misleading. The second phase occurs during operation as soon as the arterial reconstruction is completed. The third phase is the immediate postoperative period, when the surgeon wants confirmation that the arterial flow is improved. In these two latter phases, no doubt exists when distal pulses can be felt, but if there is a preexisting arterial block beyond the reconstruction, or if there is persistent arterial spasm, inability to feel distal pulses may be uninformative.

In the postoperative period, arteriography is useful but may be difficult to perform and does not yield a flow measurement. The oscillometer is a time-honored instrument for determining arterial patency, but it, too, does not provide flow data or measure pressure, and it may give falsely low readings in patients with stiff, sclerotic arteries. The square-wave electromagnetic flowmeter can supply important flow data, but it has limited clinical application because it is invasive, requires expensive equipment, and can be used for a very limited time interval. Skin thermometry, although simple and noninvasive, is highly indirect and of limited reliability. Acceptable techniques for measuring extremity flow with radioisotope or indicator-dye curves do not yet exist.

Two promising methods for noninvasive measurement of flow are (1) the electrical impedance apparatus, and (2) the ultrasonic Doppler apparatus.

has received more attention in the clinical literature than the former, but neither has received adequate emphasis. It seemed reasonable to apply the two methods concurrently in clinical cases to examine their comparative strengths and weaknesses, and to determine if such methods can supply determinant information not otherwise available at the bedside in the management of arterial insufficiency.

This patient exemplified the common problem of clinically estimating flow after aortoiliac reconstruction in lower extremities where foot pulses are absent preoperatively, and where coolness in the feet, during the early postoperative period,

may be caused by vasoconstriction of hypovolemia, hypothermia, or operative manipulation. The Doppler flowmeter, by providing objective proof of absent flow in the right leg from the femoral level distally, stimulated immediate reoperation and made arteriography unnecessary. The impedance flowmeter, lacking adequate sensitivity at low flows, could not provide accurate indication that the right leg flow was recovering, although the decrease in Z_0 was evidence that edema was accumulating in the right leg, a feature that later became obvious to examination. It was also demonstrated that restoration of flow, after this chain of events, was not immediate but gradual, requiring several days.

Preoperatively, the flowmeter readings decisively confirmed the critically low flow state present in the left foot, with neither pedal pulse being audible, although here clinical criteria alone were sufficient to warrant reconstruction. Postoperatively, the early improvement in the Doppler readings reassured the

Figure 25.8—An outline halftone versus a square halftone. Even though the square is larger, the outline draws more attention.

stable. These three basics are called control devices. A strong horizontal picture can be minimized by enclosing it within a square. A stable picture can be made to move by changing its shape to a horizontal or vertical. Let us take these control devices and utilize them in counterpoint.

A picture containing a vertical pattern, such as rows of corn, tall trees, a city skyline, or people standing in a group, can be: *accentuated* by making the containing device a vertical; *emphasized* by making the containing device also a vertical, plus adding a ruled box in a color; *minimized* by making the containing device a horizontal; and *expanded* by outlining and placing at the top of a page. A containing device does *not* mean losing control of the movement. Even an outline has a controllable form.

A picture containing a horizontal pattern, such as a broad landscape, an automobile, or anything having a naturally elongated pattern, can be: *accentuated* by making the containing device also horizontal; *emphasized* by making the containing device a horizontal and adding a ruled box, either in color or black; *minimized* by making the containing device a vertical or by adding a color or black-or-white ruled box within the containing pattern; *expanded* by outlining and placing at the top of a page.

Pictures containing patterns other than simple horizontals and verticals break down into diagonal movements, spiral or circular movements, sawtooth movements, wavy movements, and pyramid movements. The only other form might be movements which have two or more changes in direction. Almost all patterns fall into these groups. In *all* cases, changing from a halftone to line will strengthen the movement.

Most halftones are subtle. Line drawings are never subtle. Here are some counterpoints and adaptations of each.

Diagonals

Diagonal patterns move from corner to opposite corner. There are several ways to handle strong diagonal movements: *accentuate* by using a narrower width; *emphasize* by tilting or cropping to a more pronounced angle; *minimize* by complementing with color in the opposite direction or straightening out by recropping; *expand* by complementing with a color in the same direction.

Spirals and Circles

Spiral and circular patterns most often have a central point of interest, and all movement is around this point. This movement is more subdued than the strong directionals. Spirals and circles are generally used within a square container as opposed to horizontal or vertical areas. They can be handled as follows: *accentuate*, once the central point of interest has been determined, by "highlighting" the area with either a color or white space; *emphasize* by changing the shape of the container to match the general shape of the movement; *minimize* by enclosing with rules or boxes, in color; and *expand* by letting them "float" in white space, creating their own center of action.

Sawtooth Patterns

Sawtooth patterns are typified by strong up-and-down motions or forms. They are difficult to contain or even subdue. The motion causes visual vibrations that will exist even within other forms or shapes. The best way is to *use* them, accepting their form or movement as an attribute rather than a problem area. Place a sawtooth on a quiet page and see what happens! Do *not* use it with another pattern on the same page. This will only cause confusion.

Wavy Patterns

Wavy patterns are usually stronger horizontally than vertically. The horizontal shape will control the movement, while a vertical will minimize it. Here are some ways to utilize it: *accentuate* by utilizing the horizontal shape or by tilting it within a horizontal shape; *emphasize* by repeating the wavy lines in a motif, particularly in color; *minimize* by using a vertical shape or container (another method is to pacify the waves by using a dominant series of horizontal rules in color); *expand* by enlarging any or all of it.

Pyramids

Pyramids almost always act as "pointers." These are used as "leaders," drawing one's glance to another picture, across the gutter, to a title area, or to another page. Here are some ways to handle them: *accentuate* by cropping to stress the pyramid pattern and increase the value of the point; *emphasize* by outlining, to strengthen the point value; *minimize* by surrounding the point with more picture area or by containing it within a box; and *expand* by increasing its size.

Change of Direction

Change of direction occurs when there are two or more movements within the picture. Many pictures do not easily fall into one movement. Several movements within a picture will, generally, tend to cancel each other out or create a more stable feeling. This may be desirable. In some cases this can be counterpointed by mortising into another picture with movements equal to the stronger movement in the original. Very often judicious cropping can change two directions into one.

Modifying Forms

Any form can be strengthened by "shadowing" or "outlining." Any form can be minimized by reducing it in size. Any form can be emphasized by the use of color. Any form can be expanded by enlarging or using double-ruled boxes. Any form, repeated, will stabilize, particularly when in the same size. Any form will create imbalance in two different sizes. Two "same size" forms can create motion when one is dark and the other is light or when two opposite colors are used. They will do the same when one is a line drawing and the other is a halftone.

CHAPTER TWENTY-SIX

Trends and Techniques

The layout artist is rarely an isolated individual. It may be true that the magazine he or she is working on may have an extremely limited audience—like *Gladiolas for Fun and Profit* (a fictitious title)—but the good layout artist is a constant observer and keeps files, either mentally or in a morgue. Many keep file cards arranged by subject matter. A simple sketch can usually provoke sufficient recall to apply an idea.

It is a rare layout artist who initiates a trend or technique. More often than not, a good idea is pirated as soon as it's published. Many of you recall the famous Alka Seltzer commercial "I ate the *whole* thing." Within two months everyone was on the same track. The phrase was applied to almost everything. And, like a million army ants, they quickly demolished the phrase.

We have another example in posterization (covered in chapter 30). The original is lost. It might well have been an honest mistake (ordering line instead of halftone) and too late to do much about it. The result was an interesting effect that took hold and was immediately beaten to death. But, file the idea away! The interesting thing about trends is that some layout artists follow them so closely that they do not apply them correctly.

Another trend was "boxing." The follower boxes everything, sometimes even title areas. The good layout artist knows there is an application for boxing and uses it with purpose and discretion.

A relatively new trend, as this is written, is polarization. This is a technique similar to posterization in that the result is achieved by three different time sequence line negatives of the same subject. The colors are garish and vibrant. The result is eye-stopping. There may be a purpose, a once-a-year application, maybe on Halloween. The followers will also beat this into the ground, applying it everywhere.

Decorative initials come and go, being constantly rediscovered. So does Cheltenham Bold. You can almost count on a Cheltenham Bold revival every ten years or so. Decorative *initials* should be used for a purpose and not simply decorating. Decorative *rules* have a habit of reviving every so often, too. Check with any typesetter and you'll find she or he generally stocks all three, knowing full well it will only be a matter of time before they're used again.

People are "idea triggered" to symbols. Someone says "Halloween," and we think of a witch or pumpkin; goblins, ghosts, and haunted houses come next. Hardly anyone thinks in "opposites" or intimations. For instance, wouldn't a cherub and a goblin create more of an effect than just a goblin? Wouldn't a smiling grandmother make the reader wonder why this peaceful, obviously good old soul is used as a Halloween symbol?

The others are obvious—rabbits and eggs for Easter, Santa Claus and gifts for Christmas, turkey and Pilgrims for Thanksgiving, and boy babies blue, girl babies pink. I don't feel any reader is dumb. He or she doesn't need being clubbed with a symbol. I believe that a Christmas issue with only a smattering of seasonal stories and illustrations is far more effective than a conglomerate of "same-theme" stories and symbols. I feel type designs such as the word "cold" in snow-covered letters is repeated to death.

Copying a good trend or technique is not lazy, provided the results you achieve create your own special feeling. Trends, like clothing styles, are not for everyone. Find your own style. Use variations of the same theme but don't copy just to be in fashion. The results can often be disastrous.

As this is written, another art trend is starting—the "paint by numbers" style. Line drawings are made from halftones (usually people), and each area is outlined. The end result looks like one could almost add color to certain areas and create an oil painting.

Techniques vary from trends. A trend is a layout style that is repeated by all. A technique is a way, or method, of achieving a desired result by using the platemaker to develop your idea into a finished product. Some call this "mechanical art." I prefer to call it "graphics."

As an example, a simple halftone picture can be used to achieve many final results. "Fogging" certain areas by having the plate-

The Ages of Man

T lerstein in 1969 reported the results of physical training in 203 subjects who had angina pectoris or previous myocardial infarction. They participated in at least a thrice-weekly exercise program which consisted of calisthenics, run-walk sequences, and recreational activities and were followed up for an average of 2.7 years. Detailed results were presented on the first 100 patients. The average weight loss was 2.5 kg (5.5 lb) and 65 significantly improved their level of fitness as measured by bicycle ergometric testing and oxygen consumption. Sixty-three percent showed improvement in their exercise ECGs, mainly in the terms of initial slope and the junctional displacement of the S-T segment. The death rate for the exercising cardiac patients was 1.9 per 100 patients yearly, which was less than half of the expected rate; however, no comparable control group was specifically studied.

In early 1972, Rechnitzer et al reported on a group of 68 male subjects with previous myocardial infarction who participated in a program of graduated exercises over a seven-year period. A control group of 127 patients fulfilled criteria to enter the program but for various reasons were not included. Of the exercising subjects, 3.0% had nonfatal recurrence of myocardial infarction compared to 11.1% of the nonexercising control subjects who had nonfatal recurrence. The incidence of cardiac death (7.6%) was significantly less ($P<.005$) in the exercising subjects than in the 127 control subjects. Re- and 15 (11.8%) deaths in the Toronto control group.

Boyer has recently described a program of physical activity following myocardial infarction that consists of progressive intensity of exercise starting with swimming, then a walk-jog phase with calisthenics for warm-up exercises, followed later in the program by an endurance phase and group exercise. All phases of the program are monitored by heart rate check at 3, 6, and 12 months, followed by a six-month follow-up exercise testing. This program and the long-term follow-up investigation are now underway.

Currently, Morgan is studying supervised physical training in 23 men with recent myocardial infarction compared with 22 nonexercising patients with myocardial infarction. The method of selection for the nonexercisers is not specified. The exercisers trained three times weekly for three months in a hospital gym. One patient in each group has died. A significant ($P<.05$) decrease in resting and exercising heart rates occurred in the exercise group. A smaller and insignificant fall occurred in the controls.

Although no control group has been studied, the results of our program at this time are consistent in some ways, but not in others, with the aforementioned reported studies. The increase in STET time (as a measure of exercise capacity) from baseline to the three-month follow-up from three to eight minutes (Fig 1) in 33 of the 42 patients reflects notable improve- the mean value decrease for all 42 patients from initial to three-month follow-up testing was statistically significant ($P<.05$). Twenty-four of 42 patients (57%) decreased their blood pressure with peak exercise, and the mean value for all patients decreased significantly (with peak exercise) from the initial to the three-month follow-up testing ($P<.05$). Twenty-seven of 42 patients (52%) decreased their blood pressure at two minutes after exercise. Although these alterations are not too impressive, the fact that more than 50% of all 42 patients lowered their resting blood pressure after training without alteration in diet or blood pressure therapy is notable. Statistically significant changes in mean values at rest and peak exercises are also notable even with the small number of total patients.

More impressive were the data on change in resting heart rate; 25 of the 42 patients (60%) decreased their rate by five beats per minute and the mean value decrease for all patients was statistically significant ($P<.05$). This is consistent with the results of Frick and Katila and Morgan et al. Of nine patients (21%) who had an increase in resting heart rate after three months of training, two had a history of severe myocardial infarction and were thought to have considerable residual cardiac damage; three had recurrences of angina pectoris during the training period and were limited in their progress and believed not to be as well trained as the others. Of the other four with increase in

Figure 26.1—A "stand-up initial" using a decorative capital.

The Ages of Man

T times coexisting abnormalities missed. Slightly less than four of the patients with stomatitis o roentgenographic abnormalities; 71% of marginal ulcers were not seen roentgenographically and none of the patients with a double-barrel stoma and associated pathological condition were recognized. Neither patient with intussusception had roentgenographic evidence of such an event. The gastrocolic fistula was diagnosed by barium enema examination, not by upper gastrointestinal x-ray films.

Six patients exhibited persistent roentgenographic "filling defects" suggestive of ulceration; four defects were at the anastomosis and two were in the gastric pouch. Endoscopy revealed all these abnormalities to be surgical defects. All six patients exhibited vague abdominal complaints that were subsequently shown to be due to lactose intolerance in five and vascular insufficiency in one.

The combination of 25 false-negative and 6 false-positive findings (not including those patients in whom coexisting abnormalities were missed) gave a roentgenographic accuracy of 38% in evaluation of patients in this series. Roentgenographic examination was inadequate in identifying the superficial mucosal lesions and the anatomic abnormalities. Roentgenographic examination was accurate in our few cases in indicating the presence of anastomotic stenosis. It was also accurate in indicating gastric and jejunal ulcers; however, there strongly suggest that patients with postgastrectomy complaints of a mechanical-pathological nature cannot be considered to have had a thorough work-up until endoscopic examination has been performed.

Radiologic examination, long considered the mainstay of diagnosis, has been hindered by three factors: first, the creation of postsurgical anastomotic artifacts; second, the high intraabdominal anastomoses limiting the use of compression films; and third, the lack of definition of mucosal details. A review of the literature showed wide variation in the reported accuracy of radiologic examination in following up gastrectomy patients. Everson and Allen, in a review of 90 patients with marginal ulcers, reported "conclusive establishment" of diagnosis by barium x-ray studies in 70 patients. Ellis reported an 80% accuracy in those with gastroenterostomy. Hirschowitz and Luketic, on the other hand, reported an accuracy of 36% in diagnosis of marginal ulceration. The 29% accuracy in the present study was even less optimistic.

Superficial inflammatory lesions such as gastritis, stomatitis, and jejunitis as well as anatomical lesions such as double-barrel stoma were seldom detected roentgenographically. Reported results showed less than a 10% roentgenographic accuracy in diagnosis. The present study showed equally disappointing roentgenographic results.

Thirty-eight, or 76%, of our symp- orrhage, or iron deficiency anemia may be present. The endoscopic demonstration of stomatitis, however, has not been well correlated with symptom complexes. A medical regimen should be tried in that many experience symptomatic relief.

Marginal ulceration was diagnosed in 13 patients and was the second most frequent abnormality. Recurrent ulceration has been reported in from 1% to 6% of patients having vagotomy and hemigastrectomy and in 30% of patients having gastroenterostomy without vagotomy. Endoscopically, the ulcer appeared as a discrete lesion located near the stoma, generally on the jejunal side of the anastomosis. Stomatitis or jejunitis may also be present. The cause of marginal ulceration has not been fully understood; however, intestinal alkaline reflux as well as gastric acidity may be important factors. The protrusion of nonabsorbable suture material at the anastomosis (suture-line ulcer) may be of significance on occasion. Pain, hemorrhage, and obstruction were frequently associated with marginal ulcerations. Endoscopy was often required for accurate diagnosis of marginal ulceration. Medical therapy has been frequently inadequate; surgical therapy has been reviewed by Andrios et al, and Kiefer.

A double-barrel stoma was seen in four patients and was associated with mucosal inflammation in every instance. The double-barrel stoma has been recently recognized as an anatomical arrangement of the efferent

Figure 26.2—An "indented initial" using a decorative capital.

maker shoot for one area and then washing out the rest is a "technique." Using a "split image" is a technique. This involves making two identical negatives, cutting each in half, flopping one half, and stripping it together with its identical half. Making part of the halftone line, the rest halftone, and adding color to the line is also a graphic technique. Superimposing enlarged or reduced areas of the same subject within the same picture, occasionally by "flopping," is another. Enlarging the halftone proof (with the dot structure already in) and using only one interesting part with a blowup of the dot structure will give an interesting design effect.

Experiment, have frequent consultations with your platemaker, keep constantly aware of new techniques by observing and asking yourself, How was this done? Build up a morgue of techniques. You'll soon be developing your own. Just be careful with techniques or you'll start a trend.

The Ages of Man

T No one really knows what causes Bell palsy, and its treatment has for years been a matter of controversy, complicated by the high incidence of spontaneous recovery.

During the past two decades, several groups have advocated corticosteroid treatment for Bell palsy. Apparently, the most compelling published report on the benefits of such therapy is that of Kedar K. Adour, MD, and colleagues at the Facial Paralysis Research Clinic at the Kaiser-Permanente Medical Center, Oakland, Calif. The report appeared in the Dec 21, 1972, issue of *The New England Journal of Medicine*.

The Kaiser group reported that 67.5% of 194 prednisone-treated patients had complete recovery of facial function compared to 42.7% of 110 patients, studied retrospectively, who had received no treatment. A prospective double-blind study had been started but was abandoned, the investigators said, because pain relief with prednisone proved so superior. The prednisone dosage was 60 mg daily for the first four days, tapering to 5 mg by the tenth day.

Now a Pittsburgh otolaryngologist, formerly at Washington University School of Medicine in St. Louis, has taken on the Adour study and reports that his own prospective, controlled, and double-blind study of 51 patients shows that corticosteroid treatment is no better than placebo.

The two-year study was carried out by Mark May, MD, now associate professor of otolaryngology at the University of Pittsburgh, Reimut Wette, PhD, professor of biostatistics at Washington University School of Medicine, and William B. Hardin, Jr., MD, and John Sullivan, MD, both neurologists formerly associated with the Washington University School of Medicine. A report was made to the Atlanta meeting of the American Laryngological, Rhinological and Otological Society. The patients received either a prednisone-vitamin preparation—a total of 410 mg of prednisone designed to be taken in descending doses over ten days—or a vitamin preparation used as a placebo.

Only those patients were included in the study whose condition had been evaluated within two days of the onset of paralysis and whose treatment began within the same period. In the Adour study, the conditions of a quarter of the patients were initially evaluated after the third day and of another quarter after the seventh day. Dr. May believes that, to be effective, treatment must be started before any neuropathologic changes, and cited some evidence that such changes can occur within three days of onset of palsy.

Patients in Dr. May's study were followed up for six months after onset, compared to a "minimum follow-up of four months in the study by Adour. Although in most cases complications of faulty regeneration [of the nerve fibers] appears in four months," Dr. May said, "complications did not appear in five of our patients until six months postonset."

Patients in the St. Louis study were separated into four groups on the basis of results of two tests performed at the initial visit: the salivary flow test, and the maximal stimulation test (a test of nerve excitability that uses responses to maximal, rather than minimal, stimulation).

The four groups consisted of patients with (1) equal maximal stimulation response on both the normal and involved sides of the face; (2) lower (or absent) maximal stimulation response on the involved side; (3) salivary flow 26% or greater; and (4) salivary flow 25% or less. Dr. May said that the first and third groups were considered "favorable" from the prognostic viewpoint, while the second and fourth were considered "unfavorable."

The prednisone or placebo treatments were assigned at random to consecutive pairs of individuals admitted to each of these four groups. Neither the patients nor the physicians knew which treatment had been assigned. Dr. May pointed out that the latter was not true in the Adour study.

Patients were given analgesics as needed as well as ophthalmic treatment that included methylcellulose 1% ophthalmic drops, a bland ophthalmic ointment for nighttime use, and a moisture chamber eye shield.

The degree of facial motor function and any further progression of impairment was noted on

continued on next page

Figure 26.3—A "hanging initial" using a decorative capital.

CHAPTER TWENTY-SEVEN

How to Use
That Second Color

Four-color printing costs more money these days, both to process and to produce. We are all interested in ways to save money and still give fair value. There are many ways you *can* create an attractive-looking magazine without four-color. You want to do this at the least possible cost and effort simply to stay in this competitive business. Eliminating four-color and reverting to black-and-white is "polarized thinking." The reader knows the difference and might feel cheated.

Many of you may visualize a "second color" as one of the "4-A colors" or one of the process colors (process red or cyan) simply because this is what you have been accustomed to using. There is nothing wrong with this. You also are probably aware of the limitations some of these colors have in standard usage. For a few pennies more you can choose any one of the many PMS premixed colors. There are many PMS colors, but I shall illustrate this chapter with PMS 471—a warm brown.

"Warm brown" is compatible with both black and white, balances well with white space design elements, and appeals to most people. Many of you are too young to remember the Sunday newspaper supplement called the *Rotogravure* section. This was the newspaper's answer to "color" before four-color became workable. It was usually printed in a Van Dyke brown. All the type, all the halftones, and all the line drawings appeared in

this shade of brown. It was also printed on a "slick" paper to represent elegance. The only thing wrong with it was that the color so dominated the section that it became rather boring. It was used, but not used effectively.

One thing I shall try to do in this chapter is to show you how to use variations of second-color usage without getting boring. You will see that each is fully described as to technique. Since each of you is a thinking individual, I feel sure that what I describe here will bear much fruit. I will give you the tools. Once you learn how to use them, you can practice your own variables.

A magazine cover should draw attention. This may sound a little difficult using only brown, black, and white. I start out with an average halftone picture, but study it closely to determine how I might use a second color to advantage. I must be aware of the fact that white can often be thought of as a third color. The result is shown in figure 27.1. I outlined the subject on a tissue overlay and specified it to be shot as 100% PMS-471 brown. The background remains the usual gray halftone area. This makes the subject look as if it had been photographed in color. I have dropped out the background within the letters of the logo so they appear white against a darker background. I have chosen to use no story titles on this cover because the background and color detract from type identification or readability.

The illustrated table of contents shown in figure 27.2 uses a tint block, again with white helping the design. A "spot" of color will draw attention away from the advertisement. I have also been generous with white space in the contents area.

Figure 27.3 illustrates a story title in a solid color. Printing story titles in color has some ramifications. For example, yellow will not have enough substance to clearly define the letter shapes for good readability. There are few pastel shades that can be used in title areas. Be sure the color is strong enough to carry the letter shapes. One might also reverse a title out of a very dark color tint panel.

Figure 27.4 shows a simple pencil rendering of a high contrast halftone picture. It was then converted to a line photostat and the second color placed on an acetate flap to show exactly where it goes. Color is used to give a little added interest to a simple line drawing.

Figure 27.5 shows the "30 degree line technique." Tracing paper was placed over a high contrast halftone and a series of 30 degree lines were drawn in. Only enough lines were drawn to define the most important areas, primarily shadows and definition. The "blurb" bars and the lines of the drawing are then printed in a solid PMS-471.

Figure 27.6 shows the standard duotone using percentages of both black and PMS-471. A duotone is two halftone negatives of the same picture but with the dot structure

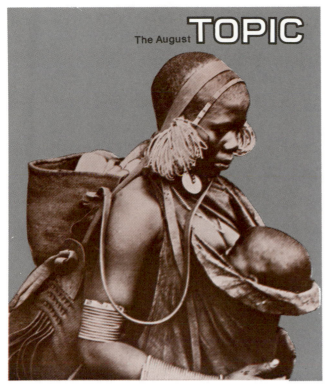

Figure 27.1—A cover using PMS-471. This combines black with white and a second color. Notice how a little preparation can give interesting results.

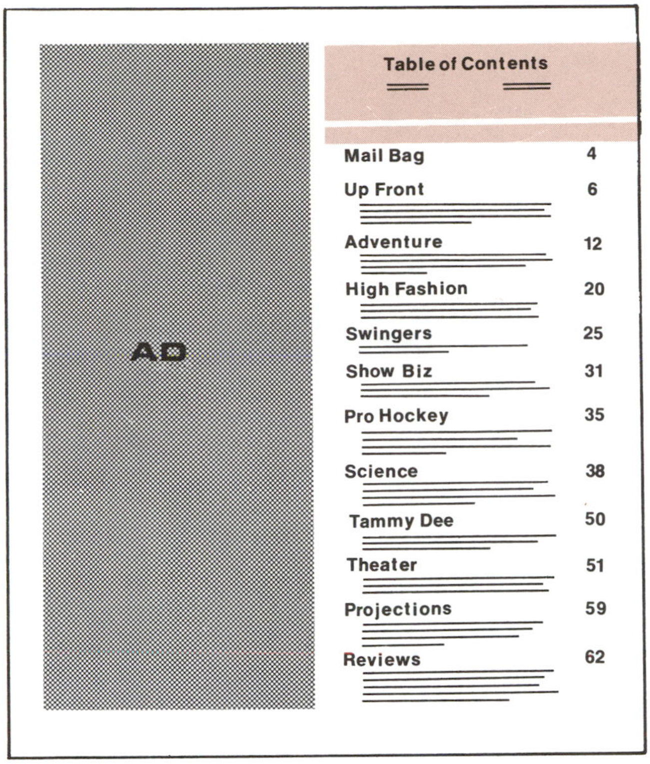

Figure 27.2—The table of contents using a tint of PMS-471.

Figure 27.3—A story title in solid PMS-471.

Figure 27.4—A pencil rendering with highlights, using a solid PMS-471.

The immigrant patiently waits contemplating a nebulous future.

Figure 27.5—The "30 degree line technique" with a color bar "blurb" using a solid PMS-471.

slightly tilted to give a dot combination of *both* colors. I have gone stronger on the brown in keeping with the subject material.

Figure 27.7 shows the same picture handled as a halftone, in black, and overprinting a PMS-471 tint block. As you can see, the duotone has more life and depth. The overprint simply lies flat.

Figure 27.8 shows how a color can be used to highlight the area. This could also have had the black halftone area "fogged" out to give a subdued effect.

Figure 27.9 shows how a "mezzotint" combined with a second color can give a new effect. There are many mezzotint patterns. All are prepared screens that give a new background to the area. Your printer can supply you with these or you can buy them at art supplies stores. They can be placed directly over a halftone prior to camera work.

Figure 27.10 illustrates "posterization." This simply means that the halftone picture is shot as a line drawing. Since there are no screen values used, the camera will pick up only white and black, with no tonal differences. The result is a rather posterlike rendering done mechanically.

Figure 27.11 shows "segmenting." The picture is pulled apart into segments that still have a relationship to the original. This can be used to tell the reader that the area segmented is important.

Figure 27.12 shows color combined with line and a halftone. It is used simply for an effect. The line part will draw attention first because it is a little unusual.

Figure 27.13 uses the outline halftone principle, but the outline is subdued. This was done by the "torn edge technique," which gives a rather muted effect rather than a hard-line edge. Color is added to highlight and give interest.

Figure 27.14 is posterization again, but placed over a tint block. In posterization, do not look for detail. Strive instead for the poster effect.

Figure 27.15 shows a technique used to draw attention to various parts *within* a picture. Frames point out various areas but still relate them to the whole.

Figure 27.16 illustrates a rather simple technique called "fragmenting" that can be used with pictures that have no important detail. The overall effect should be rather startling because it is unusual. This technique can be used on a cover or for a picture that calls for no explanation. Start with the halftone and cut it into strips of uneven widths, then rubber cement them down in a sort of "venetian blind" effect.

Figure 27.17 shows a picture di-

vided into areas by the use of tint blocks. This technique should be used sparingly.

One word of caution. These special effects lose impact with repetition. *Do not* fill the entire issue with as many techniques as you can drop in. Rather, use only one or two effectively.

Here are a few more ideas for your files: a hand-lettered title area, with almost all the letters filled in and still showing guidelines and some irregularities. This might be used to illustrate a story about an artist or the designing of a typeface. Using the "scratch technique," a picture can be created by placing a sheet of 20-gauge acetate over a photograph and, using a scratch-board knife, etching the picture on the acetate. An engraving-like quality is achieved by filling in the scratches with India ink and then rubbing it off again. Charcoal renderings can look even better if printed in a warm brown. Mortising, montages, combinations of tints in the same picture—each idea seems to have the ability to multiply within your imagination.

Your next logical question would be: What happens when we cannot specify a color of our choice?

Some second colors have limitations. Yellow, for example, can rarely be used. The lighter tints of orange and most pastel tints are too weak for second colors. Warm colors like orange, red, and brown will give entirely different results from the cold colors like some greens, blues, and purples. Some cold colors can become warm colors depending on their values, shades, or tints. Color is often an indication of personal feeling. Let us divide the techniques described in this chapter into color ranges and see how each changes the results. I shall classify the "use" as good, marginal, and negative.

1. Tint blocks with a black overprint:

Yellows—Marginal, almost negative. Very limited use.
Oranges—Marginal to good, depending on tint, shade, and tone.
Reds—Marginal to negative. Red and black tend to visually "blend," and shades and tints of red often appear pink.
Greens—Good as long as the shade is not too deep.
Blues—Good as long as the shade is not too deep.
Purples—Good in all tints (pastels) but negative in dark tones.

2. Titles printed in a solid color:

Yellows—Negative. Marginal only if outlined in black.
Oranges—Marginal to negative, depending on tint, shade, and tone.
Reds—Good to marginal. *Never* use pink.
Greens—Good, except when very dark or close to black.
Blues—Good, except when very dark or close to black.
Purples—Good up to the middle tones only.

3. Line drawings in black; white highlights over tinted backgrounds:

Yellows—Negative.
Oranges—Good to marginal, depending on tint, shade, and tone.
Reds—Good up to the middle tones, then negative.
Greens—Good, except in the very dark tones.
Blues—Good, except in the very dark tones.
Purples—Good, except in the very dark tones.

4. Lines drawn at 30 degrees to emphasize shadows:

Yellows—Negative.

Oranges—Good to marginal, depending on tint, shade, and tone.
Reds—Good, but could be very cold and "brittle" if too dark.
Greens—Good; can be warm or cold depending on tone, tint, and shade.
Blues—Good; can be warm or cold depending on tone, tint, and shade.
Purples—Good; can be warm or cold depending on tone, tint, and shade.

5. Standard duotones:

Yellows—Marginal.
Oranges—Good if results wanted are warm.
Reds—Good; results can be either warm or cold depending on tint and shade.
Greens—Good if results wanted are warm.
Blues—Good; results can be either warm or cold depending on tint or shade.
Purples—Good if results are to be warm.

6. Silhouettes:

Yellows—Negative.
Oranges—Good depending on

Figure 27.6—The standard duotone with PMS-471 and black.

Figure 27.7—An overprint on a 50% tint block. Compare the difference between this and the standard duotone. Which has more life?

Figure 27.8—A ''color highlight'' in PMS-471 over a regular halftone.

Figure 27.9—A standard duotone with a mezzotint screen.

Figure 27.10—Posterization, or a halftone shot as line.

Figure 27.11—Segmenting for emphasis.

Figure 27.12—Color combined with line and a halftone.

Figure 27.13—Color highlights over an outline halftone using the ''torn-edge'' technique for a softer outline.

tone, tint, and shade.
Reds—Good, but can be ''brittle'' or cold depending on shade.
Greens—Good in almost all shades, tints, and tones.
Blues—Good in almost all shades, tints, and tones.
Purples—Good up to the medium tints, shades, and tones.

7. Reverse silhouettes:
Same as silhouettes.

8. Tints with textured screens in black added:
Yellows—Minimal; screens will tend to dominate.
Oranges—Marginal to good.
Reds—Good, but remember that red tints often appear pink.
Greens—Good in all up to the medium values.
Blues—Good in all up to the medium values.
Purples—Good in all up to the medium values.

9. Felt-tip pen renderings with tints for special effects:
Yellows—Minimal to marginal.
Oranges—Good.
Reds—Good.
Greens—Good, except when very dark.

Blues—Good.
Purples—Good except when very dark.

10. ''Fogging'' or partial dropouts when in color:
Yellows—Negative.
Oranges—Negative.
Reds—Negative to barely marginal. Remember that red tints often appear pink.
Greens—Good in all values.
Blues—Good in all values.
Purples—Good in all values.

11. Solid-color blurbs:
Yellows—Negative.
Oranges—Good to marginal, depending on tint, shade, and tone.
Reds—Marginal. Use only very bright, nearly orange, reds. Other shades, tints, or values may appear pink.
Greens—Good up to very dark, then too close to black.
Blues—Good up to very dark, then too close to black.
Purples—Good up to medium, then too close to black.

12. Duotones with mezzotints:
See comments under Standard duotones.

13. Halftones overprinting a tint

block:
Yellows—Marginal.
Oranges—Good.
Reds—Marginal; stay away from pink tones.
Greens—Good up to the dark shades.
Blues—Good up to the dark shades.
Purples—Good up to the dark shades.

14. Line combined with tints and halftones:
Yellows—Marginal.
Oranges—Good.
Reds—Marginal; remember to avoid pink tints.
Greens—Good up to the dark shades.
Blues—Good up to the dark shades.
Purples—Good up to the dark shades.

15. Black-and-white halftones dropped into tinted background:
Yellows—Marginal.
Oranges—Good.
Reds—Marginal; remember that tints may appear pink.
Greens—Good up to the dark shades.
Blues—Good up to the dark shades.

Figure 27.14—Posterization over a tint block.

Figure 27.15—Frames used within a picture to highlight certain areas.

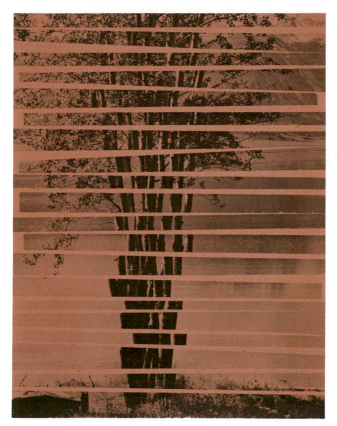

Figure 27.16—*Fragmenting over a tint block.*

Figure 27.17—*Overlapping color panels using line and a halftone.*

Purples—Good up to the dark shades.
16. Wrap-around bleed (if handled as a duotone):
   See comments under standard duotones.
17. Fracturing, if used in a second color:
Yellows—Marginal to negative.
Oranges—Good to marginal.
Reds—Marginal; depends on tint, tone, shade, and value.
Greens—Good up to very dark shades.
Blues—Good up to very dark shades.
Purples—Good up to very dark shades.
18. Segmenting:
Yellows—Marginal.
Oranges—Good.

Reds—Good.
Greens—Good up to very dark shades.
Blues—Good up to very dark shades.
Purples—Good up to very dark shades.
19. Halftones overprinted on a tinted page:
Yellows—Negative to barely marginal.
Oranges—Good.
Reds—Marginal; remember that tint values may appear pink.
Greens—Good up to dark shades.
Blues—Good up to dark shades.
Purples—Good up to dark shades.
20. Duotone with white dropouts:
Yellows—Negative; simply not strong enough to emphasize the

white areas.
Oranges—Good.
Reds—Good.
Greens—Good.
Blues—Good.
Purples—Good.

The effectiveness of color depends on the shade, tint, and value being used. Notice that yellow is rarely good, that oranges are almost always good, that reds sometimes have the bad quality of turning pink, and that the greens, blues, and purples are good only in the dark shades. If you have a problem visualizing results, by all means purchase Bourges tinted sheets and order photostats to create a ''comp'' that will be very close to the final result.

CHAPTER TWENTY-EIGHT

The "Four-Pager" —House Organs

House organs, a type of magazine, fall into the small-item, news-release classification. Stories are rarely more than one full page in length. More often they consist of no more than several short paragraphs. They usually have many "mug" shots or group pictures. This sometimes makes good graphic design difficult. Small news items with individual pictures following in relative progression often creates a "patchwork" result. A second color is, more often than not, used simply to decorate.

Many house organs seem to be poorly planned because the designer has used the simplest method. The simplest method, of course, is to order galleys, all on the same measure, and rearrange them to fit areas.

There are some good points to the house organ. People like to see their achievements and pictures in print. This creates an illusion of fame, no matter how limited. It also creates a family feeling for the company. It is a permanent, printed document to many people. None of these good points have any relationship to good design or graphics. The designer should realize these implications. He or she should follow a subtle, organized, documentary style of presentation and try not to forfeit good design for the "easiest way."

Let us start out by outlining three points applicable to any magazine design or redesign. These are "the disciplines" (type, logo, and pictures), "what the designer can see beyond the disciplines" (as well as what he wants the reader to see), and "creative layout thinking."

The typeface must be readable. It should establish a normal, easy-to-read pattern. This usually means setting the body flush left *and* right. If one sets flush left, ragged right, the design appeal may be gratifying, but the reading is slightly uncomfortable for the average reader. One also loses about 14 percent of the maximum copy area due to the "ragged right" loss. When one considers that there are usually only four pages to fill, this loss can become significant. Space is precious in the house organ. Many items are "dated"—that is, they are pertinent only to the present issue.

The logo should be simple, quickly identifiable, and rarely, if ever, contrived. Since the house organ is often mailed, it should have a return address, an issue date, and an area for either a stamp or postal permit. The logo should be readable in two sizes—the larger size for identification and a smaller size for use in the return address area. The return address can be set in type, but repeating the logo in a smaller size will add just a "touch of class."

A good type marriage between heads, copy, and captions is essential. It is usually best to keep them in the same face, but varying in size and weight. Heads can vary in size and are usually bold. Body copy should remain constant. Captions should remain constant, usually at a size smaller than the body.

Most house organs suffer from congestion. Editors and designers try to put too much into the available space. Instant improvement can be created by dropping the shortest story (if possible) and using the available space for headline areas. Most headlines are not design areas. They are treated only as necessities. Here are some ways to use them as design elements:

1. Break long headlines into two uneven lines. They can be set flush left or flush right provided the white space always occurs on the outside edge.

2. Headlines on outside columns should have white space on the outside. Headlines on the inside columns should have the white space facing into the gutter. Headlines in the well should be centered so that the white space occurs on both sides.

3. Two headlines at the top of a page will cause confusion even if separated. Try to arrange them so that this does not happen.

4. Headlines *with* a picture form a design unit and will, invariably, have white space within the arrangement.

5. Headlines need *not* be large. More often a smaller size within the same amount of space will draw more attention.

6. Headlines should be short, simple sentences. When breaking into more than one line, make each line make sense. Avoid breaking into more than three lines as this

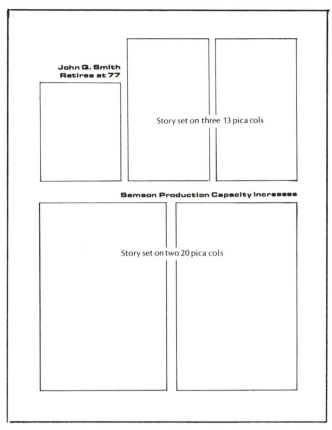

John G. Smith
Retires at 77

Story set on three 13 pica cols

Samson Production Capacity Increases

Story set on two 20 pica cols

Figure 28.1—An example of a two- and three-column "mix and match."

Picture that can be bled
on 19 picas

Copy or picture
on 13 picas

Copy or picture
on 13 picas

Figure 28.2—A format with a pattern of 19-13-13.

Picture that can be bled
on 21 picas

Copy or picture
on 13 picas

Copy or picture
on 13 picas

Figure 28.3—A format with a pattern of 21-13-13.

Picture that can be
bled on 14 picas

Copy or picture on 20 picas

Copy or picture
on 13 picas

Figure 28.4—A format with a pattern of 14-20-13.

tends to be choppy.

Pictures, because of their nature ("mug" shots or group shots), have a rather limited design appeal. They usually fall into these basic shapes:

- squares ("mug" shots)
- horizontal rectangles ("mug" shots, group shots, pictures of inanimate things)
- vertical rectangles ("mug" shots, group shots, pictures of inanimate objects)
- ovals (portraits of people)
- outline halftones

Further picture variation may include

- duotones (a second color)
- overprints (a second color)
- tint blocks

and, rarely,

- line drawings (with the possibility of a second color)

What can we see from these basics? First of all, what do we *actually see*?

- two or three gray columns of copy
- primary verticals and rectangles, usually in tones of gray
- consecutive arrangements, not always ideally arranged
- some second color usage, though not always ideally handled

What might we see beyond these basics?

- some possibilities of varying column arrangements
- little or no directional or controlled movement *within* the pictures
- consecutive arrangements that *can* be switched to give more design control
- color usage for something other than decorating

We might also ask, "What does the *reader* see?" While this is a little difficult to determine, we can rest assured readers will rarely see any design or purpose because they aren't aware of it. This is no reason to shortchange them. They are usually interested in the pictures and/or items that relate directly to them. Using the idea that "some people eat to live while others live to eat" we might well say that the key is in preparation, in other words, how we prepare the words and pictures to attract readers and invite them to read everything.

There are three steps in creative layout thinking. They narrow down to possibilities, probabilities, and practicalities. What is possible in this type of publication?

- a new size
- a new format
- a new method
- a new direction
- reorganization
- expanding or decreasing departments
- a new idea for any one department

Let us expand on each of these.

When striving for a new size, talk to your printer about what is possible from the many standard sheet sizes. You will want to avoid paper waste by using a size that doesn't cut evenly from the sheet. You must also be aware of how a size change may affect your postal rate.

The standard sizes are multiples of 8½ by 11 inches. "Legal" size is 8½ by 14 inches. This gives us a new size simply by folding it in half to 8½ by 7 inches. This immediately changes the basic shape from a rectangle to one that is nearly square. It would also change the basic format from two- or three-column to only two-column. Two-column formats have a tendency to force pictures into squares, which means repetition of the geometric shape. Two-column also restricts the pictures to either one column or two columns in width. This doesn't give many possibilities.

The standard 8½-by-11-inch size nicely accommodates three columns of 13 picas, with proportionally good alleys and borders. It also accommodates two columns of about 20 picas with the same alleys and borders. The only apparent variable might be a natural column ending or a mix of two *and* three columns within the same issue. Picture pages need not fall within the rigid two- or three-column framework, provided they are handled as complete units. This would mean clustering or grouping.

I think of communication in terms of variables of sight and sound. What about the possibility of a cheaply produced record as an occasional insert, such as a per-

sonal message from the president or Christmas carols from the company choir? This brings up the matter of cost, as well as the pertinent question, What will it accomplish on a one-time basis? What about mailing?

In order to have reorganization we must first assume that the original is *un*organized. This is hardly possible in the small size. There is usually one story handled as a feature and placed on the front page. The remainder fall into classifications or departments. Some departments can be organized by the use of a second color in the heads, tint blocks, or boxes.

Organizing the separate items into sections and complementing these sections with a picture page or center-page spread has some merit. Retraining the reader to look at the center-page spread *first* may be a little difficult.

People like pictures. Many news items can be made into a picture with a long caption, rather than a picture plus a story plus a caption. This might very well give more feature areas.

The good house organ minimizes departments. Since many house organs are literally stuck with "five-year anniversaries," "ten-year anniversaries," "twenty-five-year anniversaries," and on, *plus* "new employees" and the like, one must really stop and ask, How important are these to anyone but the persons involved? Wouldn't it be better to give "five-year anniversary awards" than take up this valuable space in every issue? Awards, suitable for framing, can be printed a lot cheaper than using this space. The argument might be, "This is a company newspaper and the anniversaries are company news!" Minimize it by supplementing it. Give the awards in a little ceremony, and delete the awards space from every issue.

A good idea is "overruns." When people achieve a newsworthy item, they invariably want extra copies, even though they may not say so. Emphasize the point! Permit purchase of up to twenty-five copies at a minimal cost. Run this fact as a specialty. Advertise it.

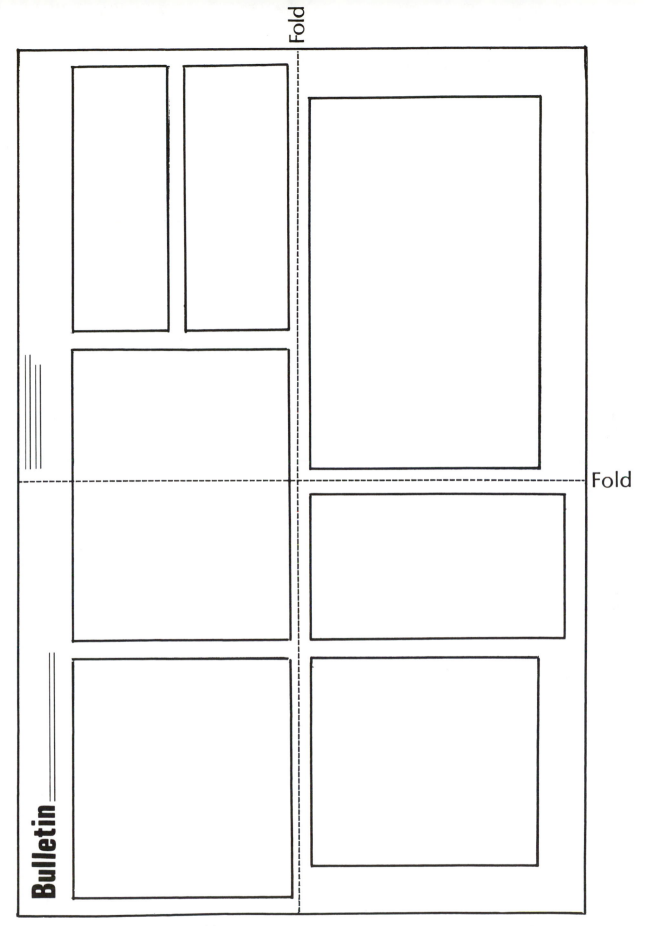

Figure 28.5—Pages 1 and 4 of a predesigned format.

Figure 28.6—Controlled organization starting from the predesigned format shown in figure 28.5. Notice how white space within each predesigned box can vary with the story.

Along with this, design the house organ to permit mailing. Make it easy and uncomplicated.

As you can well see, this chapter has not been slanted toward the professional designers. They are usually not interested in such small stuff. Or, if given the opportunity, they will overdesign, with no real forethought or planning. Instead, the chapter is directed toward the person who may have been handed the job on a "do the best you can" basis, to the person who wants to do a better job but simply doesn't know how, and to the staff editor who recognizes there are problems but doesn't know how to solve them.

I will give you three variations on the same theme. All three accomplish change. All three are design-oriented and will work with a little effort. Use them as springboards for other applications. Do not follow them implicitly. If you do, you will only exchange one stereotyped format for another.

Horizontal versus Vertical

The easiest way to change the format is to vary the geometric shapes. By this I mean a balance of *both* two and three columns within the same issue. On the surface, this seems quite easy.

We all know that two-column tends to keep the pictures relatively square within the format. We also know that three-column tends to keep the pictures relatively rectangular (either horizontally or vertically) within its format. These simple and logical changes in geometric shapes should point the way to any thinking layout person. You *can* combine horizontals with verticals and squares all within the same page framework and achieve far more interesting page results.

Since many editors may be afraid to tackle this for want of knowledge, let's outline a simple plan.

1. Call your typesetter and ask for the character count per pica in the size and face you plan to use.

2. Multiply this by 20 picas for a two-column format and by 13 picas for a three-column format. This tells you how many characters and spaces you will get in each.

3. Use any convenient method to count the characters and spaces within the story—a paragraph at a time. Enter this total on a piece of paper and attach it to the top of each story.

4. Divide the total characters and spaces of each paragraph by the number of characters per line to get a total number of lines *of each measure* in each paragraph. This now tells you how many lines you will have on the two different measures.

5. Compute the length (or, if you like, "depth") of each story in picas, again for both measures.

6. Size each picture for each story on two widths. Add this to the story length.

7. Divide the total length by two for a two-column story and by three for a three-column story.

8. You should now be ready to place and balance stories by geometric shapes. If it makes it easier for you, cut out pieces of paper showing exact placement and try arranging these on the layout form. It won't be too long before you will be able to do without this, because you will be able to visualize the spaces, making the job easier yet.

Arrange stories so that two-column stories appear at the bottom of the page and three-column stories appear at the top of a page. Do not place headlines until you have a relatively good geometric arrangement. Then, use the white space left over for headlines and/or captions. The headlines and white space will start breaking up the solid masses.

Mix and Match

The premise of mix and match is that all house organs have an unexplored area—the outside border. Most 8½-by-11-inch pages have standard borders, alleys, and column widths. They usually have a live area of 41 picas. This allows for a 5-pica page border. If I decide to use the outside margin, I now have a live area of 47 picas. I divide it into three space units: 19 picas in from the page edge, plus a 1-pica alley, plus 13 picas and a 1-pica alley, and another 13-pica unit. I use the 19-pica area for any picture that can bleed, but always to the outside edge. This gives two columns of 13 picas that can be used for copy *or* an additional 13-pica area for another picture (or an extension of the 19-pica area) plus a column for copy on the gutter side of the page. What I now have is a rhythmic pattern of 19-13-13. See figure 28.2.

If I further minimize the gutter area from the standard 5 picas on a side to 4 picas on a side, I pick up an additional 2 picas that would give still another variable of the same theme. I now have 21, 13, and 13, or 14, 20, and 13 for a little added interest. See figures 28.3 and 28.4.

Since an entire page set in this format would appear tight and crowded, I suggest that it be used only for the upper one-third of any page. The lower two-thirds would be either two even columns or three even columns. The mix and match design would then act very much like a panel with copy and/or pictures as variables.

Controlled Organization (Predesigned)

Most house organs consist of many short news items. The pictures are the obvious selling point. It is poor design to head each news item with a picture. The result can only be a patchwork arrangement.

In a predesigned format (figure 28.5), pages 1 and 4 become a picture-page spread. If any story cannot be completed within the design-oriented areas, it is permissible to jump them to pages 2 and 3. You will note that one area bridges the gutter, tying both units together. See figure 28.6.

Several questions immediately come to mind. What if you have a story without a picture? The answer is to substitute a headline for the picture, but write it within the predesigned area. Since boxes are all variables, any box can continue to include the box area next to it (but *not* below it). The only constant is that the boxes occur above and below the fold, never in the fold.

Another question might be, Are the jumps from the picture page spread to the inside pages irritating? I believe that once you catch the reader with a picture and a story he or she will not be bothered by finishing it on the inside. In this format, the inside pages are all basically copy.

The Template System

The original controlled layout has allotted positions designed to occur above and below the fold and already balanced. This design will balance equally well if a template is made and "flopped" from top to bottom. The design will still hold together although the boxes are now in opposite corners. The template can also be turned from left to right, giving still another balanced variable. It can also be turned from right to left with the same result. All four variables are still balanced. This gives at least four different layouts. Designs within the design are created by using ovals, outline halftones, pictures *plus* heads, changes in white space, and even an occasional tint block. Pictures with the least desirable impact can be placed on pages 2 and 3.

Where should a second color be used? In the logo, of course. Never in the copy. This means headlines and pictures can be in color. Duotones and overprints are naturals. The only problems are to use color to an advantage and to use the white space within the boxes to brighten it. Never run copy full in any box. Always leave some white space. This creates visual interest within each area.

CHAPTER TWENTY-NINE

Newsletters and Bulletins

Newsletters, by definition, are a way of communicating to a group of people. The general tone of a newsletter should be ''one-to-one.'' The implication is that it is addressed to one person but all others receive copies. This is sometimes rather tricky to write, but the personal touch is needed. Newsletters are often typewritten.

Bulletins, on the other hand, assume the reader already has some knowledge of the subject and the communication is being used to ''update.'' Bulletins are news-oriented, time-related, and factual. Newsletters contain news, which by implication calls for discarding it once the news has been assimilated. Bulletins may be retained for the information they contain.

News releases fall into the newsletter classification. As such they are sent out to the media (press, radio, and television). Here the news is either quoted verbatim or it may be used in a longer story. News releases should always have the name of a person to contact for further or more detailed information.

Newsletters, bulletins, and news releases must have a *strong* corporate identity. They should be well designed, positive in content, and capable of instant recognition. The premise is clear—''class'' draws attention! Design all three with this idea in mind. It is obvious that no one will pay much attention to a cheap imitation. Put yourself in the reader's shoes. Would you read every word of a mimeographed sheet? No matter how important

the communication is to *you*, it can become important to others only if they read *it*. You cannot get attention with a mediocre piece.

Disseminating newsletter information usually takes the line of least resistance. The quickest and easiest way is with a typewriter, and a piece of 8½-by-11-inch paper, and the cheapest way of reproducing the newsletter in volume. This is not necessarily wrong, but the usual results are often poor. You want it to be read—not rejected.

While newsletters are usually typewritten, bulletins are typeset. News releases can be either, depending on the time and money available. All three must be well designed. This means design with a purpose, not just the logo or corporate identity only, but the whole piece. It also means the piece should follow a well-conceived plan, with good graphics and an easy to read, concise style.

A complete knowledge of reproduction methods is a must. They usually fall into instant printing and press printing. Since the typewriter in this case is the main way of setting the copy, let's talk for a few minutes about the typewriter.

Typewritten copy is most often set flush left–ragged right. This is the easiest. Since the typewriter can set only what the keyboard has (caps, lower case, numbers, and a handful of symbols) the possibilities seem to be rather limited. The ''heads'' are usually typed in all caps, caps with an underline, or

caps and lower case with an underline. These will draw attention, but most typists forget that white space will also draw attention. A five-character indent will draw as much attention as caps or an underscore. However, an asterisk is too small to draw much attention.

Another problem area is tabular copy. The typewriter has letters and numbers that are all the same size. This makes it difficult to show any variation between the two. One could use a typewriter that has interchangeable fonts, but most offices do not want to invest in this and many typists feel the added interchanging is not worth the effort.

Tabular copy more often than not calls for rules between the lines and columns. It is easy to set a horizontal line with a typewriter, but not convenient to turn the sheet and add vertical lines. Lines can be added with a ruling pen. Both horizontals and verticals can be added with a stylus if you are mimeographing.

Let me offer an easier approach—one that will open up all kinds of new possibilities. Many art supply stores and stationery shops stock pressure-sensitive sheets of letters and symbols that are black and reproduce easily. They are applied to a sheet of paper by burnishing. Since most newsletters are reproduced from original typed copy and the pressure-sensitive additions are also black, both become a part of the original ''art.'' The variations are endless. It all depends on what you can add to create ''de-

PRINTING INSTITUTE OF CENTRAL OHIO
00 South Jackson Ave St Charles Ohio

Newsletter

Figure 29.1—A typical ''Newsletter'' designed for two-color and pre-planned so the typewritten copy will complete the page design.

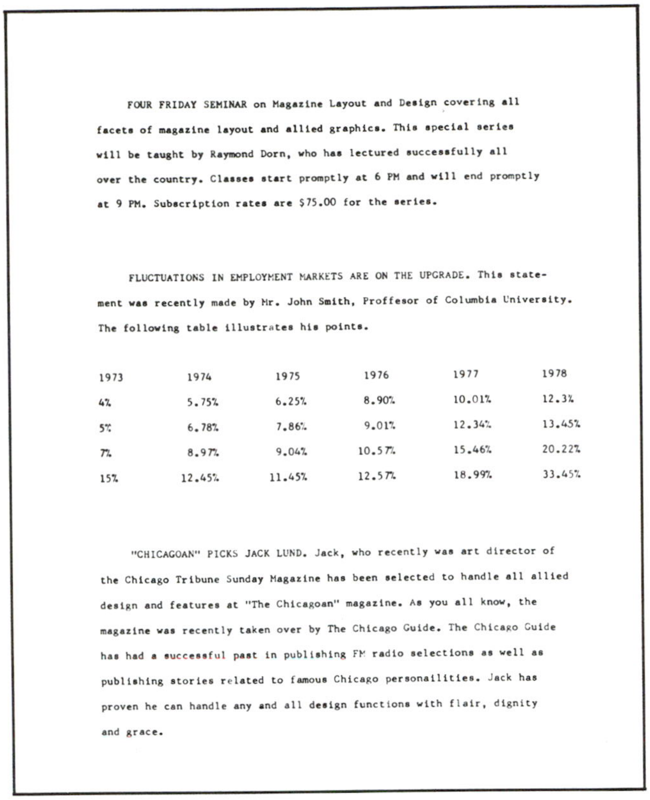

FOUR FRIDAY SEMINAR on Magazine Layout and Design covering all facets of magazine layout and allied graphics. This special series will be taught by Raymond Dorn, who has lectured successfully all over the country. Classes start promptly at 6 PM and will end promptly at 9 PM. Subscription rates are $75.00 for the series.

FLUCTUATIONS IN EMPLOYMENT MARKETS ARE ON THE UPGRADE. This statement was recently made by Mr. John Smith, Proffesor of Columbia University. The following table illustrates his points.

1973	1974	1975	1976	1977	1978
4%	5.75%	6.25%	8.90%	10.01%	12.3%
5%	6.78%	7.86%	9.01%	12.34%	13.45%
7%	8.97%	9.04%	10.57%	15.46%	20.22%
15%	12.45%	11.45%	12.57%	18.99%	33.45%

"CHICAGOAN" PICKS JACK LUND. Jack, who recently was art director of the Chicago Tribune Sunday Magazine has been selected to handle all allied design and features at "The Chicagoan" magazine. As you all know, the magazine was recently taken over by The Chicago Guide. The Chicago Guide has had a successful past in publishing FM radio selections as well as publishing stories related to famous Chicago personailities. Jack has proven he can handle any and all design functions with flair, dignity and grace.

Figure 29.2—A typical typewritten page of news items showing that simply typing the copy has no graphic interest or page impact.

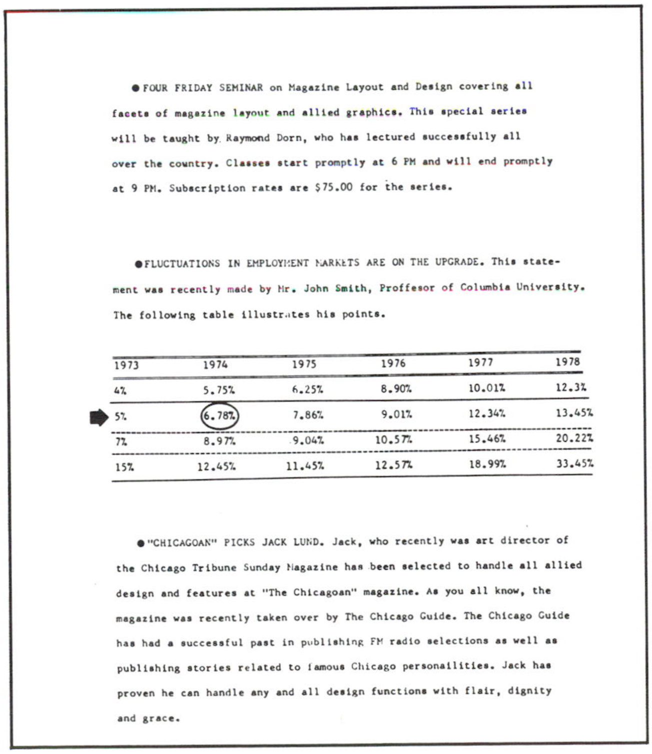

● FOUR FRIDAY SEMINAR on Magazine Layout and Design covering all facets of magazine layout and allied graphics. This special series will be taught by Raymond Dorn, who has lectured successfully all over the country. Classes start promptly at 6 PM and will end promptly at 9 PM. Subscription rates are $75.00 for the series.

●FLUCTUATIONS IN EMPLOYMENT MARKETS ARE ON THE UPGRADE. This statement was recently made by Mr. John Smith, Proffesor of Columbia University. The following table illustrates his points.

1973	1974	1975	1976	1977	1978
4%	5.75%	6.25%	8.90%	10.01%	12.3%
5%	6.78%	7.86%	9.01%	12.34%	13.45%
7%	8.97%	9.04%	10.57%	15.46%	20.22%
15%	12.45%	11.45%	12.57%	18.99%	33.45%

●"CHICAGOAN" PICKS JACK LUND. Jack, who recently was art director of the Chicago Tribune Sunday Magazine has been selected to handle all allied design and features at "The Chicagoan" magazine. As you all know, the magazine was recently taken over by The Chicago Guide. The Chicago Guide has had a successful past in publishing FM radio selections as well as publishing stories related to famous Chicago personailities. Jack has proven he can handle any and all design functions with flair, dignity and grace.

Figure 29.3—The same typewritten copy but using ''Format'' or cold type additions can add a little interest with little effort.

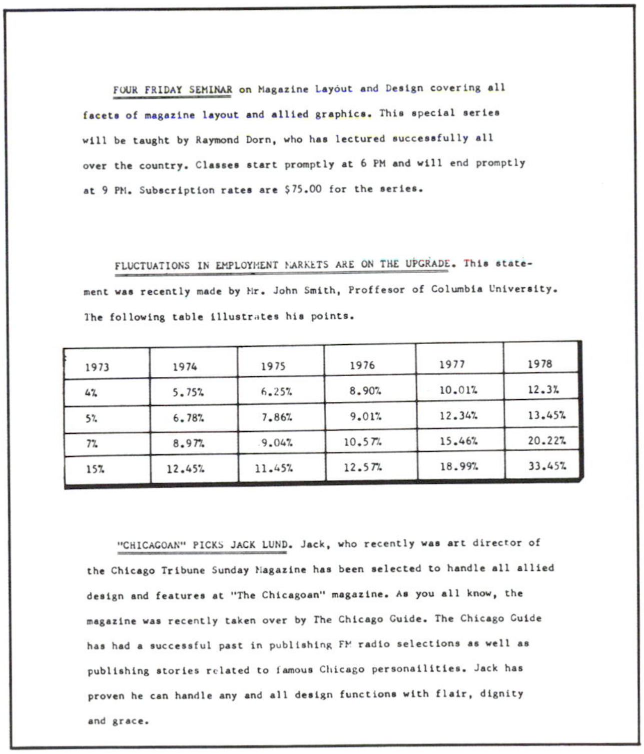

FOUR FRIDAY SEMINAR on Magazine Layout and Design covering all facets of magazine layout and allied graphics. This special series will be taught by Raymond Dorn, who has lectured successfully all over the country. Classes start promptly at 6 PM and will end promptly at 9 PM. Subscription rates are $75.00 for the series.

FLUCTUATIONS IN EMPLOYMENT MARKETS ARE ON THE UPGRADE. This statement was recently made by Mr. John Smith, Proffesor of Columbia University. The following table illustrates his points.

1973	1974	1975	1976	1977	1978
4%	5.75%	6.25%	8.90%	10.01%	12.3%
5%	6.78%	7.86%	9.01%	12.34%	13.45%
7%	8.97%	9.04%	10.57%	15.46%	20.22%
15%	12.45%	11.45%	12.57%	18.99%	33.45%

"CHICAGOAN" PICKS JACK LUND. Jack, who recently was art director of the Chicago Tribune Sunday Magazine has been selected to handle all allied design and features at "The Chicagoan" magazine. As you all know, the magazine was recently taken over by The Chicago Guide. The Chicago Guide has had a successful past in publishing FM radio selections as well as publishing stories related to famous Chicago personailities. Jack has proven he can handle any and all design functions with flair, dignity and grace.

Figure 29.4—The same typewritten copy with still more variations using ''Format'' and a little imagination.

Monthly Newsletter

WHY WE NEED P.I.I.

The main speaker in this area was Dr. Werner Hunstein, of the Medizinische Universitäts-Poliklinik, Heidelberg. He noted that very few experimental models fit the clinical description of MOS and even suggested that more than one model may be necessary, because "myelofibrosis probably encompasses at least two different etiopathogenic processes—the autonomous, proliferative, leukemia-like type and the reactive, inflammatory, scar tissue-forming type."

Spontaneous myelofibrosis seems very rare in animals, he added, but this may be due to lack of adequate hematological studies.

He analyzed a number of experimental models that produce disorders somewhat similar to human MOS: protein application, experimental infarction, saponin injection, lead acetate administration, total body irradiation, and viral infections. He also remarked that interpretation is difficult because bone marrow reacts uniformly to the most varied kinds of noxious agents: damage leads to necrosis, and necrosis to fibrosis.

Dr. Hunstein sees the most hope in experimental models that utilize whole body irradiation (with especial emphasis on whether myelofibrosis induced in this manner is reversible) and viruses. Several studies have shown that viruses appear to induce autonomous irreversible myeloproliferative disease, and so are particularly promising.

HAVE YOU TRIED KODAK'S NEW PAPER?

enmeshed in the fibrous tissue in the bone marrow. Occasionally, masses of extramedullary myeloid tissue are found as small tumor nodules in many parts of the body.

Sometimes, MOS is mistaken for chronic granulocytic leukemia, and diagnostic problems can arise with other diseases that produce massive splenomegaly, such as Gaucher disease, lymphoma, and chronic congestive splenomegaly. Secondary myelosclerosis can occur in association with tuberculosis, cancer, radiation exposure or poisoning.

According to Dr. Bouroncle, there is no specific treatment for MOS. Some patients need no therapy for some time. Both busulfan and irradiation (with the drug being more effective) have been used to treat early progressive splenomegaly. Many patients undergo splenectomy, usually because of hemolysis or thrombocytopenia resulting from their hypersplenism. This procedure is advisable only for patients with another site for the formation of red blood cells.

Progressive anemia resulting from bone marrow failure is a characteristic of the disease and androgen therapy has sometimes been helpful. When anemia is aggravated by hemolysis, treatment

In this connection, she noted that megakaryocytes and platelets concentrate serotonin. In the carcinoid syndrome, serotonin that passes through the right side of the heart is associated with fibrosis of the tricuspid and pulmonic valves. This raises the possibility that serotonin from "leaky" megakaryocytes and platelets could be responsible for the medullary and extramedullary fibrosis seen in patients with MOS.

PRESIDENT INSISTS ON QUALITY

Few participants had anything new to contribute in this area, largely because (as C. Lockard Conley, MD, put it) "Until we learn to recognize the disease earlier, we won't be able to say much about its true course."

There is still no explanation for the enlargement of the spleen. This organ has been shown to be a major site of myeloid metaplasia, the pooling of red blood cells and platelets and the sequestration and destruction of blood cells. The spleen is also associated in MOS with a great increase in circulating plasma volume (hemodilution anemia).

The majority view seems to be that the spleen's role in MOS is largely harmful, but this may not be true of the early stages of the disease. Splenectomy ideally should be postponed until there is knowledge of red blood cell destruction and production in the spleen.

THE NEW O-T REQUIREMENTS

Basophils are increased in the blood of MOS patients and also seem to be abnormal. There are now new methods of studying these cells. Prof Burkhardt has developed a new method of demonstrating the presence of mast cells in marrow, and Harriet S. Gilbert, MD, of Mount Sinai School of Medicine, New York, and co-workers have developed a new staining method (alcian blue) to facilitate the recognition of basophils in the blood.

According to Dr. Gilbert, basophils carry histamine and there is a correlation between whole blood histamine and the number of basophils. She told MEDICAL NEWS about the sometimes successful attempts to interfere with the histamine effects in MOS—such as upper and lower gastrointestinal symptoms, ulcers, headaches, and pruritus—by administering antihistamines. She added that marrow suppressive treatment can reduce both the basophil count and the serum histamine level, also relieving such symptoms.

The Mount Sinai hematologists include a basophil count in their diagnostic work-ups and regard basophil levels as indicators of disease activity in MOS.

There is still no definitive treatment for MOS. The participants concluded that emphasis should be placed on new staging and chemotherapeutic methods. Bone marrow transplants might be helpful, but this has not yet been attempted.

Figure 29.5—"Island" reading. You will notice that you read the heads first, then the stories that interest you, skipping those stories that do not interest you. This example uses all cap heads.

Figure 29.6—"Island" reading—same heads, same text but using caps and lower case heads. Compare it to Figure 29.5.

Figure 29.7—"Island" reading, but with pictures added for interest.

Newly Recognized Foreign Body in the Esophagus

To the Editor.—Foreign bodies in the esophagus are well-recognized and dreaded occurrences. A variety of objects can be swallowed, most frequently by infants and children. These include open safety pins, coins, small toys, buttons, and marbles. Pieces of meat or fish bones are frequently swallowed by adults.

A new and dangerous foreign body has emerged for due concern—namely, the pull-tab top from soda and beer cans.

We have treated a 16-year-old boy who put the pull-tab top from a soda can into the can prior to drinking and inadvertently swallowed the object. It then became lodged in his esophagus.

Our case represents the swallowing of an object that has arisen from technological advances. With the advent of metal soda and beer cans comes the convenient pull-tab top ring for opening the can. As in the case of our patient, people apparently have the habit of putting the pull tab into the can prior to drinking. As was reported, this can be a dangerous situation. The object was sharp and indeed produced a superficial esophageal laceration. There was an ever-present danger of perforation. In one series of 91 foreign bodies in the esophagus, there were two perforations.'

Typhoid Hepatitis

To the Editor.—The article, "Typhoid Hepatitis," by Ramachandran et al (230:236, 1974) is another in the series creating confusion about the nature of hepatitis. Unhappily, the term is used to describe two different entities: focal lesions that may be seen in a single lobule or may be large enough to destroy several lobules, and diffuse lesions involving virtually all lobules. The focal lesions are seen in leprosy, tuberculosis, and amebiasis, and have clinical evidence of hepatic insufficiency only rarely. Examples par excellence of diffuse lesions are those seen in viral hepatitis and yellow fever.

Amebic involvement of the liver is a focal lesion, single or multiple, small or large, and there is no such entity as diffuse amebic hepatitis. The lack of evidence for amebic hepatitis, presumably a diffuse lesion, has not pre-

To the Editor.—The recent MEDICAL NEWS article (230:903, 1974) on the problems and rewards of medical practice on an isolated Indian reservation pleased me very much. The reactions of other physicians have been pouring in from all over, and I believe that Kayenta won't have any recruitment problems for a couple more years? People have offered to help us out during their vacations; a physician in the Food and Drug Administration (at the GS-15 level) called me and said he'd "give up the $100,000 house and his city life if we had a physician slot open?" Two medical students requested that we "save them spaces" here in two or three years.

Mr. Sampson represented my opinions in a truly skillful, thoughtful, and professional manner. The article is bound to help my patients here in Kayenta, and for them, and for myself, I thank you.

Kayenta, Ariz

and the site at which it is lodged. Posteroanterior, lateral, and oblique x-ray films should be obtained and if the object is not detected, radiopaque contrast media should be used. In our case, we were able to visualize the object on plain films at the level of D-3.

Foreign bodies in the esophagus should be removed under direct vision through the esophagoscope. This was done in our case, and repeat x-ray examinations revealed absence of the foreign body.

The diagnosis is usually evident in an adult by the history of foreign body ingestion. Pain, coughing, gagging, choking, dyspnea, or vomiting may be initial symptoms. Our patient complained of a dull sticking sensation located substernally at the level where the object was lodged. Whether or not an ingested foreign body can be demonstrated roentgenologically depends on its size, opacity, articles describing it by Ramachandran and Doxiades.

For two decades, Dr. Elsdon-Dew and I—and others—have tried to "scotch" this phoenix, obviously without much success. The misconception apparently is now overlapping into other diseases such as typhoid fever, for the pathologic evidence presented in the current article describing a diffuse lesion is hardly convincing. The focal lesion is studied in most medical schools as part of the second-year course in pathology.

Dr. Aring's detached approach to the problem represents, it seems to me, an attitude that medicine should be *au dessus de la mêlée*, unconcerned about the social implications of legal and professional policies related to patient care. Dr. Aring's dictum that "abortion is not a procedure to be lofty and philosophical COMMENTARY on the subject of abortion (230:231, 1974) is a classic example of the sort of thing that continues to give medicine a bad name. It is incredible to me that he would seriously claim to have

Figure 29.8—A variation of "Island" reading but using controlled organization and white space. Compare this to the other examples. Don't you agree that this has more graphic appeal?

sign spots" that call attention to various areas. This can make copy sparkle. That's a pretty small investment for copy that moves out of the ordinary.

Newsletters, bulletins, and news releases have added impact if they can be printed in color. This invariably means having a portion of the pages preprinted. *Do not* have body copy printed in color. It's hard to read. Remember that color draws attention—it also represents "class" because it shows a little extra effort. It's "special."

Typeset copy is almost always an exercise in typography. This is better described as "functional graphics." What does it consist of? First of all, most newsletters and bulletins fall into a class called "island reading." This means that the heads are used to identify blocks of copy or reading areas. The reader scans the heads for ones that interest him, passing over those that don't. The copy for the heads must be written to draw attention rather than as simple statements of fact.

Design is as important as message. Good graphics are silent salespersons. They represent you. You certainly would not want a salesperson representing your company to have a three-day beard, sloppy clothing, and bleary eyes. Put the price of a good suit into your graphics. Don't send anything out that has a "three-day beard."

Let us summarize by making six statements:

1. Design for "class." Class sells. Mediocrity does not sell.
2. Say something, but don't fall into the trap of saying too much.
3. If you have people working for you, teach them to do the job right. Send them to classes or seminars.
4. Don't try to please everyone. Anything designed by committee is doomed to failure.
5. Develop your own style, but within the limits of good graphics. Never sell yourself short by taking the easiest way. It may be an exercise in futility.
6. Study your competition. Make them follow you, instead of you following them.

CHAPTER THIRTY

How to Be an Artist without Being an Artist

Many layout artists have had no formal art training. This does not declassify them as "artists." Art does not have to be a creative endeavor all the time. The purpose of this chapter is to provide layout artists with variations and techniques they can use to relieve the monotony of pages that have been restricted to square and rectangular forms. Each variation will assume the artist has at least one good glossy halftone print and will include subvariations plus the techniques used to achieve them.

Black and White Halftone Converted to Line Art

Nothing looks more "creative" than a line drawing. It will always look as if it were created just for the particular story in which it occurs. Converting a halftone print into a line drawing becomes a matter of abstracting and tracing. The technique is relatively simple. Study the halftone. What is the main point of interest? Visualize all background as disappearing, leaving only this main interest area. Place a sheet of tracing paper over the halftone print. With a good No. 2 pencil, trace *only* the desired part. Remove the tracing paper. Tape it to a piece of white mounting board, making sure the tracing paper is flat and tight. Send this out for a glossy photostat to the size needed in the layout. You can either accept the line drawing as it is or use screens to fill out some areas.

Black and White Halftones to Line, Plus a Second Color

There are occasions when combining *part* of the halftone with line can be very effective. A spot of color will draw interest. The technique, again, is one of abstracting and tracing. However, once the line portion is received as a glossy photostat, the artist must combine this into a new unit. This is done by using your platemaker for part of the job. First, place a piece of tracing paper over the original halftone. Trace *only the outline* of the abstracted art. Write instructions on the tracing paper overlay to the effect that you want this particular area "dropped out" of the halftone. On the line art photostat, plan your second color, and put an overlay on it. Color the overlay with colored pencil, so the platemaker will know where the second color is to go. The second color can be an overprint, or a section or even part of another related design form.

Duotones

A duotone is no more than the same negative repeated in two colors, one of which is black. This differs from a black overprint on a tint block in that the same image appears in two colors. In a black overprint, the image appears only in black. The tint block is solid. The duotone screened negatives are slightly offset, so that some of each color appears in the dot pattern. The tricky part of duotones is getting just the right percentages of black and the second color. The color should be almost solid in the very light areas and almost absent in the dark areas. The technique is not difficult. Most duotone effects can be simulated by placing a Bourges tint directly over the original halftone. Directions to the platemaker should give the exact color you want used and depend on how little or much black you want used.

Duotones can really sparkle when white is used as a third color. The technique is basically the same as ordering a duotone, except that the photograph should be examined for very light areas. These areas are then designated as "drop out" areas on a tissue overlay. The platemaker will not use black or a color in these areas. The result will be pure white areas against color, which adds sparkle.

The combination of black and a color on still a different color tinted stock can create some interesting effects. Remember that two different colors create a third color. For instance, blue and black duotones printed on yellow tinted stock will create shades of blue-green. Blue and black on blue tinted stock will tend to mute the blues. Blue and black on red tinted stock will almost destroy the duotone effect, because blue and red will tend to turn black. The technique is the same as ordering duotones. However, study the possible color com-

Figure 30.1—The original halftone picture.

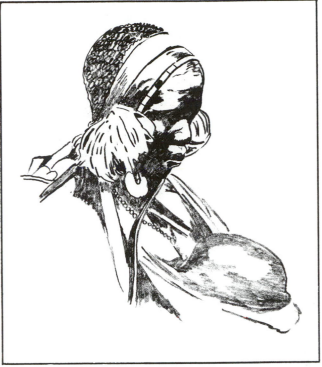

Figure 30.2—A #3 pencil rendering of the same picture.

Figure 30.3—A charcoal rendering of the same picture.

Figure 30.4—The "scratch technique" as outlined in the text.

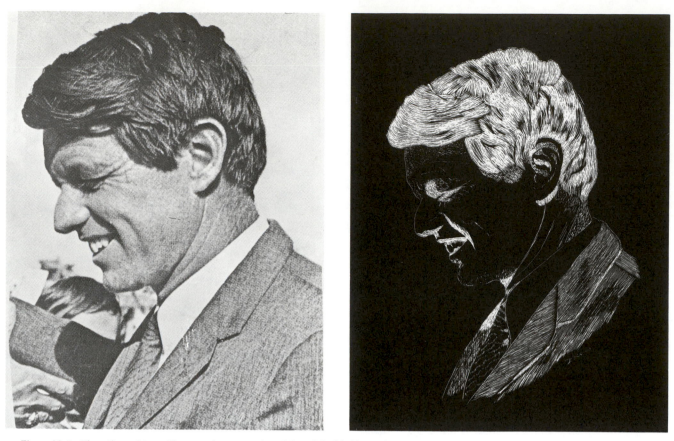

Figure 30.5—These three pictures illustrate the progression of the original halftone picture. It shows an intermediate point where the original scratched drawing was sent out for a glossy photostat. Note that this looks very much like a scratch-board drawing and could be used in that way instead of the final reproduction. Pictures of this kind can be created from any source. The original came from a four-color picture that appealed to me at the time. Once you develop a morgue of pictures you need not fall back on imagination.

binations before ordering something that may not give you the exact effect you want.

Enlarging Screen Values

A halftone print will have a dot structure. By enlarging this print three or four times, the dots will increase in size. They will not decrease in value. This can create a nice effect for large areas such as a cover. The technique is simply one of ordering a photostat sized up and then abstracting parts. The advantage is that the photostat of the subject will let you know exactly what the final result will look like.

Mezzotints

Mezzotint screens come in a wide variety of patterns: concentric circles, cross-hatching, waves, straight lines, and so on. The plate-maker, on your instructions, will substitute the mezzotint screen for the standard dot pattern screen. He can supply you with samples of the mezzotints he has available. Mezzotints are particularly effective when combined with duotones. This can give a picture an old steel-point engraving look.

Silhouettes

A silhouette is simply an outline of features. The technique is a matter of tracing just the outline, photostating to a desired size, and filling in the entire area with ink. The effectiveness of a silhouette can be greatly enhanced by having it printed in a solid color. Combining two or more silhouettes in different sizes and colors can create still dif-

ferent patterns and colors by overlapping them. Silhouettes look best in a small size.

Outlining

Outlining is a procedure where the background is dropped out completely, leaving a free-form halftone instead of a square or rectangular one.

Step and Repeat

In this technique, one picture does double duty in two widely different sizes. Often one picture can be "flopped" to create a new effect. The technique consists of ordering two different size pictures and putting them in two divergent positions.

Organized Design

This includes changing the corners or sides of a halftone to match part of the subject matter within the picture. The technique consists mainly of tracing what you want and asking the platemaker to do it for you. Organized design can also mean placing boxes, rectangles, or circles *within* the picture to highlight special areas and shapes repeated *around* the halftone, like a series of gradually increasing lines.

Fogging

Sometimes an artist may want to show only one area within the picture in sharp detail and have the rest of the picture very foggy or vague. The technique consists of tracing the one sharp area on tracing paper overlays. The platemaker is instructed to shoot this area in focus, while the rest of the picture is shot slightly out of focus. Then these are combined into one print.

Mirror or Kaleidoscope Images

Mirror images can create an interesting effect and can be achieved by having two negatives made of the same picture, but "flopping" one. A kaleidoscope effect can be created by using tracing paper and cutting pie shape parts out of one particular area. This slice of the picture is repeated enough times to make a complete circle. The "pie piece" pattern effect creates a repeated design that is most effective on color and should be used in wide white-space areas. It is used for design purposes only and never for detail.

Posterization

Posterization is nothing more than a halftone picture reproduced as line. Since there are no dots to carry tonal gradations, the print will have no tonal values. The result is a poster effect in line. If you shoot the same picture at different time sequences (such as 3 seconds, 6 seconds, and 9 seconds), each negative has greater expansion of the solid areas. Print the three negatives in three different colors. The final results can be gratifying.

Felt-Tip Pen Drawings

This is a variation of tracing with a No. 2 pencil, but the lines are heavier. If the sheet is sprayed with water afterwards, an interesting bleary effect can result. This technique is most effective in creating caricatures, because stick bodies can be added at will.

Sometimes other simple additions, depending on the story, can make the drawing likable or unlikable, depending on the magazine's editorial policy.

Scratch Technique

So far I have discussed basically mechanical ways of developing art. In the scratch technique, the layout artist who has had no formal training can appear to be a "pro." The final result looks very much like an expensive scratchboard piece of art, but the artist needs no technical training.

Start with a good halftone picture. Decide what you want abstracted from it. Place a piece of .020 gauge acetate film over the halftone. Purchase a scratchboard blade (which looks very much like an arrowhead and has sharp areas on each side as well as a needle point). Also buy a bottle of India ink and get a clean piece of cloth about a foot square. With the scratchboard knife, etch lines into the acetate sheet tracing the desired subject. Fill in areas with crosshatching, straight lines, or shading of your choice. As an area of about one inch square is completed, dip the cloth into the India ink and rub the ink into the scratches. Then immediately wipe it off. The ink will fill the scratches and create lines you can see against a piece of white paper. Keep working like this, an area at a time, filling and wiping until you have the picture you want or need.

Figure 30.6—A purposely blurred picture. This originally appeared in Photolith ScM *in February, 1975, and is used with permission. (Photographer was Danny Valdes of the* Big Spring Herald)

This technique creates a film positive that can also be printed in reverse. The platemaker must be told to shoot this *face down* and then "flop" the negative. The reason is that the acetate has thickness which, when shot face up, will not give a sharp line.

These pictures look well against a white background or over a tint block of a very light color. Backgrounds can be added to serve any purpose.

Pantone Color Films

Pantone colors come in all the colors of the rainbow, and many come in sheets that contain 100 percent, 75 percent, 50 percent, and 25 percent of the same color. These are extremely useful when used over a pencil or a felt-tip pen drawing. They can also be used without lines by putting a sheet of acetate between the subject and the Pantone film. In this way you can get exact shapes without altering or cutting the picture and just peel away the Pantone film.

One attribute of a good layout artist is constant observation and curiosity. When something appears in print that excites the imagination, the layout artist who wants to move ahead in the field will mount it on a piece of illustration board, make notes on the bottom as to how the effect was achieved, and file it. If the technique is not apparent, a call to the platemaker will usually clarify it. These should be retained in the artist's morgue.

A word about morgues—no layout artist should be without one. This is a subject file, arranged by lettering folders with titles that cover generic groups (men, women, people, animals, etc.). As the artist reads and observes, he or she should "clip" pictures and file them. You never know when you might be called on to "create" a picture that has no relationship to your daily work. This morgue can save you trips to the library or time spent in research.

Figure 30.7—A silhouette created by good camera work. This originally appeared in Photolith ScM in February, 1975, and is used with permission. The original picture was from "La Ventana," Texas Tech University of 1974. Silhouettes can also be created as outlined in the text.

Before closing, here is still another technique, called "fragmenting." This is defined as "shattering into numerous segments or parts." The creative mind has taken this concept and applied it to art, thereby developing a new way of creating pictures. Fragmentation employs magazine or news pictures (and you should have some in your morgue) to work out designs (see figure 27.16).

The object of fragmentation is to destroy something already in existence and re-create the parts imaginatively into something new. This does take practice. Before playing with one-of-a-kind prints, try fragmenting a picture that has no value. Or, use construction paper. Cut it apart and rearrange the pieces, leaving space between them. Try to create a different image from the one that exists. Clip a four-color picture from any magazine, cut it in similar-size strips, and arrange the strips in different ways.

CHAPTER THIRTY-ONE

Photojournalism

Photojournalism is a finely tuned balance between the news (presented as copy) and pictures (illustrating the news event). There are two senses involved—sight, or the pictures, and sound, or the picture captions and story. Every picture, with its caption, also carries a third element, namely, what the reader adds from his or her knowledge and experience. The picture presents irrefutable facts. Everything is captured in detail, because the camera "sees everything." The photojournalist knows there are added factors—things she or he can count on, and still others that are undetermined. One reader might pick up a little-noticed detail and magnify it into quite a different story than another reader who grasped the whole picture with only the caption as a guide. This is always a calculated decision. The layout artist must always be aware of this "third factor" and the ways it might possibly affect the readers. By actually looking for the "third factor"—planning on it and utilizing the effect of grouping and clustering—the layout artist can multiply the effectiveness of the story.

Photography is relatively "young" as a graphic form of communication. Pictures are as old as recorded time and reflect the culture of the times. The cavemen understood pictures or diagrams of important events. Pictures do not depend on knowing a language— they speak for themselves. The early photographers emulated portrait painters. That is, they posed their subjects and "shot" them with the same objective in mind— to preserve a perfect likeness. Matthew Brady did this in his pictures of the Civil War. Early examples of photojournalism indicate that the posed subject was just another way of illustrating a story. The difference between an artist's rendering and the early photographs was minimal, particularly when engravings were made.

High-speed shutters and high-speed film began cutting the time factor down. By time factor I mean the actual moment of presentation. Instead of posed subjects, action could now be caught in a fraction of a second. Acts could be documented as they happened. Photography froze the time factor into instants. It was this freezing of instants that created news photography. The camera was there, when it happened, and the visual experience did not depend on words to recreate the happening, other than to enlarge upon it or perhaps further clarify it.

What can the layout artist learn from photojournalism? The early picture magazines, and their graphic designers, experimented with visual presentation and discovered many things. One of these was "juxtaposition." This means that two pictures, unrelated in content, but related in design, can be combined into an entirely different thought. This had an entirely different impact than the "third factor" because it could be planned. Several examples may illustrate this. Picture, if you will, a row of bald heads watching a billiard match. Place a picture of the billiard balls next to this picture. The effect of similarity creates a third, entirely different and humorous variation. Another might be a picture of a professional woman model, dressed in heavy silk or satin, placed next to a pile of gravel or a wall of roughly hewn boards. The play on opposites makes the dress look silkier and the background look rougher. A tall, thin, vertical subject, such as an office building, will seem taller if placed next to an acceptable horizontal (such as a picture of wheat fields). This is a play on suggestion and two opposite directional movements, both of which tend to emphasize the other.

Picture editors (and many layout artists must assume this role) are constant observers. Their antennae are always up and sweeping. They pick up and store things by continual observation. They scrutinize detail, but are not slaves to detail. They may apply the minutiae to broader concepts. They "see" patterns and designs in the commonplace. They learn to examine every picture for points of interest. They learn the usual may not always be the best approach, because it may not always be understood. They know photographs are usually accepted as truth by most readers and must be keenly aware that truth can sometimes be disguised as only half a truth. They must always be true to readers. The good photojournalist is rarely fooled.

Photographs are exact images.

The picture editor looks for that indefinable something that makes a picture come alive for readers, something a little more than just a statement of facts. Documentary pictures have their place as a recorded slice of history. What a pity that the camera was not invented thousands of years ago. One wonders what historical facts might be much clearer.

Magazines face a very real danger from television. It is a matter of fact that television is what "killed" the picture news magazines. The public is invited, every day and night of the year, to view all major news events. They get their fiction in half-hour and one-hour segments. They get pictures and sound without mentally combining them, as they must do in magazines. Reading time gets narrowed down to the commuter train or an evening when television has little to offer. This means that a magazine must hold its readers, once they pick it up. Magazines must fight television as best they can. Pictures are the quickest persuader because the average reader is accustomed to a barrage of pictures from the television set.

The layout artist must grab the reader with a good picture before the reader can be held by a good story. This means studying pictures to get the most from them. Very often one picture will do this. Think about this when you might be tempted to flood a page with pictures. Will one picture catch the reader more positively than many? It's sort of like fishing and choosing the bait that will tempt the big ones. Actually, the layout artist may have only one chance to catch the reader, and this one chance might make the difference between reading or rejecting the story.

Study your competition—learn from it. Borrow, if necessary, but use it. As an example of just one evening of television watching, I obtained the following magazine layout "ideas."

1. The "double image." Two cameras, both at different focuses, create a picture that is a composite of the two. Converting this to magazine layout, one learns that a single-picture story can use the same picture in a variety of ways—different sizes, "flopping," or one in black-and-white, the other in color.

2. The "mirror image." Two same-size figures are placed next to each other, but with one picture overlapping the other to create a design or interesting formation. This can be easily done by using a mirror on a halftone, deciding ahead of time where to slice the picture to get the effect you want. The platemaker makes two same-size negatives instead of one and strips the two parts together.

3. Color filters are also used to create special effects. An example is a singer turned all blue for a "blues song" or red for a "hot" song. There is no problem doing this in magazines. A constant awareness of what television is doing plus a general knowledge of how to adapt television effects to the flat surface of the printed page is necessary.

Television also has weaknesses we can capitalize on. Almost everything we see must also be heard, which generally means people moving about and talking. Magazines have nearly an open field in anything except people as their subject. Antiques, though of prime interest to many, is *not* a subject for the "top ten" in the ratings game and would certainly be ignored during prime time. Sports, even though presented as they occur and with slow-motion replays, still

have an open field in magazines because there is little time on TV spent away from the action for indepth biographical sketches of the players. People want to know about their heroes. Prime-time television is much too costly to go into the interesting details about your most admired player. This means the printed word gains in importance. It is much more interesting to read than repeat to someone secondhand what you may have heard an announcer mention as an off-the-cuff observation.

Magazines in the specialty field do not have to play the ratings game and face no cancellation for lack of viewers *at a particular viewing time.* No one says you *must* read a certain magazine or story in a magazine between seven and eight o'clock Thursday evening. Reading time is up to the reader. It is this casual "enjoy me at your leisure" factor that can help keep magazines in competition with television.

In further studying the competition, we find that it has several weaknesses: the prime-time battle, the constant movement and sound, and the lack of interest in specialty fields. However, it also has many strong points. People like action. They can't get this from the printed word. People are lazy. They would rather get a one-hour condensation of a story than read it. The television cameraman and director can present views, sizes, and impositions that no magazine can possibly do.

I feel that continued study of television methods and presentations can teach us much. Keep a list of "adaptations" from the television screen and try making them work on the magazine's flat surface. Keep all your senses open for suggestions. Experiment without fear.

CHAPTER THIRTY-TWO

Tables, Graphs, and Charts

One of the more deadly forms of editorial layout is typeset tabular material found in many specialty magazines. Typographically there are few ways to make this more interesting. Both the layout artist and the typesetter are usually limited to rules, light face, bold face, italic, and regular type faces. Visually, the use of a variety of typefaces makes the final result "spotty."

The concept that typesetting is the easiest way cannot be denied. The easiest way, however, does not always mean the best way for the reader. Perhaps some of the alternatives can increase the layout artist's capabilities and give the reader some relief from masses of gray or spotty material.

Tables

Tables should always be examined for structure. Are there holes? Is information "lumped" into one or more areas? Is one area, or column, dominant? Are rules added to make reading easier? If so, do they dominate the visual appearance? Does the table spread across more than one page? Each of these questions has a graphic or visual answer.

Are there holes? This refers to areas of white space with little copy within the overall gray tabular text. There is no standard answer to this because the more columns one has, the greater the possibility there is of developing holes. There are some solutions that work in a great majority of cases. One of these is to create a diversion, to minimize the holes. In this solution, have the table preset without rules or reference lines. On receipt of the preset table, prepare a Bourges overlay. Scribe, or cut, rules creating lines or boxes and specify a 10 percent tint of gray (or color, if available). Note that the tint blocks will then fill every unit, giving the visual impression that each area is full.

Another solution (again a diversion) is to have the table preset and create a design with color tints complementing the holes. The white spaces (holes) are used as design elements, counterbalanced with color and the black type.

Still another solution is to turn the column heads vertically or on a slant. This narrows the column widths in which the holes appear.

Is information lumped into one or more columns? Since tables are rarely a balance of equally divided data, one can have the opposite of holes, a concentration of data in one area or column. Here, again, a diversion will help. When one area becomes congested with information, it is usually the one inviting the most attention. In this case, preset the table. On receipt of the preset table, prepare a Bourges overlay, creating a white "window" over the congested area. When the remainder of the table is either 10 percent gray or a light pastel color it will counterbalance the windows.

Is one area or column dominant? Dominance, in this case, is factual as opposed to visual. A column reporting final results is the crux of the table, as opposed to the others which are used to arrive at this final result. Tables should be read for final results. Color can be used to highlight certain columns.

Are rules added to make reading easier? If so, do they dominate the table's appearance? Some editorial styles specify that any table more than one column in width utilize hairline rules to make following the data easier. The danger here is that in long tables (particularly in depth) the rules subtract from good visual appearance and create bars or stripes that are not attractive. The answer is to sublimate the lines. Instead of black, they could be 40 percent of black (gray) or a light color (if color is available). Another solution is to turn to Bourges, again, and use a tint background, with the lines reversed to white.

Does the table spread across more than one page? This is often a difficult problem to solve, as the extra width will usually counteract any solution. The use of color tints increases in importance over large areas and subtracts from the data.

Color over a large area will also lose its impact and serve no real function. The most logical answer is to use color in small amounts. A 1-point rule box bridging the gutter helps. Hairline rules in a light color will also be effective.

When working with tints, percentages of gray or color, remember that tint bands can cross. If one specifies a 20 percent tint of or-

Patient	Age, yr	Ice Hockey	Street/floor Hockey	Lacerations	Fractures	Hyphema	Angle Recession	Traumatic Iritis	Corneal Abrasion	Subluxated Lens	Cataract	Retinal Edema	Retinal Detachment	Retinal Hemorrhage	Vitreous Hemorrhage	Ruptured Globe	Cerebral Concussion	Comments	Hospitalized	Possible Late Complications
1	11		*			*				*	*				*			Will need lens extraction in future	*	*
2	16		*			*													*	
3	15		*	*				*												
4	19	*		*		*	*					*	*					Required scleral buckle; permanent decrease of visual acuity to 20/40	*	*
5	41	*				*						*	*							*
6	24	*			Nose				*											
7	23	*						*	*											*
8	14	*						*												
9	17	*		*																
10	25	*			Blow out														*	
11	11		*			*		*												
12	13		*						*											
13	17		*			*													*	
14	16	*															*			
15	14	*		*	Orbit												*		*	
16	14	*							*											
17	20	*															*	Recurrence of esotropia after injury; required surgery (6 mo)	*	*
18	16	*				*													*	
19	16	*				*						*		*	*				*	
20	24	*						*										Lacerated conjunctiva		
21	16	*				*													*	
22	11	*				*	*					*		*				Permanent macula scarring	*	*
23	7	*							*											
24	19		*					*												
25	36	*				*	*			*									*	*
26	39	*				*	*												*	*
27	13	*		*																
28	17		*	*														Severe cellulitis of lids		
29	14		*					*	*											
30	16	*		*				*	*											
31	19	*						*	*											
32	15	*														*		Enucleation	*	*
33	17	*		*	Orbit			*						*				Commotio retinae with choroidal tear; final visual actuity of 20/25	*	*
34	20	*		*				*	*										*	*
35	8		*			*	*													*
36	19	*				*	*	*				*	*	*				Choroidal tear; permanent macula scar; final visual acuity of 20/200		
37	10		*											*				Surgery 3 mo after injury	*	*
38	19	*						*												
Total		26	12	9	4	13	7	12	9	3	3	5	2	4	2	1	3		16	12

* Asterisks indicate presence of injury; case 32 is that of Carter Tallman, MD, and cases 33 and 34 are those of Peter Lawlor, MD.

Figure 32.1—A table with "holes" as described in the text. Notice that there are large open areas and that it is difficult to follow some of the information.

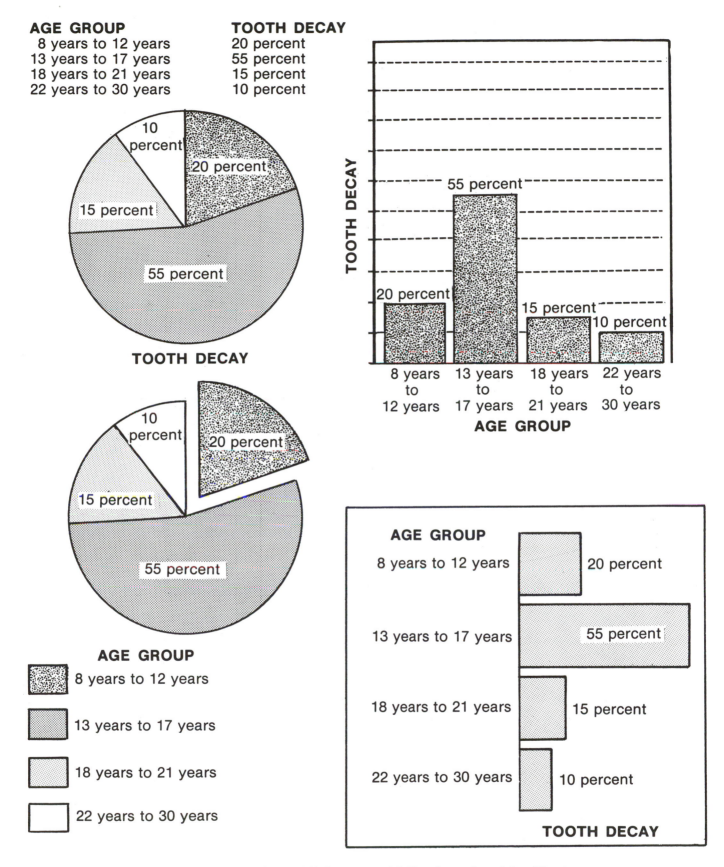

AGE GROUP	TOOTH DECAY
8 years to 12 years	20 percent
13 years to 17 years	55 percent
18 years to 21 years	15 percent
22 years to 30 years	10 percent

Figure 32.2—*The original tabular material is shown at upper left. These data are shown in four different ways: a pie graph, an exploded pie graph, vertical bars, and horizontal bars. A second color would make these more attractive.*

ange, every time the 20 percent band crosses another 20 percent band, a 40 percent tinted area will occur. This comes in handy when two columns have a common result and the result is a summation of two areas of information.

Bar Graphs

Bar graphs usually have a title or descriptive words for each measure of value. While this is usually on a one-to-one basis, there are also occasions when two or more values of the same subject occur within the same bar. Bar graphs should be studied for direction, as the horizontal bars may be too much like the text. For example, wide columns give a visual appearance of width to tables that are horizontal. The visual appearance of two horizontals only increases the feeling. Bar graphs have the quality of presenting the same information vertically *or* horizontally. Therefore, in text with wide columns, changing the direction of the bars to verticals can create interest. In narrow columns, changing the bars to verticals will only accentuate the column look. Change of direction can always add interest to any page design.

Converting tabular material to pie graphs is relatively easy with the use of a protractor. All tabular material should equal 100 percent. Each percent equals 3.6 degrees, as there are 360 degrees in a circle. Converting 20 percent into ''degrees'' is simply a matter of multiplication (20 times 3.6 equals 72 degrees). Graphically this becomes a matter of drawing a circle and dividing it into equivalent degrees, or pie slices. Pie graphs are particularly effective in color. They can have added impact by ''shadowing'' the pie cuts.

Charts

Charts are still another way of presenting tabular data. Charts have two common scales, up and down and left to right. Data are plotted on points common to both scales, creating a series of connecting lines that reflect the up-and-down courses of the accumulated data. The advantage in charts is that the common scales can present up to three lines of similar data as a single visual unit. This is also effective in color.

Table 5.—Earliest Roentgenographic Changes Observed in 153 Patients						
Roentgenographic Findings	No. of Days From Onset of First Symptom					
	1-6	7-10	11-20	21-30	31-60	>60
Destruction	5	17	31	17	5	1*
New bone formation	...	4	19	15	1	...
Destruction and new bone formation	...	...	7	6	...	1
Periosteal reaction	...	5	9	1	1	...
Sequestrum	...	...	...	1	...	...
Cortical irregularity	...	1	2	1	1	...
Demineralization	...	1	1	...	...	...

* Tuberculous osteomyelitis.

Table 6.—Infected Bones in 152 Patients With One Bone Involved and 11 Patients With Multiple Bones Involved			
Bone	No. of Cases With One Bone Involved	No. of Cases With Multiple Bones Involved	Total
Femur	49	3	52
Tibia	33	5	38
Humerus	21	4	25
Fibula	8	4	12
Phalanx	7	1	8
Radius	6	2	8
Calcaneus	5	0	5
Ulna	4	1	5
Metatarsal	3	0	3
Ischium	3	0	3
Vertebra	2	0	2
Ribs	0	1	1
Miscellaneous*	11	0	11

* Maxilla, mandible, clavicle, sternum, wrist, cuboid, metacarpal, cuneiform, sacrum, ilium, bone of piriform aperture.

Table 7.—Incidence of Recurrent or Chronic Disease in 87 Patients With Staphylococcal Osteomyelitis		
Duration of Parenteral Antibiotic Therapy*	No. of Cases	No. of Failures
Within one week†	2	2
From 8 to 14 days†	14	2
From 15 to 21 days†	21	3
From 22 to 28 days	28	0
From 29 to 35 days	8	0
From 36 to 42 days	6	0
From 43 to 49 days	3	1
More than 50 days	3‡	0
Total	**85**	**8**

* Penicillin or antipenicillinase drugs used.
† Nineteen percent failure rate in 37 patients receiving parenteral antibiotics for fewer than 21 days.
‡ Fifty-five days, 57 days, 74 days.

Figure 32.3—Three tables and three ways of drawing attention to various areas. These would be even better with a second color.

CHAPTER THIRTY-THREE

Those Invisible Construction Lines

Constant observation shows that most editorial page layouts fail because they have been planned and executed only on the basis of "good" composition. This means shifting weights and sizes around to achieve balance or an otherwise pleasing effect. There is nothing actually wrong with this premise. It just hasn't been carried far enough.

There are some very important qualities in a layout. The first is the way the elements have been grouped, clustered, balanced, or otherwise arranged. Another is what is actually in the pictures. However, there is still another quality that can either make or break a picture layout. This consists of "those invisible construction lines" *within* the pictures.

These "lines" have the ability to hold a layout together.

In well-constructed magazine layouts we are concerned with what we see and what we want the reader to see. Even more, we should also be acutely aware of what we do *not* see. I am talking about those "lines" within pictures that are not actual lines but directional movements.

Even the most prosaic layouts, those built around the simple placement of geometric shapes, have these "invisible lines." The easiest to identify is the center of balance "line" that occurs on almost every page. Elements are placed in various positions relating to the center of balance, and layouts then either strive for symmetrical or asymmetrical balance in relationship to this line. This is the prime weakness of far too many magazine layouts. Certainly there

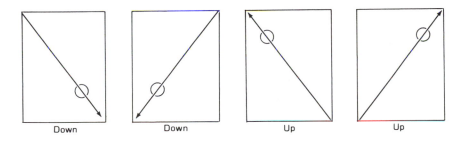

Figure 33.1—*The basic diagonal movements and how location of the "sight object" affects the movement.*

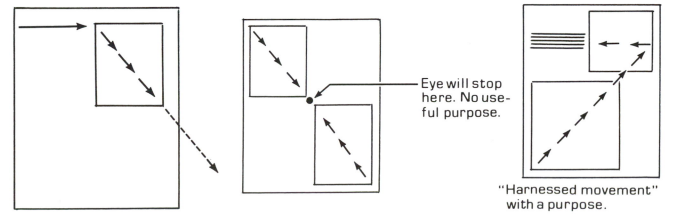

Figure 33.2—*How a "down movement" tends to carry the reader's eye off the page.*

Eye will stop here. No useful purpose.

"Harnessed movement" with a purpose.

Figure 33.3—*Some of the basic premises in the text.*

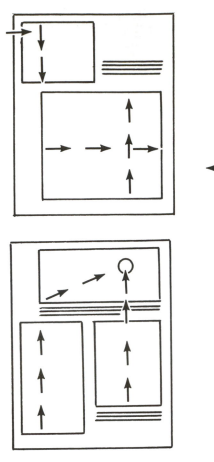

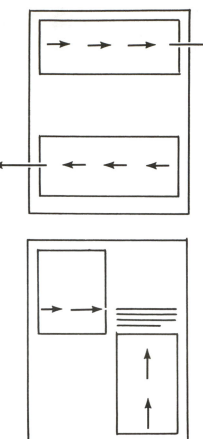

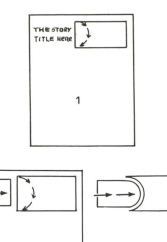

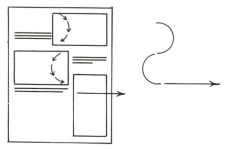

Figure 33.6—*Illustrating how circular movements can be used to include title areas or another picture into controlled organization.*

Figure 33.4—*Illustrating how you can harness the movements in more than one picture.*

Figure 33.5—*Illustrating how movements can carry you away from the story or captions (top) and how you could reorganize to control those movements to the caption (below).*

Figure 33.7—*You could even harness two or more movements.*

is balance of weights, sizes, and placement, *but* what about the visual elements *in* the pictures? How do they affect the whole layout?

When we talk about what's in pictures, we must first define our terms. All pictures have two things in common—an outside edge (defining its shape) and several structural lines within the picture itself. These structural lines are the diagonal, the vertical, the horizontal, the circular, and the directional pointer.

The Diagonal

The diagonal has two definite "movements." When the diagonal starts at either of the upper corners and moves toward the lower corners, the movement is downward. When the diagonal starts at either of the bottom corners and moves toward the upper corners, the movement is upward. Figure 33.1

will help illustrate: The circle represents a "sight object" occurring on the diagonal. In utilizing the diagonal line, look for a sight object along its axis. This will help determine the up or down movement.

How can we utilize this movement in a layout?

1. If there is only one picture, use the movement to carry the reader's eye to the title area (up), to a blurb, to a caption (down), or even into the next page. *Do not place it in any position that does not use the movement for a purpose,* for instance, a "down" diagonal movement placed at the upper right on a page. As you can see, from figure 33.2, the movement carries the reader *away* from the text and serves no purpose.

2. If there is more than one picture, use the movement to carry the reader's eye to other pictures, but study them for movements that

will create a cohesive group. *Do not use two similar movements that will cancel each other out.*

The Vertical

The vertical has two definite movements—up and down. It doesn't matter where the vertical bisects the shape. There will always be an eye movement up or an eye movement down.

How can we utilize these movements in layouts?

1. If the picture has an "up" movement, have it carry the reader's eye to the title area, a blurb, the caption, or another picture. Be sure it does *not* carry the reader's eye off the page and into a void. The oppo-

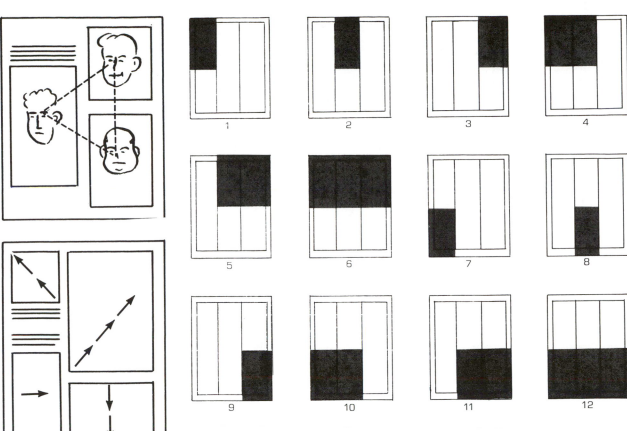

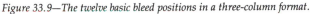

Figure 33.9—The twelve basic bleed positions in a three-column format.

Figure 33.8—How you can create a "shape within a shape" by controlled eye movements (top); how movements can "shotgun" a good picture spread when not planned (middle); and how movements can all lead to the caption, if planned (bottom).

site holds true for a "down" movement, though you will rarely use this to lead into a title area.
2. If there is more than one picture, use the movement to an advantage. In other words, make it help you control the reader's eye.

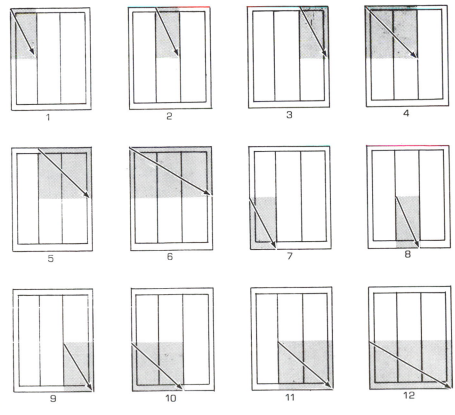

Figure 33.10—Diagonals moving from upper left to lower right.

The Horizontal

The horizontal also has two movements—to the left and to the right. They may also contain a lesser vertical movement and very often do. How can we utilize these movements?

1. A "left to right" movement will carry the reader's eye across the page. Let it lead to another picture, a blurb, or a caption. *Never let it lead into a new story.* You'll lose the eye control necessary to keep the reader within the present story.

2. A "right to left" movement will return the reader's eye much like a returning typewriter carriage. Use it to point to a title area, blurb, caption, or another picture. *Do not let it lead away from the story.*

3. If there is more than one picture, use the movement to an advantage as shown in figure 33.3.

The Circular—Spiral and Ellipse

The circular movement can be a circle or an eye-arresting spot, which causes the reader's eye to pause. The spiral will lead, or point, in one direction, usually up or down on the diagonal. The ellipse tends to encompass only a part of the picture, using the other part for peripheral balance within the shape, or outer edge, of the picture.

How do we utilize these movements?

1. If you want the reader to stop, utilize the circle.
2. If you use the spiral, see comments under "diagonals."
3. If you use the ellipse, make it "work" for you by:
   a. enclosing a title area, blurb, or caption
   b. helping form another edge to another picture (visually)
   c. helping create another movement or strengthen an existing one.

Directional Pointers

These are invariably pyramid in shape, the apex creating an arrow.

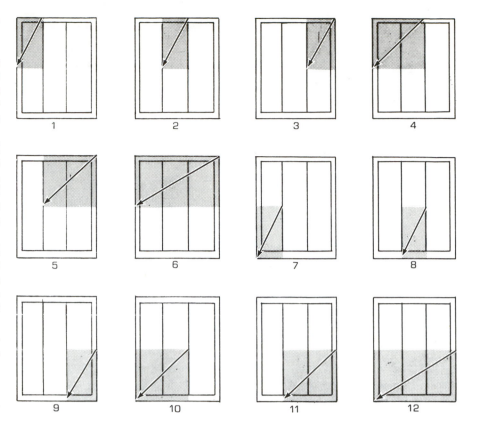

Figure 33.11—Diagonals moving from upper right to lower left.

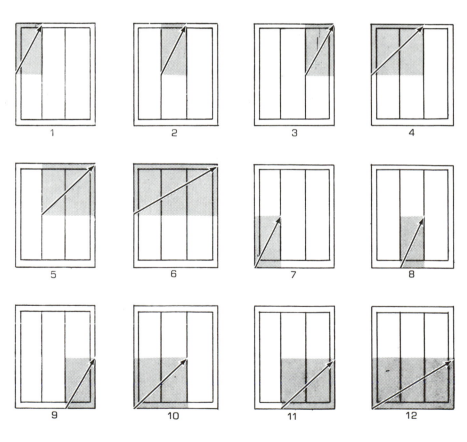

Figure 33.12—Diagonals moving from lower left to upper right.

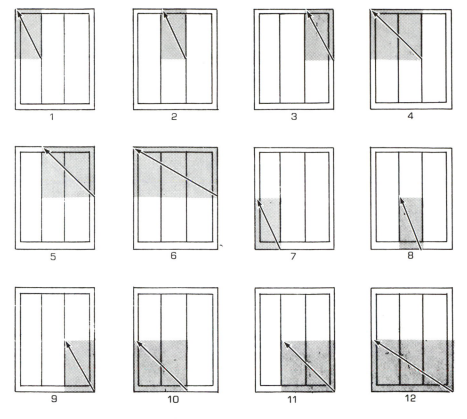

Figure 33.13—Diagonals moving from lower right to upper left.

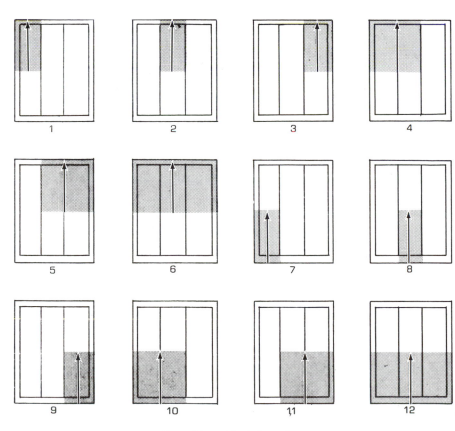

Figure 33.14—Verticals moving up.

They can be strong shapes or colors *within* a picture. They are easily identified by their "pointing" quality.

How do we utilize this movement?

1. Have the point lead the reader's eye into a title area, blurb, caption, or another picture.
2. *Never let it lead away from the story you are working on.*

People's faces, particularly the direction in which they are looking and in many cases, pointing, are very strong eye movers. Do not abuse them.

Combining Movements

All picture movements are basic. Many pictures combine one or more movements, even though one may predominate. Things to look for are:

1. Will one movement dominate? If so, use it for that movement.
2. Will two movements tend to cancel each other? If so, remember that they will also do this for the reader.
3. Will the point where two movements meet hold the reader's eye there? If so, do you want this to happen?

How can you handle combination movements in relation to movements in the other layout elements? Remember that title areas are, more often than not, horizontals and that captions, even though basically square or rectangular, are still horizontals; even blurbs are usually classified as horizontals. Conversely, columns of type are always verticals. What I want to emphasize here is that there are shapes (types of movements) *outside* the pictures that can have a direct bearing on the movements *within* the pictures.

All movements should be utilized in every layout. The best layouts are those in which the movements create shapes or designs *within* the geometric composition.

How Bleeds Affect Movements

There are twelve basic bleed positions in the three-column format.

In each case, the directional movements previously described will be affected because the bleed will tend to increase the movement. Any bleed picture is slightly out of the ordinary and will draw more attention. Figure 33.9 shows these twelve basic bleed positions, identifying each by a number. These numbers will be used to identify each of the primary movements and how they are affected by bleeding.

Diagonals moving from upper left to lower right (Figure 33.10)

1. Points to a title area, caption, or blurb. Veers slightly away from pointing to beginning of text material.
2. Points to a blurb, caption, or another picture. Because of the central position, can rarely point to a title area, as it would be away from the normal starting point.
3. Points off the page and away from almost anything.
4. Points into column three. Could point to a caption, blurb, or another picture. Leads away from the beginning of the text.
5. Points off the page and also away from any good caption, blurb, or title area location.
6. See 5.
7. See 5, but could point to a caption.
8. See 5, but could point to a caption.
9. See 5.
10. See 5, but could point to a caption.
11. See 5.
12. See 5.

Diagonals moving from upper right to lower left (Figure 33.11)

1. Points into the first column of copy. This is a good position for this movement.
2. Points somewhere into column one, but not at the beginning of the text material. Could point to a caption, blurb, or another picture.
3. Points somewhere into column two. This makes it difficult for the reader's eye to return to the

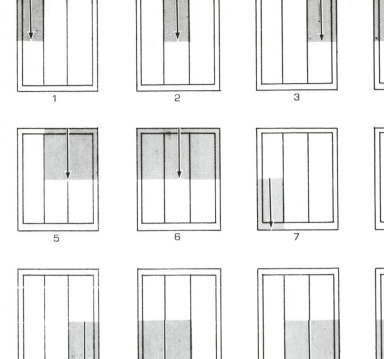

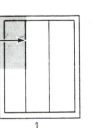

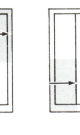
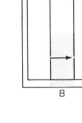

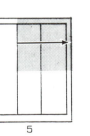

Figure 33.15—*Verticals moving down.*

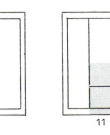

Figure 33.16—*Horizontals moving left to right.*

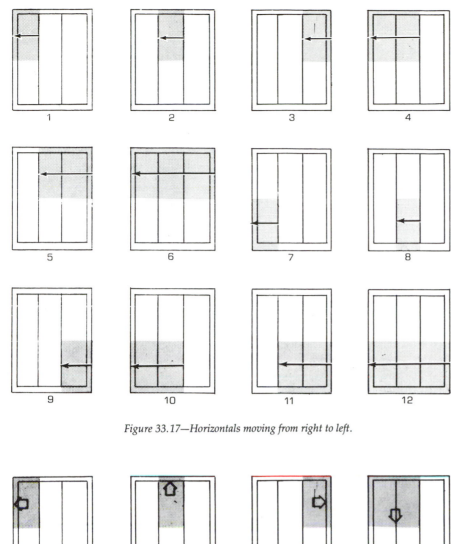

Figure 33.17—Horizontals moving from right to left.

beginning of the text without jumping over visual obstacles. Could point to a caption, blurb, picture, or title area.

4. Points into the first column of text or a caption.
5. See 1.
6. See 1.
7. Points off the page. There is no good way to return the reader's eye to the first column of text, a caption, or a blurb and really no way possible to point into a title area.
8. See 7, but could point to a caption.
9. See 7, but could point to a caption.
10. See 7.
11. See 8.
12. See 7.

Diagonals moving from lower left to upper right (Figure 33.12)

1. Points away from beginning of the text. Could point to a title area, blurb, or caption.
2. Points away from text. Could point to a blurb or caption, but rarely to a title area as the movement is away from the beginning of the text.
3. Points off the page and away from almost everything.
4. Could point to a caption or blurb.
5. Points off the page. Rarely a good position.
6. Points off the page.
7. Could point to a title area, blurb, caption, or another picture.
8. Could point to a caption or another picture.
9. See 3.
10. Could point to a title area or another picture.
11. See 3.
12. See 3.

Diagonals moving from lower right to upper left (Figure 33.13)

1. Points off the page. Never good for a first page.
2. Could point to a title area, blurb, or caption.
3. Could point to a title area, blurb, caption, or another picture.
4. See 1.

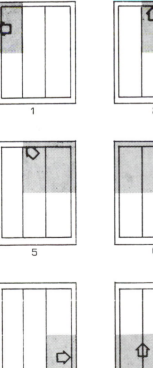
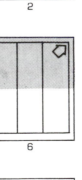
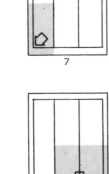

Figure 33.18—Some pointers in the basic bleed positions.

A

C

B

Figure 33.19—A, B, C, D, and E illustrate movements within pictures.

caption, blurb, or another picture.

Verticals moving down (Figure 33.15)

1. Points into text or to a title area, blurb, caption, or another picture.
2. Basically the same as number one, but a little contrived for a title area.
3. Points to a caption, blurb, or another picture, but it is very difficult to get this into a title area.
4–6. See 1.
7–12. All point off the page and away from everything.

Horizontals moving from left to right (Figure 33.16)

1. Points to title area, blurb, caption, or another picture.
2. See 1.
3. Points off the page.
4. See 1.
5. See 3.
6. See 3.
7. Could point to a caption, blurb, or another picture.
8. See 7.
9. See 3.
10. See 7.
11. See 3.
12. See 3.

5. See 2.
6. See 1.
7. Could point to a title area, blurb, or caption, but rarely to another picture as it points off the page.
8. Could point to a title area, but this might be contrived. Would ordinarily point to a caption or another picture.
9. See 8.

10. See 7.
11. See 8.
12. See 7.

Verticals moving up (Figure 33.14)

1–6. All point off the page and away from almost anything you might try to adapt to the movement.
7–12. Could point to a title area,

D

E

Horizontals moving from right to left (Figure 33.17)

1. Points away from almost everything.
2. Could point to a title area, blurb, caption, or another picture.
3. See 2.
4. See 1.
5. See 2.
6. See 1.
7. See 1.
8. Could point to a caption, blurb, or another picture.
9. See 8.
10. See 1.
11. See 8.
12. See 1.

After examining the twelve basic bleed positions and the effects of various movements on bleeds you can see that there are some preferred positions and some poor positions. There are variables, of course, because you might have a picture with more than one movement, which might remove some of the stigma from the positions indicated as "poor."

I have not covered circles, spirals, or "pointers" in bleed positions because the location *within* the rectangle can affect its movement. For example, in "position one," a pointer could have many more than eight variations.

I have not covered irregular shapes either, such as outline halftones, oval framing, free form, and the like, because the outer edge of the form will always draw more attention than what's inside the form, thereby cancelling it.

CHAPTER THIRTY-FOUR

The "Mini-Magazine" Format

There is a growing tendency in the publishing industry to look for ways to minimize paper and postage costs for the subscription magazine. Eliminating half the bulk might be a beginning toward solving the problem. This points the designer to the "digest" size, 5³/₈ by 7¹/₂ inches.

Reader's Digest has been with us for many years. The designer's first impulse should be to study a win-

ner. It has two equal columns set on 12¹/₂ picas, a 1-pica alley, 2¹/₂-pica borders at the top and sides, and a 4-pica area at the bottom to carry the folio number. The magazine is perfect-bound because of its bulk, or number of pages involved. It has a wrap-around cover, and the table of contents on the cover. It has been this way for as long as I can remember.

There are several valid points in

this format. There is really no good column arrangement other than two equal columns. Anything smaller would create rivers and hyphenated words in profusion. Anything wider, such as one column on 25 picas, would tend to make reading difficult and limit pictures to include "run-around copy." This is always difficult and time consuming.

Reader's Digest is a copy-oriented

Figure 34.1—The basic mini-magazine format.

A

Topical steroids are contraindicated in vac
cinia, varicella, and in patients hypers
ensitive to any components of

If irritation develops, discontinue
and institute this preparation.
appropriate therapy. If infection is present

If a favorable response does
priate antifungal or antibacterial agent,
, institute use of an appro

little or no effect. In addition to ot
differences, cow's milk contains th
times as much tryptophan per mil
ter as breast milk, suggesting
possibility that the increased tr
tophan load enhanced metabol
through the quinolic metabolic pa
way with the accumulation of x
thurenic acid or of a similar meta
lite considered to be toxic (Fig
Since diiodohydroxyquin and x
thurenic acid are both substitu
quinoline compounds, Hansson s
gested that diiodohydroxyquin a
by competitive inhibition, there
preventing the accumulation of x
thurenic acid in toxic amounts.
found normal xanthurenic acid exc
tion in one case of AE, and noted
clinical change following the or:
administered tryptophan load.[11] C
and Berger[10] measured kynure
acid excretion in a patient with
during an exacerbation and foun
to be normal. We found all tryp
phan metabolites to be normal foll
ing tryptophan loading, with :
without pyridoxine stimulation.

Pyridoxine is essential for seve
of the steps in the metabolism
tryptophan. Cash and Berger[10] no
exacerbation of clinical symptoms
lowing intravenous administratior
pyridoxine (100 mg daily for six da
in their case. Nicotinamide (200
administered intramuscularly
seven days) was without effect.[11]
noted no clinical change after oral
ministration of 5.0-gm tryptopl
loads or of 100 mg of intramuscula

given pyridoxine. Patients w
known defects in tryptophan meta
lism, such as those affected with
droxykynureninuria[32] and pyridoxi
dependent infantile convulsior
have unquestionable and large qu
titative abnormalities in the urin
metabolites, particularly xanthure
acid and 3-hydroxyanthranilic aci

Freier and associates[11] repor
"deterioration" of an otherwise
treated patient after five days
intravenously administered tryp
phan. The patient was undergoin
series of therapeutic trials with p
enterally administered amino ac
and routinely worsened each time
amino acid infusions were stopp
Since the tryptophan was admi
tered during the time when
amino acid infusions were discont
ued and deterioration might h.
been expected, it is difficult to det
mine whether the worsening was
to the tryptophan or simply to the
sence of effective therapy.

Robertson and co-workers[34] are
only investigators to report an abn
mality in tryptophan metabolism
AE. They observed an accumulat
of kynurenine following tryptopl
loading experiments and normal l
els of metabolites below kynuren
in the metabolic pathway, suggest
a possible deficiency in kynuren
hydroxylase. As with other investi
tors, no clinical exacerbation
noted following oral tryptophan
gestion. Interpretation of tryptop
studies is difficult because of dif

B

Design News

Mini Magazine Format in action

mucosal cells and more typica!
those seen in an actively metaboli:
state. We have also observed a s
lar picture with numerous inclus:
(presumably lipid) in jejunal muc
tissue obtained at least 15 hours p
prandially. Moynahan et al[46] repor
weak staining for succinic d
drogenase and leucine amino;
tidase activity in jejunal muc
cells. This finding has been repor
in a variety of unrelated gastr
testinal disorders and is prob:

In treating extensive areas, the possibility exists of
until the infection is adequately controlled.
not occur promptly, discontinue the corticosteroi

eral consensus that the morpholog;
the GI tract is essentially norma
AE, except for the irregular and
consistent areas of focal mucosal
generation. The ultrastructural
clusions observed in jejunal muc
cells under fasting conditions may
meaningful but they will require 1
ther elucidation.

A single and highly questiona
association of AE with fibrocystic
ease of the pancreas was reported
Ugland[48] in 1952, prior to the use
diiodohydroxyquin. His patient d
and showed pancreatic fibrosis on
topsy. The only possible link to
was the presence of acral dermat
during the terminal stages of the
tient's disease. Since no other such
stance has ever been reported,
one case is probably fortuitous. (
patient had normal amounts of p
creatic lipase, amylase and tryp:
normal fecal fat, and sweat chloric
all of which are grossly abnormai
fibrocystic disease.

Others have suggested pancre:
dysfunction in AE, although
claims have never been substantia
or considered significant. Rodin :
Goldman[44] described a cribriform ;
tern of the islets of Langerhans in
autopsied patient. Bloom[49] stud
pancreatic proteolytic enzymes :
measured absorption of ^{131}I-labe
neutral fat and oleic acid and fou
all tests normal although the abs
tion of ^{131}I-labeled neutral fat \

are not similar to those we have
served in our patient. The promin
insulin spike seen early in the
GTT on several occasions is simila
the excessive insulin release seer
various GI diseases or following
surgery. This type of hyperinsulin
is due to excessive activity of
various factors that stimulate or
tentiate insulin release, includ
secretin, gastrin, pancreozyminch
cystokinin, and intestinal glucag
like immunoreactive material. R
tive hypoglycemic symptoms, wh
may be seen with this type of hy
insulinism, were not encountered
our patient.[23] At the time of this w
ing, our patient is six months pr
slightly reduced. The absorption
[131]I-labeled triolein was normal in
patient, indicating sufficient p
creatic lipase to break triolein and
equate mucosal surface for absorpt
of the by-products.

The observation of glucose into:
ance and abnormal insulin respo
in our patient also suggests the p
sibility of pancreatic dysfuncti
although we were unable to dem
strate any other evidence of p
creatic insufficiency. Ilic and Lalev
and Bloom and Sobel[50] found nor
GTTs in their patients, although D
bolt[51] reported a case with an abn
mal glucose curve demonstratin;
sharp and rapid initial rise. Our
tient has a family history of diabe
making interpretation of the d
difficult. However, it should be e
phasized that in a prediabetic w
chemical diabetes the insulin patte
1942, the disease was generally c
sidered to be a form or variant of

dermolysis bullosa of the dystror
or letalis type.

Following recognition of the
ease as a separate clinical entity,
merous theories of its cause were ;
posed over the years.

In 1963, Hansson combined sev
previous observations into a the
proposing an abnormality in tryr
phan metabolism.[11] It was known
early as 1936 that cow's milk agg
vated AE[28] and that human bre

of topical steroids has not absorption of
taken. In pregnant females, the safe use
increased systemic

Figure 34.2—A, B, and C (next page) show how the "half pyramid" placement falls neatly within the mini- magazine format.

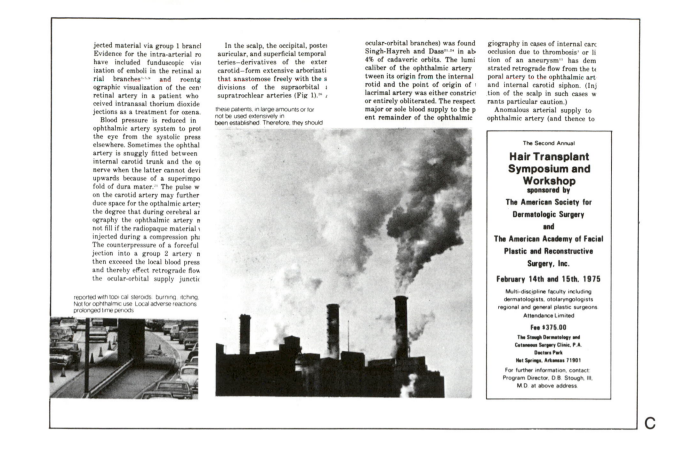

C

magazine and uses "fillers" to great advantage. If one were to faithfully copy this format and try to adapt it to a picture-oriented magazine one would find the picture sizes limited to one column, two columns, a full page, or any multiple equaling 25 picas. This would result in pictures about 8½ picas wide, or postage stamp size.

A natural impulse would be to follow the line of least resistance—copy the format and squeeze a picture-oriented magazine into a copy-oriented format. The trouble is—it will look like just that.

There is a solution that is not a faithful following of a *Reader's Digest* format. It lies in a slight difference in the handling of the gutter area. Now is also a valid time to point out that almost *all* magazines handle pages—even double page spreads—as individual pages. They all have equal borders at the top and sides and a slightly larger area at the bottom. But you know that *no* page exists as an individual page, except the cover and back cover. Every other page *faces* another page.

In the illustrated layout sheet (figure 34.2), I have changed the gutter area from 2½ picas on each side (totaling 5 picas) to 2 picas on each side (totaling 4 picas). I have decreased the column widths to 12 picas from 12½ picas. We have also used a 1½-pica alley instead of a 1-pica alley. While these small changes don't sound like much, they give us a white space panel at the outside edge of each page 2 picas wide. They also moved facing pages slightly closer together, making them a more cohesive unit.

In the examples shown, I use this white space panel area for titles, pictures, and picture captions. The result is clean, neat, and functional, all the basic requirements for good design. Ads may be full page or 13 picas wide.

I call this the "half-pyramid" format because almost all the sight elements can occur at the base of the pyramid, the bottom of the page area, and decrease in steps toward the top. The magazine would have to be produced in eight-page signatures and perfect-bound to retain the narrower gutter area.

CHAPTER THIRTY-FIVE

Tabloids

More and more internal publications are using the tabloid size. There are two possible reasons for this—the concept of a newspaper style and the availability of paper in 11-by-14-inch multiples. It is also somewhat easier to locate a local printer, as most local newspapers are geared to handle the tabloid, with both typesetting and printing available in one place. The tabloid, however, is neither a newspaper nor a magazine.

Look at the diagrams of facing pages in a tabloid format (figures 35.1 and 35.2). Here we see the ad sizes most frequently used—the full page, the one-column vertical, and the two-thirds island. Note that these ad sizes will fit the usual four-column tabloid format—namely, 13-pica columns separated with 1-pica alleys. Not shown is the half-page horizontal because that will fit within the full page (as will two quarter-page ads or four quarter-page ads).

Why the discussion on ad sizes? Here is where we often find the beginning of how and why a design has been used—money to finance the publication. It also points up the fact that there are tabloid column formats that will accept ad sizes if you want them—even if yours is an in-house publication. So there is a beginning to tabloid design—column sizes determined by ad sizes. Another very impor-

Figure 35.1—Lefthand page with four 14-pica columns and 1-pica alleys.

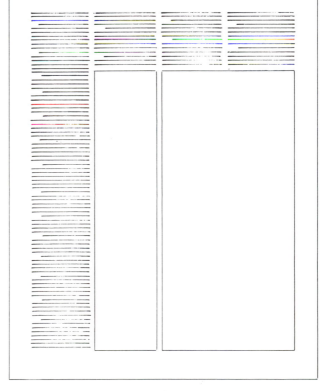

Figure 35.2—Righthand page with four 14-pica columns and 1-pica alleys.

Tabloids 157

tant remark is in order. The ad sizes and the four-column format always create an "L" shape on each page and combine into a "T" shape on facing pages. This predetermined shape is formidable.

Let us assume, for the balance of this discussion, that the tabloid design is for an internal publication, and no ads are being used.

In a tabloid the page size is 11 by 14 inches. This breaks down to 66 by 84 picas. The "live area" is this size less the borders. The usual borders are 5 picas at the top and sides and 6 at the bottom, the additional pica being for the folio and running foot. The "live area" width is 56 picas. Our design problem now distills down to what column formats can we get within the 56-pica width. It is apparent that the depth will not be affected by column designs, since columns are vertical in pattern and of lengths that can vary depending on the paper size.

First of all we can fit three 18-pica columns with 1-pica alleys in the format. This is illustrated in figure 35.3. What is different in this illustration is that the designer has pur-

posely gone to a "horizontal feeling." Many tabloid designers use the modular system within the vertical columns and end up with an increased vertical feeling. We propose that the designer purposely divide the page into unequal units of space, the largest at the top, followed by a medium size unit and a smaller unit. This not only creates visual interest, but also gives areas suitable to the headline importance.

The next variable is a format consisting of four columns of 13 picas with $1^{1}/_3$-pica alleys. This accommodates most magazine ads. It should also be handled as "uneven" horizontal units, as figure 35.4 illustrates. There is a large space at the top for the major headline area, followed by two areas, one slightly larger than the other for the two minor headline areas and pictures. In this case I have shown how a hairline rule can be used to separate the horizontal areas.

Note that in both of the illustrations I have purposely used white space in the headline areas. This is highly desirable from a design

standpoint and helps break up the strong column arrangements. The white space subtly divides the page into horizontal units. Hairline rules are used only as an aid to help those designers who feel the white space must be filled with "something." Also note that I have not used banners or logos to identify the tabloid by name. The banner can be placed anywhere in an in-house publication.

Within the 56-pica width, I can use five 10-pica columns with $1^{1}/_2$-pica alleys. This is illustrated in figure 35.5. The subtle switch from a strong horizontal arrangement can now be discarded in favor of the more conventional vertical arrangement. The headline areas are not strong enough to favor a horizontal movement, and the columns are narrow enough to emphasize the vertical feeling.

Figure 35.6 has six columns. They are $8^{1}/_2$ picas wide with 1-pica alleys. There is no way to keep a horizontal arrangement within this column format. There is one other design factor of note: $8^{1}/_2$ picas is as narrow as you can get a column of 8/10 or 9/11 copy and not create

Figure 35.3—Three 18-pica columns with 1-pica alleys.

Figure 35.4—Four 13-pica columns with $1^{1}/_3$-pica alleys.

"rivers" of white due to word spacing. I have thrown in an arrangement of headline areas in this illustration. The major headline is at a point well under the top of the live area leaving a minor headline area at the top of the page.

With the six-column format, I have exhausted the column width possibilities within the 56-pica measure. In the past, designers and layout artists have used these

Figure 35.5—Five 10-pica columns with 1½-pica alleys.

Figure 35.6—Six 8½-pica columns with 1-pica alleys.

Figure 35.7—A mix-and-match of five columns and three columns.

Figure 35.8—A combination of four columns with six columns.

column widths but have always been consistent in using the same format throughout the publication. This is a design error.

Look at figure 35.7. This is a "mix and match" of three columns with five columns. Right away we notice that there is a visual change—the areas separate into viable units independently. They are held together by the common live-area width (56 picas) but stand free as units. This is further emphasized by a change in headline locations and sizes. This could also be three columns, three columns, and five columns (instead of three, five, and five). It could also be five, three, and five. The idea, of course, is that you can "mix" the two on the same page with good design results.

Figure 35.8 combines four columns with six columns. These can also be four-six-six or four-six-four or six-six-four instead of four-four-six. The idea here is that one can get some pretty interesting column formations and different designs within the same area.

So far I've described "horizontal" designs. What if I want to go "vertical"?

Figure 35.9 is a combination of a 20-pica column and three 11-pica columns, separated with 1-pica alleys, again within the "56-pica live area" width. This combines a feature column with news items. While I have used only two headlines, there could be three. This design creates a visual backbone (the 20-pica column enclosed with a hairline rule box), while the news items and their headlines literally "hang" from it. If this were a double-page spread, the 20-pica columns would be next to the gutter, giving the pages a pica combination of 11-11-11-20/20-11-11-11. We have now combined a vertical design with horizontals.

Figure 35.10 takes the feature column (a horizontal) and combines it with six columns of news articles. Even though the design seems horizontal, the narrow columns "hang" from the feature box, creating verticals.

No doubt there are many other combinations that would create good designs. What I have attempted to do here is to show you that you need not restrict yourself to a single column-width format.

Typography can constitute a design element in tabloids. I am frequently asked which is better, justified or flush left, ragged right? As you will note from the examples and discussions preceding, justified columns have a purity that blends well with the designs shown. But let's also be practical. Many people like the sans-serif typefaces as body copy. And the design feeling for sans-serifs is that they look better set flush left, ragged right. And we always have the designer who says (as if he personally discovered it), "Sans-serif, flush left, ragged right is 'modern.'" (As a historical note—sans-serif typefaces are *not* new. I have a Civil War typeface book in which almost half of the typefaces shown are sans-serifs.)

Let's look at the different column

Figure 35.9—A combination of one 20-pica column and three 11-pica columns with 1-pica alleys.

Figure 35.10—A combination of a horizontal feature with six-column format.

formations and see which might adapt to flush left, ragged right. Three columns? Yes, if the ragged lines do not vary by more than five or six characters and spaces. If more than six, the alleys get too large and irregular. What you end up with are large "rivers" of white space between columns. This can be compensated for with hairline rules, but fails to look clean, neat and functional.

Four columns? Only if the ragged setting is within the five to six character and space "rag" *and* if hairline rules are used between columns. Five and six column are already set too narrow to call for anything but justified copy.

What about sans-serif body copy versus a standard Roman face? I am not opposed to sans-serif body copy, but prefer Roman. If you look at sans-serif body copy, particularly in long columns (as tabloids certainly are), you will notice that they have a tendency to emphasize the vertical feeling. The circular letters are very close to a perfect circle, while the ascenders and descenders are almost all straight lines. There is no softness to sans-serifs. They are brittle and hard. For a comfortable feeling, a Roman typeface (like Times Roman) cannot be beat. It reads well as 9/11 and also 8/10—two common type sizes and leading used.

Headlines are another matter. The Roman typefaces larger than 18 point tend to become art forms instead of letters. There is nothing better than sans-serif for headlines. They look good in all display sizes (though not as good in body sizes). A headline assortment of 36 point, light, regular, and bold, 24 point, light, regular, and bold, and 18 point, light, regular, and bold is all you need for any headline in a tabloid. Avoid italic. Italic headlines look like a last resort instead of good typographic planning.

Captions? No reason why they can't be italic and set one size smaller than the body copy. A good mix is Helvetica headlines (all nine variables) with 9/11 Times Roman body copy and 8/10 Times Roman italic captions.

CHAPTER THIRTY-SIX

Using Blurbs as Fillers

There are several ways to expand a story so that it will fill the allotted space and give a full-page ending. You can use a natural column ending, or irregular column endings, to give space at the bottom of each column. We can use the natural story ending that is then filled with a line drawing or cartoon. You can use a "filler" device as in *Reader's Digest*, where short items pad out each page ending. However, the best way to give your pages a designed feeling is the use of "blurbs."

"Blurbs" are short, concise abstracts from the text. The principle is good, but we see the same one or two designs used over and over again. We also see them placed at optical center on a page, which tends to deaden their impact.

This chapter shows some "blurbs" as purposely designed sight elements. There are eighteen designs for the 13-pica column measure and twelve designs for the 20-pica measure. Have a film negative made of these designs by your printer. He should then supply you with a set of same size prints. When you want to use one in your story to help pad it out to fill that last page, photocopy a set of prints, place the copy on your page dummy, and identify it by code letter. Your printer will then strip in the design from the negative. Try to use the copy suggested for best results.

"A" in the 13-pica size is a 6-point rule, top and bottom. This should rarely appear in black be-cause the "color" is much too heavy, pulling the reader into that area and holding him there by sheer force. Use a second color or tints of a second color combined with a solid color bar and a tint block that squares it off. Copy can be Roman, boldface, italic, sans-serif italic, or any typeface compatible with the story/headline typography.

A

"B" in the 13-pica size is often called a "Bodoni Rule" as it consists of a hairline rule plus a 2-point rule, top and bottom, but in reversed position. It is clean, neat, and functional. It is best used when copy is stiff and formal, too. Copy can be Roman italic or sans-serif italic, preferably a thin stroke typeface. Keep the typography close to the thick/thin feeling of the rules. Can be either black or a second color, but not tints.

B

"C" in the 13-pica size is a variation of "B" with limited usage be-cause it is composed of dashes, or broken lines. I suggest the copy block be 18-point type or larger, with a boldface italic for best results in a sans-serif.

C

"D" in the 13-pica size is a strong design blurb and makes use of extra large quotation marks. It should never appear in black; use a second color. The second color should be carefully chosen. Stay away from strong reds, bright oranges, and any color that will hold attention to the design and prevent seeing the copy. I suggest pastels or tints for the quote marks and black for the rules and copy for the best results. Copy will look best as a sans-serif in a medium weight.

D

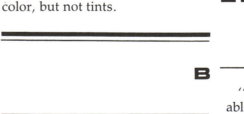

"E" in the 13-pica size is a variable of "D" and should also appear in a second color. While "D" should be in the AAAA colors, "E" could be in PMS colors, provided the registration is exact.

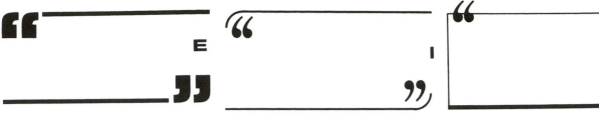

E

"F" combines some of the design factors used in "D" and "E" but will help when copy is short and you need an enclosure to keep it from floating. Copy will look best as a medium weight sans-serif.

F

"G" in the 13-pica size is a design in which black can be used. It is best for very short statements. Copy looks good in a Roman italic boldface. Any AAAA color can be used, but no PMS colors, as the thin lines will not screen well.

G

"H" in the 13-pica size can be black or a solid AAAA color. Since this uses an enclosure, copy should be short and brief. Choose a boldface Roman or a condensed sans-serif.

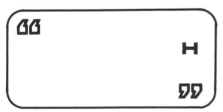

H

"I" in the 13-pica size can be either black or a solid AAAA color. It, too, is clean, neat, and functional. Copy should be a thin line sans-serif or a Roman boldface italic.

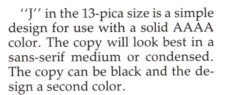

I

"J" in the 13-pica size is a simple design for use with a solid AAAA color. The copy will look best in a sans-serif medium or condensed. The copy can be black and the design a second color.

J

"K" is a lighter variable "J." Copy should dominate. I suggest a boldface sans-serif, not italic, or a boldface Roman, not italic, with good leading (4 to 6 points). Can appear in black.

K

"L" is the same basic design as "J" and "K" but with dots instead of squares. See "K" for copy suggestions.

L

"M" is a shadowed box with quotation marks breaking the box design. It should rarely be used as black. A solid AAAA color is best, but stay away from dominant colors like bright red. Copy should be a boldface Roman italic.

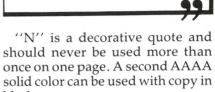

M

"N" is a decorative quote and should never be used more than once on one page. A second AAAA solid color can be used with copy in black.

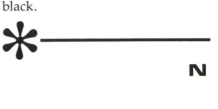

N

"O" can be used as is or reversed out. It can also be filled with a tint block, with the arrow white and copy overprinting in black.

O

"P," "Q," and "R" are mug shots combined with areas for quotes. Keep the pictures black and white, the designs in a solid AAAA color, and the copy in black. You can also use a duotone for the picture. Copy should be the same type face as used in the story headline.

P

Remember—blurbs are to be used with discretion. Simply placing them on a page at optical center does not look good. I suggest irregular placement, closer to the top than the bottom.

As you can see, there are differences in the designs for 20-pica wide columns. "A" and "B" are the same in both 13-pica and the 20-pica widths, but the similarity ends there.

"C" in the 20-pica size should have the quote marks in a solid AAAA color, the lines in black, and the copy either a condensed Roman thin line or a sans-serif thin line, printed in black.

"D" in the 20-pica size can have a solid AAAA color for the design and black for the copy. A Roman italic looks good here. A sans-serif will not.

"E" can be used as is or with a tint block inside and the quote marks in white. This is an enclosed area so the copy should be short.

"F" is an enclosed box. Print the quote marks and box outline in either black or a solid AAAA color with copy a sans-serif thin line and in black.

"G" is for solid AAAA colors only, though beware of bright colors. Could also be tints of 50 percent with copy black. Copy can be any that matches the text copy.

"H" is a stylized quote design and will look good with a thin-line sans-serif.

"I" should have only a tint of a solid AAAA color as the design is strong and might detract from the copy. Copy should be black and a Roman typeface.

"J" will look great as a solid AAAA color, preferably cyan. You can also use almost any match color. Copy can be the text copy face, but larger in size.

The mug shots are the same as 13-pica mug shots in content, color, and face.

A final word of caution. The law of diminishing returns works exceptionally well with the use of blurbs. The second time you use a blurb as a design element in an issue, you get a return of 50 percent. The third time you use it, the reader response drops to 25 percent and the fourth time—zilch. Redundancy is dull. Also, watch your colors. If you want good results, don't make the color too bright as it detracts from the copy. Cyan is good if not used excessively. Yellow is too pale to hold the design. Metallic inks can cause problems.

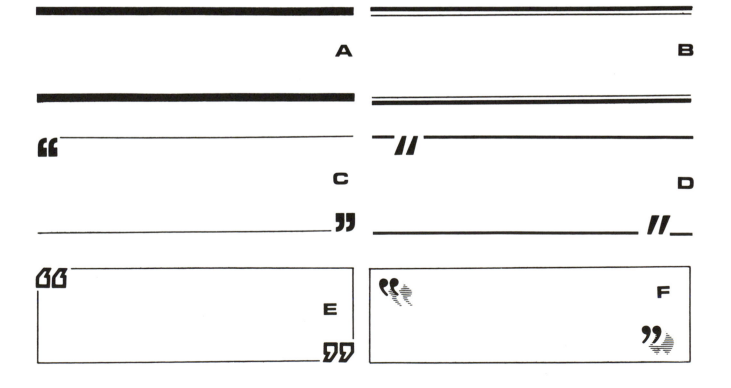

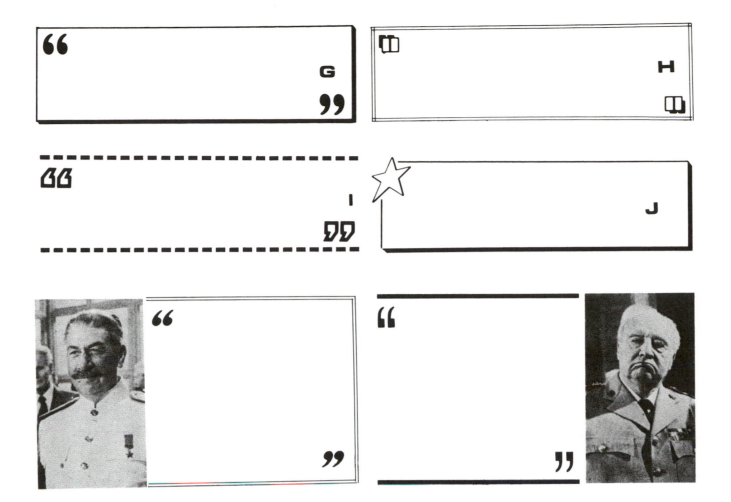

G

H

I

J

CHAPTER THIRTY-SEVEN

Using Modules and Grids

There are three ways of doing publication layouts. The first and most common is called the "galley system." In this method, copy is set on column measure with the length determined only by how much the typesetter can get on a printed sheet. If there is more, a second sheet is used. The copy is proofread on receipt to make sure no errors occur. It is then "dummied up" on layout sheets, so many lines per column, until the story copy runs out. Pictures are interspersed. Headlines are dropped in. Captions are placed in position. This is a rather haphazard method, since any copy that won't fit is edited out. It must be proofread again before it is sent to the typesetter to make up into page proofs.

When the "dummy" is converted into final form by paste-up and/or keylining, it must proofread again to make sure all changes and alterations have been made. This page proof is the final step before making a negative and then a printing plate. Even then, there may be author alterations and corrections of mistakes not caught in the previous proofreading stages. This is the most accurate method because you can "see" it every step of the way. It is very good for people who can't visualize in their minds what the final product will look like.

The second method is the "page layout system" described in chapter 10, "Methods of Layout" (copy + pictures + title area + space = layout). This entails estimating the copy for length and making a page layout showing the typesetter how many lines you want placed in different areas of the page. You go immediately to page proofs and proofread only one time. This system is probably the cheapest since you don't have many alterations. You may eliminate a widow, and increase or decrease to compensate for a lost line or a few lines overset, but the alteration charges are minimal.

The third method is called "writing to fit" and is a little more complicated. This requires planning layouts with visuals—headlines, pictures, breakouts, design motifs, sidebars, and so on. The body copy is written last, not first, as in the two previous methods.

How do you write copy to fit? First of all, you must know the character count per pica in the size and face you are using. Then, regardless of the line width, you know how many characters and spaces will occur within a given line. Let us assume, for example, that you are planning to use a three-column format. If you are using a standard Roman typeface in 9 point, this will come very close to a character count per pica of 3.0. That means there will be about 39 characters and spaces on each 13-pica line.

Let's assume the page is planned with 55 lines per column, and a picture takes up an area two columns wide and 21 picas deep. That depth is the equivalent of 23 lines set 9/11. Allow another 3 lines of 9/11 to take up caption and spacing. Now we have 24 lines taken out of two columns, leaving 31 lines, plus a column of 55 lines. This is a total of 137 lines. You are now going to write copy to fit that area.

You know that 137 lines of 39 characters and spaces each will be a total of 4,543 characters and spaces. Set the typewriter for 45 characters and type 101 lines at that measure. Or set for 90 characters and type 51 lines (half of 101). It will be better to set the tabs for 78 (twice the average line set of 39) and type 60 lines.

The lead paragraph should answer the questions, Who? What? When? Why? How? and Where? The last paragraph summarizes what has been said in between. So, when writing to fit, you already know the beginning and end. You have to fill in only the middle. As soon as you have used up about 4,200 characters and spaces, you had better plan on summarizing. This method can save on "authors alts," since you are doing the editing before typesetting and not after.

Modules

In a modular system of layout, the page is divided into equal units of any number. Figure 37.1 shows a basic module of twelve units. The format is three columns. The modules are created by dividing the columns in half and then dividing each half again. This gives four units to each column, or twelve to the page.

If you want twenty-four units, you divide each unit again to give eight to the column. It now becomes obvious that modules are horizontally constructed since the column format does not change in this system. You can create modules by line increments. Since there are 55 lines in a column, there are five units of 11 lines each. You now have a fifteen-unit page. This is often the best way of doing it, because it allows one to write to fit in smaller units of 11 lines.

Figure 37.1 is the module plan for the page in figure 37.2, which shows you how the items are planned to fill a module or group of modules in space. The headline takes up the top three modules. The largest picture takes up two modules. The smallest picture takes up one module. This leaves six modules for copy. Copy is set 9/11. The typeface is Roman with a character count of 3.0, giving 39

characters and spaces per line. You need 93 lines of 39 characters and spaces. This layout shows no captions. It illustrates only how body, headline, and pictures fit.

The basic premise in a modular system is that everything takes up a module or group of modules. You cannot use the galley system for this method of layout. You can use the page layout system and the writing-to-fit system.

Grids

The grid system is one of perspective. Imagine yourself standing at the right-hand corner of figure 37.1 and looking up. If the grid were the skeleton of a highrise building, the first floor is closer and visually larger than the second floor. The second floor looks smaller because things look smaller as distance increases. The third floor looks smaller yet, while the

fourth floor seems to be the smallest. The grid is an illustration of this perspective. Let's try the same perspective application from right to left. The right column looks larger than the second, and the third appears to be the narrowest.

An illustration of this is shown in figure 37.3. The page is still divided into twelve units, but none of them is equal. This is important because it defines the difference between modules and grids. Uneven units make better design. You can see that the page shown in figure 37.2 does not have the flair or interest that the page in figure 37.4 has.

To lay out a grid page, fill grids or combinations of grids just as you did modules. Grids can be even more complex than those shown in this illustration. Grids are not just arbitrarily drawn. They should be planned and based on content. Study previous issues of the publication you are working on to determine whether they had more pic-

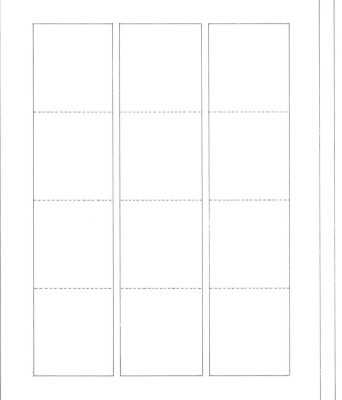

Figure 37.1.—A basic module of twelve units. This is the simplest form of a modular layout sheet: three units across and four units deep. The units are interchangeable since they are all the same size.

Figure 37.2.—The page elements here are arranged by modules or groups of modules. This is a highly regimented layout.

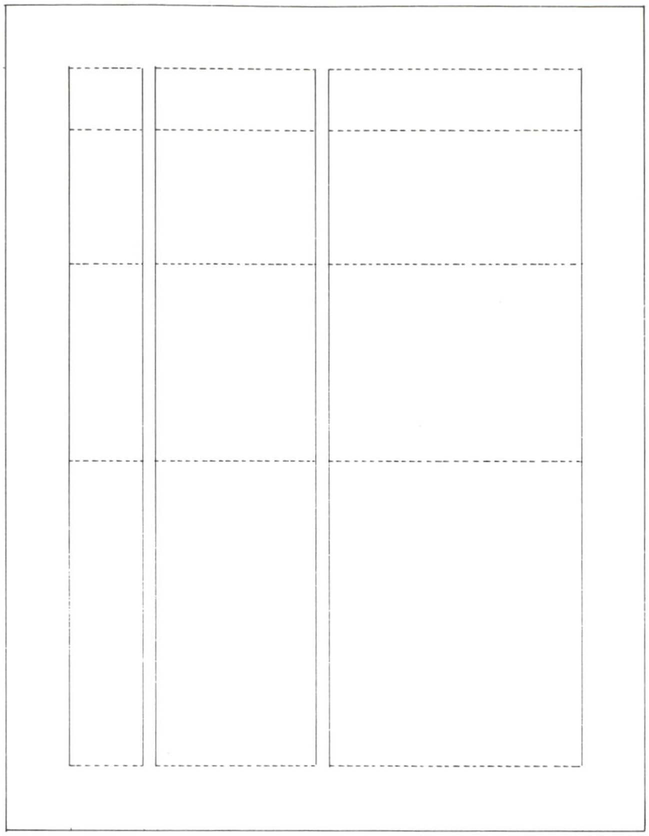

Figure 37.3.—*A simple grid layout sheet composed of three units across and four units deep. However, the units are not interchangeable since no two are the same size.*

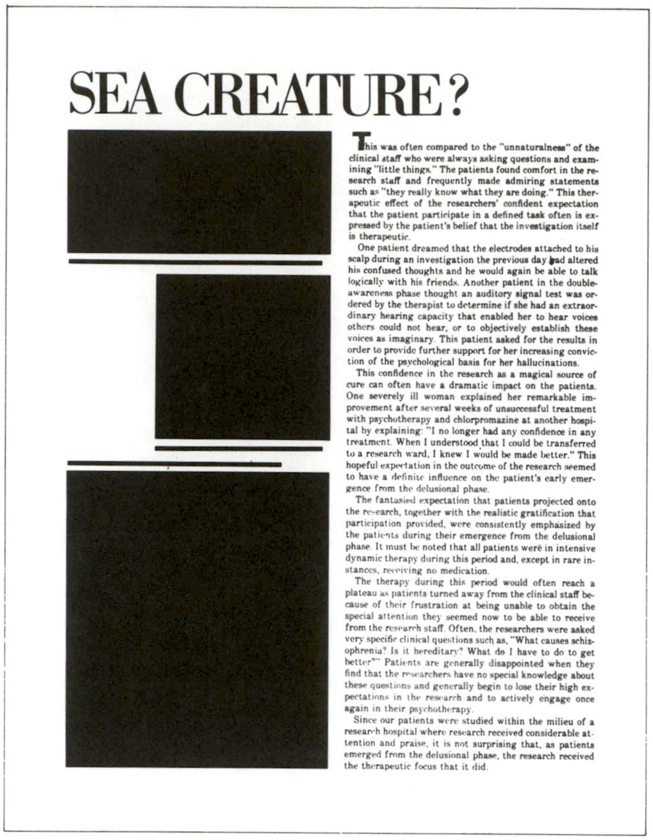

SEA CREATURE?

This was often compared to the "unnaturalness" of the clinical staff who were always asking questions and examining "little things." The patients found comfort in the research staff and frequently made admiring statements such as "they really know what they are doing." This therapeutic effect of the researchers' confident expectation that the patient participate in a defined task often is expressed by the patient's belief that the investigation itself is therapeutic.

One patient dreamed that the electrodes attached to his scalp during an investigation the previous day had altered his confused thoughts and he would again be able to talk logically with his friends. Another patient in the double-awareness phase thought an auditory signal test was ordered by the therapist to determine if she had an extraordinary hearing capacity that enabled her to hear voices others could not hear, or to objectively establish these voices as imaginary. This patient asked for the results in order to provide further support for her increasing conviction of the psychological basis for her hallucinations.

This confidence in the research as a magical source of cure can often have a dramatic impact on the patients. One severely ill woman explained her remarkable improvement after several weeks of unsuccessful treatment with psychotherapy and chlorpromazine at another hospital by explaining: "I no longer had any confidence in any treatment. When I understood that I could be transferred to a research ward, I knew I would be made better." This hopeful expectation in the outcome of the research seemed to have a definite influence on the patient's early emergence from the delusional phase.

The fantasied expectation that patients projected onto the research, together with the realistic gratification that participation provided, were consistently emphasized by the patients during their emergence from the delusional phase. It must be noted that all patients were in intensive dynamic therapy during this period and, except in rare instances, receiving no medication.

The therapy during this period would often reach a plateau as patients turned away from the clinical staff because of their frustration at being unable to obtain the special attention they seemed now to be able to receive from the research staff. Often, the researchers were asked very specific clinical questions such as, "What causes schizophrenia? Is it hereditary? What do I have to do to get better?" Patients are generally disappointed when they find that the researchers have no special knowledge about these questions and generally begin to lose their high expectations in the research and to actively engage once again in their psychotherapy.

Since our patients were studied within the milieu of a research hospital where research received considerable attention and praise, it is not surprising that, as patients emerged from the delusional phase, the research received the therapeutic focus that it did.

Figure 37.4.—*Page elements here are laid in by grids or groups of grids. This layout form is irregular in shape and far more interesting than modules.*

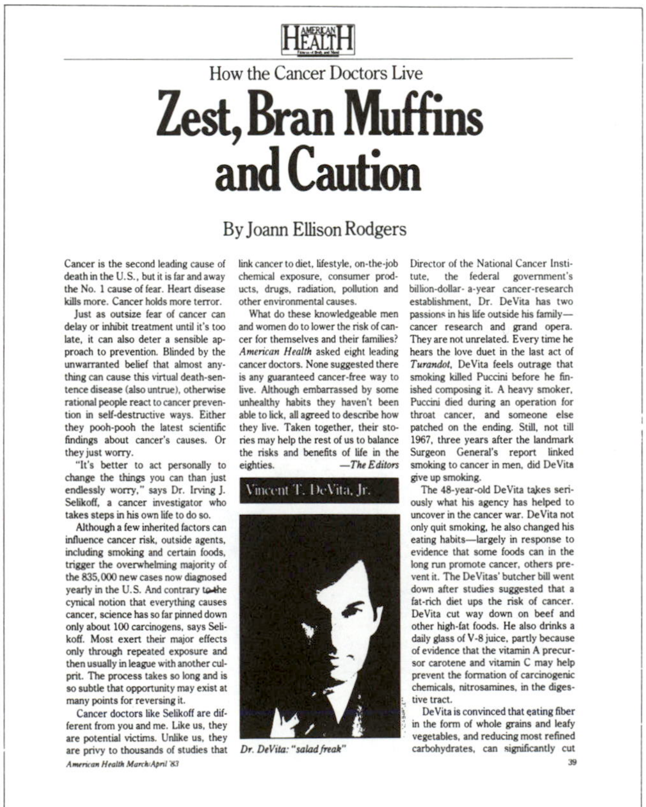

AMERICAN HEALTH

How the Cancer Doctors Live

Zest, Bran Muffins and Caution

By Joann Ellison Rodgers

Cancer is the second leading cause of death in the U.S., but it is far and away the No. 1 cause of fear. Heart disease kills more. Cancer holds more terror.

Just as outsize fear of cancer can delay or inhibit treatment until it's too late, it can also deter a sensible approach to prevention. Blinded by the unwarranted belief that almost anything can cause this virtual death-sentence disease (also untrue), otherwise rational people react to cancer prevention in self-destructive ways. Either they pooh-pooh the latest scientific findings about cancer's causes. Or they just worry.

"It's better to act personally to change the things you can than just endlessly worry," says Dr. Irving J. Selikoff, a cancer investigator who takes steps in his own life to do so.

Although a few inherited factors can influence cancer risk, outside agents, including smoking and certain foods, trigger the overwhelming majority of the 835,000 new cases now diagnosed yearly in the U.S. And contrary to the cynical notion that everything causes cancer, science has so far pinned down only about 100 carcinogens, says Selikoff. Most exert their major effects only through repeated exposure and then usually in league with another culprit. The process takes so long and is so subtle that opportunity may exist at many points for reversing it.

Cancer doctors like Selikoff are different from you and me. Like us, they are potential victims. Unlike us, they are privy to thousands of studies that link cancer to diet, lifestyle, on-the-job chemical exposure, consumer products, drugs, radiation, pollution and other environmental causes.

What do these knowledgeable men and women do to lower the risk of cancer for themselves and their families? *American Health* asked eight leading cancer doctors. None suggested there is any guaranteed cancer-free way to live. Although embarrassed by some unhealthy habits they haven't been able to lick, all agreed to describe how they live. Taken together, their stories may help the rest of us to balance the risks and benefits of life in the eighties. *—The Editors*

Vincent T. DeVita, Jr.

Dr. DeVita: "salad freak"

Director of the National Cancer Institute, the federal government's billion-dollar- a-year cancer-research establishment, Dr. DeVita has two passions in his life outside his family—cancer research and grand opera. They are not unrelated. Every time he hears the love duet in the last act of *Turandot*, DeVita feels outrage that smoking killed Puccini before he finished composing it. A heavy smoker, Puccini died during an operation for throat cancer, and someone else patched on the ending. Still, not till 1967, three years after the landmark Surgeon General's report linked smoking to cancer in men, did DeVita give up smoking.

The 48-year-old DeVita takes seriously what his agency has helped to uncover in the cancer war. DeVita not only quit smoking, he also changed his eating habits—largely in response to evidence that some foods can in the long run promote cancer, others prevent it. The DeVitas' butcher bill went down after studies suggested that a fat-rich diet ups the risk of cancer. DeVita cut way down on beef and other high-fat foods. He also drinks a daily glass of V-8 juice, partly because of evidence that the vitamin A precursor carotene and vitamin C may help prevent the formation of carcinogenic chemicals, nitrosamines, in the digestive tract.

DeVita is convinced that eating fiber in the form of whole grains and leafy vegetables, and reducing most refined carbohydrates, can significantly cut

American Health March/April '83

39

Figure 37.5.—*This page is set Roman, justified. Body copy is squared on both sides. Columns are rigid in form, and the page layout is centered to keep it formal.*

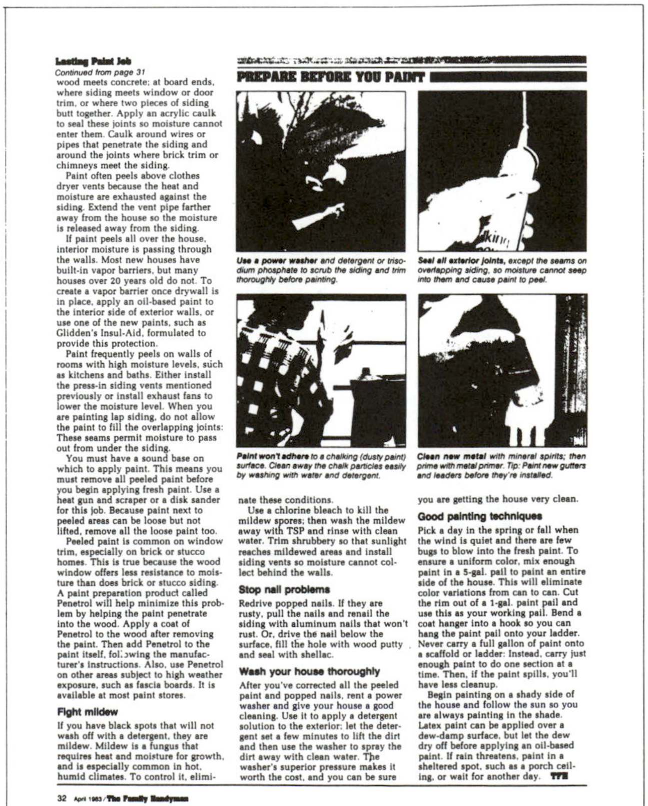

Lasting Paint Job

Continued from page 31

wood meets concrete; at board ends, where siding meets window or door trim, or where two pieces of siding butt together. Apply an acrylic caulk to seal these joints so moisture cannot enter them. Caulk around wires or pipes that penetrate the siding and around the joints where brick trim or chimneys meet the siding.

Paint often peels above clothes dryer vents because the heat and moisture are exhausted against the siding. Extend the vent pipe farther away from the house so the moisture is released away from the siding.

If paint peels all over the house, interior moisture is passing through the walls. Most new houses have built-in vapor barriers, but many houses over 20 years old do not. To create a vapor barrier once drywall is in place, apply an oil-based paint to the interior side of exterior walls, or use one of the new paints, such as Glidden's Insul-Aid, formulated to provide this protection.

Paint frequently peels on walls of rooms with high moisture levels, such as kitchens and baths. Either install the press-in siding vents mentioned previously or install exhaust fans to lower the moisture level. When you are painting lap siding, do not allow the paint to fill the overlapping joints: These seams permit moisture to pass out from under the siding.

You must have a sound base on which to apply paint. This means you must remove all peeled paint before you begin applying fresh paint. Use a heat gun and scraper or a disk sander for this job. Because paint next to peeled areas can be loose but not lifted, remove all the loose paint too.

Peeled paint is common on window trim, especially on brick or stucco homes. This is true because the wood window offers less resistance to moisture than does brick or stucco siding. A paint preparation product called Penetrol will help minimize this problem by helping the paint penetrate into the wood. Apply a coat of Penetrol to the wood after removing the paint. Then add Penetrol to the paint itself, following the manufacturer's instructions. Also, use Penetrol on other areas subject to high weather exposure, such as fascia boards. It is available at most paint stores.

Fight mildew

If you have black spots that will not wash off with a detergent, they are mildew. Mildew is a fungus that requires heat and moisture for growth, and is especially common in hot, humid climates. To control it, eliminate these conditions.

Use a chlorine bleach to kill the mildew spores; then wash the mildew away with TSP and rinse with clean water. Trim shrubbery so that sunlight reaches mildewed areas and install siding vents so moisture cannot collect behind the walls.

Stop nail problems

Redrive popped nails. If they are rusty, pull the nails and renail the siding with aluminum nails that won't rust. Or, drive the nail below the surface, fill the hole with wood putty and seal with shellac.

Wash your house thoroughly

After you've corrected all the peeled paint and popped nails, rent a power washer and give your house a good cleaning. Use it to apply a detergent solution to the exterior; let the detergent set a few minutes to lift the dirt and then use the washer to spray the dirt away with clean water. The washer's superior pressure makes it worth the cost, and you can be sure you are getting the house very clean.

Good painting techniques

Pick a day in the spring or fall when the wind is quiet and there are few bugs to blow into the fresh paint. To ensure a uniform color, mix enough paint in a 5-gal. pail to paint an entire side of the house. This will eliminate color variations from can to can. Cut the rim out of a 1-gal. paint pail and use this as your working pail. Bend a coat hanger into a hook so you can hang the paint pail onto your ladder. Never carry a full gallon of paint onto a scaffold or ladder: Instead, carry just enough paint to do one section at a time. Then, if the paint spills, you'll have less cleanup.

Begin painting on a shady side of the house and follow the sun so you are always painting in the shade. Latex paint can be applied over a dew-damp surface, but let the dew dry off before applying an oil-based paint. If rain threatens, paint in a sheltered spot, such as a porch ceiling, or wait for another day. TFH

PREPARE BEFORE YOU PAINT

Use a power washer *and detergent or trisodium phosphate to scrub the siding and trim thoroughly before painting.*

Seal all exterior joints, *except the seams on overlapping siding, so moisture cannot seep into them and cause paint to peel.*

Paint won't adhere *to a chalking (dusty paint) surface. Clean away the chalk particles easily by washing with water and detergent.*

Clean new metal *with mineral spirits; then prime with metal primer. Tip: Paint new gutters and leaders before they're installed.*

32 April 1983/The Family Handyman

Figure 37.6.—*This page is set Roman, flush left, ragged right, which gives an informal look to the columns as well as to the page design.*

ture area than text and, if so, how much more. What kind of pictures were used? What sizes were used most often? What other visuals were used and what kind of space did they take up? If you are starting a new publication and have nothing to fall back on, I suggest using the grid shown in figure 37.3 as a beginning. It is made for a two-column format, each column 20 picas wide. Divide the outside column into pica units of 6-1-13 (totaling 20). The heights are pica measures of 5-11-16-24. This should accommodate most pictures and simplify picture sizing. In laying this out, pictures *with* captions equal the grid.

Ways to Set Body Copy

''Justified'' means that the copy is set column width and is aligned on both sides. This is done by varying the letter and word spacing within the lines. It gives a rather rigid column, straight up and down, and clean. You get the maximum characters per line and per page setting justified. This is shown in figure 37.5.

''Flush left, ragged right'' means that the copy is set aligned on the left side but not on the right side, much as you do with a typewriter. The theory is that this simulates conversation and avoids hyphenation. You will have about 14 percent less copy per page than with justified copy, since there are fewer characters and spaces in most lines. You can see this loss in figure 37.6.

''Sans-serif'' letters are created mechanically. The circular letters are perfect circles instead of the softer and more casual ovals of Roman, or serif, letters. The up-and-down strokes are straight and emphasize the verticals of the columns. Sans-serif type looks and feels rather rigid (see figure 37.7). Sans-serif, set flush left, ragged right means that the copy is aligned at the left, but has an irregular right edge. In figure 37.7, the headline, side heads, and copy are all flush left. Figure 37.8 shows a variation of this. Although headlines are set flush left, ragged right (and in Roman), there is some variation in the body setting. The first paragraph is set flush left, and succeeding paragraphs are indented.

''Swiss'' is another typesetting style. The Swiss people often use hyphenated words, such as *Castle-on-the-Rhine.* This may result in reading confusion when type is set justified, since additional hyphens are often required. Swiss typesetters developed their own style of setting each line to the end of a word or hyphenated phrase. This means setting flush left, ragged right, since line widths vary. In a two-column format they found that often there were two lines that nearly touched when set long, so they put in a hairline rule to prevent reading across two or more columns. This divided the page perfectly, and to make the page look better, they added a hairline rule to the left so that both columns looked alike.

In Swiss style, then, we have a sequence: hairline rule, 1 pica of

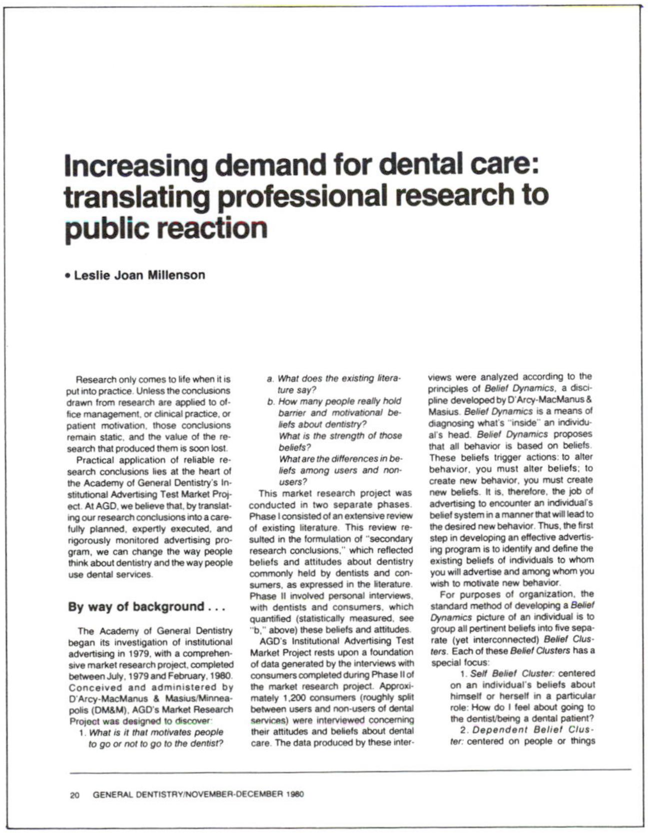

Increasing demand for dental care: translating professional research to public reaction

• Leslie Joan Millenson

Research only comes to life when it is put into practice. Unless the conclusions drawn from research are applied to office management, or clinical practice, or patient motivation, those conclusions remain static, and the value of the research that produced them is soon lost.

Practical application of reliable research conclusions lies at the heart of the Academy of General Dentistry's Institutional Advertising Test Market Project. At AGD, we believe that, by translating our research conclusions into a carefully planned, expertly executed, and rigorously monitored advertising program, we can change the way people think about dentistry and the way people use dental services.

By way of background . . .

The Academy of General Dentistry began its investigation of institutional advertising in 1979, with a comprehensive market research project, completed between July, 1979 and February, 1980. Conceived and administered by D'Arcy-MacManus & Masius/Minneapolis (DM&M), AGD's Market Research Project was designed to discover:

1. *What is it that motivates people to go or not to go to the dentist?*
   a. *What does the existing literature say?*
   b. *How many people really hold barrier and motivational beliefs about dentistry?*
   What is the strength of those beliefs?
   What are the differences in beliefs among users and non-users?

This market research project was conducted in two separate phases. Phase I consisted of an extensive review of existing literature. This review resulted in the formulation of "secondary research conclusions," which reflected beliefs and attitudes about dentistry commonly held by dentists and consumers, as expressed in the literature. Phase II involved personal interviews, with dentists and consumers, which quantified (statistically measured, see "b," above) these beliefs and attitudes.

AGD's Institutional Advertising Test Market Project rests upon a foundation of data generated by the interviews with consumers completed during Phase II of the market research project. Approximately 1,200 consumers (roughly split between users and non-users of dental services) were interviewed concerning their attitudes and beliefs about dental care. The data produced by these interviews were analyzed according to the principles of *Belief Dynamics*, a discipline developed by D'Arcy-MacManus & Masius. *Belief Dynamics* is a means of diagnosing what's "inside" an individual's head. *Belief Dynamics* proposes that all behavior is based on beliefs. These beliefs trigger actions: to alter behavior, you must alter beliefs; to create new behavior, you must create new beliefs. It is, therefore, the job of advertising to encounter an individual's belief system in a manner that will lead to the desired new behavior. Thus, the first step in developing an effective advertising program is to identify and define the existing beliefs of individuals to whom you will advertise and among whom you wish to motivate new behavior.

For purposes of organization, the standard method of developing a *Belief Dynamics* picture of an individual is to group all pertinent beliefs into five separate (yet interconnected) *Belief Clusters*. Each of these *Belief Clusters* has a special focus:

1. *Self Belief Cluster:* centered on an individual's beliefs about himself or herself in a particular role: How do I feel about going to the dentist/being a dental patient?
2. *Dependent Belief Cluster:* centered on people or things

20 GENERAL DENTISTRY/NOVEMBER-DECEMBER 1980

Figure 37.7.—This page is set sans-serif, justified. The body copy is stiff and formal. Most people find sans-serif type harder to read than Roman.

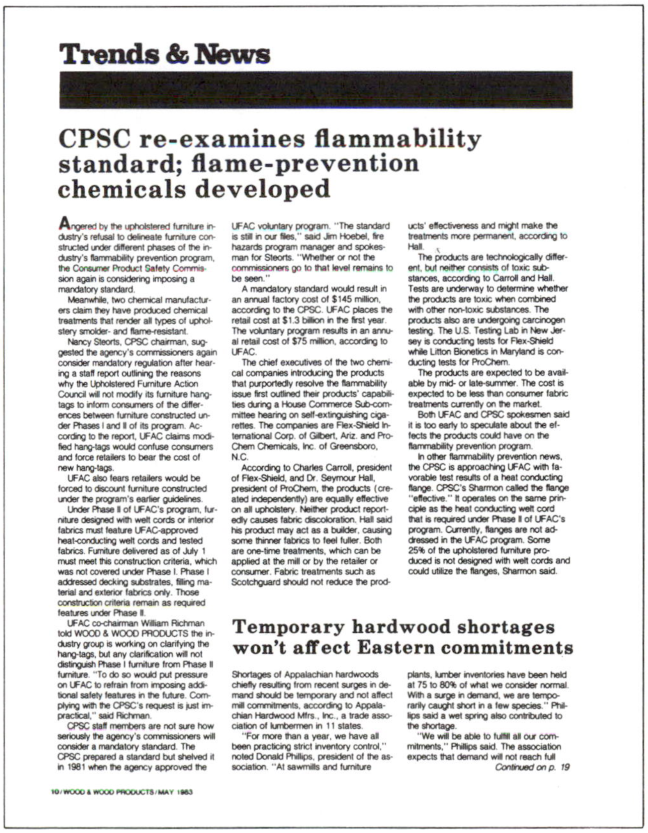

Trends & News

CPSC re-examines flammability standard; flame-prevention chemicals developed

Angered by the upholstered furniture industry's refusal to delineate furniture constructed under different phases of the industry's flammability prevention program, the Consumer Product Safety Commission again is considering imposing a mandatory standard.

Meanwhile, two chemical manufacturers claim they have produced chemical treatments that render all types of upholstery smolder- and flame-resistant.

Nancy Steorts, CPSC chairman, suggested the agency's commissioners again consider mandatory regulation after hearing a staff report outlining the reasons why the Upholstered Furniture Action Council will not modify its furniture hang-tags to inform consumers of the differences between furniture constructed under Phases I and II of its program. According to the report, UFAC claims modified hang-tags would confuse consumers and force retailers to bear the cost of new hang-tags.

UFAC also fears retailers would be forced to discount furniture constructed under the program's earlier guidelines.

Under Phase II of UFAC's program, furniture designed with welt cords or interior fabrics must feature UFAC-approved heat-conducting welt cords and tested fabrics. Furniture delivered as of July 1 must meet this construction criteria, which was not covered under Phase I. Phase I addressed decking substrates, filling material and exterior fabrics only. Those construction criteria remain as required features under Phase II.

UFAC co-chairman William Richman told WOOD & WOOD PRODUCTS the industry group is working on clarifying the hang-tags, but any clarification will not distinguish Phase I furniture from Phase II furniture. "To do so would put pressure on UFAC to refrain from imposing additional safety features in the future. Complying with the CPSC's request is just impractical," said Richman.

CPSC staff members are not sure how seriously the agency's commissioners will consider a mandatory standard. The CPSC prepared a standard but shelved it in 1981 when the agency approved the UFAC voluntary program. "The standard is still in our files," said Jim Hoebel, fire hazards program manager and spokesman for Steorts. "Whether or not the commissioners go to that level remains to be seen."

A mandatory standard would result in an annual factory cost of $145 million, according to the CPSC. UFAC places the retail cost at $1.3 billion in the first year. The voluntary program results in an annual retail cost of $75 million, according to UFAC.

The chief executives of the two chemical companies introducing the products that purportedly resolve the flammability issue first outlined their products' capabilities during a House Commerce Sub-committee hearing on self-extinguishing cigarettes. The companies are Flex-Shield International Corp. of Gilbert, Ariz. and Pro-Chem Chemicals, Inc. of Greensboro, N.C.

According to Charles Carroll, president of Flex-Shield, and Dr. Seymour Hall, president of ProChem, the products (created independently) are equally effective on all upholstery. Neither product reportedly causes fabric discoloration. Hall said his product may act as a builder, causing some thinner fabrics to feel fuller. Both are one-time treatments, which can be applied at the mill or by the retailer or consumer. Fabric treatments such as Scotchguard should not reduce the products' effectiveness and might make the treatments more permanent, according to Hall.

The products are technologically different, but neither consists of toxic substances, according to Carroll and Hall. Tests are underway to determine whether the products are toxic when combined with other non-toxic substances. The products also are undergoing carcinogen testing. The U.S. Testing Lab in New Jersey is conducting tests for Flex-Shield while Litton Bionetics in Maryland is conducting tests for ProChem.

The products are expected to be available by mid- or late-summer. The cost is expected to be less than consumer fabric treatments currently on the market.

Both UFAC and CPSC spokesmen said it is too early to speculate about the effects the products could have on the flammability prevention program.

In other flammability prevention news, the CPSC is approaching UFAC with favorable test results of a heat conducting flange. CPSC's Sharmon called the flange "effective." It operates on the same principle as the heat conducting welt cord that is required under Phase II of UFAC's program. Currently, flanges are not addressed in the UFAC program. Some 25% of the upholstered furniture produced is not designed with welt cords and could utilize the flanges, Sharmon said.

Temporary hardwood shortages won't affect Eastern commitments

Shortages of Appalachian hardwoods chiefly resulting from recent surges in demand should be temporary and not affect mill commitments, according to Appalachian Hardwood Mfrs., Inc., a trade association of lumbermen in 11 states.

"For more than a year, we have all been practicing strict inventory control," noted Donald Phillips, president of the association. "At sawmills and furniture plants, lumber inventories have been held at 75 to 80% of what we consider normal. With a surge in demand, we are temporarily caught short in a few species." Phillips said a wet spring also contributed to the shortage.

"We will be able to fulfill all our commitments," Phillips said. The association expects that demand will not reach full

Continued on p. 19

10/WOOD & WOOD PRODUCTS/MAY 1983

Figure 37.8.—This page is set in sans-serif type, flush left, ragged right. It is informal, but hard to read, since sans-serif typefaces are not as comfortable for the eye as Roman faces are.

white space, followed by copy set flush left, ragged right, and no hyphens at the end of a line. This is repeated for as many columns as you have on the page. All copy is set flush left, ragged right—headlines, captions, breakouts, side heads, and body copy. This is shown in figure 37.9. Whenever there is a paragraph, the copy is not indented as we usually do in American typesetting. Instead, each paragraph is set flush left, and a full line of space is left between paragraphs. This space is equal to the type size with leading. If the type is 9/11, the space will be 11 points. The visual impression is that the type ''hangs'' from the hairline rule, much like a flag flying from a mast.

''Modified Swiss'' is an Americanized version of Swiss. This is shown in figure 37.10. The Swiss, for example, use sans-serif type with their design. The typeface of choice would be Helvetica with all copy set in a variation of that face—light, bold, italic, regular, and so on. Modified Swiss allows Roman typefaces, as shown in figure 37.10. There are paragraph indentations and no full line space between paragraphs. Compare figures 37.9 and 37.10. You can see that Swiss is rather loose in feeling, but when it has been Americanized, it looks tighter.

Now that you know the five basic styles, let's see how they fit into either modules or grids as a design complement. In the modular system we are almost wedded to a typesetting style that will help the design. This means setting justified. Justified also gives us the feeling that there is a positive attitude prevailing—no nonsense, straightforward, facts up front. When we use flush left, ragged right, we are more informal and casual. Look at newspapers. How many have you seen set flush left, ragged right? Not many, because readers want the ''facts,'' and many readers feel that flush left, ragged right is an affectation that does not belong in a serious publication.

While the feeling in modules is stiff and formal, the feeling in grids is loose and informal. Flush left, ragged right is appropriate in most grid systems. And how about Swiss? I have seen it used in both systems, and it looks good in both. Remember, however, that the shorter the line measure, the more you need to hyphenate.

The Horizontal Grid

The horizontal grid is shown in figure 37.11. This has a very definite design. The figure sizes are defined by usage and proportion and are ''stacked.'' Why are these proportions used? If you go through copies of your publication for the past year and size all the figures used, you will develop averages. For example, you will find mug shots occur more often than grin-and-shakes. You will find new products occur more than group shots or larger pictures. Cutting up

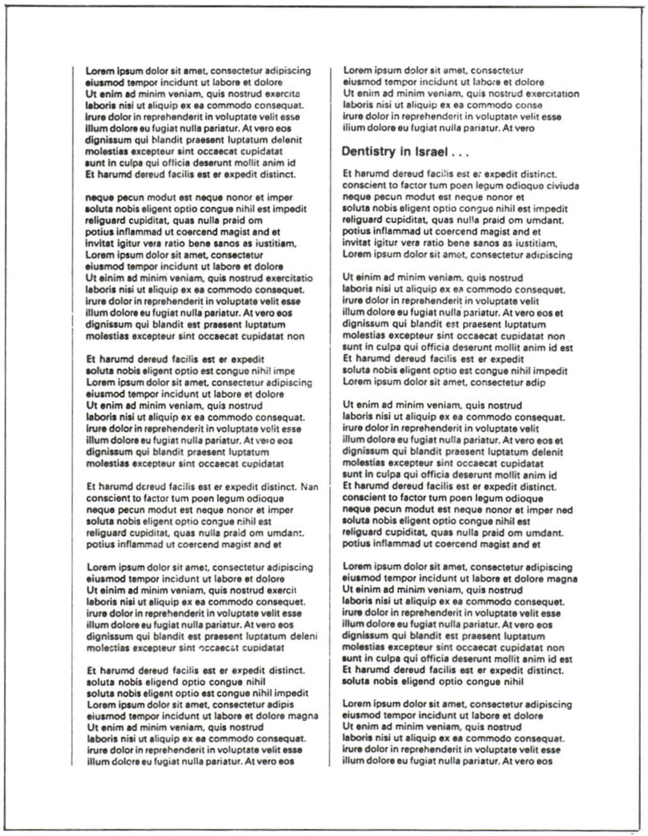
Lorem ipsum dolor sit amet, consectetur adipiscing eiusmod tempor incidunt ut labore et dolore Ut enim ad minim veniam, quis nostrud exercita laboris nisi ut aliquip ex ea commodo consequat. Irure dolor in reprehenderit in voluptate velit esse illum dolore eu fugiat nulla pariatur. At vero eos dignissum qui blandit praesent luptatum delenit molestias excepteur sint occaecat cupidatat sunt in culpa qui officia deserunt mollit anim id Et harumd dereud facilis est er expedit distinct.

neque pecun modut est neque nonor et imper soluta nobis eligent optio congue nihil est impedit religuard cupiditat, quas nulla praid om potius inflammad ut coercend magist and et invitat igitur vera ratio bene sanos as iustitiam, Lorem ipsum dolor sit amet, consectetur eiusmod tempor incidunt ut labore et dolore Ut einim ad minim veniam, quis nostrud exercitatio laboris nisi ut aliquip ex ea commodo consequet. irure dolor in reprehenderit in voluptate velit esse illum dolore eu fugiat nulla pariatur. At vero eos dignissum qui blandit est praesent luptatum molestias excepteur sint occaecat cupidatat non

Et harumd dereud facilis est er expedit soluta nobis eligent optio est congue nihil impe Lorem ipsum dolor sit amet, consectetur adipiscing eiusmod tempor incidunt ut labore et dolore Ut enim ad minim veniam, quis nostrud laboris nisi ut aliquip ex ea commodo consequat. irure dolor in reprehenderit in voluptate velit esse illum dolore eu fugiat nulla pariatur. At vero eos dignissum qui blandit praesent luptatum molestias excepteur sint occaecat cupidatat

Et harumd dereud facilis est er expedit distinct. Nan conscient to factor tum poen legum odioque neque pecun modut est neque nonor et imper soluta nobis eligent optio congue nihil est religuard cupiditat, quas nulla praid om umdant. potius inflammad ut coercend magist and et

Lorem ipsum dolor sit amet, consectetur adipiscing eiusmod tempor incidunt ut labore et dolore Ut einim ad minim veniam, quis nostrud exercit laboris nisi ut aliquip ex ea commodo consequet. irure dolor in reprehenderit in voluptate velit esse illum dolore eu fugiat nulla pariatur. At vero eos dignissum qui blandit est praesent luptatum deleni molestias excepteur sint occaecat cupidatat

Et harumd dereud facilis est er expedit distinct. soluta nobis eligend optio congue nihil soluta nobis eligent optio est congue nihil impedit Lorem ipsum dolor sit amet, consectetur adipis eiusmod tempor incidunt ut labore et dolore magna Ut enim ad minim veniam, quis nostrud laboris nisi ut aliquip ex ea commodo consequat. irure dolor in reprehenderit in voluptate velit esse illum dolore eu fugiat nulla pariatur. At vero eos

Lorem ipsum dolor sit amet, consectetur eiusmod tempor incidunt ut labore et dolore Ut enim ad minim veniam, quis nostrud exercitation laboris nisi ut aliquip ex ea commodo conse irure dolor in reprehenderit in voluptate velit esse ilium dolore eu fugiat nulla pariatur. At vero

Dentistry in Israel . . .

Et harumd dereud facilis est er expedit distinct. conscient to factor tum poen legum odioque civiuda neque pecun modut est neque nonor et soluta nobis eligent optio congue nihil est impedit religuard cupiditat, quas nulla praid om umdant. potius inflammad ut coercend magist and et invitat igitur vera ratio bene sanos as iustitiam, Lorem ipsum dolor sit amet, consectetur adipiscing

Ut einim ad minim veniam, quis nostrud laboris nisi ut aliquip ex ea commodo consequet. irure dolor in reprehenderit in voluptate velit illum dolore eu fugiat nulla pariatur. At vero eos et dignissum qui blandit est praesent luptatum molestias excepteur sint occaecat cupidatat non sunt in culpa qui officia deserunt mollit anim id est Et harumd dereud facilis est er expedit soluta nobis eligent optio est congue nihil impedit Lorem ipsum dolor sit amet, consectetur adip

Ut enim ad minim veniam, quis nostrud laboris nisi ut aliquip ex ea commodo consequat. irure dolor in reprehenderit in voluptate velit illum dolore eu fugiat nulla pariatur. At vero eos et dignissum qui blandit praesent luptatum delenit molestias excepteur sint occaecat cupidatat sunt in culpa qui officia deserunt mollit anim id Et harumd dereud facilis est er expedit distinct. conscient to factor tum poen legum odioque neque pecun modut est neque nonor et imper ned soluta nobis eligent optio congue nihil est religuard cupiditat, quas nulla praid om umdant. potius inflammad ut coercend magist and et

Lorem ipsum dolor sit amet, consectetur adipiscing eiusmod tempor incidunt ut labore et dolore magna Ut einim ad minim veniam, quis nostrud laboris nisi ut aliquip ex ea commodo consequet. irure dolor in reprehenderit in voluptate velit esse illum dolore eu fugiat nulla pariatur. At vero eos dignissum qui blandit est praesent luptatum molestias excepteur sint occaecat cupidatat non sunt in culpa qui officia deserunt mollit anim id est Et harumd dereud facilis est er expedit distinct. soluta nobis eligend optio congue nihil

Lorem ipsum dolor sit amet, consectetur adipiscing eiusmod tempor incidunt ut labore et dolore Ut enim ad minim veniam, quis nostrud laboris nisi ut aliquip ex ea commodo consequat. irure dolor in reprehenderit in voluptate velit esse illum dolore eu fugiat nulla pariatur. At vero eos

Figure 37.9.—This is an example of Swiss style using sans-serif. It also uses the full increment between paragraphs making it more of a true Swiss than figure 37.10.

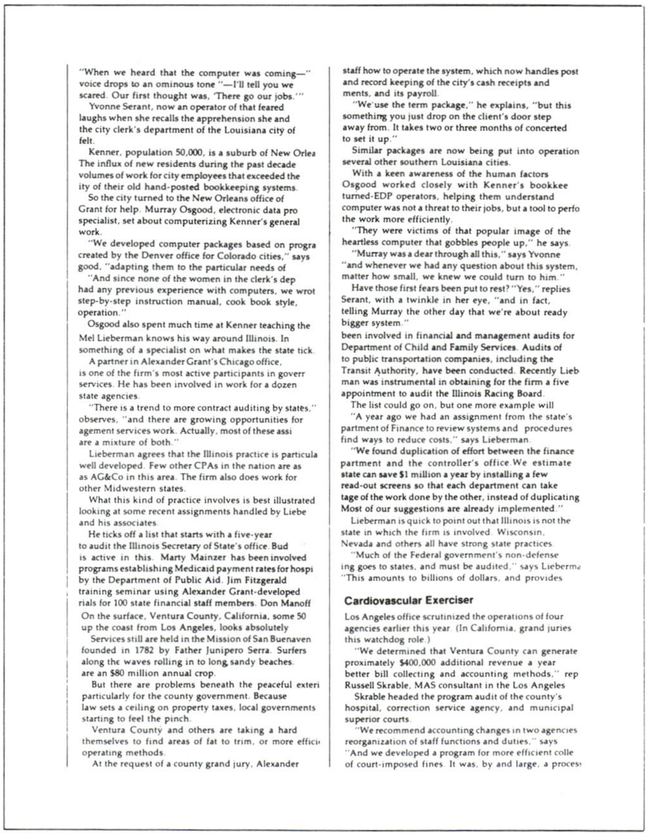
"When we heard that the computer was coming—" voice drops to an ominous tone "—I'll tell you we scared. Our first thought was, 'There go our jobs.'"

Yvonne Serant, now an operator of that feared laughs when she recalls the apprehension she and the city clerk's department of the Louisiana city of felt.

Kenner, population 50,000, is a suburb of New Orlea The influx of new residents during the past decade volumes of work for city employees that exceeded the ity of their old hand-posted bookkeeping systems.

So the city turned to the New Orleans office of Grant for help. Murray Osgood, electronic data pro specialist, set about computerizing Kenner's general work.

"We developed computer packages based on progra created by the Denver office for Colorado cities," says good, "adapting them to the particular needs of

"And since none of the women in the clerk's dep had any previous experience with computers, we wrot step-by-step instruction manual, cook book style, operation."

Osgood also spent much time at Kenner teaching the

Mel Lieberman knows his way around Illinois. In something of a specialist on what makes the state tick.

A partner in Alexander Grant's Chicago office, is one of the firm's most active participants in goverr services. He has been involved in work for a dozen state agencies.

"There is a trend to more contract auditing by states," observes, "and there are growing opportunities for agement services work. Actually, most of these assi are a mixture of both."

Lieberman agrees that the Illinois practice is particula well developed. Few other CPAs in the nation are as as AG&Co in this area. The firm also does work for other Midwestern states.

What this kind of practice involves is best illustrated looking at some recent assignments handled by Liebe and his associates.

He ticks off a list that starts with a five-year to audit the Illinois Secretary of State's office. Bud is active in this. Marty Mainzer has been involved programs establishing Medicaid payment rates for hospi by the Department of Public Aid. Jim Fitzgerald training seminar using Alexander Grant-developed rials for 100 state financial staff members. Don Manoff

On the surface, Ventura County, California, some 50 up the coast from Los Angeles, looks absolutely

Services still are held in the Mission of San Buenaven founded in 1782 by Father Junipero Serra. Surfers along the waves rolling in to long sandy beaches. are an $80 million annual crop.

But there are problems beneath the peaceful exteri particularly for the county government. Because law sets a ceiling on property taxes, local governments starting to feel the pinch.

Ventura County and others are taking a hard themselves to find areas of fat to trim, or more effici operating methods.

At the request of a county grand jury, Alexander

staff how to operate the system, which now handles post and record keeping of the city's cash receipts and ments, and its payroll.

"We use the term package," he explains, "but this something you just drop on the client's door step away from. It takes two or three months of concerted to set it up."

Similar packages are now being put into operation several other southern Louisiana cities.

With a keen awareness of the human factors Osgood worked closely with Kenner's bookkee turned-EDP operators, helping them understand computer was not a threat to their jobs, but a tool to perfo the work more efficiently.

"They were victims of that popular image of the heartless computer that gobbles people up," he says.

"Murray was a dear through all this," says Yvonne "and whenever we had any question about this system, matter how small, we knew we could turn to him."

Have those first fears been put to rest? "Yes," replies Serant, with a twinkle in her eye, "and in fact, telling Murray the other day that we're about ready bigger system."

been involved in financial and management audits for Department of Child and Family Services. Audits of to public transportation companies, including the Transit Authority, have been conducted. Recently Lieb man was instrumental in obtaining for the firm a five appointment to audit the Illinois Racing Board.

The list could go on, but one more example will

"A year ago we had an assignment from the state's partment of Finance to review systems and procedures find ways to reduce costs," says Lieberman.

"We found duplication of effort between the finance partment and the controller's office. We estimate state can save $1 million a year by installing a few read-out screens so that each department can take tage of the work done by the other, instead of duplicating Most of our suggestions are already implemented."

Lieberman is quick to point out that Illinois is not the state in which the firm is involved. Wisconsin, Nevada and others all have strong state practices.

"Much of the Federal government's non-defense ing goes to states, and must be audited," says Lieberma "This amounts to billions of dollars, and provides

Cardiovascular Exerciser

Los Angeles office scrutinized the operations of four agencies earlier this year. (In California, grand juries this watchdog role.)

"We determined that Ventura County can generate proximately $400,000 additional revenue a year better bill collecting and accounting methods," rep Russell Skrable, MAS consultant in the Los Angeles

Skrable headed the program audit of the county's hospital, correction service agency, and municipal superior courts.

"We recommend accounting changes in two agencies reorganization of staff functions and duties," says "And we developed a program for more efficient colle of court-imposed fines. It was, by and large, a proces

Figure 37.10.—This is an Americanized version of Swiss using a Roman typeface and set flush left, ragged right, with 1 pica of space between the hairline rule and type and no increment between paragraphs.

past issues and counting picture sizes will point out some interesting things. One is that pictures have been sized to column width. That's natural, though not the best design.

Sizes of illustrations often are related to their content. Mug shots, for example, will invariably be 6 by 9 picas. Grin-and-shakes will be very close to 9½ by 11 picas. New products will be 13 by 13, and other categories will tend to fall into one of these three or 20 by 20 picas. It's true you will have some odd sized pictures, but examine those and see if they could be a combination of these four.

The reason we want pictures to fall into these four sizes is that they will also fall into totals that equal both the live area width of 41 picas and the live area depth of 55 picas. And they will tend to fall into occurrence ratios. For example, there will be a ratio between sizes—six mug shots to four grin-and-shakes to three new products to two large shots. These can then be aligned

across and stacked as in figure 37.11.

Once you have created your own ratios and stacks, you can alter them to vary the page designs. Look at figure 37.12; the sizes and occurrences are the same, but the stacking has been changed to give variety. You can change this in any way you see fit. Do you have twice as many new products sizes as we have shown? Then create your own horizontal using two layers of that size and none for mug shots or none for the smaller sizes like grin-and-shakes.

I mentioned at the beginning of this section that sizing all pictures to column width is not good design application. I much prefer to consider the total width or height and to create panels composed of uneven sizes. A panel across the top can have many multiples in width, though the height stays the same. Instead of three pictures, each 13 picas wide, set across the 41-pica live area, have a pattern of 11-1-18-1-10 picas.

Interlocking Designs

Figure 37.13 shows a combination of two designs—standard three-column with the "Double-18." The area where they overlap—that is, the Double-18—should be less than two-thirds of the page. Copy should cover no more than two-thirds of the page. This allows for about one-third of the page on which they overlap, or interlock.

This design can also be called "actors-on-a-stage," because body copy is set on 13 picas for a three-column stage. Pictures are set on 18 picas and run across the stage created by the body copy, as shown in figure 37.14. The key to its use is to consider all stories as units. The body copy total is divided by the number of columns needed for the story. If you need a three-page story, there would be nine columns involved, three for each page. If the total story length is 297 picas, there will be 33 picas in each of the nine columns. This creates the "stage"

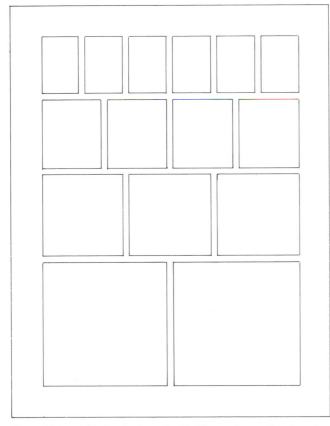

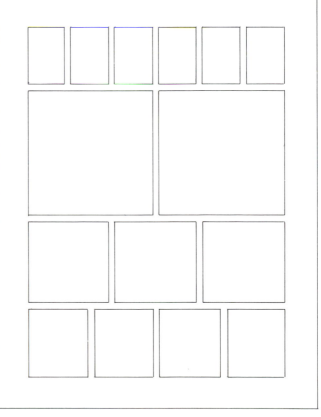

Figure 37.11.—This is a horizontal grid. Picture sizes are based on sizes used previously. In this case, there is a ratio of six mug shots to four "grin-and-shakes" to three group shots (or new products) and two vista or action shots.

Figure 37.12.—The layering can be altered to suit each issue. We now have the mug shots across the top and the grin-and-shakes at the bottom. You can alter the layers at will, once you have determined the ratios.

for the illustrations. All pictures are sized to multiples that equal 37 picas in width—18-1-18 in the figures. There should always be white space to the outside of the page. Filling in the white space destroys the design.

This design application can also include a "movable sink," where the white space at the top of the page can be raised or lowered to suit an all-copy story.

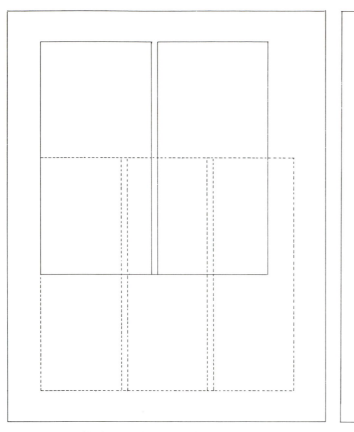

Figure 37.13.—This shows the layout sheet for an interlocking layout grid. It uses "Double-18" at the top and "standard three" at the bottom.

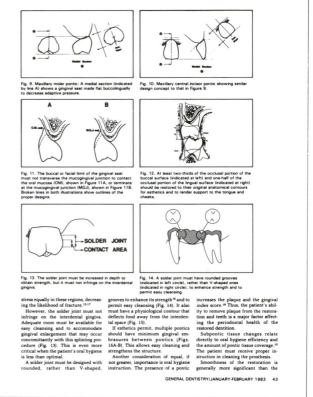

Figure 37.14.—This is the interlocking grid system used by General Dentistry. Note the extra white space at the top where visuals are used.

CHAPTER THIRTY-EIGHT

Four-Column Design

It is surprising that a four-column format was not used in magazines on a regular basis until recently. *Self* magazine was the first that I know of that incorporated it into their design. They used a mix of two-column, three-column, and four-column design, and showed that the three variables married well in constant usage. Since then we have seen more and more of four-column.

Four-column design is based on a live area of 41 picas. Discussion of a new design must begin with the premise that it fits within the live area—usually 41 picas, since that fits so well on the page sizes most frequently used. In four-column designs, the columns are set on 9½ picas, with 1-pica alleys, totaling 41 picas.

Certain column widths fit certain subject matter. A wide column—such as 30 picas—is used in books. This width is associated with more serious content. The next commonly used width is 20 picas. Readers place this width in the "thoughtful" class. Indeed, many scientific publications are set on 20 picas because of this and because it is the best width to use when you have formulas that must be seen as entities.

When we see a 13-pica-wide column, we immediately think of news. There are several reasons for this. Newspapers for years have set news on a short measure. We have become accustomed to reading news that way. And there is another reason. We know from a study done years ago in England that the most readable typeset line is one-and-a-half alphabet lengths of type size used. Since the majority of what we read is set in one of the conventional Roman style typefaces and in 9-point size, the usual column has 39 characters and spaces on a 13-pica line. Why? Because 9-point Roman typefaces have a character count of very close to 3 per pica ($3 \times 13 = 39$).

And where do we use a 9½-pica column? You might be thinking that this is only half of "serious" column width and only a part of "news" column. Let's see where it is being used. In "how-to-do-it" stories it helps to divide the story into small step-by-step parts or sections. In the classified ads section it helps concentrate the smaller set copy into more readable chunks. It is a natural for "new products," where there is a small picture plus a copy block. It is also a natural for "bits-and-pieces," those short news items that just don't look important when set on 20 or 13 picas and are only a few lines deep. A news item set 10 lines deep on 13 picas will set 14 lines deep when set on 9½ picas. This makes it *look* longer and *seem* more important. A four-column format is excellent for fractional ads, particularly those set in type by the publisher. We are seeing more and more "letters" sections being set in four-columns. Again, the letters look longer and seem more important.

Finally, we are seeing four-column used more and more in "recipe" sections. The reasons are obvious. When you have copy that says: "½ tsp. salt," you have 11 characters and spaces. When this is set on 13 picas you have 28 characters and spaces blank! A chunk of white space results. Increase that white space by the number of lines needed to describe ingredients, and you can see that a lot of space is wasted when the copy is set on a 13-pica measure. However, when you set "½ tsp. salt" on 9½ picas, little space is wasted.

From what we have already discussed, the idea that we can design a magazine by sections should be obvious. We can do stories on 13 and 20 picas or we can use both. We can have an editorial section set on 20 picas as well as a news section set on 13, and we can mix three-column and four-column design in the various special sections.

In a typical ninety-six-page magazine there would normally be three thirty-two-page signatures. Or, depending on the circumstances, there might be six sixteen-page signatures. Since newsstand magazines have ads in both three- and two-column widths we must also consider where they are placed within the issue. There is no reason why we cannot plan an issue to accommodate ads, sections, stories, and so on by signatures—each size being assigned to a signature.

For example, the first sixteen pages could be assigned to copy to be set on a three-column design. This would include three-column editorial material and three-column ads. The next thirty-two pages could accommodate two columns, three columns, or both. The next thirty-two pages could be the editorial "well" where the only ads that occur would be full-page ads to separate stories. The last sixteen pages would be used for three-column, four-column, and other fractional material.

Figure 38.1, taken from *McCall's*, shows a four-column page. It has three small articles all under a heading of "You and the Law." It is set flush left, ragged right, which allows about five words per line. We know from experience that setting flush left, ragged right also gives a loss of 14 percent in copy length as compared to setting justified. This is a good example of making copy look longer. If the copy had been set on 20 picas, the lines in the second section (presently 44 lines long) would have been only 21 lines long. If set on 13 picas, it would have been 32 lines long. It looks twice as long by setting it on half the 20-pica width.

Notice that each column has a hairline rule dividing the columns. This prevents confusion when reading lines set on short measure. If there were no hairline rule, the reader would tend to read right across the page, seeing the space between columns as word spacing.

In figure 38.2, a page taken from *Esquire*, the four columns are set justified. This gives about six words per line. It also tends to look more formal, or serious. Included are two halftone pictures. This is very much like a new products section found in many trade publications. Note that *Esquire* has used a natural column ending well.

Figure 38.3 shows a page called "Reader Input" from *American Health* magazine. This is a magazine that uses a mix of two, three, and four columns in one issue, and does a beautiful job of it. There are some slight differences between this page and what we have previously discussed. For one, the rules go up and down, but not across. Therefore, the page lacks the enclosed feeling of the previous examples and is free and light. For another, the designer used a full line (or increment) of space between items. This works very well in a "letters" section. Readership surveys have shown that letters are popular. The thermometer to the right-hand side might bother some readers, but, in fact, the reader's temperature is being measured, is it not?

Figure 38.4, taken from *Esquire*, shows how to handle various sections within the same area. Each section has a head, a headline, a stand-up initial, and body copy. Notice that one picture is column width and that the other is wider and ties the third and fourth columns together.

Much of what is done in page design today can be traced directly to computerized typesetting. Once the keystrokes have been captured they can be set on *any* measure. When type was set once in hot metal, Heaven help you if you wanted it reset on another measure. The cry to typesetters now is save the tape or disc until what,

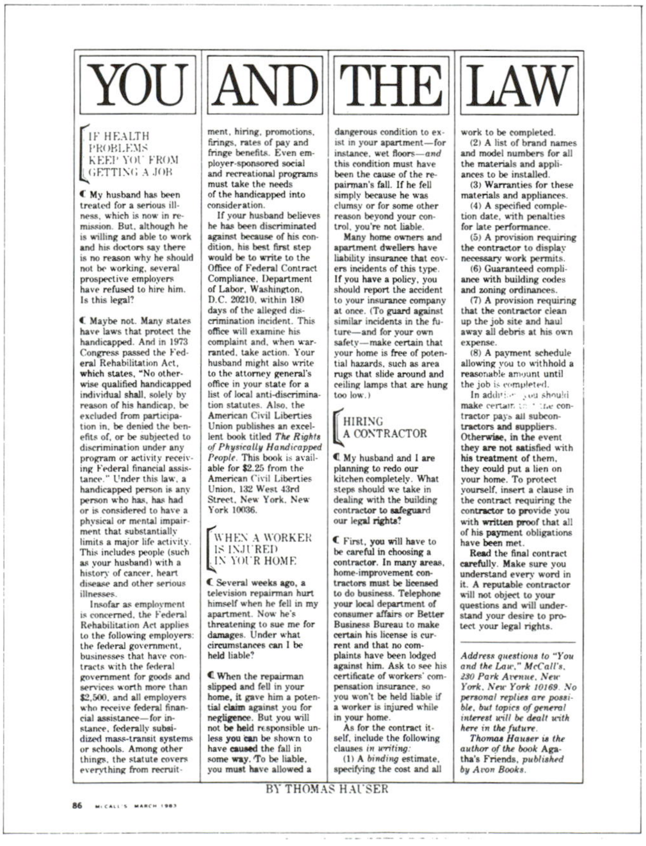

YOU AND THE LAW

IF HEALTH PROBLEMS KEEP YOU FROM GETTING A JOB

My husband has been treated for a serious illness, which is now in remission. But, although he is willing and able to work and his doctors say there is no reason why he should not be working, several prospective employers have refused to hire him. Is this legal?

Maybe not. Many states have laws that protect the handicapped. And in 1973 Congress passed the Federal Rehabilitation Act, which states, "No otherwise qualified handicapped individual shall, solely by reason of his handicap, be excluded from participation in, be denied the benefits of, or be subjected to discrimination under any program or activity receiving Federal financial assistance." Under this law, a handicapped person is any person who has, has had or is considered to have a physical or mental impairment that substantially limits a major life activity. This includes people (such as your husband) with a history of cancer, heart disease and other serious illnesses.

Insofar as employment is concerned, the Federal Rehabilitation Act applies to the following employers: the federal government, businesses that have contracts with the federal government for goods and services worth more than $2,500, and all employers who receive federal financial assistance—for instance, federally subsidized mass-transit systems or schools. Among other things, the statute covers everything from recruitment, hiring, promotions, firings, rates of pay and fringe benefits. Even employer-sponsored social and recreational programs must take the needs of the handicapped into consideration.

If your husband believes he has been discriminated against because of his condition, his best first step would be to write to the Office of Federal Contract Compliance, Department of Labor, Washington, D.C. 20210, within 180 days of the alleged discrimination incident. This office will examine his complaint and, when warranted, take action. Your husband might also write to the attorney general's office in your state for a list of local anti-discrimination statutes. Also, the American Civil Liberties Union publishes an excellent book titled *The Rights of Physically Handicapped People*. This book is available for $2.25 from the American Civil Liberties Union, 132 West 43rd Street, New York, New York 10036.

WHEN A WORKER IS INJURED IN YOUR HOME

Several weeks ago, a television repairman hurt himself when he fell in my apartment. Now he's threatening to sue me for damages. Under what circumstances can I be held liable?

When the repairman slipped and fell in your home, it gave him a potential claim against you for negligence. But you will not be held responsible unless you can be shown to have caused the fall in some way. To be liable, you must have allowed a dangerous condition to exist in your apartment—for instance, wet floors—*and* this condition must have been the cause of the repairman's fall. If he fell simply because he was clumsy or for some other reason beyond your control, you're not liable.

Many home owners and apartment dwellers have liability insurance that covers incidents of this type. If you have a policy, you should report the accident to your insurance company at once. (To guard against similar incidents in the future—and for your own safety—make certain that your home is free of potential hazards, such as area rugs that slide around and ceiling lamps that are hung too low.)

HIRING A CONTRACTOR

My husband and I are planning to redo our kitchen completely. What steps should we take in dealing with the building contractor to safeguard our legal rights?

First, you will have to be careful in choosing a contractor. In many areas, home-improvement contractors must be licensed to do business. Telephone your local department of consumer affairs or Better Business Bureau to make certain his license is current and that no complaints have been lodged against him. Ask to see his certificate of workers' compensation insurance, so you won't be held liable if a worker is injured while in your home.

As for the contract itself, include the following clauses *in writing:*

(1) A *binding* estimate, specifying the cost and all work to be completed.

(2) A list of brand names and model numbers for all the materials and appliances to be installed.

(3) Warranties for these materials and appliances.

(4) A specified completion date, with penalties for late performance.

(5) A provision requiring the contractor to display necessary work permits.

(6) Guaranteed compliance with building codes and zoning ordinances.

(7) A provision requiring that the contractor clean up the job site and haul away all debris at his own expense.

(8) A payment schedule allowing you to withhold a reasonable amount until the job is completed.

In addit[illegible] you should make certain [illegible] the contractor pays all subcontractors and suppliers. Otherwise, in the event they are not satisfied with his treatment of them, they could put a lien on your home. To protect yourself, insert a clause in the contract requiring the contractor to provide you with written proof that all of his payment obligations have been met.

Read the final contract carefully. Make sure you understand every word in it. A reputable contractor will not object to your questions and will understand your desire to protect your legal rights.

Address questions to "You and the Law," McCall's, 230 Park Avenue, New York, New York 10169. No personal replies are possible, but topics of general interest will be dealt with here in the future.

Thomas Hauser is the author of the book Agatha's Friends, *published by Avon Books.*

BY THOMAS HAUSER

86 McCALL'S MARCH 1983

Figure 38.1.—A typical four-column page design used by McCall's. *Copy is set Roman, flush left, ragged right. This gives a word count of four to the typeset line, which is a little thin. I prefer five.*

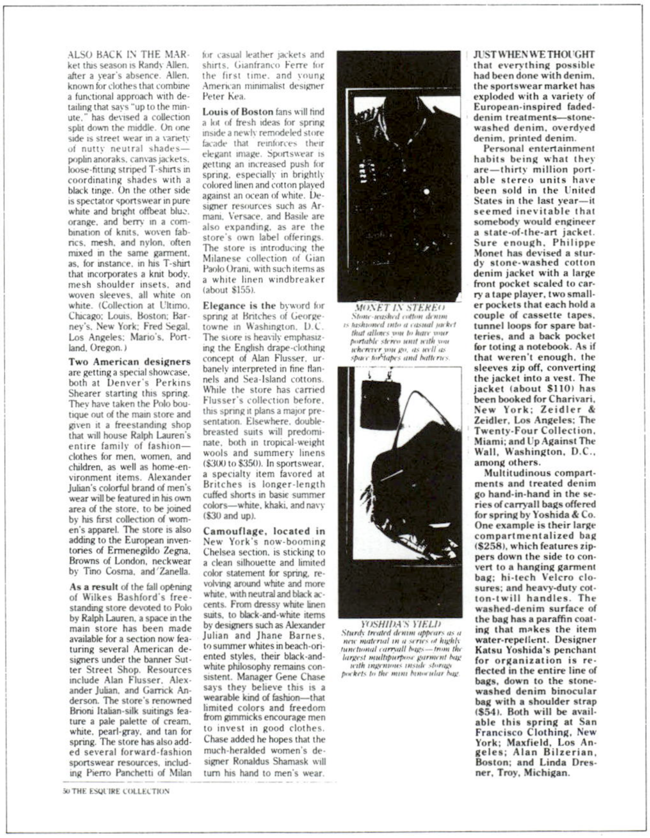

ALSO BACK IN THE MARKET this season is Randy Allen, after a year's absence. Allen, known for clothes that combine a functional approach with detailing that says "up to the minute," has devised a collection split down the middle. On one side is street wear in a variety of nutty neutral shades—poplin anoraks, canvas jackets, loose-fitting striped T-shirts in coordinating shades with a black tinge. On the other side is spectator sportswear in pure white and bright offbeat blue, orange, and berry in a combination of knits, woven fabrics, mesh, and nylon, often mixed in the same garment, as, for instance, in his T-shirt that incorporates a knit body, mesh shoulder insets, and woven sleeves, all white on white. (Collection at Ultimo, Chicago; Louis, Boston; Barney's, New York; Fred Segal, Los Angeles; Mario's, Portland, Oregon.)

Two American designers are getting a special showcase, both at Denver's Perkins Shearer starting this spring. They have taken the Polo boutique out of the main store and given it a freestanding shop that will house Ralph Lauren's entire family of fashion—clothes for men, women, and children, as well as home-environment items. Alexander Julian's colorful brand of men's wear will be featured in his own area of the store, to be joined by his first collection of women's apparel. The store is also adding to the European inventories of Ermenegildo Zegna, Browns of London, neckwear by Tino Cosma, and Zanella.

As a result of the fall opening of Wilkes Bashford's freestanding store devoted to Polo by Ralph Lauren, a space in the main store has been made available for a section now featuring several American designers under the banner Sutter Street Shop. Resources include Alan Flusser, Alexander Julian, and Garrick Anderson. The store's renowned Brioni Italian-silk suitings feature a pale palette of cream, white, pearl-gray, and tan for spring. The store has also added several forward-fashion sportswear resources, including Pierro Panchetti of Milan for casual leather jackets and shirts, Gianfranco Ferre for the first time, and young American minimalist designer Peter Kea.

Louis of Boston fans will find a lot of fresh ideas for spring inside a newly remodeled store facade that reinforces their elegant image. Sportswear is getting an increased push for spring, especially in brightly colored linen and cotton played against an ocean of white. Designer resources such as Armani, Versace, and Basile are also expanding, as are the store's own label offerings. The store is introducing the Milanese collection of Gian Paolo Orani, with such items as a white linen windbreaker (about $155).

Elegance is the byword for spring at Britches of Georgetowne in Washington, D.C. The store is heavily emphasizing the English drape-clothing concept of Alan Flusser, urbanely interpreted in fine flannels and Sea-Island cottons. While the store has carried Flusser's collection before, this spring it plans a major presentation. Elsewhere, double-breasted suits will predominate, both in tropical-weight wools and summery linens ($300 to $350). In sportswear, a specialty item favored at Britches is longer-length cuffed shorts in basic summer colors—white, khaki, and navy ($30 and up).

Camouflage, located in New York's now-booming Chelsea section, is sticking to a clean silhouette and limited color statement for spring, revolving around white and more white, with neutral and black accents. From dressy white linen suits, to black-and-white items by designers such as Alexander Julian and Jhane Barnes, to summer whites in beach-oriented styles, their black-and-white philosophy remains consistent. Manager Gene Chase says they believe this is a wearable kind of fashion—that limited colors and freedom from gimmicks encourage men to invest in good clothes. Chase added he hopes that the much-heralded women's designer Ronaldus Shamask will turn his hand to men's wear.

MONET IN STEREO
Stone-washed cotton denim is fashioned into a casual jacket that allows you to have your portable stereo unit with you wherever you go, as well as space for tapes and batteries.

YOSHIDA'S YIELD
Sturdy treated denim appears as a new material in a series of highly functional carryall bags—from the largest multipurpose garment bag with ingenious inside storage pockets to the mini binocular bag.

JUST WHEN WE THOUGHT that everything possible had been done with denim, the sportswear market has exploded with a variety of European-inspired faded-denim treatments—stone-washed denim, overdyed denim, printed denim.

Personal entertainment habits being what they are—thirty million portable stereo units have been sold in the United States in the last year—it seemed inevitable that somebody would engineer a state-of-the-art jacket. Sure enough, Philippe Monet has devised a sturdy stone-washed cotton denim jacket with a large front pocket scaled to carry a tape player, two smaller pockets that each hold a couple of cassette tapes, tunnel loops for spare batteries, and a back pocket for toting a notebook. As if that weren't enough, the sleeves zip off, converting the jacket into a vest. The jacket (about $110) has been booked for Charivari, New York; Zeidler & Zeidler, Los Angeles; The Twenty-Four Collection, Miami; and Up Against The Wall, Washington, D.C., among others.

Multitudinous compartments and treated denim go hand-in-hand in the series of carryall bags offered for spring by Yoshida & Co. One example is their large compartmentalized bag ($258), which features zippers down the side to convert to a hanging garment bag; hi-tech Velcro closures; and heavy-duty cotton-twill handles. The washed-denim surface of the bag has a paraffin coating that makes the item water-repellent. Designer Katsu Yoshida's penchant for organization is reflected in the entire line of bags, down to the stone-washed denim binocular bag with a shoulder strap ($54). Both will be available this spring at San Francisco Clothing, New York; Maxfield, Los Angeles; Alan Bilzerian, Boston; and Linda Dresner, Troy, Michigan.

50 THE ESQUIRE COLLECTION

Figure 38.2.—This four-column format is set Roman and justified. It gives a word count of five, which is easier to read than a four-word line.

Figure 38.3.—In this four-column format, note that the hairline rules do not run across the bottom. This gives the page a little more "air."

Figure 38.4.—This four-column design uses Roman type, justified, and has some wrap-around copy. Notice how the picture ties the two columns together.

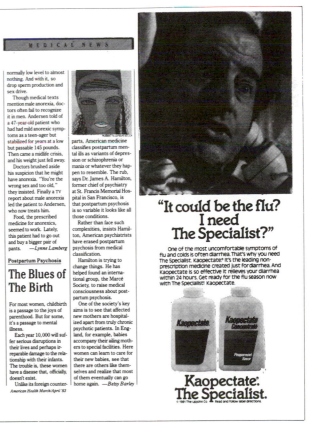

Figure 38.5.—Four-column body copy (editorial) mixes well with a half-page ad.

Figure 38.6.—Another successful mix of four-column copy and a vertical ad.

where, when, how wide, how long, what size, and all the other design intangibles have been settled. The type wrap-around of the second picture, though a little tight at top and bottom, could have been done only with planning.

How are ads handled in four-column design? Figure 38.5 shows a horizontal half-page ad with four-columns of body copy above it, and figure 38.6 shows a vertical half-page ad with four-column-width copy next to it. They both work well. This again points up the fact that magazine issues can be planned by signatures and *should* be planned that way.

And what happens when you forget that hairline rules are needed to separate the lines? Look at figure 38.7, taken from *House & Garden*. Sixteen sight objects are floating. The typesetting has been specified as "no hyphenation," which means that words are not to be broken and hyphenated at the end of a line. If the word doesn't fit, it is carried into the next line. This gives more space at the end of each line, and there is an average of four words per typeset line instead of five or six. *House & Garden* does a marvelous job of designing as a rule. Figure 38.8, a page from *McCall's*, shows what has now become the accepted way to typeset recipes and set-by-step procedures in four-column design. There is also a trend toward making tables of contents in four-column design.

THE SCREEN AS ART: GOOD IDEA GONE WRONG

The Rizzoli Gallery in New York recently asked four architects and one artist to design decorative screens now on display through April 11 at the Rizzoli Gallery in Chicago. It was a worthwhile exercise, but as sometimes happens with specially commissioned efforts of this sort (as opposed to spontaneously created works that are later exhibited together), the results were rather disappointing. Architect Thomas Beeby's entry was a bizarre convertible table/chair/screen in a flamboyant style that might be termed Neo-Tolkien. Architect Stanley Tigerman came up with a screen in the form of cartoonlike stylized Classical columns incongruously incorporating electrified sconces. Architect Robert Stern produced a vapid green composition said to represent a partially open French balcony window. More successful was Michael Graves's Classical screen draped with his own Sunar fabric. Best of show: painter Richard Haas's sharp but affectionate take-off on Art Deco. This vibrantly zig-zagged lacquer screen, strong in presence and coherent in line, was ironically, as its creator correctly boasted, "the most architectural" of them all. □ *M.F.*

Top to bottom: Screens by Richard Haas, Michael Graves, and Stanley Tigerman.

WIDE-ANGLE LOOK AT A PHOTOGRAPHER OF FASHION

Norman Parkinson, the photographer most famous for his gauzy portraits of British royals, has a much broader range, shown in this 1975 double take of model Jerry Hall in Russia. His best work is assembled in *Fifty Years of Style and Fashion* by Norman Parkinson (Vendome, $30), including a hilarious photo of novelist Barbara Cartland posed more regally than the Queen.

THE ARCHITECTURAL EYE OF CERVIN ROBINSON

Farish Gallery, Rice University, Houston, through April 17; Wellesley College Art Gallery, Wellesley, Massachusetts, Fall 1983.

There are but a handful of architectural photographers whose pictures are as much works of art as the objects they represent. Among contemporary practitioners of the art, none is more distinguished than Cervin Robinson, whose photographs of the past 25 years are now the subject of a retrospective exhibition that brings together 100 of his black-and-white images and 15 color works. They demonstrate Robinson's remarkable ability to create photographs that are themselves the embodiment of Vitruvius' famous triad of architectural values: firmness, commodity, and delight. Robinson's photographs typically are composed with an architectonic solidity (*Continued on page 176*)

Art Deco towers, N.Y.C., 1966

British Art Center, Yale University, New Haven, 1978

APRIL 1983

175

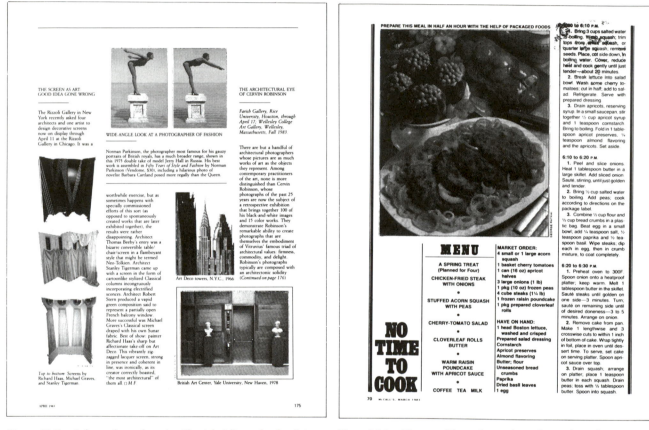

Figure 38.7.—*A four-column format without hairline rules for "structure." Note that the elements look rather loose and disconnected.*

PREPARE THIS MEAL IN HALF AN HOUR WITH THE HELP OF PACKAGED FOODS

GEORGE RATKAI

NO TIME TO COOK

MENU

A SPRING TREAT
(Planned for Four)

CHICKEN-FRIED STEAK WITH ONIONS
•
STUFFED ACORN SQUASH WITH PEAS
•
CHERRY-TOMATO SALAD
•
CLOVERLEAF ROLLS
BUTTER
•
WARM RAISIN POUNDCAKE WITH APRICOT SAUCE
•
COFFEE TEA MILK

MARKET ORDER:
4 small or 1 large acorn squash
1 basket cherry tomatoes
1 can (16 oz) apricot halves
3 large onions (1 lb)
1 pkg (10 oz) frozen peas
4 cube steaks (1¼ lb)
1 frozen raisin poundcake
1 pkg prepared cloverleaf rolls

HAVE ON HAND:
1 head Boston lettuce, washed and crisped
Prepared salad dressing
Cornstarch
Apricot preserves
Almond flavoring
Butter; flour
Unseasoned bread crumbs
Paprika
Dried basil leaves
1 egg

[illegible] to 6:10 P.M.

1. Bring 3 cups salted water to boiling. Wash squash; trim tops from small squash, or quarter large squash; remove seeds. Place, cut side down, in boiling water. Cover, reduce heat and cook gently until just tender—about 20 minutes.

2. Break lettuce into salad bowl. Wash some cherry tomatoes; cut in half; add to salad. Refrigerate. Serve with prepared dressing.

3. Drain apricots, reserving syrup. In a small saucepan, stir together ½ cup apricot syrup and 1 teaspoon cornstarch. Bring to boiling. Fold in 1 tablespoon apricot preserves, ¼ teaspoon almond flavoring and the apricots. Set aside.

6:10 to 6:20 P.M.

1. Peel and slice onions. Heat 1 tablespoon butter in a large skillet. Add sliced onion. Sauté, stirring, until just golden and tender.

2. Bring ½ cup salted water to boiling. Add peas; cook according to directions on the package label.

3. Combine ½ cup flour and ½ cup bread crumbs in a plastic bag. Beat egg in a small bowl; add ¼ teaspoon salt, ½ teaspoon paprika and ½ teaspoon basil. Wipe steaks; dip each in egg, then in crumb mixture, to coat completely.

6:20 to 6:30 P.M.

1. Preheat oven to 300F. Spoon onion onto a heatproof platter; keep warm. Melt 1 tablespoon butter in the skillet. Sauté steaks until golden on one side—3 minutes. Turn; sauté on remaining side until of desired doneness—3 to 5 minutes. Arrange on onion.

2. Remove cake from pan. Make 1 lengthwise and 3 crosswise cuts to within 1 inch of bottom of cake. Wrap tightly in foil, place in oven until dessert time. To serve, set cake on serving platter. Spoon apricot sauce over top.

3. Drain squash; arrange on platter; place 1 teaspoon butter in each squash. Drain peas; toss with ½ tablespoon butter. Spoon into squash.

70 McCALL'S, MARCH 1983

Figure 38.8.—*The use of four columns for recipes and step-by-step procedures is commonplace. Note how little wasted space there is after the item descriptions.*

CHAPTER THIRTY-NINE

The Double-18 Design

It seems to me that two- and three-column formats have been with us for a very long time. The Code of Hammurabi was posted in three columns in the three most commonly used languages of the day, and we can certainly look back to illuminated manuscripts and Gutenberg's Bible as examples of two-column design.

When we think of designing publications we must think of column arrangements. Advertisers plan ads based on a certain amount of live area. To ignore ads is to ignore a fact of life: ads are needed to pay the bills. Advertisers make ads to fit the live area of a publication. In a magazine, the live area is usually 7 by 10 inches. In other publications, such as tabloids, the live area depends on column arrangements.

A look at a publication's rate card will show how ads are fitted into columns. A standard two-column design will have ads that are half-column, or quarter-page; full-column, or half-page, vertically; half-page, horizontally; and full-page. The same holds for the standard three-column format. The ads are made in column widths and multiples of column widths.

If you design your publication without considering advertisers, you'll soon have no funds to work with. There have been magazines published in the 11-by-11-inch size that were beautiful to look at and a joy to work with, but they were economic disasters because advertisers would not make square ads. And you simply cannot make a 7-by-11-inch ad fit an 11-by-11-inch space.

In the standard two- and three-column formats, the live area is 41 picas wide. The depth usually comes close to 10 inches. In a two-column design there is a 20-pica column, a 1-pica alley, and another 20-pica column. In a three-column design, there is a 13-pica column, a 1-pica alley, another 13-pica column, a 1-pica alley, and a final 13-pica column. Both total 41 picas across. That's very important, since most publication design on an 8½-by-11-inch page will have that live area.

What If?

Designers frequently experiment. They play a game called "What if?" For example, what if we have two columns in a page design, but they are *not* 20 and 20? What if they are 18 and 18? Can this still fall within the live area of 41 picas? The answer, of course, is yes. We can add 18 and 1 (for the alley) and 18 and get 41, but we have 4 picas left over.

Where do we put this 4 picas? We could put it in the middle, but that would give us a 5-pica alley, which separates the two columns with too much space. They no longer are seen as an entity, but rather as two individual units. We could split the 4 picas and put 2 picas at each side. This does nothing more than increase the borders from the normal 5 picas to 7. It also increases the

gutter to 14 picas. Can you envision a 14-pica gap between the live areas of two facing pages? No. The only place the 4 picas can go is on the outside edge of the page. This creates what used to be called a "scholar's margin." The margin was purposely wide to allow the reader to make notes on the text.

Figure 39.1 shows an editorial page in the two-column format or design. The columns are 20 picas wide, the alley is 1 pica, and the borders are 5 picas. This is called a standard two-column format. Now look at figure 39.2, which shows two 18-pica columns with the additional white space to the outside. This creates a white band running from top to bottom that is 9 picas wide—4 picas plus the usual 5-pica border. The white space is always added to the outside margin. I call this format the "Double-18."

Using the White Space

If I want to be noticed when I walk down the street, I can do something out of the ordinary, such as hold my right arm straight out. You can imagine the comments: "Why is he walking with his arm out like that?" It is quite obvious that I am drawing attention without explanation. What if you could draw attention and then explain it?

Look at figure 39.2 again. No matter what I place in that white outside margin, it will be surrounded with white space and will be noticed. There are several forces at work here. One is gravity. Your eye will drop down to see what breaks up the vertical shapes. Another is that any irregular shape is more interesting than a regular shape. The key idea in this design is to place items where they will be noticed more than if they were in a standard position.

Figure 39.3 shows the simplest application of this theory. The headline and "kicker" are placed in the white space, to the outside of the live area. Notice that the headline is the first thing you see on that page for three reasons: it is where the reader normally starts on any page (upper left), it is in large boldface type, and it hangs out into the white space creating an irregular edge within the page.

Figure 39.4 shows a righthand page with two 18-pica columns. The reader may start at upper left, but finds only white space there. The eye moves to the right to the "kicker phrase," then to the slight overhang into the white space. De-

signing is very much like fishing—once we have caught the reader, we direct the reader to the story beginning, in this case the boldface letter O. Look this over again. Track the reader's eye. Squint a bit to get the shape in your mind's eye. That slight "bump" caused by the overhanging headline is just enough to make it interesting. Note that the page number (called the folio) is also hanging into white space where it is very much apparent. Compare this folio to one on a standard two-column design, where it aligns with the column edge.

Type Visuals

How do you get the reader into the story when you have no pictures? Figure 39.5 uses a "breakout," or "in-text quote," or "blurb" (whatever you care to call it) as an all-type visual. The break-

out actually sticks out into the white space, practically shouting to be noticed and read. This would not be so apparent in a standard two-column design. The breakout is given added depth and emphasis by the shadowing technique—that is, a thin line on two sides and a thick line on the other two sides. A second color can be used here. You can overprint the copy on a 10 percent tint block, such as blue or beige. I challenge you to look at this page and *not* see the breakout.

Another type visual is the "sidebar," an aside to the story—something not very long, certainly not long enough to be a story in itself. In figure 39.6, I not only use the sidebar design (shadowing, again) but also have it bumping out into the white space to the outside of the page. This creates an irregular shape and looks especially fine if it is overprinted on a 10 percent tint block, particularly in a second color. I have also added a dash of design by using a boldface beginning initial.

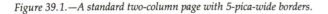

Figure 39.1.—A standard two-column page with 5-pica-wide borders.

Figure 39.2.—A Double-18 format with two columns of 18 picas. The leftover white space is added to the outside margin, which is called a "scholar's margin."

Profiles in College

Meet five people who've picked up the school spirit.

One patient dreamed that the electrodes attached scalp during an investigation the previous day had a his confused thoughts and he would again be able t logically with his friends. Another patient in the d awareness phase thought an auditory signal test w dered by the therapist to determine if she had an ex dinary hearing capacity that enabled her to hear others could not hear, or to objectively establish voices as imaginary. This patient asked for the res order to provide further support for her increasing c tion of the psychological basis for her hallucination

This confidence in the research as a magical sou cure can often have a dramatic impact on the pat One severely ill woman explained her remarkable provement after several weeks of unsuccessful treat with psychotherapy and chlorpromazine at another tal by explaining: "I no longer had any confidence i treatment. When I understood that I could be transl to a research ward, I knew I would be made better." hopeful expectation in the outcome of the research so to have a definite influence on the patient's early gence from the delusional phase.

The fantasied expectation that patients projected the research, together with the realistic gratificati participation provided, were consistently emphasiz the patients during their emergence from the delu phase. It must be noted that all patients were in int dynamic therapy during this period and, except in ra stances, receiving no medication.

The therapy during this period would often be plateau as patients turned away from the clinical st cause of their frustration at being unable to obtai special attention they seemed now to be able to r from the research staff. Often, the researchers were very specific clinical questions such as, "What causes ophrenia? Is it hereditary? What do I have to do better?" Patients are generally disappointed when find that the researchers have no special knowledge these questions and generally begin to lose their hi pectations in the research and to actively engage again in their psychotherapy.

Since our patients were studied within the milie research hospital where research received considera tention and praise, it is not surprising that, as pa emerged from the delusional phase, the research re the therapeutic focus that it did.

Jacobs and Kotin[1] have described the "research i apy" belief as a fantasy characteristic of research Our material suggests that this is not entirely fants reflects and contributes to the recovery process. Sin

the change in her beliefs, she suggested to us a nam the first phase of the recovery process.

Double-Awareness Phase

The appearance of reality testing into a delusiona ation creates a double awareness. In this phase, th tient becomes increasingly able to establish distance his delusions and is no longer totally immersed in He either questions his delusions or simultaneous cepts and rejects them. Often he may conceal them other ways try to suppress them."

During this phase the patient may still be fearfu procedure, but is often able to participate with some ence to the double-awareness experience. This may the form of an explanation that the fear was "pro crazy" or "49% of me knows that what I am thinking weird to be real." One patient, seeing a child perform reaction time procedure, felt more convinced that haps it wasn't really a dangerous apparatus." Anoth tient insisted on examining the room adjoining the laboratory "just to be sure" his fears that the head were connected to the devil he was still hallucinating really imaginary.

The patient is still delusional but increasingly nizes the delusion as a symptom and is able to entiate his perceptions from his ideas. This is accomp by an increased capacity to relate to people and to their support for his still impaired reality testing. quent occurrence during this period is the patient's ning to seek more information about his delusion. H ask a trusted staff member to take him on the ho grounds in order to test his belief that the hospi really a political prison.

The clinical staff is quite sensitive to the patient's into the double-awareness phase and experiences i marily as his "being in contact." Although these p are not continuous, they are welcomed as early evide improvement. Participation in intricate research dures now occurs regularly and is praised by the sta taken as evidence of recovery. This enhances the pat self-esteem and the research becomes a source of c erable narcissistic gratification. One lonely adolesce said it was like being "Queen for a Day." Another p boasted that his reaction time was as fast as that of perior athlete.

The possible therapeutic effect of research on psy patients has been noted by several authors.[1,2] One of research participation that our patients emph during the double-awareness phase was how impi they were with the confidency of the research staff ir

119 Arch Gen Psychiatry/Vol 30, Jun 1974   Recovery From Delusions/Sacks et al

Figure 39.3.—An example of the Double-18 format. The headline extends into the white space to create a visual hook.

Are You Overinsured?

Insurance is a gamble: Like Las Vegas, the odds are stacked in the company's favor.

One patient dreamed that the electrodes attached scalp during an investigation the previous day had al his confused thoughts and he would again be able to logically with his friends. Another patient in the d awareness phase thought an auditory signal test w dered by the therapist to determine if she had an ex dinary hearing capacity that enabled her to hear others could not hear, or to objectively establish voices as imaginary. This patient asked for the resu order to provide further support for her increasing c tion of the psychological basis for her hallucination

This confidence in the research as a magical sour cure can often have a dramatic impact on the pat One severely ill woman explained her remarkabl provement after several weeks of unsuccessful treat with psychotherapy and chlorpromazine at another tal by explaining: "I no longer had any confidence i treatment. When I understood that I could be transf to a research ward, I knew I would be made better." hopeful expectation in the outcome of the research so to have a definite influence on the patient's early gence from the delusional phase.

The fantasied expectation that patients projected the research, together with the realistic gratificatior participation provided, were consistently emphasiz the patients during their emergence from the delu phase. It must be noted that all patients were in inte dynamic therapy during this period and, except in ra stances, receiving no medication.

The therapy during this period would often re plateau as patients turned away from the clinical sta cause of their frustration at being unable to obtai special attention they seemed now to be able to r from the research staff. Often, the researchers were very specific clinical questions such as, "What causes ophrenia? Is it hereditary? What do I have to do t better?" Patients are generally disappointed when find that the researchers have no special knowledge these questions and generally begin to lose their high pectations in the research and to actively engage again in their psychotherapy.

Since our patients were studied within the milie research hospital where research received considerat tention and praise, it is not surprising that, as pa emerged from the delusional phase, the research re the therapeutic focus that it did.

Jacobs and Kotin[1] have described the "research i apy" belief as a fantasy characteristic of research Our material suggests that this is not entirely fants reflects and contributes to the recovery process. Sin

This was often compared to the "unnaturalness" clinical staff who were always asking questions and ining "little things." The patients found comfort in t search staff and frequently made admiring states such as "they really know what they are doing." This apeutic effect of the researchers' confident expect that the patient participate in a defined task often pressed by the patient's belief that the investigation is therapeutic.

refusing to do so for a month. Later, she explaine she did so despite believing that it would result death, since there was no longer any hope of escapi persecutors. She had decided that death would be than further resistance. Another young woman wi delusion that her former employer was transmittin ual thoughts to her participated—despite her certai the danger involved—because the investigators "we her, she was astonished and, for the first time, ques the reality of her delusions. Through this recognit the change in her beliefs, she suggested to us a nan the first phase of the recovery process.

Double-Awareness Phase

The appearance of reality testing into a delusiona ation creates a double awareness. In this phase, t tient becomes increasingly able to establish distanc his delusions and is no longer totally immersed in He either questions his delusions or simultaneous cepts and rejects them. Often he may conceal them other ways try to suppress them."

During this phase the patient may still be fearfu procedure, but is often able to participate with some ence to the double-awareness experience. This may the form of an explanation that the fear was "pr crazy" or "49% of me knows that what I am thinking weird to be real." One patient, seeing a child perforr reaction time procedure, felt more convinced that haps it wasn't really a dangerous apparatus." Anoth tient insisted on examining the room adjoining the laboratory "just to be sure" his fears that the head were connected to the devil he was still hallucinating really imaginary.

The patient is still delusional but increasingly nizes the delusion as a symptom and is able to entiate his perceptions from his ideas. This is accomp by an increased capacity to relate to people and to their support for his still impaired reality testing. quent occurrence during this period is the patient's ning to seek more information about his delusion. H

Arch Gen Psychiatry/Vol 30, Jun 1974   Recovery From Delusions/Sacks et al 119

Figure 39.4.—An example of the Double-18 format on a right-hand page. The white space should always be added to the outside.

ing with them and the often elaborate equipment they employed.

This was often compared to the "unnaturalness", clinical staff who were always asking questions and ining "little things." The patients found comfort in t search staff and frequently made admiring states such as "they really know what they are doing." This apeutic effect of the researchers' confident expect that the patient participate in a defined task often pressed by the patient's belief that the investigation is therapeutic.

One patient dreamed that the electrodes attached scalp during an investigation the previous day had a his confused thoughts and he would again be able t logically with his friends. Another patient in the d awareness phase thought an auditory signal test w dered by the therapist to determine if she had an ex dinary hearing capacity that enabled her to hear others could not hear, or to objectively establish voices as imaginary. This patient asked for the rest order to provide further support for her increasing c tion of the psychological basis for her hallucination

This confidence in the research as a magical sour cure can often have a dramatic impact on the pat One severely ill woman explained her remarkabl

refusing to do so for a month. Later, she explaine she did so despite believing that it would result i death, since there was no longer any hope of escapi persecutors. She had decided that death would be than further resistance. Another young woman wi delusion that her former employer was transmitti ual thoughts to her participated—despite her certai the danger involved—because the investigators "wer trolling her movements." When testing did not elect her, she was astonished and, for the first time, ques the reality of her delusions. Through this recognit the change in her beliefs, she suggested to us a nan the first phase of the recovery process.

Double-Awareness Phase

The appearance of reality testing into a delusiona ation creates a double awareness. In this phase, tl tient becomes increasingly able to establish distance his delusions and is no longer totally immersed in He either questions his delusions or simultaneous cepts and rejects them. Often he may conceal them other ways try to suppress them."

During this phase the patient may still be fearfu procedure, but is often able to participate with some ence to the double-awareness experience. This may the form of an explanation that the fear was "pro crazy" or "49% of me knows that what I am thinking weird to be real." One patient, seeing a child perform reaction time procedure, felt more convinced that haps it wasn't really a dangerous apparatus." Anoth tient insisted on examining the room adjoining the laboratory "just to be sure" his fears that the head were connected to the devil he was still hallucinating really imaginary.

The patient is still delusional but increasingly nizes the delusion as a symptom and is able to entiate his perceptions from his ideas. This is accomp by an increased capacity to relate to people and to their support for his still impaired reality testing. quent occurrence during this period is the patient's ning to seek more information about his delusion. H ask a trusted staff member to take him on the ho grounds in order to test his belief that the hospi really a political prison.

The clinical staff is quite sensitive to the patient's into the double-awareness phase and experiences i marily as his "being in contact." Although these p are not continuous, they are welcomed as early evide improvement. Participation in intricate research dures now occurs regularly and is praised by the sta taken as evidence of recovery. This enhances the pat self-esteem and the research becomes a source of c erable narcissistic gratification. One lonely adolesce said it was like being "Queen for a Day." Another p boasted that his reaction time was as fast as that of perior athlete.

The possible therapeutic effect of research on psy patients has been noted by several authors.[1,2] One of research participation that our patients empha during the double-awareness phase was how impi they were with the confidency of the research staff in

> 'People who live in a stressful environment—an inner city, for instance—have a higher rate.'

The fantasied expectation that patients projected the research, together with the realistic gratificatior participation provided, were consistently emphasiz the patients during their emergence from the delu phase. It must be noted that all patients were in inte dynamic therapy during this period and, except in ra stances, receiving no medication.

The therapy during this period would often re plateau as patients turned away from the clinical sta cause of their frustration at being unable to obtai special attention they seemed now to be able to re from the research staff. Often, the researchers were very specific clinical questions such as, "What causes ophrenia? Is it hereditary? What do I have to do t better?" Patients are generally disappointed when find that the researchers have no special knowledge these questions and generally begin to lose their hig pectations in the research and to actively engage again in their psychotherapy.

Since our patients were studied within the milie research hospital where research received considera tention and praise, it is not surprising that, as pa emerged from the delusional phase, the research re the therapeutic focus that it did.

Jacobs and Kotin[1] have described the "research i apy" belief as a fantasy characteristic of research Our material suggests that this is not entirely fants reflects and contributes to the recovery process. Sin

119 Recovery From Delusions/Sacks et al   Arch Gen Psychiatry/Vol 30, Jun 1974

Figure 39.5.—A "break-out," or blurb, bumping out into the added white space. There is no way the reader can ignore this. Don't abuse it by using it for unimportant items.

refusing to do so for a month. Later, she explaine she did so despite believing that it would result death, since there was no longer any hope of escapi persecutors. She had decided that death would be than further resistance. Another young woman wi delusion that her former employer was transmittin ual thoughts to her participated—despite her certai the danger involved—because the investigators "wer trolling her movements." When testing did not elect her, she was astonished and, for the first time, ques the reality of her delusions. Through this recognit the change in her beliefs, she suggested to us a nan the first phase of the recovery process.

Double-Awareness Phase

The appearance of reality testing into a delusiona ation creates a double awareness. In this phase, t tient becomes increasingly able to establish distanc his delusions and is no longer totally immersed in He either questions his delusions or simultaneous cepts and rejects them. Often he may conceal them other ways try to suppress them."

During this phase the patient may still be fearfu procedure, but is often able to participate with some ence to the double-awareness experience. This may the form of an explanation that the fear was "prr crazy" or "49% of me knows that what I am thinking weird to be real." One patient, seeing a child perform reaction time procedure, felt more convinced that haps it wasn't really a dangerous apparatus." Anoth tient insisted on examining the room adjoining the laboratory "just to be sure" his fears that the head were connected to the devil he was still hallucinating really imaginary.

The patient is still delusional but increasingly nizes the delusion as a symptom and is able to entiate his perceptions from his ideas. This is accomp by an increased capacity to relate to people and to their support for his still impaired reality testing. quent occurrence during this period is the patient's ning to seek more information about his delusion. H ask a trusted staff member to take him on the hc grounds in order to test his belief that the hosp really a political prison.

The clinical staff is quite sensitive to the patient's into the double-awareness phase and experiences i marily as his "being in contact." Although these p are not continuous, they are welcomed as early evide improvement. Participation in intricate research dures now occurs regularly and is praised by the sta taken as evidence of recovery. This enhances the pat self-esteem and the research becomes a source of c erable narcissistic gratification. One lonely adolesce said it was like being "Queen for a Day." Another p boasted his reaction time was as fast as that of perior athlete.

The possible therapeutic effect of research on psy patients has been noted by several authors.[1,2] One of research participation that our patients empha during the double-awareness phase was how impi they were with the confidency of the research staff in

ing with them and the often elaborate equipmen they employed.

This was often compared to the "unnaturalness" clinical staff who were always asking questions and ining "little things." The patients found comfort in t search staff and frequently made admiring state such as "they really know what they are doing." This apeutic effect of the researchers' confident expec that the patient participate in a defined task often pressed by the patient's belief that the investigation is therapeutic.

One patient dreamed that the electrodes attached scalp during an investigation the previous day had a his confused thoughts and he would again be able t logically with his friends. Another patient in the d awareness phase thought an auditory signal test w dered by the therapist to determine if she had an ex dinary hearing capacity that enabled her to hear others could not hear, or to objectively establish voices as imaginary. This patient asked for the rest order to provide further support for her increasing c tion of the psychological basis for her hallucination

This confidence in the research as a magical sou cure can often have a dramatic impact on the pat One severely ill woman explained her remarkabl provement after several weeks of unsuccessful treat with psychotherapy and chlorpromazine at another tal by explaining: "I no longer had any confidence in treatment. When I understood that I could be transl to a research ward, I knew I would be made better." hopeful expectation in the outcome of the research so

> R esearch, together with the realistic gratification that participation provided, were consistently emphasized by the patients during their emergence from the delusional phase. It must be noted that all patients were in intensive dynamic therapy during this period and, except in rare instances, receiving no medication.
>
> The therapy during this period would often reach a plateau as patients turned away from the clinical staff because of their frustration at being unable to obtain the special attention they seemed now to be able to receive from the research staff. Often, the researchers were asked very specific clinical questions such as, "What causes schizophrenia? What do I have to do to get better?" Patients are generally disappointed when they find that the researchers have no special knowledge about these questions and generally begin to lose their high expectations in the research and to actively engage once again in their psychotherapy.
>
> Since our patients were studied within the milieu of a research hospital where research received considerable attention and praise, it is not surprising that, as patients emerged from the delusional phase, the research received the therapeutic focus that it did.
>
> Jacobs and Kotin[1] have described the "research is therapy" belief as a fantasy characteristic of research units. Our material suggests that this is not entirely fantasy. It reflects and contributes to the recovery process. Since it is

Arch Gen Psychiatry/Vol 30, Jun 1974   Recovery From Delusions/Sacks et al 119

Figure 39.6.—An example of the Double-18 with a sidebar placed in the soft corner, where the reader's eye leaves the page.

Selling Your Home in the New Mortgage Market

Figure 39.7.—A double-page spread using the Double-18 format. This shows the best placement of the white space—to the outside.

Figure 39.8.—In this double-page spread, note that the caption is used in the white space on the left and a line drawing is used on the right. The design also uses the pyramid method of layout, with the weight at the bottom.

Pictures

So far I have covered those visuals described as "type"—headlines, teasers, trailers, breakouts, initials, and sidebars. The best visuals, of course, are good pictures. When you combine pictures with the type visuals and use one or the other, or both, in the white space, you create attractive page layouts. Figure 39.7 is a double-page spread using a headline and three pictures. The left-hand page also uses gravity as a layout device. Your eye picks up on the headline because it is where the eye normally starts on the page. The headline bumps out into the white space to make it even more obvious. You can't get away from the headline. Since there is nothing but space underneath the breakout, your eye drops to the next slight element—a picture. You are hooked with a one-two punch—headline and picture.

On the right-hand page are two more pictures, one column width and the other bumping out, creating enough of an irregularity to be interesting. Note that the two pictures counterbalance the one at lower left on the first page. We now have a balanced design including interesting sight elements (type and pictures) and a reading patterns that leads the reader from sight element to sight element and doesn't turn the reader loose until all items have been looked at. This would not happen if the design elements were within a "standard two" since they would line up on all sides.

Figure 39.8 shows a typical double-page spread in the middle of a story. Here there is no headline to attract attention. We now have to use the Double-18 format without the "big club." The picture at lower left is not exactly one or two columns wide—it falls in between. The caption is written to fit a certain space and bumps out into the white space. This creates an irregularity that pulls the reader's eye down.

The line drawing at lower right uses another layout device—the caption is within the picture area, not above or below it. This uses some blank white space, but helps concentrate the sight element. And either picture could be at the top or bottom. I prefer using both of them at the bottom. When you have the widest design element at the bottom and the "lightest" at the top you have a solid design structure.

Pictures draw attention. The normal viewing sequence is pictures, captions, and then text. Pictures are the cheese that baits the trap. Remember—if you can't get the reader to read the story, you have failed. You must use every device possible to persuade the reader you have something to say.

The Double-18 is the simplest layout to typeset since body copy and, usually, captions are set on 18 pica widths. You can vary breakouts and sidebars to fit the circumstances. Captions have two variables: they can be set on 18 or on 22 picas, so they are column width or column width plus the 4 picas of white space.

CHAPTER FORTY

The Arbitrary Column

In the arbitrary-column layout design, pages need no longer be a standard three or two columns. Instead, the column arrangement can serve a specific purpose. We can have a narrow column followed by two medium-width columns, or a wide column followed by two narrow ones.

Using the concept of arbitrary, the designer can plan a page around a specific idea instead of making the idea fit a pre-established form. This opens up new design possibilities. One need not puzzle over planning a page for new products or "mug" shots or bits and pieces of news items, trying to force them into a preplanned design.

Anyone who has worked in publications knows that there are design areas in a publication. Some ads fit a two-column format; some ads fit a three-column format. Then there are fractional ads and special departments, such as letters, new products, people sections, editorial areas, and the like. Furthermore, stories often call for special handling. Even if we divide a magazine into only two sections, advertisements and editorial, we still need more than one format to separate them from each other.

Some time ago, it was determined that a designer could mix two-column format with a three-column one, since the live area did not change in any given publication. Designers then added a four-column format to the design possibilities. It, too, fit within the same live area. As long as one could fit a column arrangement into the live area, it was acceptable.

Now, add to this concept the new advances in typesetting. Once we have captured the keystrokes, we can do anything we want to with that copy. This means that the story, captions, headlines, and whatever else you have set in type is captured on tape or disk. Every letter, space, punctuation mark, capital or lower case letter, and number is available to be set on *any measure*. That's the key to new designs—the fact that type can be set on any measure simply by rerunning the file.

The advantages are tremendous. In the old days, once type was set in lead, you were stuck with it. If you had decided on setting copy 20 picas wide, that's where it stayed. If you wanted it reset on 13 picas, it meant dumping the 20-pica copy and starting over on 13 picas. That doubled expenses. Now you can set copy on 20 picas, then change it to 13 or 11 or 9 or anything you want at only a 10 percent or so increase in cost.

How Can We Use It?

As you will see from the examples, the arbitrary column can be used to solve any design problem. You can plan issues by areas (or signatures). You can decide within any issue how many pages to give to a two-column format, including the two-column ads, and how many to give to a three-column format, including the ads. You can decide how many pages to use in the editorial section and in the "back of the book" in a variety of column widths. You have complete design freedom. You can now accept any size ads so long as they fit within the live area.

I suggest that the average sixty-four-page magazine be sectioned off as follows. The first sixteen pages should be two-column (this will include all two-column ads), the second sixteen should be three-column, including three-column ads. The middle thirty-two pages should be editorial, interspersed with full-page ads, and the final thirty-two pages should incorporate the arbitrary columns to take care of special sections.

What's the Key to Doing This?

The key to doing this is shown in figure 40.1, which is one page from the Universal Layout Sheet (copyrighted by the Ragen Report, Chicago, Illinois, and sold by them). The Universal Layout Sheet shows the live area and the normal borders. It has 62 lines that are 11 points apart. Experience has shown that the most readable type size is 9 point in most conventional Romans with a character count of 3.0. I know of fifteen Romans that can be used with no problem: Baskerville, Bodoni, Bookman, Caledonia, Caslon, Century Schoolbook, Cheltenham, Garamond, Goudy Old Style, Korinna, Melior, Palatino, Souvenir, Tiffany, and Times Roman.

The lines are used to get perfect alignment across with all copy that has been set. You will note that there are no vertical lines on the Universal Layout Sheet. That's because you create each sheet or spread to serve your own purpose. You draw in the verticals.

Let's Get Down to Specifics

Most publications have a letters section, which gets a lot of reader attention. Engineers write about engineers and their problems, nurses write about nursing problems, and pollution engineers write about their concerns. The quickest way to point out the specifics of an arbitrary column is here. In figure 40.2, the arbitrary column has been used as a 3-pica vertical in which to place the department head. If you placed this on a page with a standard two- or three-column arrangement, it would have to lie outside the live area. This is awkward and crowds the page margin. Instead, I planned the page around this arbitrary 3 picas (4 with the alley). I subtracted 4 picas from the live area of 41 to get 37 picas. Allowing 1 pica for another alley, I now have two columns of 18 picas each. Therefore, 18-1-18-1-3 is the design combination that will fit the live area. I draw in those vertical lines and now have a layout sheet to suit a specific area and purpose.

How about New Products

"New products" is material that traditionally was used as filler around ads. The new-products pictures were cropped to column width, the ad was put in, and then new-products copy plus pictures were arranged around it.

Now I'll show you three variables of the new-products page using the arbitrary column. In figure 40.3 I use a combination of 9-1-15-1-15, totaling 41 picas. Each new-product picture can be 9 by 10 picas. You can change from a vertical design to a horizontal design with no problem whatsoever. In the example shown, a few lines of copy introduces the new-products area, followed by four pictures and commentary handled horizontally. If you use ads in this section you can see how this will also accommodate a half-page horizontal ad or a pair of quarter-page ads. Once you have determined the column widths you want, draw them in on the Universal Layout Sheet. Do not use standard layout sheets—you'll only get confused because of the many vertical lines.

Figure 40.4 shows another variation of the new-products page. Here the pictures are larger, and the copy is set in one column. The design is back to vertical. The pattern is 11-1-17-1-11, totaling 41 pi-

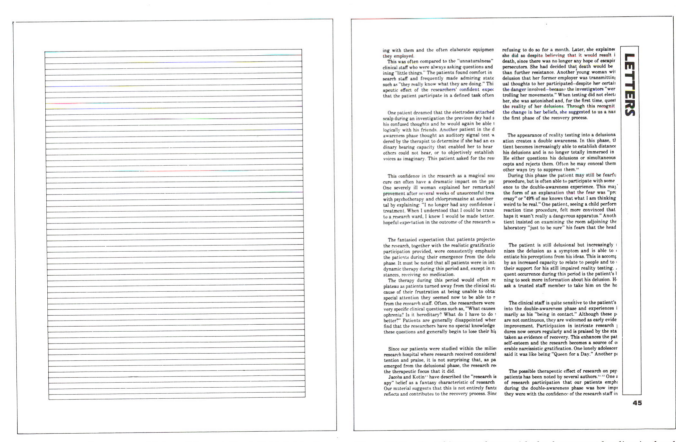

Figure 40.1.—The one-page Universal Layout Sheet divided into increments for layout, paste-up, and keyline. You draw in the verticals.

Figure 40.2.—An arbitrary column with the department heading is placed first. The column widths are determined by dividing the remaining space by two.

Figure 40.3.—How to place new-product pictures using the arbitrary column format.

Figure 40.4.—The arbitrary column in reverse—that is, the pictures are placed first and the arbitrary column fills the space left over. This is useful for new-product areas in the back of a publication.

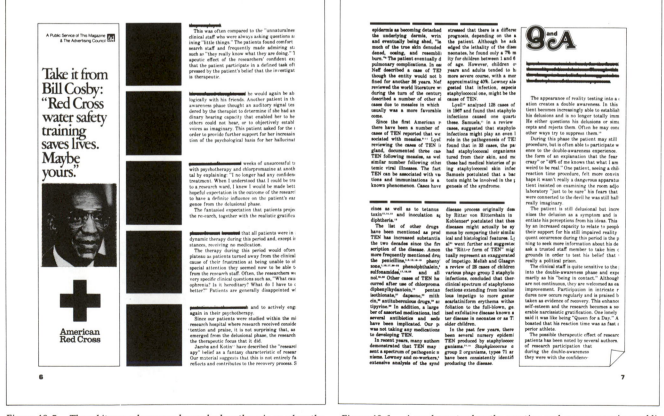

Figure 40.5.—The arbitrary column can be used when there is an ad on the page. This example shows three different column widths.

Figure 40.6.—A good way to place the question-and-answer area in a publication.

cas. Eight pictures fit on the page instead of four, as shown in the previous figure. Some new products need more copy than others. You now have a choice of designs, one showing more copy than picture, the other showing more picture than copy. Can you mix them within an issue? You might have some flack from the advertisers as to picture sizes reflecting importance, so my suggestion is that you use one or the other but not both within one issue.

Figure 40.5 shows a three-column ad in its usual position, the outside column. Now, instead of using two more columns set on 13 picas to fill in the live area of this page, divide the remaining 27 picas into 9-1-17. Now the design reads 13-1-9-1-13, totaling 41 picas.

How about "Bits and Pieces"?

Those small news items that have no place else to go are often called bits and pieces. Set them on 17 picas, flush left, ragged right, and place them to the outside edge. Then have short news items in two 11-pica columns. Figure 40.6 shows an 11-1-11-1-17 arrangement where the 17-pica column is used for a question-and-answer section. Questions and answers are basically the same as bits and pieces since the paragraphs are short.

Note one other thing before we leave this figure. The wide column is a vertical, and the narrow columns become horizontal stories. We have now combined two changes of direction on the page as well as a new design. The "tip" at the bottom of the question-and-answer column can be added to draw attention.

How about Mug Shots?

The mug-shot area has been ignored by most designers with the attitude that we're stuck with them, so let's just ignore them. But you can use the arbitrary column to design this problem with finesse.

Figure 40.7 shows mug shots that measure 6 by 9 picas. This size is neither too big nor too small. If we have only a few mug shots on a page, for example, five, we would arrange them on the outside edge of the page. Start with 6 picas and add 1 for the alley to make 7. Subtract 7 from 41 to get 34. Add 1 pica for an alley. We now have 32 picas. If we divide 32 by 2, we have two 16-pica columns. So, column widths for five mug shots would be 6-1-16-1-16. But mug shots seldom come in such small groups. More often there will be ten. Using 6-1-6 picas to accommodate two columns of mug shots, we now have 13 picas, or the equivalent of one column in the standard three-column format. But instead of putting the photos all on the outside, we move that "13" to the middle and put a 13-pica column of type on each side. We now have 41 picas, but the mug shots are gathered in the middle.

Figure 40.8 uses the same concept as figure 40.7, except the arrangement is 6-1-13-1-6-1-13. We

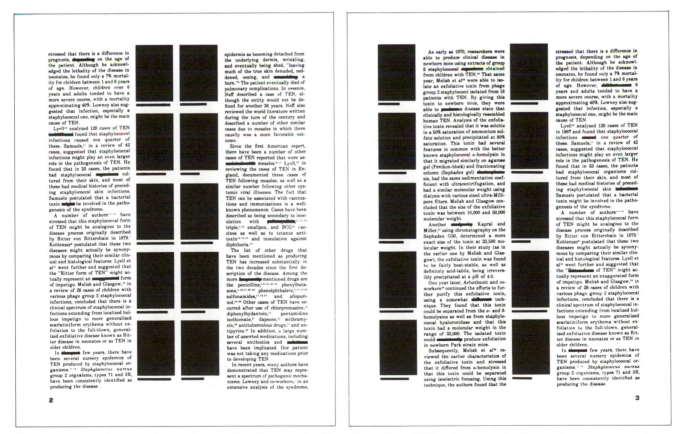

Figure 40.7.—Mug shots are no longer a layout problem if you use the arbitrary column.

Figure 40.8.—Still another way to handle mug shots or new products.

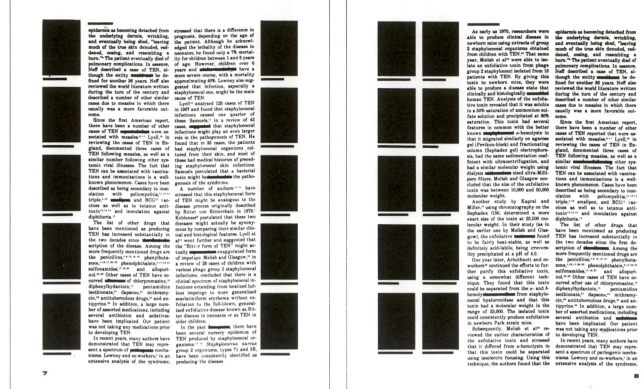

Figure 40.9.—*Splitting the mug shots can be done with an arbitrary column format.*

Figure 40.10.—*Mug shots again, but this time arranged all on one side.*

Figure 40.11.—*The arbitrary column works well in a newsletter.*

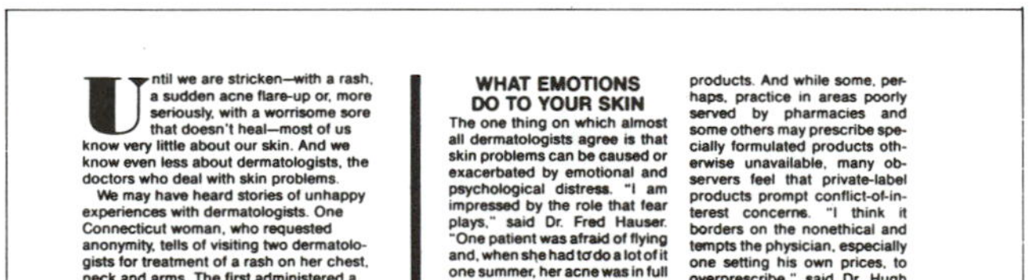

Figure 40.12.—*The arbitrary column used in a newsstand publication.*

Figure 40.13.—The arbitrary column may be used for captions and a small picture.

Figure 40.14.—Here the arbitrary column is used for a listing.

Figure 40.15.—Note how this page uses the arbitrary column as a design foil. It appears to the left, to the right, and in the middle.

Figure 40.16.—Another use of the arbitrary column as a sidebar area.

now have alternating columns of copy and mug shots.

Figure 40.9 uses a 6-1-13-1-13-1-6 format, but now the mug shots are on the outside and the copy is on the inside. Figure 40.10 shows still another variable, 6-1-6-1-13-1-13, totaling 41 again, but in a different arrangement.

Can mug shot formats be mixed in a publication? Of course, since the only thing changing is the arrangement. How much more interesting this can be than the postage stamp album arrangement.

Figure 40.11 shows a page from *Focus*, a school newsletter that uses the arbitrary format for mug shots on the outside edge. Copy is set on 18 picas, flush left, ragged right, so there is some freedom within the design area.

Figure 40.12 is a page from *Mc-Call's* magazine which uses one column set on 17 picas, flush left, ragged right, and two columns set on 11 picas, justified. This incorporates two column widths and typesetting styles. Does it look good? Sure it does. It may take some getting used to if you have been a purist and think that there are only two column arrangements—two-column and three-column—and only five ways of handling body copy.

Figure 40.13 shows the arbitrary column used for captions. The column arrangement is 13-1-6-1-20, totaling 41 picas. This is good page design and shows a great use of the arbitrary column to solve a specific design problem.

The page shown in figure 40.14, also from *McCall's*, uses a medium-medium-narrow column arrangement to give design impact to the page. It also uses justified copy as a foil for flush left, ragged right copy.

Figures 40.15 and 40.16 show pages from *50 Plus*, examples of how to use the arbitrary in still different ways. Figure 40.15 shows an arbitrary 9 picas wide in the top third of the page, a 9-pica one in the next layer, and a 10-pica one in the bottom section. Copy is split into two equal parts in each section. This is good thinking and good design. In figure 40.16 we have $8\frac{1}{2}$-1-16-1-16, which is just over 41 picas. Notice the type style of the arbitrary—boldface, sans-serif, set flush left, ragged right as opposed to Roman, justified, in the other columns. This is a fine design and a good choice of faces.

The possibilities of the arbitrary column have barely been tapped.

CHAPTER FORTY-ONE

Table of Contents Design

If you were asked, "What is a table of contents?" you would most likely say it is a list showing what is where. Contents pages are basic. They offer good opportunities for functional design. Yet newsstand magazines insist on making them selling tools. I have watched both my wife and daughter look at magazines for years. Neither one gives a hoot for the table of contents. They do, however, look at every page in the magazine, and most often from the back forward.

The original intention of a contents page was to show the story headline, author, and page location. But then designers decided that it would be nice to have a "teaser" following the headline to help it out. This was followed by a synopsis—often several sentences. *Psychology Today* used this in the 1970s.

Then, in the late 1970s, the table of contents was "discovered" as a place for special design attention. We began to see not only the basic "what is where," but also abstracts and pictures. Pictures in the table of contents? But, of course. We had cover-story pictures. We had pictures from the first page of the story. We had parts of pictures from the story. We had subliminal implantation of picture, phrase,

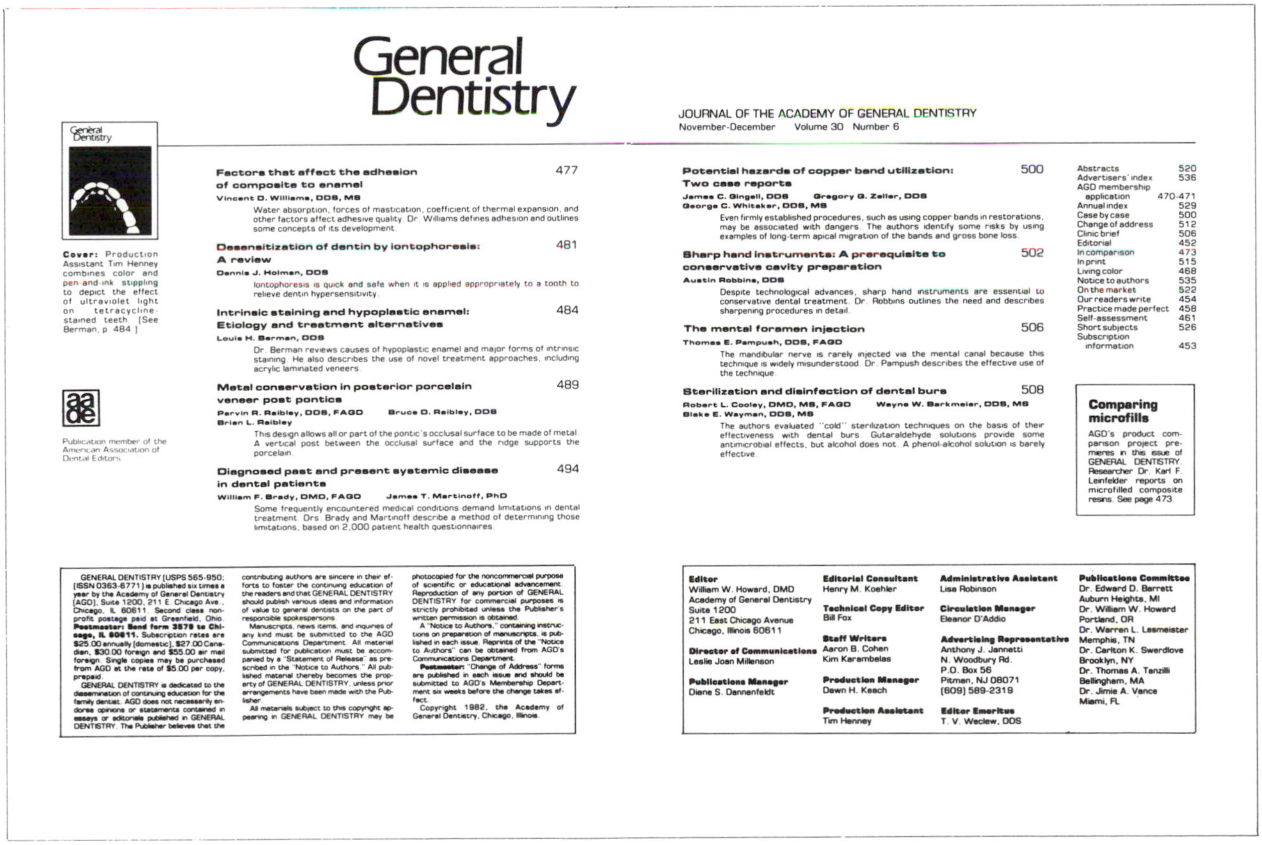

General Dentistry

JOURNAL OF THE ACADEMY OF GENERAL DENTISTRY
November-December Volume 30 Number 6

Cover: Production Assistant Tim Henney combines color and pen-and-ink stippling to depict the effect of ultraviolet light on tetracycline-stained teeth. (See Berman, p. 484.)

Factors that affect the adhesion of composite to enamel 477
Vincent D. Williams, DDS, MS
Water absorption, forces of mastication, coefficient of thermal expansion, and other factors affect adhesive quality. Dr. Williams defines adhesion and outlines some concepts of its development.

Desensitization of dentin by iontophoresis: A review 481
Dennis J. Holman, DDS
Iontophoresis is quick and safe when it is applied appropriately to a tooth to relieve dentin hypersensitivity.

Intrinsic staining and hypoplastic enamel: Etiology and treatment alternatives 484
Louis H. Berman, DDS
Dr. Berman reviews causes of hypoplastic enamel and major forms of intrinsic staining. He also describes the use of novel treatment approaches, including acrylic laminated veneers.

Metal conservation in posterior porcelain veneer post pontics 489
Parvin R. Raibley, DDS, FAGD **Bruce D. Raibley, DDS** **Brian L. Raibley**
This design allows all or part of the pontic's occlusal surface to be made of metal. A vertical post between the occlusal surface and the ridge supports the porcelain.

Diagnosed past and present systemic disease in dental patients 494
William F. Brady, DMD, FAGD **James T. Martinoff, PhD**
Some frequently encountered medical conditions demand limitations in dental treatment. Drs. Brady and Martinoff describe a method of determining those limitations, based on 2,000 patient health questionnaires.

Potential hazards of copper band utilization: Two case reports 500
James C. Gingell, DDS **Gregory G. Zeller, DDS** **George C. Whitaker, DDS, MS**
Even firmly established procedures, such as using copper bands in restorations, may be associated with dangers. The authors identify some risks by using examples of long-term apical migration of the bands and gross bone loss.

Sharp hand instruments: A prerequisite to conservative cavity preparation 502
Austin Robbins, DDS
Despite technological advances, sharp hand instruments are essential to conservative dental treatment. Dr. Robbins outlines the need and describes sharpening procedures in detail.

The mental foramen injection 506
Thomas E. Pampush, DDS, FAGD
The mandibular nerve is rarely injected via the mental canal because this technique is widely misunderstood. Dr. Pampush describes the effective use of the technique.

Sterilization and disinfection of dental burs 508
Robert L. Cooley, DMD, MS, FAGD **Wayne W. Barkmeier, DDS, MS** **Blake E. Wayman, DDS, MS**
The authors evaluated "cold" sterilization techniques on the basis of their effectiveness with dental burs. Gutaraldehyde solutions provide some antimicrobial effects, but alcohol does not. A phenol-alcohol solution is barely effective.

Abstracts	520
Advertisers' index	536
AGD membership application	470-471
Annual index	529
Case by case	500
Change of address	512
Clinic brief	506
Editorial	452
In comparison	473
In print	515
Living color	468
Notice to authors	535
On the market	522
Our readers write	454
Practice made perfect	458
Self-assessment	461
Short subjects	526
Subscription information	453

Comparing microfills
AGD's product comparison project premieres in this issue of GENERAL DENTISTRY. Researcher Dr. Karl F. Leinfelder reports on microfilled composite resins. See page 473.

Publication member of the American Association of Dental Editors

GENERAL DENTISTRY (USPS 565-950; (ISSN 0363-6771) is published six times a year by the Academy of General Dentistry (AGD), Suite 1200, 211 E. Chicago Ave., Chicago, IL 60611. Second class non-profit postage paid at Greenfield, Ohio. **Postmaster: Send form 3579 to Chicago, IL 60611.** Subscription rates are $25.00 annually (domestic), $27.00 Canadian, $30.00 foreign and $55.00 air mail foreign. Single copies may be purchased from AGD at the rate of $5.00 per copy, prepaid.

GENERAL DENTISTRY is dedicated to the dissemination of continuing education for the family dentist. AGD does not necessarily endorse opinions or statements contained in essays or editorials published in GENERAL DENTISTRY. The Publisher believes that the contributing authors are sincere in their efforts to foster the continuing education of the readers and that GENERAL DENTISTRY should publish various ideas and information of value to general dentists on the part of responsible spokespersons.

Manuscripts, news items, and inquiries of any kind must be submitted to the AGD Communications Department. All material submitted for publication must be accompanied by a "Statement of Release" as prescribed in the "Notice to Authors." All published material thereby becomes the property of GENERAL DENTISTRY, unless prior arrangements have been made with the Publisher.

All materials subject to this copyright appearing in GENERAL DENTISTRY may be photocopied for the noncommercial purpose of scientific or educational advancement. Reproduction of any portion of GENERAL DENTISTRY for commercial purposes is strictly prohibited unless the Publisher's written permission is obtained.

A "Notice to Authors," containing instructions on preparation of manuscripts, is published in each issue. Reprints of the "Notice to Authors" can be obtained from AGD's Communications Department.

Postmaster: "Change of Address" forms are published in each issue and should be submitted to AGD's Membership Department six weeks before the change takes effect.

Copyright 1982, the Academy of General Dentistry, Chicago, Illinois.

Editor
William W. Howard, DMD
Academy of General Dentistry
Suite 1200
211 East Chicago Avenue
Chicago, Illinois 60611

Director of Communications
Leslie Joan Millenson

Publications Manager
Diane S. Dannenfeldt

Editorial Consultant
Henry M. Koehler

Technical Copy Editor
Bill Fox

Staff Writers
Aaron B. Cohen
Kim Karambelas

Production Manager
Dawn H. Keach

Production Assistant
Tim Henney

Administrative Assistant
Lisa Robinson

Circulation Manager
Eleanor D'Addio

Advertising Representative
Anthony J. Jannetti
N. Woodbury Rd.
P.O. Box 56
Pitman, NJ 08071
(609) 589-2319

Editor Emeritus
T. V. Weclew, DDS

Publications Committee
Dr. Edward D. Barrett
Auburn Heights, MI
Dr. William W. Howard
Portland, OR
Dr. Warren L. Lesmeister
Memphis, TN
Dr. Carlton K. Swerdlove
Brooklyn, NY
Dr. Thomas A. Tanzilli
Bellingham, MA
Dr. Jimie A. Vance
Miami, FL

Figure 41.1.—A double-page table of contents.

and page number. We suddenly had more to put into the table of contents than the art director had time for. It became the showplace for everything the magazine had to offer. The airline magazines, especially, made heavy use of this. The concept that if one is good, two had to be better prevailed. We had two- and three-page tables of contents. And, as suddenly as it appeared, it disappeared—in the January issues of 1981, to be exact. Everyone seemed to have had the same idea. It had gone too far.

Let's look at what is now popular in tables of contents. First, the different types of magazines basically can be grouped into newsstand and controlled circulation or business publications. Figure 41.1 shows a table of contents from *General Dentistry*. It consists of two pages. Why two pages? Look at what is included in this magazine: nine feature stories; eighteen special departments; a cover story and picture; the indices; the masthead; and the logo. Would you really like

to see all that on one page? The next question has to be, Why so much? Dentists are busy people. When they have time to read their journals, they want to read what they are most interested in and to go to it without struggling through page after page of advertising. In other words, they don't want to turn pages to search for things. They want the table of contents to serve a valuable function: to save time. This is one thing most designers never even think about. They get lost in the overall look of the result.

Figure 41.2 is from *Consulting Engineer* magazine. This table of contents epitomizes "clean, neat, and functional." It has four features, two "briefs," and twelve special departments and is a good example of how to save the reader time and yet give the reader everything needed in a well-designed manner. The second color often changes but remains functional.

Figure 41.3, from *Pollution Engineering*, also combines design with

function. There are eighteen places for the reader to go, some features, some special areas. If you look at this table of contents you may also notice that the magazine is only a few pages more than seventy-four, including the four covers. This is not a big magazine, but the table of contents certainly makes the content *seem* large. The symbols remain constant with each issue. They can be one color, two color, or four color depending on the signature.

The *Folio* magazine table of contents in figure 41.4 illustrates the use of pictures in an area not usually known for illustrations. The thing I find weak in this design is that the pictures have only a page number, no title. This means one of two things—you can look over the table of contents to see if there is a possible connection between the page number and a subject, or you can turn to the page to see what the picture is about. In this case, design fails to follow function.

Figure 41.5 is from *House & Gar-*

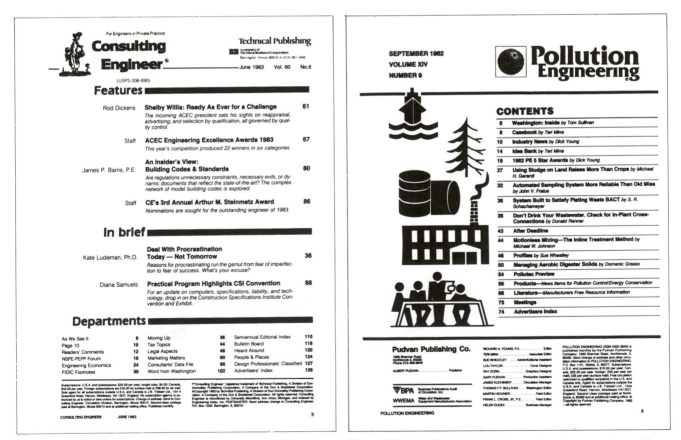

Figure 41.2.—A well-designed table of contents is clean, neat, and functional.

Figure 41.3.—An illustrated table of contents, or how to make a small area look bigger.

Figure 41.4.—An illustrated table of contents.

Figure 41.5.—A plain but effective table of contents.

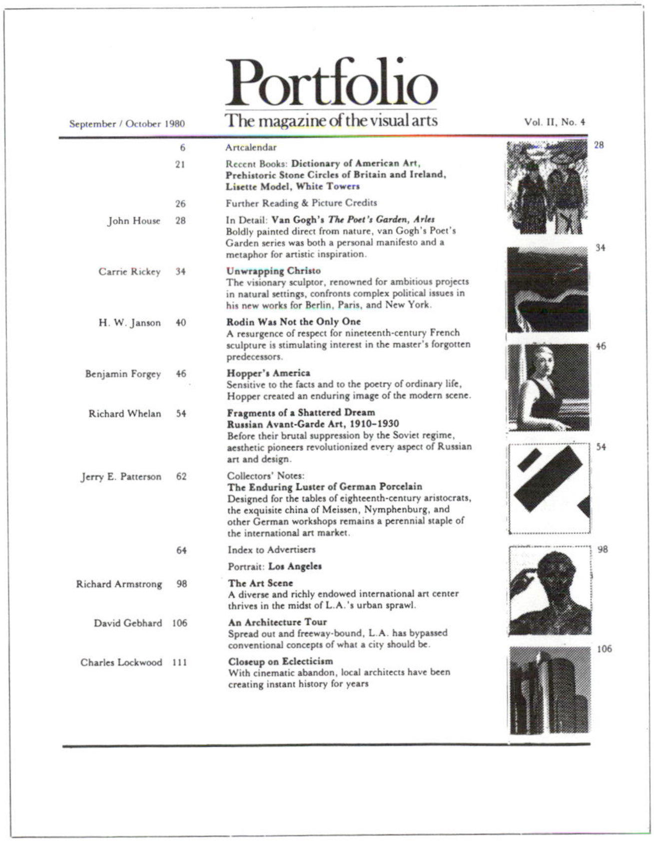

Figure 41.6.—Author first, title next, followed by pictures and a number. Notice the extra eye movements needed to go from the page number to the picture and back again.

Figure 41.7.—Pictures again, but they are there simply to decorate. The design is obvious and good.

Figure 41.8.—A departmentalized table of contents. The page appears cluttered because the contents area is competing with the outside ad.

Figure 41.9.—A table of contents that promises a lot for your money.

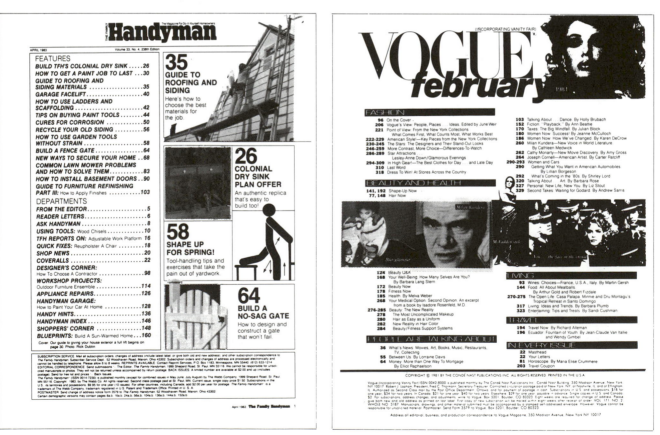

Figure 41.10.—Here's an example of a magazine telling you, up front, that it is full of information.

Figure 41.11.—"New Wave" design also affected tables of contents.

den. There is nothing fancy about this table of contents. Note that there is no real type contrast between the parts. Headlines, teaser, author, and page number are all the same size and face. The only change is all caps and italic. The special departments are one size smaller, but the type size and face stay the same. This example fits the rest of the magazine in style and temperament.

Next are two more examples of the good, crisp, "pure" table of contents. In figure 41.6 from *Portfolio* magazine, note that the sequence has changed. That is, the author's name comes before instead of after the title of the story. The story headline is followed by a short abstract. This faces a picture that, again, has nothing going for it but a page number. You can tie in the page number with the page numbers following the headline-synopsis, but why?

Figure 41.7 from *Texas Homes* is a beauty. It's clean, neat, and functional. White space has been used well; pictures are there, but merely to decorate.

Newsstand magazines have a different viewpoint about tables of contents. Figure 41.8 is from *Better Homes & Gardens*. This magazine has been around for many years. It has a good table of contents for its audience. It is "departmental-ized," meaning the magazine has specific areas of interest. There are stories or articles under each department. Pictures are included, but they make design sense, as the picture has a headline and a caption-type story. No guesswork here.

Figure 41.9 is from *Ladies Home Journal*, another old-timer. Magazines such as this know their audience and know what they want. I would guess that the average woman doesn't have a lot of money to spend on magazines. It is therefore prudent buying to get as much as she can for the money she spends. A look at the cover, as well as the table of contents, indicates you get a lot for the price—although what a good definition of "a lot" is I can't really say. But the visuals *promise* a lot.

And talk about a lot for your money, look at figure 41.10 from *Handyman* magazine. Now there's "a lot"! Fourteen features! Sixteen special departments! And four special articles! Considering all the items involved with this table of contents, the design is very good. I don't like the very small type at the bottom of the page set on 42 picas, but then I can't have everything.

Figure 41.11 from *Vogue* shows a classic example of a new design called "New Wave" that hit in the late 1970s and early 1980s. This is a combination of everything at once, a design shrieking for attention no matter what the device used. If you look closely at this page, for example, you see the department headings in thin-line type, reversed out of a solid black background. You see a panel of pictures across the middle consisting of four black-and-white shots, all blended into one montage. The heads are in

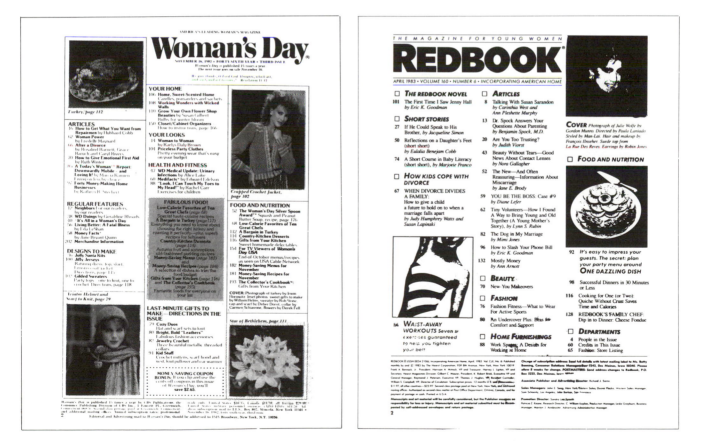

Figure 41.12.—Another example of offering a lot in a small space.

Figure 41.13.—Still another table of contents that offers many subjects.

small sans-serif type, making reading difficult. The titles are in small type and one wide measure.

For contents pages that make the buyer feel he or she is getting a lot of value for the price, look at figures 41.12 and 41.13. These are from newsstand magazines. Just one look and you know that there has to be something in each issue to please you. Could we do without this table of contents? I doubt it. There's too much content. How can you tell what is where without a table of contents? This illustrates that there are certain kinds of magazines that need certain kinds of tables of contents. The business press wouldn't allow this for a moment.

One other thing before we leave this subject. Look at figures 41.14 and 41.15, both from *50 Plus* magazine. Figure 41.14 is "before" and 41.15 is "after" a design change. Examine them and see what has happened. First of all, this is a magazine for older people. That's why the typeface is bold and large. Know your audience. But even more, there is a different philosophy expressed in each. Figure 41.14 was designed by an outside designer. Figure 41.15 was designed by the art director of the magazine. Notice how many special departments "lost their heads." And we now have ten stories instead of fourteen. Notice the change from caps and lower case to all-cap heads. This is a good example of knowing your audience and designing for them, something the outside designer does not always know.

50plus VOL. 21 NO. 11 NOVEMBER 1981

How to plan for the quality years. How to enjoy them.

Cover photo: Mark Wallach. **Other credits: p. 8** CIBA Pharmaceutical, **10** Wide World, **37** Wide World (3), **61** George Wolfe, **62** David Kendrick, **84-85** Joseph Farris, W. A. Vanselow

50 Plus (ISSN 0163-2027) © 1981 by Retirement Living Publishing Co. Inc., a member of the Magazine Division of Whitney Communications Corp., 850 Third Ave., New York, NY 10022. All rights reserved. Published monthly. Indexed in Readers' Guide to Periodical Literature. Controlled circulation postage paid at New York, NY and additional mailing offices. Postmaster please send Form 3579 to 99 Garden St., Marion, Ohio 43302

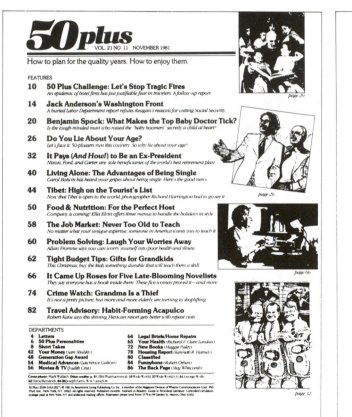

Figure 41.14.—A table of contents for 50 Plus, *a magazine for an older audience, uses large type. Compare this with figures 41.12 and 41.13.*

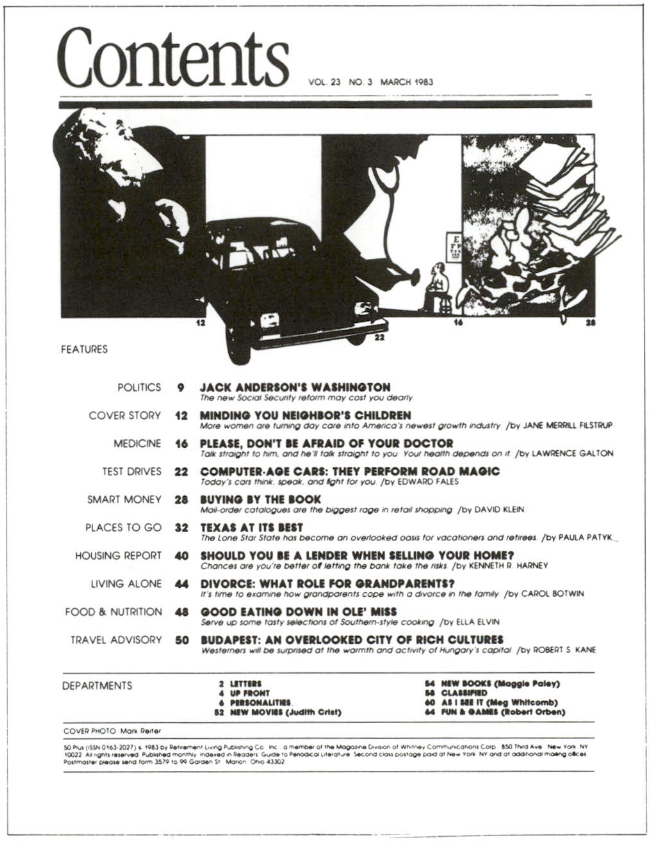

Contents VOL. 23 NO. 3 MARCH 1983

COVER PHOTO Mark Reiter

50 Plus (ISSN 0163-2027) © 1983 by Retirement Living Publishing Co. Inc., a member of the Magazine Division of Whitney Communications Corp., 850 Third Ave., New York, NY 10022. All rights reserved. Published monthly. Indexed in Readers' Guide to Periodical Literature. Second class postage paid at New York, NY and at additional mailing offices. Postmaster please send form 3579 to 99 Garden St., Marion, Ohio 43302

Figure 41.15.—The 50 Plus *table of contents redesigned. Can you pick out the changes?*

CHAPTER FORTY-TWO

Sidebars

The sidebar is a ''little story'' relating to the feature but not long enough to be a story of itself. It falls into a class halfway between a caption or legend and a short story—never more than a full page and more often less than half. It has been ignored as a design area for years.

The usual way to handle a sidebar is to enclose it with a hairline or a 1-point-rule box. The other way is to overprint the story on a tint block of gray or another color available in the signature. Both are permissible; both are static.

Several magazines asked me to do something about their sidebar design problems. They felt that their readers were due more than the simple box or tint block treatment. *Kiwanis* magazine, for example, has feature stories, short stories, and news areas. The sidebar treatment is used half a dozen times per issue as part of their design package.

In the ten examples shown you will see my solutions to the problem. Each sets off the sidebar as special. Figure 42.1, for example, uses a design principle called the ''bump-out.'' Here, the headline area bumps out from the rest of the copy; in this case it is above the block of body copy. The design

Two devices used to treat leg injuries are the isokinetic dynamometer (left), which measures a person's leg strength and weakness, and the arthroscope (below), a telescope-like instrument that allows a surgeon to examine and operate on a knee without surgically opening the joint.

University of Chicago photos

as thousands of recreational runners, himself included.

"Alberto tried to kill the treadmill," says Costill, discussing the experiment with the marathon champion. "Not many runners can tolerate running uphill at that speed."

What the experiment documented was an incredibly high maximum oxygen uptake, which when measured with a scuba-like breathing apparatus is a basic indicator of a person's ability to process oxygen and generate energy.

The average jogger in fairly good shape might have a maximum oxygen uptake of fifty milliliters of oxygen per kilogram of body weight per minute. Salazar's oxygen uptake was seventy-six.

"What this means is that Alberto can generate more energy than almost anyone else. It's like having a supercharged engine inside a Volkswagen body," says Costill. "He's also extremely efficient."

Besides treadmill testing, Costill took a tiny tissue sample from Salazar's calf muscle and measured the ratio of slow-twitch and fast-twitch muscle fibers. Everyone has both types, usually in a fifty-fifty ratio.

The former type has the capacity of contracting over and over without becoming fatigued. The latter contracts faster and more powerfully but tires more quickly. Not surprisingly, Salazar had 92 percent slow-twitch fibers.

Says Costill: "All good distance runners are on the high end of the slow-twitch spectrum. Sprinters, on the other hand, have a higher per-

Kiwanians tackle injury prevention

Sports medicine has made impressive advances in recent years, but most experts would agree: Prevention is still the best medicine.

The Kiwanis Club of Greenhills-Forest Park, Ohio, has put that philosophy to work in a recent Share Good Health project.

"We wanted to bring the number of high school sports injuries down," explains Jim Treadway, club president. "The best way to do that seemed to be to bring the experts together."

The club sponsored three workshops—one for athletes, another for parents and trainers, and a third for coaches. The club invested $1,000 to bring in professionals from the Cincinnati Sports Medicine and Orthopaedic Clinic to cover topics like nutrition for athletes, the prevention of injuries, and the care of the injured athlete.

Hundreds of area high school athletes attended the first workshop, which was directed at them. "We would have liked even more students to have been there," says Jim. "We realize now that the first workshop should have been directed to the coaches. That way they could go back and encourage the students to attend the second. We'll know better next year."

Next, coaches from twenty-four area schools attended their workshop and, Jim says, they were unanimous in their praise of the project: "A new state law requires that coaches pass a CPR, or cardiopulmonary resuscitation, class, so we included that in the workshop. That added to its success."

At their workshop, parents learned how the home environment could be supportive of the athlete's goals, Jim says. Parents were shown which foods are best for the young athlete, how minor injuries can be treated, and how to be sure their son or daughter is not letting athletics interfere with schoolwork.

Jim says he is especially pleased with the large turnout of coaches because "what they learn isn't just helping them. They're putting it to use with the students they're coaching."

A flea market and lobster and grapefruit sale raised the money needed to sponsor the project. The forty-five club members are enthusiastic about the workshops. Says Jim: "We're working to improve the health of our young people. It has to be worthwhile."

AUGUST 1982/KIWANIS MAGAZINE/17

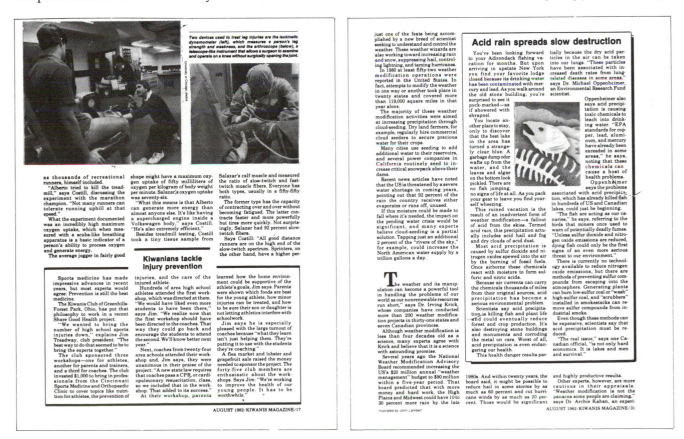

Figure 42.1.—One of a series of sidebar designs with the headline ''bumping out.''

just one of the feats being accomplished by a new breed of scientist seeking to understand and control the weather. These weather wizards are also working toward increasing rain and snow, suppressing hail, controlling lightning, and taming hurricanes.

In 1980 at least fifty-two weather modification operations were reported in the United States. In fact, attempts to modify the weather in one way or another took place in twenty states and covered more than 119,000 square miles in that year alone.

The majority of these weather modification activities were aimed at increasing precipitation through cloud-seeding. Dry land farmers, for example, regularly hire commercial cloud seeders to secure precious water for their crops.

Many cities use seeding to add additional water to their reservoirs, and several power companies in California routinely seed to increase critical snowpack above their dams.

Recent news articles have noted that the US is threatened by a severe water shortage in coming years, pointing out that 92 percent of the rain the country receives either evaporates or runs off, unused.

If this moisture could be made to fall where it's needed, the impact on the pending water crisis would be significant, and many experts believe cloud-seeding is a partial solution. Tapping just an additional 2 percent of the "rivers of the sky," for example, could increase the North American water supply by a trillion gallons a day.

The weather and its manipulation can become a powerful tool in handling the problems of our world as our nonrenewable resources run short," says Dr. Irving Krick, whose companies have conducted more than 200 weather modification projects in thirty-one states and seven Canadian provinces.

Although weather modification is less than four decades old as a science, many experts agree with Krick and believe that it is a science with astounding promise.

Several years ago the National Weather Modification Advisory Board recommended increasing the US's $20 million annual "weather management" budget to $90 million within a five-year period. That board predicted that with more money and hard work, the High Plains and Midwest could have 10 to 30 percent more rain by the late 1980s. And within twenty years, the board said, it might be possible to reduce hail in some storms by as much as 60 percent and cut hurricane winds by as much as 20 percent. Those would be significant and highly productive results.

Other experts, however, are more cautious in their appraisals. "Weather modification is not the panacea some people are claiming," says Dr. Archie Kahan, an experi-

Acid rain spreads slow destruction

You've been looking forward to your Adirondack fishing vacation for months. But upon arriving in upstate New York you find your favorite lodge closed because its drinking water has been contaminated with mercury and lead. As you walk around the old stone building, you're surprised to see it pock-marked—as if showered with shrapnel.

You locate another place to stay, only to discover that the best lake in the area has turned a strangely clear blue. A garbage dump odor wafts up from the water, and the leaves and algae on the bottom look pickled. There are no fish jumping, no signs of life at all. As you pack your gear to leave you find yourself wheezing.

This ruined vacation is the result of an inadvertent form of weather modification—a fallout of acid from the skies. Termed *acid rain*, this precipitation actually includes acid hail and fog and dry clouds of acid dust.

Most acid precipitation is caused by sulfur dioxide and nitrogen oxides spewed into the air by the burning of fossil fuels. Once airborne these chemicals react with moisture to form sulfuric and nitric acids.

Because air currents can carry the chemicals thousands of miles from their original sources, acid precipitation has become a serious environmental problem.

Scientists say acid precipitation is killing fish and plant life and could eventually reduce forest and crop production. It's also destroying stone buildings and monuments and corroding the metal on cars. Worst of all, acid precipitation is even endangering our health.

This health danger results partially because the dry acid particles in the air can be taken into our lungs. "These particles have been associated with increased death rates from lung-related diseases in some areas," says Dr. Michael Oppenheimer, an Environmental Research Fund scientist.

Oppenheimer also says acid precipitation is causing toxic chemicals to leach into drinking water. "EPA standards for copper, lead, aluminum, and mercury have already been exceeded in some areas," he says, noting that these chemicals can cause a host of health problems.

Oppenheimer says the problems associated with acid precipitation, which has already killed fish in hundreds of US and Canadian lakes, could just be beginning.

"The fish are acting as our canaries," he says, referring to the birds that miners once used to warn of potentially deadly fumes. "Unless sulfur dioxide and nitrogen oxide emissions are reduced, dying fish could only be the first signs of an even more serious threat to our environment."

There is currently no technology available to reduce nitrogen oxide emissions, but there are methods of preventing sulfur compounds from escaping into the atmosphere. Generating plants can burn low-sulfur coal or "wash" high-sulfur coal, and "scrubbers" installed in smokestacks can remove sulfur compounds from industrial smoke.

Even though these methods can be expensive, scientists say that acid precipitation must be reduced.

"The real issue," says one Canadian official, "is not only hard economics. It is lakes and men and survival."

Illustrated by John Lambert

AUGUST 1982/KIWANIS MAGAZINE/31

Figure 42.2.—This sidebar design uses the shadowing technique.

consists of a 4-point tint line above and below the copy and a 1-point line at the sides. The bump-out plus the break in the design call attention to the headline and create interest in the material. They also serve as a counterweight to the pictures on the same page.

Figure 42.2 uses another design application called "shadowing." The sidebar now has 1-point rules at the top and left with 6-point rules at the right and bottom. Note that these are cut 1 pica in from the corners—not at the corners. This sidebar now acts as a visual on an otherwise dull page. The design can be in solid color; it can also be in black with a tint of color in the sidebar area, say 10 percent green. It could also be 10 percent with a solid green design, green and green, or green and black. The picture could be four-color or black and white.

Figure 42.3 uses a 4-point rule at the top and bottom and a 1-point rule on the two sides. Inside is a line drawing with round corners to add interest. Again, the design could be in color, the story overprinted on a 10 percent tint of gray or color, or both could be in color. Remember when using a picture within a tint block to leave 4 points of space around the picture to frame it with white space. Otherwise it will blend into the background.

Figure 42.4 uses another design treatment, the "curled edge." The sidebar should be only one column wide when using this, since the wider the copy gets, the less impact the "curl" has. The curl is no more than an indication that the sidebar has been made separately and pasted into position with the curl sort of an accident. This looks best when printed in a solid color with a 10 percent color background, though it does not look bad when done in black. Remember that the body copy must be set 1 pica in from each side. If you are using a 13-pica column, this means setting the body copy on 11 picas. The curl can be drawn on the hard copy and made to fit. I suggest the last four lines be set on a shorter measure, as shown in the example.

Figure 42.5 uses still another design treatment. The headline is part in and part out of the design area. Neither the headline nor the design can stand without the other. The ribbon effect at the top adds weight to the headline area. The 2-point and 1-point rules finish the enclosure. This looks good when printed in color. In the example shown, the color was cyan, or process blue. The blue-black combination works very well.

Figure 42.6 asks the question, Can a sidebar bleed? and the answer is that it most certainly can. In this case I have used a design that interlocks. The story copy forms an inverted "L" shape. The sidebar fits into it, spoon fashion. The design consists of a 6-point rule and a hairline rule at the top. The picture and remainder of the design are bordered with a 1-point rule. The design bleeds to the left. Even though there is no design printed,

Figure 42.3.—Thick bars at the top and bottom and a round-cornered picture give this page still another design twist.

Figure 42.4.—The "curled edge" design for a sidebar. The background can be a 10 percent tint of gray or a pastel, or the curl can be a solid color.

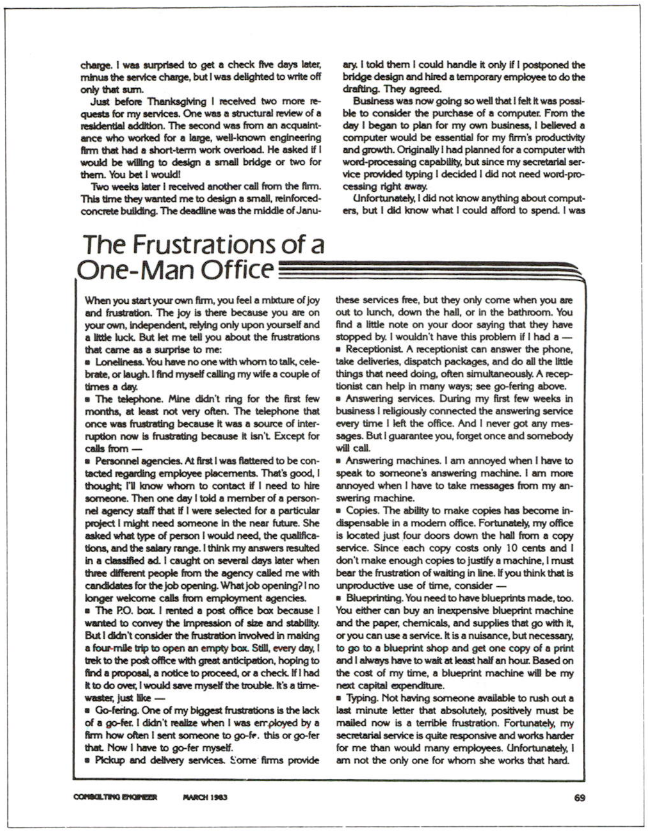

charge. I was surprised to get a check five days later, minus the service charge, but I was delighted to write off only that sum.

Just before Thanksgiving I received two more requests for my services. One was a structural review of a residential addition. The second was from an acquaintance who worked for a large, well-known engineering firm that had a short-term work overload. He asked if I would be willing to design a small bridge or two for them. You bet I would!

Two weeks later I received another call from the firm. This time they wanted me to design a small, reinforced-concrete building. The deadline was the middle of January. I told them I could handle it only if I postponed the bridge design and hired a temporary employee to do the drafting. They agreed.

Business was now going so well that I felt it was possible to consider the purchase of a computer. From the day I began to plan for my own business, I believed a computer would be essential for my firm's productivity and growth. Originally I had planned for a computer with word-processing capability, but since my secretarial service provided typing I decided I did not need word-processing right away.

Unfortunately, I did not know anything about computers, but I did know what I could afford to spend. I was

The Frustrations of a One-Man Office

When you start your own firm, you feel a mixture of joy and frustration. The joy is there because you are on your own, independent, relying only upon yourself and a little luck. But let me tell you about the frustrations that came as a surprise to me:

- Loneliness. You have no one with whom to talk, celebrate, or laugh. I find myself calling my wife a couple of times a day.
- The telephone. Mine didn't ring for the first few months, at least not very often. The telephone that once was frustrating because it was a source of interruption now is frustrating because it isn't. Except for calls from —
- Personnel agencies. At first I was flattered to be contacted regarding employee placements. That's good, I thought; I'll know whom to contact if I need to hire someone. Then one day I told a member of a personnel agency staff that if I were selected for a particular project I might need someone in the near future. She asked what type of person I would need, the qualifications, and the salary range. I think my answers resulted in a classified ad. I caught on several days later when three different people from the agency called me with candidates for the job opening. What job opening? I no longer welcome calls from employment agencies.
- The P.O. box. I rented a post office box because I wanted to convey the impression of size and stability. But I didn't consider the frustration involved in making a four-mile trip to open an empty box. Still, every day, I trek to the post office with great anticipation, hoping to find a proposal, a notice to proceed, or a check. If I had it to do over, I would save myself the trouble. It's a time-waster, just like —
- Go-fering. One of my biggest frustrations is the lack of a go-fer. I didn't realize when I was employed by a firm how often I sent someone to go-fer this or go-fer that. Now I have to go-fer myself.
- Pickup and delivery services. Some firms provide these services free, but they only come when you are out to lunch, down the hall, or in the bathroom. You find a little note on your door saying that they have stopped by. I wouldn't have this problem if I had a —
- Receptionist. A receptionist can answer the phone, take deliveries, dispatch packages, and do all the little things that need doing, often simultaneously. A receptionist can help in many ways; see go-fering above.
- Answering services. During my first few weeks in business I religiously connected the answering service every time I left the office. And I never got any messages. But I guarantee you, forget once and somebody will call.
- Answering machines. I am annoyed when I have to speak to someone's answering machine. I am more annoyed when I have to take messages from my answering machine.
- Copies. The ability to make copies has become indispensable in a modern office. Fortunately, my office is located just four doors down the hall from a copy service. Since each copy costs only 10 cents and I don't make enough copies to justify a machine, I must bear the frustration of waiting in line. If you think that is unproductive use of time, consider —
- Blueprinting. You need to have blueprints made, too. You either can buy an inexpensive blueprint machine and the paper, chemicals, and supplies that go with it, or you can use a service. It is a nuisance, but necessary, to go to a blueprint shop and get one copy of a print and I always have to wait at least half an hour. Based on the cost of my time, a blueprint machine will be my next capital expenditure.
- Typing. Not having someone available to rush out a last minute letter that absolutely, positively must be mailed now is a terrible frustration. Fortunately, my secretarial service is quite responsive and works harder for me than would many employees. Unfortunately, I am not the only one for whom she works that hard.

CONSULTING ENGINEER MARCH 1983 69

Figure 42.5.—Still another sidebar design.

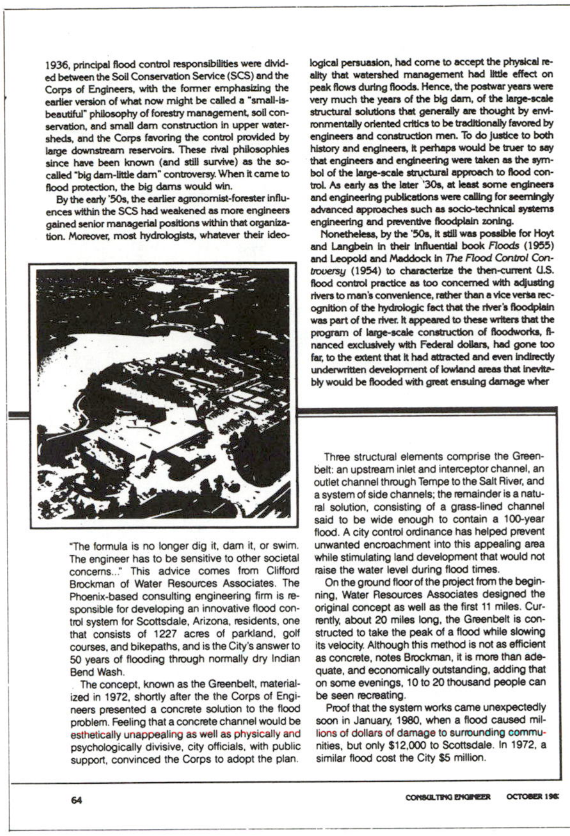

1936, principal flood control responsibilities were divided between the Soil Conservation Service (SCS) and the Corps of Engineers, with the former emphasizing the earlier version of what now might be called a "small-is-beautiful" philosophy of forestry management, soil conservation, and small dam construction in upper watersheds, and the Corps favoring the control provided by large downstream reservoirs. These rival philosophies since have been known (and still survive) as the so-called "big dam-little dam" controversy. When it came to flood protection, the big dams would win.

By the early '50s, the earlier agronomist-forester influences within the SCS had weakened as more engineers gained senior managerial positions within that organization. Moreover, most hydrologists, whatever their ideological persuasion, had come to accept the physical reality that watershed management had little effect on peak flows during floods. Hence, the postwar years were very much the years of the big dam, of the large-scale structural solutions that generally are thought by environmentally oriented critics to be traditionally favored by engineers and construction men. To do justice to both history and engineers, it perhaps would be truer to say that engineers and engineering were taken as the symbol of the large-scale structural approach to flood control. As early as the later '30s, at least some engineers and engineering publications were calling for seemingly advanced approaches such as socio-technical systems engineering and preventive floodplain zoning.

Nonetheless, by the '50s, it still was possible for Hoyt and Langbein in their influential book *Floods* (1955) and Leopold and Maddock in *The Flood Control Controversy* (1954) to characterize the then-current U.S. flood control practice as too concerned with adjusting rivers to man's convenience, rather than a vice versa recognition of the hydrologic fact that the river's floodplain was part of the river. It appeared to these writers that the program of large-scale construction of floodworks, financed exclusively with Federal dollars, had gone too far, to the extent that it had attracted and even indirectly underwritten development of lowland areas that inevitably would be flooded with great ensuing damage wher

"The formula is no longer dig it, dam it, or swim. The engineer has to be sensitive to other societal concerns..." This advice comes from Clifford Brockman of Water Resources Associates. The Phoenix-based consulting engineering firm is responsible for developing an innovative flood control system for Scottsdale, Arizona, residents, one that consists of 1227 acres of parkland, golf courses, and bikepaths, and is the City's answer to 50 years of flooding through normally dry Indian Bend Wash.

The concept, known as the Greenbelt, materialized in 1972, shortly after the the Corps of Engineers presented a concrete solution to the flood problem. Feeling that a concrete channel would be esthetically unappealing as well as physically and psychologically divisive, city officials, with public support, convinced the Corps to adopt the plan.

Three structural elements comprise the Greenbelt: an upstream inlet and interceptor channel, an outlet channel through Tempe to the Salt River, and a system of side channels; the remainder is a natural solution, consisting of a grass-lined channel said to be wide enough to contain a 100-year flood. A city control ordinance has helped prevent unwanted encroachment into this appealing area while stimulating land development that would not raise the water level during flood times.

On the ground floor of the project from the beginning, Water Resources Associates designed the original concept as well as the first 11 miles. Currently, about 20 miles long, the Greenbelt is constructed to take the peak of a flood while slowing its velocity. Although this method is not as efficient as concrete, notes Brockman, it is more than adequate, and economically outstanding, adding that on some evenings, 10 to 20 thousand people can be seen recreating.

Proof that the system works came unexpectedly soon in January, 1980, when a flood caused millions of dollars of damage to surrounding communities, but only $12,000 to Scottsdale. In 1972, a similar flood cost the City $5 million.

64 CONSULTING ENGINEER OCTOBER 198[illegible]

Figure 42.6.—A sidebar design that bleeds.

KIWANIS SCENE

Task force studies service role

A blue-ribbon Task Force on Voluntarism that will analyze the various areas in which Kiwanis clubs serve their communities has been named by International President E. B. "Mac" McKitrick.

"Today, when voluntarism is so vital, it is essential that we understand our proper service roles," says President Mac. "This task force will help Kiwanis maintain and seek out effective avenues of community service."

The task force, which is comprised of International Board members, is charged not only with evaluating the extent of Kiwanis clubs' service work but also with proposing new directions in voluntarism.

In addition, the Task Force on Voluntarism plans to cooperate with US President Ronald Reagan's Task Force on Private Sector Initiatives, which is encouraging greater involvement by private citizens and organizations in solving public problems, particularly at the community level.

President Mac named International Trustee Raymond B. Allen as chairman of the Kiwanis task force. Other International leaders serving as members are Vice-President Raymond W. Lansford, Treasurer Aubrey E. Irby, and Trustees Mark Arthur Jr. and Albert L. Cox. President Mac is an ex officio member.

"The task force has an opportunity to accomplish a great deal for Kiwanis," says Chairman Ray. "We will be working hard to determine exactly where Kiwanis is today and where it can and will go in the future.

"We also stand ready to provide the President's Task Force on Private Sector Initiatives with the benefit of Kiwanis' sixty-seven years of volunteer experience. Our community analysis program alone should make a substantial contribution to that group's efforts."

The Task Force on Voluntarism will present a report of its findings at the International Convention in Minneapolis, Minnesota, in June.

Kiwanians pledge building gifts

Donors of $500 or more receive this plaque and their names will be on display at the new General Office.

Gifts already pledged range from flagpoles to sofas, from massive emblems to bookcases.

The beneficiary of this spirit of goodwill and organizational pride is the new General Office of Kiwanis International currently under construction in Indianapolis, Indiana. The donors are the proud clubs, divisions, and districts that comprise Kiwanis.

However, plenty of items remain available for such groups eager to ensure the success of this ambitious building project.

Individuals, too, are getting in on the act of giving. And a recent legal opinion obtained by Kiwanis International indicates that individual gifts to the fund are tax deductible in the US.

Contributions from individuals should be sent to the Kiwanis International Foundation Building Fund, 101 E. Erie Street, Chicago, Illinois 60611. Gifts from clubs, divisions, and districts should be sent to the building fund at the same address. All contributions will be acknowledged.

Gifts from individuals of at least $25 but less than $100 will earn the donor a wallet-size "Cornerstone Club" membership card and a replica of the new headquarters' cornerstone. The gold plate on marble replica is inscribed "We Build."

Donors of at least $100 but less than $500 will be distinguished as "Builders," and their names will be inscribed on a bronze plaque mounted in the new office building. A gift of at least $500 merits "Major Builder" status, and the contributor's name will be so noted on the bronze plaque. He also will receive the eight-by-ten-inch plaque shown at left.

Monetary gifts from individual donors will cover the cost of constructing those areas of the building related to Kiwanis' various service and educational activities.

Once these specific building costs are met, any subsequent gifts will support the continued operation of these activities.

8/KIWANIS MAGAZINE/JUNE-JULY 1982

Figure 42.7.—In this example, the picture bleeds, but the sidebar design does not.

responsibility, since they are likely to have the practical knowledge required. Larger companies hire industrial engineers exclusively to evaluate suggestions, which eliminates the possibility that a jealous supervisor might routinely reject good ideas recommended by underlings.

How should a company calculate awards? Many companies give 10 to 50 percent of the first year's savings. Others manage the suggestion system as a contest—prizes are awarded for the best ideas.

Channels through which a worker may appeal if he feels his suggestion is not given fair consideration must also be established. "Channels for appeal are essential for any suggestion system," says NASS executive secretary Hallett. People will maintain confidence in the system when they can get clear answers about why their ideas weren't adopted.

Detailed recordkeeping is another essential element of a successful suggestion system. Nothing can put a knife in the back of a suggestion system faster than making an award to one employee for an idea that was submitted two months earlier by another. Personnel must believe that the program plays no favorites, that the suggestions are accepted or rejected on their merits alone, and that personalities play no part in the evaluators' decisions.

Smart suggestions help small firms

A small business entrepreneur might feel a suggestion system is a luxury that only a General Motors can afford and an impractical tool for his own "Ma and Pa" company of twenty-five employees.

But Oliver Hallett, executive secretary of the National Association of Suggestion Systems (NASS) in Chicago, believes big ideas spring from small companies, too, and not just from the boss.

Although NASS generally recommends companies have a minimum of 200 employees for an ongoing suggestion system, Hallett says some NASS members employ as few as fifteen.

Says Hallett, "The existence of a suggestion system opens a two-way communication between management and entry level or higher personnel because every suggestion has to be answered.

"A communication channel is more important in smaller companies," Hallett says, because many small businesses lack a middle management level to serve as a liaison between the employer's ideas and input from the workers.

"The rules for a suggestion system are exactly the same, whether a company is large or small," says Hallett. And so is the system's basic premise that "the person actually doing the job has the best ideas on how to recognize and deal with problems."

Hallett concedes that the expense of installing a system may appear prohibitive to the management of a small company, but each adapted idea on the average realizes five dollars in savings for every dollar spent on a firm's suggestion system.

Last February NASS began marketing the "Team Idea Plan" (TIP) that is specifically aimed at smaller companies.

TIP, the brainchild of Robert Schwarz of Purdue University, involves small groups of employees who are given special training in creative problem solving. The groups meet twice monthly to generate ideas that improve job performance. Awards are made to teams based on projected first-year savings or increased earnings derived from adapted ideas.

NASS promotes TIP as a means of encouraging peer support and positive interaction between employees as well as training workers to identify needs and solve problems. "The beauty of TIP is that you set it up with a finite conclusion," says Hallett, which spares a long-term commitment on the part of the small business entrepreneur.

The TIP program has enjoyed success in hospitals where it has been adapted, and its boosters claim it is equally effective among production personnel as it is with clerical and administrative employees.

"Suggestion systems will also work as well in a service industry (such as restaurants) as in a manufacturing industry, but the rewards will be smaller," Hallett says.

Virtually all companies can benefit from a suggestion system with the exception of the construction industry, which NASS says is not a good outlet because of its transient labor force.—*S.T.*

Good records help to ensure that, especially if suggestions are submitted to supervisors for appraisal identified only by letters and numbers. Detailed records begin with formal suggestion forms that should include the employee's name, job title, his or her suggestion, and the date the idea is submitted.

The suggestion form should also allow space for the evaluator's name and his comments, the date and amount of the award given the employee, and the date the company implemented the idea and the amount of savings realized from its enactment.

Obviously, filing, cross-filing, and retrieving records is what the computer was born to do, and even small companies can save high administrative costs by putting the suggestion system into a computer.

Don Simmerman, vice-president of Crocker National Bank of San Francisco, put the corporation's suggestion system into an already-owned computer and was so satisfied with the results that, after two-and-a-half years, he says, "If it's worth having a suggestion system, it's worth having it automated."

The bank receives more than fifty suggestions a month and one staff member manages the entire program in a bit more than one hour a day. Without the computer, the same work would take at least one full-time staffer. Simmerman says that the computer could handle almost 600 suggestions a month.

Placing an "idea box" in the company cafeteria is a simple step, but establishing a suggestion system is a multiphase process that requires considerable time to prepare and to gain acceptance. Except in the smallest of companies, there should be a lead time of at least five months (continued on page 54)

38/KIWANIS MAGAZINE/JUNE-JULY 1982

Figure 42.8.—This sidebar design has a large tint bar at the top, a smaller tint bar at the bottom, and narrow lines at the sides.

the enclosure seems to continue outside the page edge at the left. This was used in *Consulting Engineering* magazine.

Figure 42.7 uses the same principle—a bleed. The picture bleeds to the left, outside the sidebar design and off the page. It is half in, half out, and it creates interest. The design is a 4-point rule at the top and bottom with 1-point rules at the sides. The rule was cyan (process blue), and the picture, four-color.

Figure 42.8 shows a 12-point tint block running across the top of the sidebar. This provides a hanger for the sidebar treatment. Figure 42.9 shows a sidebar with a corporate logo included. There are two things going on here. The bump-out is now in clear sight at the top and cannot be ignored. You see that headline the instant you look at the page. Then you see the corporate logo, even before you read the copy. Fine, you say, but do you want to have three or four sidebars in an issue, all with the logo included? By placing the logo in that particular spot you have implanted the "signature" used most often in ads. A logo gives the idea of corporate approval, like the president's name signed at the end of a letter. Do not abuse this device. You certainly don't want corporate approval on every sidebar.

Figure 42.10 is an obvious sidebar. The design says so. The position says so. This looks good when done in color.

Can we have sidebars in tabloids? Certainly. The only difference is that tabloids have different column widths. Magazines usually have a 13-pica column and a 20-pica column—two kinds of designs, one narrow, one wide. Tabloids have even more column widths—18, 13, 11, and 9½ picas. Almost all of the designs shown here will work in a tabloid except those that bleed.

What about using more than one sidebar per page? Like anything that is out of the ordinary, repeating too often destroys the impact. My suggestion is one per page and no more than two designs per issue, but you can certainly change every issue.

Sidebars can also be used instead of fillers. The filler invariably follows the story and quite obviously is used to fill out the page space. The sidebar looks and feels designed. Sidebars are often written to fit an area, much as fillers are. If you have a story that is 30 picas short of filling the last page and you want a design feature to fill the space, a sidebar is the answer. How do you write to fit an area? Know the character count per pica and figure out how many characters and spaces will be needed to fill it. Then write some copy.

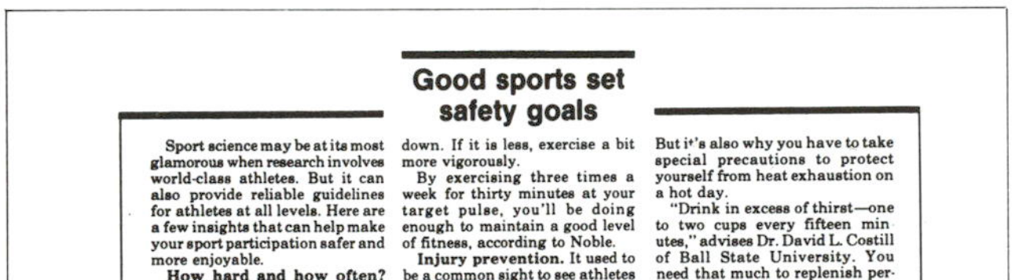

Good sports set safety goals

Sport science may be at its most glamorous when research involves world-class athletes. But it can also provide reliable guidelines for athletes at all levels. Here are a few insights that can help make your sport participation safer and more enjoyable.

How hard and how often? When a person exercises at a moderate level, his or her heart and lungs can provide the necessary amount of oxygen to keep the muscles working. This is *aerobic* exercise.

But as effort becomes more strenuous, the muscles need more oxygen than the cardiovascular system can supply. Called *anaerobic* exercise, such activity is accompanied by the build up of lactic acid, a waste product that impairs muscle function.

The ideal level of exercise, then, is just short of the aerobic-anaerobic threshold. But how do you recognize this point if you don't happen to have access to an exercise laboratory?

"Use your pulse as a guide," says Dr. Bates Noble of Northwestern University. By keeping your heart rate at 70 percent of maximum, you're exercising at a safe, effective level.

First determine your maximum heart rate by subtracting your age from 220. Then multiply by 0.7. The result is your target pulse rate per minute.

After a few minutes of exercise, take your pulse for ten seconds and multiply by six. If the result (your heart rate per minute) is above your target pulse, slow down. If it is less, exercise a bit more vigorously.

By exercising three times a week for thirty minutes at your target pulse, you'll be doing enough to maintain a good level of fitness, according to Noble.

Injury prevention. It used to be a common sight to see athletes warming up by bending at the waist, reaching for the ground and bobbing up and down. Less so nowadays, says Noble.

"Muscle research shows that bobbing triggers a reflex action in the tendons that actually leaves the muscles tighter and more prone to injury," he says. "You have to overcome that reflex reaction with gentle, yoga-like stretching."

For example, to stretch your hamstrings (backs of the legs), you would do best to sit on the ground, slowly reach toward your toes to a point just short of discomfort, and hold the position for thirty to sixty seconds.

Noble recommends five minutes of stretching and light calisthenics before and after a workout or game. Not only does this reduce risk of injury, it minimizes the feeling of stiffness the next day. That's because cool-down exercise helps clear the muscles of lactic acid.

Fluids. The human body is roughly 25 percent efficient, which means that 75 percent of the energy you generate to perform work turns into heat. That's why you feel comfortable jogging on a cold day wearing only a windbreaker and sweat pants. But it's also why you have to take special precautions to protect yourself from heat exhaustion on a hot day.

"Drink in excess of thirst—one to two cups every fifteen minutes," advises Dr. David L. Costill of Ball State University. You need that much to replenish perspiration and keep your natural cooling system in operation.

Costill recommends drinking plain water, preferably cold. Fruit juices, soda, and most athletic beverages are absorbed more slowly from the stomach due to their sugar content.

Diet. The primary muscular fuel is glycogen, a form of sugar derived from carbohydrates in your diet. When you exercise regularly, you've got to replenish your glycogen.

"Eating steak and eggs doesn't really make much sense," says Costill, since athletes have no greater need for protein than non-athletes. Moreover, the body uses protein as an energy source only in dire situations.

For an optimal training diet, increase your carbohydrate consumption, says Costill, adding that the complex carbohydrates of breads, pasta, and vegetables are better than the simple carbohydrates in sugary, junk foods that are virtually worthless.

On the day before a race or key event you might want to eat extra carbohydrate food. Called "carbohydrate loading,"

Air Products

than ever before. In 1980, he hurled the discus 229 feet, nearly twenty feet farther than his best Olympic throw. (The current world record is 233.5 feet.)

For the world-class athlete there's probably no greater hazard than injuries.

One false move can knock him or her out of the game for life. But thanks to advances made in sports medicine, more and more injured athletes are going on to play another day.

"Far fewer careers are terminated by injuries nowadays. Better diagnosis and rehabilitation permit a much more rapid return to function," says Dr. Bates Noble, director of Northwestern University's Center for Sports Medicine and team physician for the Chicago Bulls basketball team.

Possibly the most important new gadget in the sports doctor's black bag is the arthroscope. It permits a surgeon to look inside an injured joint through a tiny incision.

Through it the surgeon can check for torn cartilage or ligaments, calcium deposits or bone chips. And in many cases damage can be repaired with tiny surgical tools inserted through the scope.

"We definitely do not cut as much as we used to," says Noble. "Eighty percent of the cases I see are done without opening the joint."

One of his recent patients was Artis Gilmore, star center for the Bulls, who injured his knee early in the 1981-82 season.

"We had to open the knee," recalls Noble, "but the arthroscope showed us exactly where the damage was, so we could keep the incision to a minimum."

As a result Gilmore was back in action in early 1982. In the past an open-knee operation would probably have knocked him out for the season.

(continued on page 48)

AUGUST 1982/KIWANIS MAGAZINE/19

Figure 42.9.—A sidebar treatment can use a corporate logo as a signature.

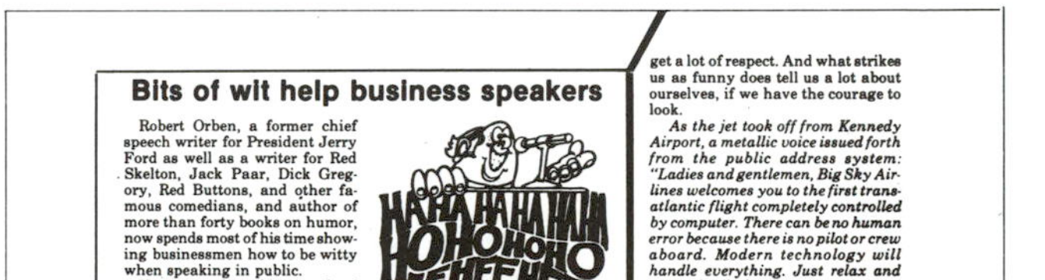

Bits of wit help business speakers

Robert Orben, a former chief speech writer for President Jerry Ford as well as a writer for Red Skelton, Jack Paar, Dick Gregory, Red Buttons, and other famous comedians, and author of more than forty books on humor, now spends most of his time showing businessmen how to be witty when speaking in public.

Here are a few of his words of wisdom:

• Humor can do a lot of things. It can drive home a point, illustrate a problem, humanize the speaker and the company he represents, build rapport with others, win over an audience, or defuse a tense situation.

• Humor is a social lubricant. That's its principal value to the businessman. It helps put him on the same plane as the people he is speaking to.

• If you are an executive speaking to the average audience, there's a gap you have to bridge. Humor is the best way to do it.

• If you can, tell a story about yourself that pokes fun gently. You want your listeners to poke each other in the ribs and say, "Hey, he's a regular guy."

• Because of television, people's standards have changed. People expect more. You have to come up with better material.

• Shun puns. Audiences have become conditioned to groan at the cleverest of puns.

• Don't step on your lines. Stop, smile, and wait after telling a story.

• Don't be afraid to lay an egg. Some jokes die. Acknowledge the fact that your story bombed.

• Don't be intimidated by the fact that you have used a story or joke many times before. The only old joke is the one told by the previous speaker. If an audience laughed the first time, the chances are they will laugh again.

realize that life is not nearly so serious as we sometimes pretend.

"In a world where many people have abandoned the restraints of good manners for self-assertiveness, it's better to be amused than to be annoyed," says Fromme. Perhaps this is why the universal humor of Chaplin, Laurel and Hardy, Keaton, and others remains appealing today.

Sigmund Freud devoted a great deal of thought to sexual humor and its popularity in Western cultures. In his treatise, "Wit and Its Relation to the Unconscious," Freud expressed the view that humor was all bound up with sex and aggression, but that people felt it necessary to repress these connections to an unhealthy degree.

Society, he believed, compelled men and women to confine their fantasies in these areas to dreams. Only young children openly acted out their sexuality and were often punished by their parents for doing so.

In 1905, Freud reasoned that jokes were a verbal formulation of aggression. In other words, a joke is funny to the extent that it allows hostile or sexual feelings to bubble harmlessly to the surface and be evaporated in laughter. Laughter, in this view, is the relief that follows anxiety. The unacceptable becomes acceptable.

"In personal relationships, humor can be a very important safety valve," says Professor Grotjahn. "The joke teller commits the sin of expressing a dangerous thought, but in a wittily disguised way. The listener recognizes the hostility in the joke and laughs to release his own aggressive impulses. The more energy released, the louder and deeper the laughter."

Just like steam from a boiler. A lot of heat, but nobody gets burned.

"Impropriety is the soul of wit," said the late author Somerset Maugham. A professional comic is someone who expresses a lot of pent-up anger in wit and not in deeds, and thus earns the appreciation and forgiveness of the rest of us through our laughter.

Rodney Dangerfield, in fact, does get a lot of respect. And what strikes us as funny does tell us a lot about ourselves, if we have the courage to look.

As the jet took off from Kennedy Airport, a metallic voice issued forth from the public address system: "Ladies and gentlemen, Big Sky Airlines welcomes you to the first transatlantic flight completely controlled by computer. There can be no human error because there is no pilot or crew aboard. Modern technology will handle everything. Just relax and enjoy the flight. Every contingency has been foreseen and nothing can go wrong . . . go wrong . . . go wrong . . .

In addition to ethnicity, sexuality, and absurdity, a great deal of contemporary humor is based on human fears, suffering, and death.

"Some people can always fight the anxiety of death by finding something to joke about," says Professor Grotjahn.

Humor allows us to take a benign view of human misery and frustration. It is—above all else—therapeutic.

When we can laugh a great deal we feel differently about things. Psychologists tell us that by changing our behavior we can alter our mood. Laughter distracts. Things are not so upsetting. Our blood pressure stays down.

We accept the impossibility of the human condition. Yes, life can be, after all, a slowly sinking ship. It's so sad that it's funny.

Some years ago, Norman Cousins, editor of the Saturday Review of Literature, was told that he was suffering from an irreversibly crippling and ultimately fatal disease. He had, said his doctors, maybe one chance in 500 to survive.

Refusing to accept this verdict, Cousins focused on an upbeat philosophy. He joked with his friends, read humorous literature, watched Candid Camera on television.

"I discovered that ten minutes of genuine belly laughter would give me two hours of pain-free sleep," Cousins reported at the time. He also took massive doses of ascorbic acid—vitamin C—believing in the research of Dr. Linus Pauling.

Perhaps you already know the result. He recovered. The astonished medical world read the account of his battle against illness in the New England Journal of Medicine. Laughter, claimed Cousins, was the key to his cure. His case history is still a matter of controversy among

(continued on page 55)

24/KIWANIS MAGAZINE/JUNE-JULY 1982

Figure 42.10.—A novel sidebar treatment.

CHAPTER FORTY-THREE

More about Trends

There are as many trends in publication design as there are in fashion. One can trace these trends back to 1950 when Fleur Fenton Cowles published *Flair* magazine. This magazine published thirteen issues; each was a publishing adventure. There was always a die-cut cover that gave the reader a peephole into the inside. This meant coordinating the cover with the first righthand page. There were pages slit up the middle, so one would read a half page at a time. There were pages slit across, so the reader could see a constant and read half pages by turning only the bottom half. There were four-page foldouts. There were tip-ins of brochures or even smaller magazines. There was a purple page with gold ink, a handwritten note from Fleur to the readers. *Flair* was a magazine pitched to the rich. It sold for fifty cents when most magazines were a nickel or a dime. Although *Flair* ceased publication, it showed the publishing world that there was indeed much that was exciting to be done in the area of visuals.

In Olden Times

Before the 1960s, type was set either by hand or by linotype. The letters were formed by pouring molten lead into a matrix. Type was set according to rigid rules and rarely beyond three "measures"— books at 30 picas, magazines at 20 picas, and news on 11 or 13 picas.

Not only were the rules rigid but so were the layouts. Type was simply not thought of as being anything but lead lines in solid block formations. Pictures were either line or halftones, with a few combinations of the two thrown in. Printing was usually black and white; the Sunday supplement was printed in Van Dyke brown and called the rotogravure section.

About the same time, a change was taking place in printing from letterpress to offset. We were passing from the stiffness and rigidity of lead and locked-up forms to a great deal more freedom by using negatives. Ads that were to be printed letterpress, for example, were set in lead using both type and cuts (blocks of wood with line drawings or halftones mounted on them). If these had to be shipped, a "matte" was made to save money and weight. This was an impression of the type and cut made by pouring a material over them that created a mold. The mold was shipped and then lead poured into it at the new destination. The system was awkward, cumbersome, and time consuming. Offset printing and film negatives did away with much of this. Pages were made up and simply photographed. The film was shipped in place of mattes or lead. Letterpress soon became obsolete for many purposes.

Another change in typesetting was phototypesetting. Setting type on film did away with the weight of lead. This was closely followed by computerized typesetting. Once the keystrokes had been captured, the typesetting equipment could set on any measure, any size, and set or reset as many times as one wished. Computer assisted typesetting has paved the way for a design revolution. Designs changed from two and three columns to four and five columns, arbitrary columns, wrap-around copy, and the multitude of type variables we see today.

Spotting Trends

Spotting trends is no more than noticing the unusual, the variables from the norm. Trends are most apparent in newsstand magazines. Close observation will show you that many trends start in advertisements and move to the editorial pages. All-cap headlines, for example, occurred in ads about a year before they appeared in story headlines. We are seeing more and more design innovations, no doubt because designers are feeling comfortable with the new equipment and constantly testing it to see what it can do for them.

Trends of the 1980s

Figure 43.1 shows a trend, a break-out (or in-quote or blurb). There is not a lot new about break-outs. However, prior to March of 1983 they were column width. In a three-column page, the break-out was usually in the middle column, at or above optical center. While there are a number of blurb designs in this book, figure 43.1 shows a new way of doing it. The blurb has been moved from its conventional position into the soft-design corner area. The capital letter "B" in red draws the reader's attention. Figure 43.2, a page from a different magazine, shows the use of the same idea. This is from *Esquire*. Here are two art directors who used a new idea at the same time.

Not only did these two magazines use the Band-aid break-out treatment, but here comes *50 Plus* with the same thing, shown in figure 43.3. All three magazines are published in New York. I doubt that the three art directors had the same idea at the same time; probably they all read the same book or trade magazine, or heard the same speaker at a design conference or luncheon.

Figure 43.3 uses a break-out to tie three columns together (compare it with figure 43.1), but the effect is the same. The boldface italic, in a larger size than text, is a good choice.

Figure 43.4 shows a page from *Esquire*. Notice the type handling in the break-out—an all-cap introductory word, followed by condensed Roman, ragged left and right. The break-out is used here to tie two columns together.

Figure 43.5 shows a slightly different treatment: the visual at optical center is handled much like a break-out and ties the three columns together. There is also a touch of something new in this page from *Plain Truth*. It might become a trend or it might die on the vine. Did you notice it? Look at the first paragraph—it is set in a large-size type. The second paragraph is set in type that is one size smaller, and the text is smaller yet. This graduated type funnels you into the story. When I see something like this I tear it out and save it, and I watch for other instances of its use.

In figure 43.6, we see a break-out, but what else do we see? Let's go back one step: we enter a page visually at upper left and we see the department head, "Medicine." The headline is not flush left, ragged right, or centered; the first letters of the three lines form a curve from "Medicine" to the large standup initial of the text. Now we move on to the break-out. This is a good example of design controlling eye movement.

Tabloids

Trends start in ads, move to magazine pages, and then are picked up by tabloids, particularly those that deny that they are newspapers. *Parade* is a Sunday supplement in many newspapers. It is a tabloid in design, but has many magazine attributes.

Look at figure 43.7, a page from *Parade*. Here is a break-out, one column wide. The design duplicates the 4-point rule from the outer frame. The type is set bold-

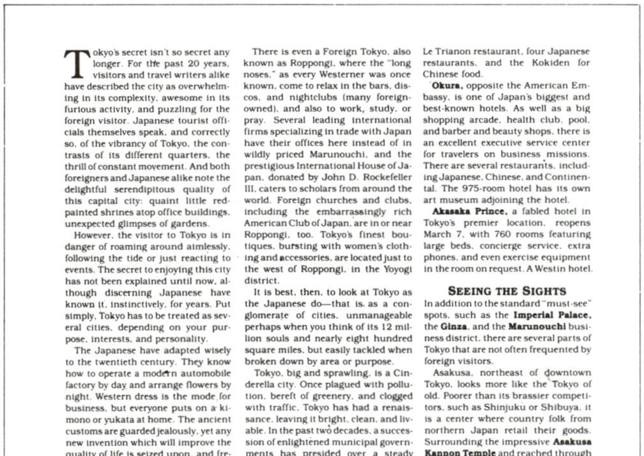

Figure 43.1.—The Band-aid treatment uses a break-out to tie two columns of body copy together.

Figure 43.2.—This is another Band-aid application of a break-out.

Figure 43.3.—How to tie three columns together.

Figure 43.4.—Two columns can be tied together with a break-out.

Figure 43.5.—Notice the introductory paragraphs in different type sizes and the break-out treatment in this example.

Figure 43.6.—With this break-out three columns are tied together visually.

face italic, flush right, ragged left (a little hard to read because of the irregular line starts), and is nicely handled. The only step missing is to use this break-out to tie two or more columns together, as was done in the previous examples.

Figure 43.8 shows still another design: the bold 1-pica bars at top, bottom, and break-out are all the same width and have the same starting point. This is no accident. The large boldface "When" certainly draws attention. It is followed by boldface italic. Notice the wrap-around copy. One cannot read the story and get away from the break-out. There is also a nice balance on this page between ad and editorial copy in design and structure. That takes planning and know-how. The art director should be congratulated.

Figure 43.9 shows another break-out. The type here is set more traditionally—flush left, ragged right—with wrap-around story copy. If you compare figures 43.7 and 43.9 you will see that the designer used a mix of three- and four- column design. I believe the

extra large "T" is a bit much in light of all that's happening on the page, but even that tends to hold it all together. My advice is to stay away from large decorative motifs unless you feel capable of handling the subtleties needed to balance all sight elements. This takes a great deal of practice and should not be done as a last-minute gesture.

Illustrated Break-Outs

Now you are ready for the next step in sighting the trends on break-outs—illustrating the subject matter of the break-out. Figure 43.10 shows a page that was handled properly—the subject matter matches the text very well. The page is from *In-Plant Reproductions* and shows how the break-out and illustration at optical center become a cohesive unit. This is particularly effective when the story has no other visual.

In figure 43.11, a page from *ZIP* magazine, the illustration looks very much like the kind one gets from a clip-art service. You sub-

scribe to the service, and every month you get a series of line drawings on different subjects. You file them and use them as you see fit. This art could have been done by a staff artist or freelancer, though the drawing reflects the style you usually get from a clip-art service. Whatever the source of the art, the result is an illustrated unit. Line art can be more effective when a spot of color is added.

Figure 43.12 shows that you can make a break-out look special with just a little art—the quote marks have been elongated to suit the design, and the oak leaf adds a decorative touch. This page is from *World Wide Printer* magazine. Figure 43.13, from *Plain Truth* magazine, shows what a staff artist can do. The art is printed in full color with wrap-around copy and is placed at optical center.

Figure 43.14, from *Consulting Engineer* magazine, shows another trend. This is the "illustrated movable sink." The sink is the area from the trim line at the top of the page to the live area. In this magazine, the stories must take up a full

Figure 43.7.—The tabloids have picked up on the break-out treatment also.

Figure 43.8.—Another successful tabloid treatment of the break-out.

page, which often means that the artist must pad out the stories in some manner. This can be accomplished by break-outs as well as the movable sink area. This particular movable sink takes up 10½ picas over each column, or 42 picas on the spread. There are few layout devices that can absorb that much space on a double-page spread. The illustrations are simple in execution since they are not meant to be descriptive. The break-out copy carries the theme.

You will recall that we spotted a trend in figure 43.5 in the use of type as a "funnel" lead-in. Another example of the same technique is shown in figure 43.15. Now, two instances do not make a trend, but more layout artists may pick up on this. A design like this would not have been possible in handset type or in linotype, but it is easy to do in computerized typesetting. The type is enlarged photographically from the basic 12-point size.

Figure 43.9.—This example uses the break-out as well as other design elements. Notice how many visuals there are and how well they balance each other.

Research Is the First Step Of Quality Control Program

by Ben E. Grey

There can be no doubt about a manager's success when patrons are proud of every job the in-plant printing department does for them. Establishing quality control can be a manager's challenge; especially if workers are being upgraded from quick and dirty production. Bad habits must be broken. The job becomes easy when quality-control standards are established and new methods are accepted as routine.

Misconceptions about quality control cause problems for managers. Quality control should guarantee that work reaching the patron is something of which he or she can be proud. It means every piece of every job must be inspected to ensure quality. Inspection prior to delivery is necessary—it is the final step of insurance. However, throwing away finished work is expensive and should not be considered part of a quality-control program.

Rather, quality control must start with the patron. The manager's mandate, "Make every job meet the end user's need," requires research. Only the patron can provide this information, so that proper quality standards can be implemented by the managers from design through delivery.

Answers to a simple list of questions can provide quality-control standards for every step of each project. Some managers use a form which patrons complete; others depend on their order takers to ask the following questions.

For whom is the work intended? What must it accomplish? What is the age and education level of the user and from what geographic area does he come? Against what does the printed piece have to compete? What must the work endure? (Trace each step through which the work goes: printing, bindery, shipping and being returned, filed in, sorted, filed and reused.) What is the work's life expectancy? Answers to these questions provide guidelines for design—type size, color, language, paper weight and quality. With additional information on estimating job costs and establishing a budget for the desired quality requirement, work can begin.

Recognized as an in-plant printing authority, Ben Grey is graphic coordinator for the Chesapeake Public Schools.

Quality Standards. Once quality standards have been set, workers need tools to obtain the quality.

Since many in-plant patrons furnish the manager with materials, a show-and-tell book is one of the ways to ensure quality control. The book simply shows samples of originals and how they will reproduce. Examples should include: broken type, light type, filled-in letters, 10th generation copy machine output, light blue printing, color work reproduced in one color, such as red art inside a black seal, and color stock such as pink or goldenrod. Make a special section in the book for photography including color prints reproduced in black, extreme enlargement and reduction, Polaroid or washed-out prints and mistakes in focus, exposure and development. It is a strong sales point to be able to say, "If it looks like this, it will reproduce like this."

Throwing away finished jobs is expensive and should not be considered a way to regulate the standards of printed work

Then ask the patron: Is this what you really want? Will it do the job which you want it to do? Will you be proud of the work? Often it is wiser to address these questions to the person who wants the work or who will have to use the work rather than to the person submitting the work.

The gray scale is a quality-control tool that can be used from design through press. In design, it can be used to evaluate copy, determine what will require screening and what can be reproduced as a line shot. A positive gray scale is also necessary when working with black and white photography. The eye loses control and often will accept gray as black and gray or cream as white. Comparing photography with the gray scale proves the colors and their printing ability.

On the process camera, gray scales are used to set and monitor the lights. Simply position five or six scales in the center and around the edge of the copyboard. When the lights are the same intensity and in proper position, all the scales develop equally. If you use a scale with fine line grids, such as the Stouffer, it will also indicate fine focus and the ability to hold fine line work.

When the positive gray scale is used with each piece of copy and properly interplated with the copy density, every piece of film can be developed to the same density.

In-Plant Reproductions

Figure 43.10.—The illustrated break-out.

Figure 43.11.—Another illustrated break-out. This one is very effective.

Figure 43.12.—You can illustrate effectively with just a few lines.

Figure 43.13.—The break-out treatment with contoured copy is very effective.

Figure 43.14.—An illustrated movable sink used as a break-out area.

204   *How to Design and Improve Magazine Layouts*

Editor's Notebook

WITH JOHN MACK CARTER Almost as much work gets done around this table in the Good Housekeeping Institute dining room as in my office—here, for example, you see the planning session with Muriel Kennedy (left), president, and Phyllis Tritsch (right), executive director, of American Women in Radio and Television, that resulted in GH's sponsorship of AWRT's Certificate of Commendation Awards Program. On May 6 I'll be presenting this year's awards, for radio and television programs that contribute to the education of women and to the improvement of society's image of them, at another luncheon—this time for 500 people attending AWRT's thirty-first annual convention in San Francisco. That's about 480 more than will fit comfortably around the table above. But it all started there, and our participation is a good example of the kind of interaction that constantly goes on between GH and influential women's groups in many fields.

Just three Mays from now, *Good Housekeeping* will be celebrating its hundredth anniversary, and in preparation we have started to fill the gaps in our file of past issues. All the missing magazines are from the early years, like the August 1904 issue little Henrietta Gainer (later Wilfong) is holding here. "I was almost four years old and couldn't read yet but loved to look at the lovely pictures," Mrs. Wilfong writes. "A widow now, I have three children, eleven grandchildren, and seven great-grandchildren. . . . Just want you to know that *Good Housekeeping* has been a friend of the family all these years." Mrs. Joan Downey, of Thousand Oaks, Calif., sent us a copy of our September 1906 issue, which she found, she says, "at a sale, in a box of odds and ends." And she adds, "Did you ever touch something old and want it to speak to you—tell you all it's seen? Like the rock we found on the hill behind our new home that has etched into it: 'Bear & deer found here. Love was felt. 1897.' I look out on my hill and know I'm not the first to do so and not the last. . . . It's a little like how I feel about this old issue of GH. I have spent many hours with it, wondering about the woman who read it first. And now it has found its way home." We hope more missing issues will find their way here, too, and for each one we will pay the sender $10. The issues we need are all those between the following dates: May 1885 to Dec. 1899; Jan. 1902 to Dec. 1903; Jan. 1908 to June 1910; Jan. 1912 to June 1913; Jan. to June 1914. Jan. to June 1915; July to Dec. 1917. IMPORTANT: Before sending *any* magazine, please write, giving date(s) to: Miss Joan Munroe, Room 531, 959 Eighth Avenue, New York, N.Y. 10019, so she can send you a special mailing envelope.

The woman having her hair done here is the talented young actress Sharon Gabet; the hairdresser is Bill Westmoreland, nephew of General William Westmoreland. If that sounds like the incipient plot of a soap opera, it's quite appropriate: Sharon, who plays Raven Whitney in *The Edge of Night*, and the other beauties who model our *25 Romantic Hairdos* (see pages 142-153) are all leading TV soap-opera stars. They loved the new hairdos Bill and other experts created for this feature, and we think you will too.

4

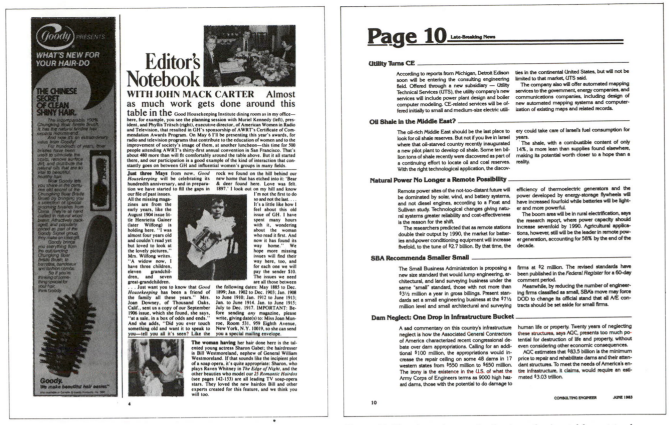

Figure 43.15.—Another example of graduated type leading the reader into the text.

Page 10 Late-Breaking News

Utility Turns CE

According to reports from Michigan, Detroit Edison soon will be entering the consulting engineering field. Offered through a new subsidiary — Utility Technical Services (UTS), the utility company's new services will include power plant design and boiler computer modeling. CE-related services will be offered initially to small and medium-size electric utilities in the continental United States, but will not be limited to that market, UTS said.

The company also will offer automated mapping services to the government, energy companies, and communications companies, including design of new automated mapping systems and computerization of existing maps and related records.

Oil Shale in the Middle East?

The oil-rich Middle East should be the last place to look for oil shale reserves. But not if you live in Israel where that oil-starved country recently inaugurated a new pilot plant to develop oil shale. Some ten billion tons of shale recently were discovered as part of a continuing effort to locate oil and coal reserves. With the right technological application, the discovery could take care of Israel's fuel consumption for years.

The shale, with a combustible content of only 14%, is more lean than supplies found elsewhere, making its potential worth closer to a hope than a reality.

Natural Power No Longer a Remote Possibility

Remote power sites of the not-too-distant future will be dominated by solar, wind, and battery systems, and not diesel engines, according to a Frost and Sullivan study. Technological changes giving natural systems greater reliability and cost-effectiveness is the reason for the shift.

The researchers predicted that as remote stations double their output by 1990, the market for batteries and power conditioning equipment will increase fivefold, to the tune of $2.7 billion. By that time, the efficiency of thermoelectric generators and the power developed by energy-storage flywheels will have increased fourfold while batteries will be lighter and more powerful.

The boom area will be in rural electrification, says the research report, where power capacity should increase sevenfold by 1990. Agricultural applications, however, still will be the leader in remote power generation, accounting for 58% by the end of the decade.

SBA Recommends Smaller Small

The Small Business Administration is proposing a new size standard that would lump engineering, architectural, and land surveying business under the same "small" standard, those with not more than $3½ million a year in gross billings. Present standards set a small engineering business at the $7½ million level and small architectural and surveying firms at $2 million. The revised standards have been published in the *Federal Register* for a 60-day comment period.

Meanwhile, by reducing the number of engineering firms classified as small, SBA's move may force DOD to change its official stand that all A/E contracts should be set aside for small firms.

Dam Neglect: One Drop in Infrastructure Bucket

A sad commentary on this country's infrastructure neglect is how the Associated General Contractors of America characterized recent congressional debate over dam appropriations. Calling for an additional $100 million, the appropriations would increase the repair ceiling on some 48 dams in 17 western states from $550 million to $650 million. The irony is the existence in the U.S. of what the Army Corps of Engineers terms as 9000 high hazard dams, those with the potential to do damage to human life or property. Twenty years of neglecting these structures, says AGC, presents too much potential for destruction of life and property, without even considering other economic consequences.

AGC estimates that $83.5 billion is the minimum price to repair and rehabilitate dams and their attendant structures. To meet the needs of America's entire infrastructure, it claims, would require an estimated $3.03 trillion.

10 CONSULTING ENGINEER JUNE 1983

Figure 43.16.—A good example of using a horizontal layout to showcase small news items.

Figure 43.16 may not really be a trend, but rather a good answer to the problem of small copy in a business press magazine. The designer has changed the copy from a series of tag-on verticals to a designed set of horizontals. The copy is broken up into two blocks instead of one and arranged horizontally. Headlines hang out into white space—always to the outside (that's why this is always done on a lefthand page).

The more you get into publication layout and design, the more you realize that all layout artists and designers face the same problems. When you have a new problem, go to your library and look through the magazines. See if anyone has solved your problem for you. If so, buy that issue at the newsstand and start building a trend file. It will pay off.

GLOSSARY

Ads (advertisements). Ads are created to fit the column and page widths. Ads may be sold by the column inch or a fraction of the page, i.e., 1/8, 1/4, 1/2, or full page.

Agate. Originally a type size (5½ point). The term also was used as the basic unit in measuring the depth of advertising space. There are approximately 14 agate lines to the inch. Modern publications measure depth by inches.

Alley. The white space between two columns of copy on the same page.

Antique Paper. A rough finish, high quality printing paper. See your paper supplier for specific texture and colors.

Art. All pictorial matter in a publication. Includes photographs, illustrations, cartoons, charts, graphs, etc.

Art Deco. An art style of the 1920s and 1930s. Simple, repeated forms and symmetry are aspects of art deco.

Art Director. The person in charge of all visual aspects of a publication. This includes typography as well as art.

Ascender. That part of a typeset letter that is higher than the lower case letter ''x.''

Back of the Book. The section of a magazine following the main articles and stories. This consists of continuations of articles and stories, ads, and filler material.

Balance. The arrangement of various elements on a page or spread such that the weight of the various elements is equal.

Banner. The main, one-line headline running across a page or spread.

Bar Graph or Bar Chart. Art that shows statistics by using bars of various lengths. Bars may be horizontal or vertical.

Baseline. The invisible line the type sits on, usually defined as the bottom of the x-height.

Bauhaus. A German school of design (1919–1933). Bauhaus is characterized by a highly ordered, no-frills, functional style in architecture, art, and typography. Helvetica is the most famous Bauhaus typeface.

Benday or Ben Day. A pattern or tone added to a line drawing. Benday comes in a variety of patterns (dots, squares, crosshatching, etc.). A Benday can be applied to artwork or directly to film. Bendays come in dots-per-inch percentages, usually in 5 percent increments. A mix of Bendays creates a tonal/textural contrast.

Binding. The mechanical process of stitching or gluing forms or signatures to produce a complete magazine. Binding includes adding the cover.

Bleed. Elements that go to the page edge or gutter edge. A bleed may be a picture, tint block, rule, etc., but *never* typeset material. Bleeds to a page edge are actually printed beyond the page boundary, then trimmed after the page has been folded into its signature.

Blind Embossing. Die stamping without ink to produce an image that is raised on one side of a sheet and indented on the other side.

Block. A chunk of copy of any length that is considered to be one unit. One or more blocks of copy constitute some of the elements of a page.

Blue Line. A paper proof taken from the film in a direct image process to show how the final page will look. It is called a blue line because image areas are usually blue in this proofing process. Other methods are in use now that may produce different colors, but the proof from film often is still called a blue line.

Blue Pencil. To make corrections or edit, so-called because nonreproducing blue pencil may be used to mark corrections on camera-ready copy and need not be removed after the correction is made. The camera does not ''see'' nonrepro blue, and it will not appear on the film.

Blurb. (1) A short phrase from or synopsis of any section in a story. (2) A short, definitive phrase relating to the story. (3) A follow-up title for a magazine article longer than the main title but in smaller type, often italic. (4) A title or phrase displayed on the cover.

Body Copy. Text material. Does not include headlines, subheads, captions, cutlines, or blurbs.

Boldface. A weight of a type face that is heavier than body type.

Bond Paper. Paper used for business stationery; often has a rag content.

Border. The white space between the live area and page edge. Also a rule, tint block, or other frame for a photo, blurb, or caption.

Box. A design element composed of rules (or another type of frame), with type or art inside.

B.R.C. Business reply card.

Bridge the Gutter. A method of relating the pages of a spread visually by using the gutter area as live area and filling it with a visual bridge such as a banner headline. A photograph or blocks of type may be used as a bridge successfully only on the center spread.

Bulk. The thickness of paper. Paper can be high bulk and still be relatively light in weight.

Bullet. A typographical device used to add emphasis. Solid or open squares and circles are the most often used bullets. May be used in a list instead of numbers.

Calendering. A paper manufacturing process that runs paper between rollers to increase its smoothness.

Camera Ready. A page or spread with all elements affixed in their correct positions, ready for the camera to shoot.

Cap Height. The height of a capital letter. Sometimes used as a specification instead of type size. See *Indented Initial*.

Caps. Capital letters. Also known as upper case; when type was hand set, capital letters were stored in the upper part of the type case.

Caption. A short descriptive block of copy or a phrase that describes an illustration.

CRT. Cathode ray tube—a vacuum tube used by phototypesetting machines to transmit the letter image onto the film or sensitized paper.

Centered Head. A headline centered over a story. It may be centered over one or more columns, depending on the page design.

Centerfold. A center-page spread with one or both of the pages opening up into an additional page.

Center Spread. The two facing pages in the center of a magazine that are printed on one sheet of paper. The center spread is usually treated as a unit. Often the gutter is considered live area and contains a banner headline, photograph, rules, and even a copy block.

Change of Direction. When two different shapes that occur on the same page cause the eye to move in one direction, then another (e.g., from horizontal to vertical).

Character per Pica. The average number of characters of a font, in a particular point size, that occur in a pica measure. (Your typesetter should be able to give you this information.) By knowing the character per pica count, you can fairly accurately determine from typewritten copy how long the typeset copy will be (copy fitting) *or* write copy to fill a space.

Character. Each typeset letter, number, punctuation mark, space, and symbol.

Clip Art. Illustrations sold in book or sheet form that may be added to a layout: art not created for a specific use.

Cluster. Several pictures, usually of various sizes, that are planned as one visual unit. They are held together by a 1-pica separation in the form of a cross, H, U, or T. The captions are usually set toward the outside—never as one block with indentifiers.

Cold Type. Phototypesetting or strike-on typesetting (as an automatic typewriter).

Collage. A mixture of various elements to create a unit or to present a single idea. For example, a collage on flight might contain photographs and drawings of airplanes and birds, airplane structures, and bird skeletons.

Color Corrected. Changing the ink colors when printing on colored stock so the printed piece is true to the actual colors desired. Not necessary for opaque inks.

Color Scanners. Electronic instruments that produce color-corrected, continuous tone separations for use in four-color reproduction.

Color Separations. Film negatives, one for each of the four colors in four color process reproduction. These are magenta, cyan (process blue), yellow, and black. See also *Four-Color Reproduction*.

Column. An area on a page defined by a specific width and depth. All columns on a page may or may not have the same specifications.

Column Inch. An area that is one column wide and one inch deep.

Column Rule. A thin vertical rule separating columns of type on a page.

Combination. A piece of art combining both line and halftone processes.

Company Publication. A periodical produced by a company to promote its own interests. See also *External Publication* and *House Organ*.

Comprehensive Layout. A layout plan finished to look as close to the final piece as possible.

Condensed Type. A vertically compressed typeface. Condensed type may be one of the fonts in a type family. Condensed type can be produced from an existing font or may be electronically created on some phototypesetting machines.

Contents Page. The page or pages containing a list of the articles in a publication and the numbers of the pages on which they begin.

Continuous Tone. A photographic print that has all tones or values of a hue gradually blending into one another.

Contrast. The difference between one tonal value or texture and another that defines each as a distinct unit.

Copy. Manuscript, headlines, captions, blurbs, text—anything that will be typeset.

Copy Block. See *Block*.

Copy Editing. Making corrections and changes in the manuscript. May include correcting facts, grammar, and changing copy to conform to a publication's house style.

Copy Fitting. Using the character per pica information to determine how many column inches typewritten copy will take. Also, using the character per pica information to write copy to fill a specific space.

Cover. There are four covers. The outside front cover has the logo, title, and art. It is used to sell the magazine. The three ad covers are the inside front cover, inside back cover, and outside back cover.

Cover Stock. The heavier or thicker paper used to form the magazine cover. Cover stock helps hold the shape of the magazine on the rack and in the mail.

Credit Line. The typeset name next to a photograph or illustration that credits the photographer or artist.

Cropping. Specifying with crop marks that part of a picture to be used.

Crop Marks. Straight lines at the top and one side of a picture that tell the cameraperson what part of the picture is to be used. In addition to cropping, the picture editor should give the dimensions of the printed photo so the cameraperson can determine the percentage to enlarge or reduce the photo.

Cutline. A short descriptive block of copy or a phrase that describes an illustration.

Cyan. One of the colors used in four-color process printing. Also called process blue.

Densitometer. An instrument that measures the density of colors on a color proof or transparency. This measurement allows exact comparison between proof and printed material for accurate reproduction of originals.

Descender. That part of letters in a font that descends below the baseline of the lower case "x."

Design. A plan to organize elements proportionately with contrast and to promote the articles, ads, and other elements present. The design takes into account the parts of a page—columns, alleys, gutter, margins, folio line, etc.

Die. The form that is used to die-cut shapes from paper; the form used for embossing or blind embossing.

Die Cut. A hole or outline punched out of the paper. See *Die*.

Digital Type. Phototypesetting system that is computer generated instead of using a film font. Type images are formed on the surface of a cathode ray tube from digital records of the type. The images are then transferred to photosensitive paper or to film.

Dingbat. A decorative typographical device such as a star, circle, pointing hand, etc., used to add interest to a headline, fill isolated white space, as an end-of-story device, and to add emphasis (sometimes used in place of a bullet).

Display Face. A typeface designed to be set 18 points or larger and used for headlines, blurbs, etc. These faces are not used for body copy. See also *Display Heads*.

Display Head. A headline set 18 points or larger. A display head may be a display face or it may be a typeface suitable for body copy but enlarged for headline use.

Double Page Spread. Left and right facing pages, designed to be seen as one unit. A banner headline may be used as a unifier. See also *Center Spread* and *Printer's Spread*.

Drop Out. Type that appears as space dropped out of a dark background. To produce a drop out, type is set on an overlay, which is placed over a photograph when the cameraperson shoots the film. Because the type blocks some of the photo from appearing on the film, the type image, when printed, appears as the color of the paper.

Dummy. A rendering of a page or pages provided to the printer or keyline artist to show the location of various elements. A photocopy of typeset galleys may be used to dummy to be sure of page fit. See also *Printer's Dummy*.

Duotone. A halftone printed in two colors, one of which is usually black. Two halftone plates are made of the same illustration.

Edit. See *Copy Editing*.

Editorial. A short, unsigned essay stating the publication's opinion on some issue. Also designates the non-advertising space in a magazine.

Element. Any unit that makes up a page design, e.g., copy, headline, subhead, art, rule, border, photo, color tint block, caption, blurb, cutline, folio line, etc.

Em or Em Space. The width of the capital "M" in the type size used. When the term originated, all typefaces were designed such that the capital "M" equaled the type size, i.e., an "M" in 9-point type equaled 9 points. With modern typeface design, this may not be strictly true, but the em space still equals the point size for most use, such as a one-em paragraph indent. Two common exceptions are a condensed and an expanded typeface where the em space supplied with the face is altered proportionately.

Emboss. To print an image on paper and stamp it, so that it rises above the surface of the paper. A die is used to emboss.

En. One half of an em.

Enamel Stock. Very smooth paper with a slick coating. Often used as cover stock. Desirable with photographs because there is no texture to the paper to compete with the details in the photo.

Expanded Type. Typeface that is altered to be wider than the regular font of its family. Expanded type may be produced for a specific font or may be electronically or digitally altered from the regular font on a phototypesetting machine.

External Publication. A company magazine prepared for and circulated to a group of readers, such as customers or investors, outside the organizational structure. An annual report or prospectus is an external publication.

Face. See *Typeface*.

Family. See *Type Family*.

Filler. Small pieces of copy used to avoid isolated white space after story endings. Fillers should be compatible with the purpose of a magazine or at least with the surrounding stories. For example, a suitable filler for a typography magazine might be the dates of activity of the Bauhaus School of Design.

Flat. An opaque, gridded sheet of paper, with page negatives taped on it, positioned according to the printer's dummy. The flat is "opened up" (the opaque paper is removed from the page negatives), placed on a metal plate, and exposed to intense light to create the printing plate.

Flop. Turning a negative over so the printed photograph is the reverse of the original. Often used to change the way a person faces so the subject will not be looking off the page. Cannot be used when words appear in a photo.

Flush Left (or Right). Copy set even on one edge or side only; the other side is ragged.

Folio. Page number.

Folio Line. The position of the page number on the page design. The folio line may also contain the publication name and/or publication date.

Font. All the letters—both caps and lower case—numbers, punctuation, and symbols of one typeface. In phototypesetting the font is photographically or digitally proportioned according to the desired type size. In hand-set type, each point size must have a separate font. Each subdivision of a type family (regular, italic, bold, condensed, etc.) must have its own font.

Format. See *Design*.

Four-Color Process Reproduction. A printing process using four basic colors (magenta, cyan (process blue), yellow, and black) to produce the full color spectrum. Each color has its own printing plate. The imprints are overprinted in various areas and in various proportions to create other colors, e.g., blue and yellow combine to create green, but less blue and more yellow create olive green.

Fourth Cover. The back cover. See also *Cover*.

Frame. See *Border*.

Galley. Copy typeset to specifications (typeface, type size, column width, leading, etc.) ready for proofreading or pasting on a layout. When making a dummy, a photocopy of the reproduction galley is usually used.

Gatefold. A fold on the outer edge of a page that, when extended, creates a wider page. Usually folded like a gate, toward the center fold.

Glossy. A photograph with a slick finish.

Grid. A page design created to form preplanned areas of unequal dimensions. Grids can be horizontal, vertical, or a combination of both. Elements are placed to fill the grid areas. See also *Modular Design*.

Grin-and-Shake Pictures. Those pictures taken of two people grinning at each other and shaking hands. These are the most stereotyped of photos and the bane of every page designer.

Grouping. Arranging pictures so that there is a leader, or focal point and followers.

Gutter. That area that is composed of the inside margins of two facing pages. It is also the area used to bind a magazine into pages. On a center spread, the gutter area may be used as live area. See *Center Spread*.

Hairline Rule. A line ½ point thick. This is approximately the width of a very fine pencil-drawn line.

Halftone. A film process in which a photograph is converted into a series of same size dots of various densities to create tone values.

Hand Lettering. Lettering done by an artist. Used when there is no comparable typeface available for the desired result and to create a special effect, such as lettering on a curve.

Headline or Head. A story title. See also *Subhead*.

Highlight. In a halftone reproduction an area from which all dots have been removed.

Horizontal Look. Lines of type, rules, and/or pictures handled in such a way as to give the visual appearance of width as opposed to height.

Hot Type. Type cast in a matrix with hot lead. Used for letterpress printing. Usually Linotype or Ludlow, but increasingly falling from use with the advent of photo-typesetting.

House Organ. A company publication released on a regular schedule for distribution to employees.

House Style. Specifications of layout or typesetting peculiar to a publication. For example, in a house organ, the company name may be set in small caps every time it appears.

Impression. Each contact of the printing plate to paper. A page with four-color reproduction will have four impressions for each side of the printing sheet.

In a Well. Said of a headline placed between the two outside columns (in a three-column format) to surround the title with columns of copy. The headline will usually be centered.

Indented Initial. The first letter of a paragraph, typeset larger than the body copy, proportionate to the number of lines to be indented. For example, a three-line initial will sit on the same baseline as the third line of type and the top of the letter should be at the same height as an ascender in the first line. The first three lines will be indented for this initial to fit in the "well" created by the indent. This device can add contrast to an all-type page. The initial is sometimes specified to the typesetter as cap-height.

In-House. Something produced by the publisher's staff rather than purchased from an outside supplier.

Insert. A preprinted piece that has been inserted (tipped in) between signatures and bound into the magazine. An insert may be a single page, such as a subscription reply card, or a signature prepared by an advertiser and shipped to a publication already printed, ready for insertion in the binding process.

Issue Date. A periodical's publication date.

Italic. A typeface that slants to simulate handwritten copy.

Jump. To continue copy on another page, usually at the back of the magazine.

Jump Line. The typeset line, usually smaller or a different typeface than the body copy, which tells on what page a story has been continued. No jump line is necessary when the story is continued on the following page.

Justified. Type that has been set to align on both sides, usually by changing the size of the space bands.

Keyline. The camera-ready layout, including crop marks for the page boundaries and for any items to be stripped in by the printer. May include flaps, or overlays, with items printed in another color, to be printed on the page. See also *Overlay* and *Stripping*.

Layout. A master plan or blue print for a page or spread.

Leader. (1) Rows of periods used in tables, price lists, tables of contents, etc., to help carry the reader's eye across empty space. (2) In a photo "grouping," the leader is the picture that gets immediate attention, because of its size, shape, or color.

Lead-In. The first few words of a block of copy that are set in a different type style from the rest of the copy. The lead-in may be italic, all caps, etc.

Leading. The space between typeset lines which prevents ascenders and descenders from touching. If 8-point type has 1 point of leading, it is written as 8/9 and read as "8 on 9."

Legibility. The ease with which you can identify letters and words in lines of copy.

Letterpress. The method of printing from raised surfaces. The ink is spread over these raised surfaces and imprinted onto paper. Letterpress has been replaced by offset printing in many uses. See also *Offset Printing*.

Letterspace. The space between letters. Letterspacing may be increased or decreased to suit a design.

Ligature. Two or more characters on a single piece of type that join or overlap. The same effect may be created for a phototypesetting font. The most common ligatures are fi, ff, and ffi.

Line Art. Art work composed entirely of line and dots. It can give the impression of tonal values when screens or Bendays are used, but does not actually have continuous tone.

Line Conversion. Changing a continuous tone glossy picture into a halftone with dots. See also *Screen*.

Line Gauge. A printer's ruler marked off in picas and points. It usually will have scales of 9-point lines, 10-point lines, etc., to facilitate determining how many lines of copy are typeset. To use these scales properly, measure from baseline to baseline.

Linotype. A hot-type casting machine that produces raised letters for letterpress printing.

Lithography. A planographic printing process that relies on the mutual resistance of water and ink to achieve printing. In modern usage, a synonym for *Offset Printing*.

Live Area. That area on a page that includes all the space ordinarily used for copy and pictures. It does not include margins or borders. The live area is usually about 7 by 10 inches on an 8½-by-11-inch magazine page. See also *Center Spread.*

Logo or Logotype. The name or symbol of a publication, set in a particular typographic style, as run on the cover, table of contents, on company letterheads, envelopes, bills, invoices, etc. It is the publication image. Magazines often will have a special font produced for their phototypesetting machines so the title is always produced in the logo format.

Lower Case. Non-capital or ''small'' letters; a reference to when type was hand set and small letters were stored in the lower part of the type case.

Magazine. A publication of eight pages or more, bound with a cover of some kind (self-cover or added). Magazines come in a variety of sizes, but they are usually close to 8½ by 11 inches.

Magenta. One of the four colors used in four-color process printing. This color is not red, as we ''see'' red, but a sort of purple shade of red that combines with yellow, cyan (process blue), and black to give full color.

Manuscript. Typewritten copy; the form in which a story or article is submitted to an editor. The manuscript is copyedited before it is sent to the typesetter. See also *Copy Fitting.*

Marriage. A term used to mean type compatibility between two faces that creates a good design when viewed together. Depending on the goal of the designer, a good marriage may produce a blended effect or a contrast.

Masthead. A list of all the persons responsible for publishing a magazine. These include editors, art directors, writers, production people, etc.

Match Color. Any color that must have ink mixed to match a swatch or sample. A match color usually is a solid; that is, it cannot be created from the four-color process colors.

Matrix. A brass or bronze die, or mold, used in a hot-type casting machine to produce the letter shape.

Measure. The width of a line or column of type when set. On ragged or centered copy, the measure is the maximum width.

Mechanical. A layout or dummy with all type and other elements pasted into position ready to be photographed as one unit. See *Camera Ready.*

Mezzotint. A picture created by overlaying a patterned screen on a conventional halftone. Mezzotint screens come in a variety of patterns and can be used to create effects that enhance the photo's message.

Modular Design. Modules are even units, all with the same dimensions. Design elements are placed to fill a module or group of modules. Highly regimented. See also *Grid.*

Moire. An undesired pattern caused when a screened photograph is screened a second time. May also occur when a line drawing depicting a pattern—such as herringbone or crosshatching—is screened. Cannot be corrected. The photo or drawing must be shot again from the original.

Monotype. A process in which a casting machine makes the letters one at a time; the letters cast by such a process. In contrast, the familiar Linotype machine makes a line of type, not individual letters.

Montage. Several photos pasted together to form a single photo mass to create an effect or reinforce a story's message. For example, a biography might contain a montage of photos of the subject from childhood to adulthood. See also *Collage.*

Mood Typefaces. Display typefaces chosen to create a special mood or feeling. Old English, for instance, is often used for biblical text.

Mortise. A section cut out of the edge of a picture to make room for another picture. These cuts are usually square cornered and take the place of an overlap. Mortising reinforces the relationship between the individual photos.

Mug Shot. A portrait or picture that shows only a person's head.

Natural Column Endings. Columns that are not vertically justified to fit the live area, but are allowed to end irregularly. Can make paste-up and typesetting much easier and, therefore, less expensive.

Natural Story Ending. The story copy is allowed to end with no attempt to square off the column with other columns on the page or spread. This leaves a ''hole'' at the end of the story, which is filled with some kind of *Filler* or a *Dingbat.*

Newsprint. A low quality, cheap paper used for newspapers and sometimes for preliminary layouts.

Nonreproducing Blue. A color that, when used to write corrections or instructions on camera-ready copy, does not appear on the film when the page is shot.

Offset Lithography. A system of printing. The surface of a printing plate is treated to accept ink in image areas and water in nonimage areas. The plate is pressed against a rubber blanket transferring the ink design to the blanket. Then the rubber blanket is pressed against the paper, and the ink is transferred to the paper, creating an exact reproduction of the image on the printing plate.

Offset Paper. Paper manufactured especially for offset lithography presses.

Opaque. To eliminate flaws on a film negative by painting them over with an opaque liquid. This is done before making the printing plate from the film.

Optical Center. A spot two-fifths down from the top of the page and equidistant from the sides of the live area. This is where the eye will seek to ''balance'' the page elements rather than at the exact, mechanical center.

Outlining. Dropping the background away from a photo subject. The outline is then free-form instead of having a ''mechanical'' form such as a square, rectangle, or circle.

Overlay. In keylining, a ''flap'' of either paper or acetate placed over the black ink layout. Art to be printed in a second color is pasted on the overlay. Subsequent colors are treated the same way on separate overlays. Each overlay must be registered, or keyed, to the black plate by registration marks.

Overprint. Type printed over a picture or photograph.

Page Dummy. A layout sheet on which galleys of type and other elements have been placed to give the platemaker an exact guide to all elements. See also *Printer's Dummy.*

Panel. A group of pictures arranged in a line with one common measure—either all the same height or the same width. Creates a ''strip'' on the page.

Paste-Up. Camera-ready copy. All elements of a page or spread are pasted into exact position and ready to be mounted on a copyboard in front of a camera.

Perfect Binding. A method of gluing forms together at their spine edge to hold them together, resulting in a magazine or book with all pages in order. Perfect binding creates a flat spine on which the magazine title and date may be printed.

Perspective. Quality in a photograph or picture that creates the illusion of depth.

Photocomposition. See *Phototypesetting.*

Photoengraving. Printing plate with raised images or areas created by acid etching.

Photojournalism. Photography used in mass media to report news, express opinion, and entertain, with the emphasis on pictures rather than words.

Photostat. A reproduction process involving a paper negative and a paper positive. The final result is a positive print in either matte or glossy finish. As ''stats'' may be enlarged or reduced, they are sometimes pasted onto camera-ready layouts and shot with the rest of the page, rather than stripping-in the photos later. See *Stripping.*

Phototypesetting. Type set directly onto photosensitive film or paper. Most systems use film that has the letters, numbers, and symbol forms for a type font. Type sizes are created by using the film font in conjunction with various lenses. See also *Digital Type.*

Pica. A printer's measure. One pica is 12 points. There are 6 picas to an inch and 72 points to an inch.

Pica Stick. A ruler divided into increments based on the point system. See *Pica.*

Pictograph. A simplified drawing using symbols to illustrate a message. International warning signs (no smoking, for example) are examples of pictographs.

Plate. The metal or paper surface that carries the image in a printing process. There is one plate for each color. See *Letterpress* and *Offset Lithography.*

P.M.T. A reproduction process similar to photostats but lacking the paper negative step. Direct image reproduction results in a positive print only. You cannot get a reverse or negative P.M.T. unless you start with a negative image.

Pockets. (1) the space between signatures where tip-ins and inserts can be bound. (2) The area in the binding equipment where the signatures are stacked, prior to binding.

Point. A printer's measure. There are 12 points to a pica, and 72 points to an inch.

Pre-Prep. All production steps prior to making printing plates. These include typesetting, dummying, photo sizing, creating illustrations, laying out, pasting up, creating mechanicals, proofreading, and shooting final film and/or film stripping.

Press Proof. A proof, pulled on the press, showing exactly how the printed page will look. It is often used when color and/or photographs are of prime importance. Making any changes at this point is very expensive and should be avoided. A representative of the magazine should be on hand to see the first proof as it comes off the press.

Press Run. The number of copies of a magazine printed at one time.

Primary Colors. Red, yellow, and blue. Mix any two primary colors and you get secondary colors, orange, green, and violet. Tertiary colors are made by combining secondary colors with primary colors. *Note:* Primary colors are not to be confused with four-color process colors, which are magenta, cyan (process blue), yellow, and black.

Printer's Dummy. A dummy that shows the placement of pages on the press sheet and how that sheet will be folded, so that the pages will be in the proper order. If a designer wants to use an extra color on a page, the printer's dummy will show on which pages a second color will be ''free''—if a second color is already being printed on one side of a press sheet, color can be added to all the pages on that side at no extra cost.

Printer's Spread. A spread that shows which pages will face each other on the press sheet, rather than in the magazine (a *Page Spread*). On a cover spread, for instance, the front cover will appear on the right and the back cover on the left because that is how they are printed.

Process Blue. One of the four color process colors; also called cyan. This is a rather bright blue.

Proof. A reproduction in some form that shows production instructions have been followed. See also *Press Proof*.

Proofread. To check typeset copy for errors.

Ragged. Type that is set flush on one side only, with the lines ending at different measures on the other side, within the maximum line length allowed. Usually, but not always, ragged copy is set flush left, ragged right.

Reader Service Card. A postcard tipped into a publication with direct number references to the ads. The reader circles numbers referring to products or services about which the reader would like more information. The card is mailed to the publisher for handling, through the advertiser. Often referred to as a ''BRC'' or ''Bingo Card.'' See also *Tip-In*.

Ream. Five hundred sheets of paper.

Register. Positioning of elements so they are printed in exactly the right place. Registration marks (usually crossed lines inside a circle) are placed on the base copyboard. Each overlay has matching registration marks. This allows the printer to make plates and to make adjustments on the press so all elements are positioned correctly on the printed piece.

Reverse. Printed so that the part that usually prints in color is the tone of the paper and the background is in color. This can be done with type and with pictures.

Roman. (1) Of or relating to the Latin alphabet; i.e., an alphabet with serifs. (2) A type style with upright characters; not italic.

Rough. A simplified layout plan, lacking details. See *Thumbnail*.

Rule. A line used to separate columns, pictures, blurbs, and captions; to underscore; or to create a box. A rule may be of various thicknesses and is measured in points. A hairline rule is ½ point.

Run. The number of printed pieces produced at one time.

Running Foot. The magazine's title line running across the bottom of a page. This usually is combined with the folio (page number) and the date of the issue.

Running Head. A title line that runs across the top of the page and that usually is combined with the folio.

Saddle Stitch. A method of binding where a wire is stitched into the spine to hold the signatures together.

Sans Serif. A typeface without serifs, or ''tails.''

Screen. A printer's device consisting of a clear base and dots. Different screens will have dots of various densities. A screen's value, expressed as a percentage, is determined by how many same-size dots there are to the inch. A screen breaks a continuous-tone photograph or tint block into dots, which then can be printed as line art.

Scribe. To scratch or etch a line into film.

Script. A typeface that looks like handwriting.

Second Color. Any color other than black.

Separation. See *Color Separation*.

Serifs. The small lines that define the tops and bottoms of letters of some typefaces.

Set Solid. To set type with no leading between lines.

Sheet Fed. A method of printing in which the paper is printed one sheet at a time and on one side of the sheet at each impression.

Shot or Shoot. A term applied to camera work. Camera-ready art or photographs are ''shot'' or exposed on film.

Sidebar. A short story relating to a major story and run nearby; usually set off with rules, set in a different typeface, and/or backed with a tint block.

Side Stitch. A method of binding a signature with the staple on the side instead of in the fold. See also *Saddle Stitch; Perfect Binding*.

Signature. All the pages printed on both sides of a single press sheet. The press sheet is folded and then trimmed to form the pages. Signatures usually come in multiples of 8 (i.e., 8, 16, 24, 32). The layout of pages on a signature is called a *Printer's Dummy*.

Sign Off. A symbol indicating the end of a story.

Silhouette. A subject outlined, and the outline filled with black, like a shadow. Also, such an outline reproduced in any color or Benday.

Sink. That distance from the top of the page to the beginning of the live area.

Sizing. Determining what size an illustration will be when enlarged, reduced, or cropped by camera to fit a page layout.

Slug. A set line of hot type. Also, an identifying line—the author's name or story title—for a galley of type.

Specifications or Specs. Exact instructions to the typesetter or printer.

Spine. The backbone of any publication. This is where all the folds occur. See also *Perfect Binding*.

Spread. Facing pages. See also *Printer's Spread*.

Stand-Up Initial. The first letter of a paragraph that stands up above the first line of copy. See also *Indented Initial*.

Story Spread. The total number of pages in a story.

Stripping. Adding an element to the film after shooting the mechanical. For instance, a layout may block out an area for a photo, creating a "window" in the film. The photo negative is then stripped in before the printing plate is made.

Subhead. A minor headline occurring within the text rather than at the beginning. There may be more than one "level" of subhead, determined by the importance of the subhead and its relationship to other subheads. Each level must have its own specifications.

Symmetrical Balance. Occurs when all elements are balanced down the middle of a page or spread, either horizontally or vertically.

Table of Contents. A listing of all articles, stories, columns, and other editorial material within a publication, with the number of the page on which each begins.

Teaser. A headline or blurb on the cover intended to encourage the reader to purchase the magazine. Also, a title or blurb printed in one issue to encourage purchase of the next issue.

Text. Stories, columns, and articles of a publication. Does not include advertising.

Thumbnail. A rough plan, less than full size, used to determine the design or placement of all the items on a page.

Tint. A shade or value of a color that is not full density. In a halftone, the density of the screen determines the intensity of the color. Screening a color allows it to be printed as line art.

Tint Block. A prescribed area printed with a tint. A tint block may be used instead of rules or a box to set off a sidebar or a headline, to add interest to an all-type page, or to help balance a page.

Tip-In. A preprinted piece that is bound into a magazine. A reader's service card is an example of a tip-in.

Title. The name of a publication; also, a story headline.

Title Area. The headline, blurb, byline, and/or other elements, excluding text, that define the beginning of a story.

Trailer. A phrase accompanying a headline; also called a blurb.

Trim. To cut a bound publication to its final size. This is done after the signatures have been folded and bound together and the cover affixed. The trim is usually one-eighth of an inch. Trimming *after* binding

eliminates the irregular edge produced by paper shifting on the press during folding and binding.

Typeface. A particular style and weight of type design, e.g., Bodoni *or* Bodoni Italic *or* Bodoni Bold.

Type Family. All of the styles and weights of a type design, e.g., Bodoni *and* Bodoni Italic *and* Bodoni Bold, etc.

Type Size. The height of a typeface. Type size is designated in the printer's measure of points. The size is measured from the top of the ascenders to the bottom of the descenders. A type size may also be specified by cap height, especially for display faces or an indented initial.

Typography. The "art" of typesetting. Typesetting denotes changing manuscript into typeset copy. Typography includes letter and word spacing to create eye-pleasing copy.

Upper Case. See *Caps*.

Vandyke. A photographic proof, brown in color, made from a negative.

Velox. A glossy print made from a film negative. See also *Photostat*.

Web Offset. A method of printing two sides at once of the sheet of paper on a continuous roll. The paper is then cut and folded into signatures.

Weight. (1) Thickness of a typeface, usually designated in relation to that face's "regular" or "book" weight. (2) The value of an element when balancing it with other elements on a page or spread. (3) A paper specification designating how much a ream (500 sheets) of a particular paper weighs.

White Space. An unprinted area. White space may be an element when balancing a page or spread.

Widow. (1) A less-than-full-width typeset line that appears at the top of a column. (2) A word ending, a single word, or two very short words appearing at the end of a paragraph. Avoid widows.

Wrap-Around. Copy set around a picture or blurb. In magazines, copy is often contoured around a photo of a regular columnist.

"x" Height. The height of the lower case "x" in a typeface. The x-height is used to describe a typeface. For instance, a typeface with a large x-height has ascenders and descenders that are less than one-third of the face in any size, so the area designated by the lower case "x" may be larger. A book face with a large x-height is usually more readable than one with a small x-height. The base of the "x" and other lower case letters is usually used for measuring the baseline-to-baseline leading in a block of typeset copy.

INDEX